Latinity and
Literary Society
at Rome

Latinity and
Literary Society
at Rome

W. Martin Bloomer

PENN

University of Pennsylvania Press

Philadelphia

Copyright © 1997 University of Pennsylvania Press
All rights reserved
Printed in the United States of America on acid-free paper

10   9   8   7   6   5   4   3   2   1

Published by
University of Pennsylvania Press
Philadelphia, Pennsylvania 19104-6097

Library of Congress Cataloging-in-Publication Data

Bloomer, W. Martin.
  Latinity and literary society at Rome / W. Martin Bloomer.
    p.   cm.
  Includes bibliographical references and index.
  ISBN 0-8122-3390-5 (cloth : alk. paper)
    1. Latin literature—History and criticism.   2. Latin language—Social
aspects—Rome.   3. Literature and society—Rome.   4. Books and reading—
Rome.   5. Rome—Civilization.   6. Rhetoric, Ancient.   I. Title.
PA6019.B58   1997
870.9'001—dc21   96-45632
                                                                     CIP

Contents

Preface

THIS BOOK EXAMINES THE WAYS Roman literature used representations of and reflections on proper and improper language to create a society of reading. It begins with questions about the sociology of Latin literature—what social interests were served by the creation of high style, how literary stylization constituted a system of social decorum—and proceeds by offering readings of whole texts. Latinity emerges not as marble language—the unchanging formal sheen of language and literature—but as an artificial, contested field of identity and social polemic. I hope I have suggested what the allure of Latinity has been: why authors have chosen to highlight issues of purity of style, how they have sought to create and perpetuate a linguistic lineage.

I thank the friends at the University of California, Berkeley, and Stanford University especially who have encouraged me to write a book that ranges from the first practitioners of Latin literature to the greatest ancient theorist on Latin to a not-so-grand writer of fables. Colleagues at the Stanford Humanities Center urged that I make this book accessible to a wide community of humanists. To that end I have translated nearly all the Latin that appears in the book and described the cultural and social contexts of the ancient texts and institutions. In addition, those who read portions of this book have rendered me a great *beneficium*: Keith Bradley, Mark Griffith, Maud Gleason, Robert Gregg, Elaine Fantham, Joseph Farrell, Thomas Habinek, Ralph Hexter, Leslie Kurke, J. E. Lendon, Elizabeth Meyer, Charles Murgia, Andrea Nightingale, Patricia Parker, Haun Saussy, Daniel Selden, Susan Stephens, Susan Treggiari, Michael Wigodsky, Gordon Williams. Finally, for their many good deeds and constant good humor I thank my research assistants Livia Tenzer and Brendon Reay.

Introduction:
The Contested Ground of
Latinitas

LATINITAS IS THE "LATINNESS" OR Latinity of speech and, especially, the literary style that marked the high literature of Rome and those who sought to perpetuate it. Latinity also stands as a metonymy for the mediating and intermediate culture between the Greeks and the moderns, primarily because Latin became a learned and learnéd language, with the concomitant definition of culture as an ancient, literary learning recovered from Latin texts and conducted in Latin. The cultured man, the educated man, was one who knew Latin, just as earlier in Rome the authoritative speaker was one whose purity of speech declared him a native—a well-trained master of his tongue and of his subordinates. Latinity has by definition and by its history, then, a double pose: it is both the medium of culture and culture itself. Further, while it presents its practitioners and perfected works as tokens of native style, it is itself both an act of diligent training and artifice and an act of translation; for the Latin term translates or operates as the cultural correlate for what Hellenistic scholars called *Hellenismos*, the quality of classical Greekness prized by later Hellenistic authors.[1]

The invention of *Hellenismos* makes an alluring story: In the far-flung Greek-speaking world that was the legacy of Alexander the Great, scholars and poets established a literary language on the basis of classical Athenian literary models and so, in one fertile and brilliant moment, preserved the classics for us, founded the practices of textual scholarship, refined orthography, introduced

the idea of a standard literary language, and not incidentally produced another great flowering of literature and the arts. Should
we extend this highly romantic notion of artistic fertility by asking whether the Romans similarly invented a standard or literary
language, even if one founded upon different pressures of empire
and a newfound sense of linguistic disorder, variety, or decay? Or
was Latinity simply one of many adoptions from the cultural practices of the Hellenistic experts who increasingly came to Rome
from the mid-third century B.C. to the reign of Augustus Caesar?
For the church father Jerome, or the Protestant reformer, or the
Jesuit educator, Latinity was a prized possession. Jerome worried
that he was too addicted: in a famous dream an angel accuses him
of being a Ciceronian, not a Christian. To the saint's Renaissance
heirs Latinity provided the genuine voice of antiquity. But these
are pretexts for continuing a traditional code.

Whether in the well-scripted dream of the great translator or
in writings of ancient linguistic experts, the search for Latinity is
an exercise in phantoms. Latinity is a topic with many possible beginnings; indeed, it lends itself to a search for origins. High style,
like many an elite code, often maintains that it is natural, natal,
genuine. In addition, Latinity has always been able to be represented as a return—to a lost time, to pristine norms, or to the
genuine expression of the individual. If we accept this prejudice,
then the writing of a history of style becomes the archaeology
of an imaginary community of language users—those, unlike us,
without anxiety about the propriety of their speech, perhaps a
group for whom writing and speaking are one, who have no need
of manuals of style or books about Latinity. We must be wary of
answers to the question "Where do we locate this community?"
for the responses range from the aboriginal Latins to the first literary Latins and beyond. In fact, the quest for what is simulta-
neously native, correct, and a return to high style may be essential
to poetics in the West.

Latinity mattered to the ancients because it was a crucial part
of the linguistic self-artifice of the ancient orator or poet—its most
basic premise is that the speaker's or writer's expression is com-

prised of the words of an approved community. It is not good logic that good Latin makes an argument good, but it is excellent rhetoric that the display of language as a natural, legitimizing possession advances the speaker's authority while it excludes other styles and speakers as corrupt, barbarian, or vulgar. For us, and even for the Romans from the second century B.C. on, Latinity is also something scholarly—the language that allows access to the classical or ideal past and that distinguishes that classicism and the scholar's practice from the intervening stages of the language. Finally, Latinity is a cultural calque, a translation of Greek literary practice. All three manifestations hold out the promise that Latinity is eminently learnable. A "proper" Latin establishes the authority of the ancient orator, the practice of the belated scholar, and indeed the very possibility of cultural transmission.

Latinity differs in many respects from its parallel in the Greek-speaking world. At the very time Greek scholars in Alexandria and Pergamum were editing Homer and reflecting, both in theoretical fashion and in poetic works, on the nature of language and the essential differences of literary language, the Romans had no "literature." This alone makes the Roman invention of a native style more problematic than the Hellenistic creation of a Greek one had been. Of course, Rome had its own linguistic traditions—legal, religious, and political. However, like the ephebeia (the final stage of formal education for freeborn adolescent males) or the gymnasium, Hellenistic Greek was a transnational institution to be found in any community that wished to be a polis; these places and practices, once confined to the local city-state, were now pan-Mediterranean marks of Greekness. Culture itself, paideia, was an index of identity for the Greek speaker, whether he lived in North Africa or in the Peloponnese.[2] It is easy indeed to point out that one language does not mean one culture, and likewise to query the very idea of a single language. When scholar or native identifies a ritual or a phrase or a bucket as Greek or indigenous, the process of identification operates with difficult tolerances. What range of vocabulary or syntax or accent is acceptable for one speaker or writer to be recognized as using our language? Upon what criteria do we assign a vase to this or that period? Clearly, the Hellenistic scholars, with their invention of accent marks and refinements of punctuation, were trying to make reading a text less ambiguous, and yet this scholarly urge to fix a reading has at least as many consequences for the community as for the object of research. The text being made plain is not quite the same as the pot restored by the archaeologist, as the Hellenistic scholars were part of a practicing community and their museum activities guided not simply the gaze of the tourist or pilgrim but the gaze and the pen of reader and writer. Like the well-ruled margin, the comma, or the obelisk, stylistic prescriptions try to shape the reader, the language user too.

At Rome, authors would found complex claims of identity and status on the issue of proper language in ways fundamentally different from their predecessors and significant for their aspirant heirs. A sense of Latinness developed at the same time as literature was being invented. Neither of these is a natural process or event. Not every community or every group in a community has a strong sense of linguistic difference or advertises language, dialect, or sociolect as a blazon of identity. In foregrounding the important role played by language in such acts of identity, the Romans had the example of Greek practices. At the same time the peninsula of Italy had its own richly diverse linguistic circumstances. As Roman literature was first written, colonies were being founded and foreign territories seized and made into provinces. Foreign peoples, Italic peoples, and descendants of Roman citizens or allies in new communities would use the language of their administrators, at least in the drawing up of contracts, or when serving in the legions, or in erecting honorific inscriptions. Against this richly layered landscape—and not in the stark cameo world of Latin versus Greek—a linguistic politics developed at Rome which had its own role to play in the evolution of Roman literature, in the developing ideologies of what it was to be a Roman, and in the social and civil strife between Romans of different classes and statuses. Reflections on language use and language boundaries are not the sole province of the linguist or the poet;

sneers and slurs about the language of a political opponent, an underclass, or the opposite gender attempt to reinforce structures of social oppression as natural distinctions of that allegedly transparent and legible expression of identity—language itself. Noble and base, man and woman, slave and master, foreigner and native can be defined and redefined by those with the authority to make prescriptive statements about language. Of course, such manipulation of discourse and its categories can fall short of its intent: linguistic prescription is one instrument of power, only part of the polemics of social practice.

The claim to *Latinitas* was not the same as the legal right to citizenship or the social right to participate in a citizen's activities. Language alone does not necessarily constitute social or national identity. Among other social practices, dialect or sociolect can communicate group solidarity or identity. Yet only some will want that fluid medium, rather than place or status of birth or some combination of these, to ally men. The society of letters, however, is one type of assertion of authority wherein the literate is ranged against the illiterate but where, too, author and reader, citizen and citizen, author and author forge or sunder public, legible connections. At Rome as elsewhere, the equality of speech, and the equality made possible by acquiring proper speech, might level inherited social distinctions or might serve as a vehicle for social and political change. As a legacy from the Hellenistic world, strictures about style and proper language in Rome can be seen as a translation of a process of cultural rivalry: the Hellenistic literary elite had reinforced their own eliteness by distinguishing their Greek and their writing in what was at least a bilingual world. In constructing a native literary language the Romans adopted, along with so much from Hellenistic literary practice, notions and techniques of purity of style. However, the circumstances of the invention of Latin literature and the social uses of literature were far different, and under these pressures expertise about language and the representation of such expertise served far different purposes.

Writing about the literary styles of the Romans has fallen into at least two potent genres: scholarly display of the Latinity of the author studied and of the studious critic himself, and the systematized manual of speech and conduct, the idealized and well-ordered behavior exhibited in didactic works ranging from Quintilian's *Institutio Oratoria* to Erasmus's *De duplici copia verborum ac rerum*. In contrast, my book considers the conflicting rhetorics and targets of the claims to genuine style deployed in Roman literature. Within Roman literature claims to an authenticating style structure and reinforce the ambitious status of literature: the text promises that it confers Romanness. What did and did not constitute solecism, where lay the breach of decorum, are stylistic and sociolinguistic queries. In special monographs and literary works, even in the funerary inscriptions of former slaves whose freeborn children displayed their own claim to citizen status by imitating the Latin of the aristocrat's epitaph, Romans themselves drew attention to issues of propriety of speech. The subject of how and why Roman literature employed linguistic protocols has dimensions different from the strictly linguistic because Roman culture, like so many others, found stylistic strictures to be a vehicle for anxieties about ethnicity, social order, social status, and gender. Generations of scholars have catalogued the lexicon of true Latin against barbarism, archaism, vulgarism.[3] But in approaching the construction of walls of decorum within and between literary texts, we must ask who is excluding whom, and why and by what means. One generation, like one class or dialect or sociolect, may feel that its language is inferior, but this sense of inadequacy can become a technique for creating various alliances: the present writer or speaker identifies himself with the past or enlists for his project those knowledgable fellows who disdain the vulgar and socially pretentious.

This book examines the social fiction behind the claims for cultured language at its Western, Roman beginnings. Any sociology of literature begins from the realization that there is no single language, no single culture, and that both of these fictions are mystifications of a particular elite. More particularly, as a vibrant, polemical social institution, Roman literature could negotiate complex and conflicting claims of power, access, and identity. The book proceeds by examining the attitudes of several Roman authors toward the Latin of their characters, their critics, and their own works. Native explanations of language, literature, or any other social institution do not inspire confidence, especially in the present age, so sensitive to discovering "true" structure. Today the professional linguist uses the chief ancient authority, the scholar Varro, only as a compendium of vocabulary. In this respect, the old text serves the same function that the older republican texts had served for Varro himself or the glossarists and encyclopedists of the late Roman Empire; they are mines for the contemporary scholar to excavate and reassemble. I am concerned with something different: not with ranking and categorizing old words or augmenting Latin by nonclassical diction, nor even in erecting a progressive intellectual history of thinking about language, with the Hellenistic scholars as pioneers, the Romans as poor copyists, and the post-Enlightenment as arrived science.

Instead, this book investigates what and whom the Roman authors' professed interest in language served. Theories of language, for the most part, I leave aside; such prescriptions seem to me a genre of social and intellectual protocols that demands separate treatment. The primary focus is the social and intellectual force of *Latinitas*, especially as manifested in Roman literary works. I take such reflection not as literary gamesmanship (self-contained tropes about language) but as part of a wider, social consideration about the powers of discourse. In addition, such textual declarations on the state of language recognizably practice social analysis, reflection, and polemics. To discuss Latinity requires and exhibits decisions about who, not just what, constituted valid practice. The power to confer legitimacy of speech wielded strong symbolic power, for in a polyglot empire where education was rare, expensive, and time-consuming, proper Latin was a symbol of being a citizen, an owning, commanding member of the most powerful group in the world. That was the claim of *Latinitas*.

The worries about Latinity are correspondingly large. Native language, the citizen's birthright, can be taught and hence appropriated as surely as the toga or some other cultural and social symbol can be conferred on an outsider. Language as a fixer of status is especially fluid at certain times and under certain historical and social conditions. Ever worrying to the Roman master was the fact that language was taught by slaves, freedmen, and women. Language training belonged to domestic space and to the houses or rented shops of freedmen teachers. From here the male elite developed the habits and techniques of speech that were idealized as the essential attributes of the governing class—the magistrates' tongues that supposedly swayed the less verbal and nonverbal body politic.

The various studies of this book begin by asking how professed expertise and indicted failures of Latinity invent, confer, and evaluate status. At times these textual representations of linguistic relations represent social structuring (idealizations or models of how society or some subset of it should work, interact, or talk). Clearly these representations spill out from the text to construct a society of reader and author. In the scenes, characters, and motifs under consideration, Roman texts reflect upon literature's own mediating and transforming role within Roman society. The power of speech, in such representations, resides in its potential to fix or unfix status, and indeed to cement social harmony. Roman writers write of communication in ways that are contaminated with social terms. The *officium* of a writer, like the inclusion of deference to a named patron, includes the writer in a recognizable hierarchy. But something more is meant. Almost as a synecdoche, communication figures society. "Civil speech" nicely blends and metaphorizes the two realms. By means of such insistent tropes, social order becomes inextricable from linguistic order, and both, at least in the text or according to the text, depend upon the writer as constituter of that Roman order.

The beginning of my first chapter treats the elder Cato, who in the formative era of Latin literature chose to represent problems of social and political policy as issues of proper and improper language and culture. Quite simply, Cato founded prose literature for the Romans, and in his celebration of native land, ancestral

virtues, local farming, and original language he left the powerful ideological legacy of Latinity as nativism. In this first chapter
I consider how two other practitioners of early Roman literature
defined their poetic personae and their audience in terms of mastery of Latinity. Proper Latin's ability to leap over divisions of ethnicity, status, and time (and religion) is then explored in a work of
another pretender to Latinity, the English Victorian poet Robert
Browning, whose "Tomb at St. Praxed's" both perpetuates and attacks the fiction that fine, marble Latin defines the poet. Browning
unmasks the interestedness, the linguistic politics, behind writers'
claims to be Rome's continuator, preserver, or restorer.

The strong focus of this book, however, is a single hundred
years of Roman literary and social life, the period from the Augustans to their first inheritors. The Romans themselves recognized
the importance of language to the social and political transforma-
tions of their world. A century after the first political transition of
the new age of the emperors, the historian Tacitus would maintain
that the names had stayed the same while the realities of power
now centered upon one man. At the same time, the historian
would locate in the second emperor, Tiberius, and in other members of the imperial family, various diseases of language. Tacitus
perpetuated both the perception that language is an index to character, individual and imperial, and the strong polemical practice
that sought to influence political and social life through prescriptive representations about language and style. With the inclusion
of Tacitus, I violate my chronological span of one century, in part
to frame my period with a synthetic reflection on its linguistic
politics and to counterbalance the treatment of the late republican
Varro, who serves, in Chapter 2, to usher in the discussion of the
new culture that came with the Caesars. In this way I seek to suggest the strength of Roman anxieties about status, social change,
and language without hanging these on the handy peg of the emperors.

Tacitus and those who follow his strong line would have us
believe that this political change ushered in a new, derivative culture. I stress that new practitioners appropriated and reshaped

culture, and so begin my account of the new practices of Latinity with Varro of Reate, the chief Roman theorist of the Latin language and the authority recognized by his illustrious rivals, Caesar and Cicero, as the greatest scholar.[4] Their recognition had much to do with the powerful symbolic value of definitions of Romanness, which they vigorously contested against one another in their own publications. I detach Varro's authoritative project from the intellectualist tradition of theoretical works on language so as to describe its affinities with other, contemporary literary works that portray the role of language in social upheaval. In order to define the context of the rivalry of these experts of high status, I present Roman cultural notions of the teacher of language, which constitute the foil for Varro's project and the vehicle for some of his polemic with his social peers Caesar and Cicero. Thus Chapter 2 treats two responses to claims to the authority of Latinity in which masters of prose confront the poets' power of Romanizing speech. The first half of the chapter examines Varro's polemics in his monumental *De lingua latina*. In the second, I discuss one of his targets, the freedmen who taught the freeborn their most proper Latin, and consider the ambivalent representation of these authorities in the sections of Suetonius's *De viris illustribus* devoted to grammarians and rhetoricians.

Chapters 3 through 6 study the ways in which linguistic exchange and mastery function within literary genres (verse fable, rhetorical treatise, historiography, the novel) to construct a Roman society of letters which, while textual, stems from and spills over into the "real." I have chosen for these chapters texts that do not so ostensibly have language as their subject, in order to show the preoccupation, if not anxiety, with which Roman authors presented the social dynamics of the role of speech. These studies of the Augustan freedman poet Phaedrus, the Spanish equestrian Seneca, and the high magistrates Tacitus and Petronius clarify how Roman literature functioned as a resonant, vital system within Roman society. Literature is, then, decidedly not a separate sphere of human activity, the realm of the mind, estheticism, or social dissent, but a functioning element of a social and cultural system.

Although I approach Roman literature as a part of a cultural or literary economy, these studies do not seek to erect an autonomous space for the practice of literature. Roman literature was not a fixed and orderly method of establishing values; although it aims to be self-sufficient, literature participates in the social institutions and practices as a result of which identity and status arise, shift, and are appropriated.

In Rome of the Punic Wars, where Roman literature was conceived, fundamental shifts in social structure were allied to infusions of capital, currency, goods, technologies, and people. Roman literary reflections on literature as a system of exchange—for example, Greek for Roman, client's service for master's bidding, reward or applause or gratitude for finished work—reflect other transitions and substitutions in Roman culture. In the middle of the second century B.C. the playwright Terence would be celebrated as a master of Latinity. By this point the rhetoric of Latinity was ascendant. The playwright, who was an African freedman, was recognized as writing a citizen's Latin. Writing, Latinity, and Roman identity were now enmeshed, whereas before the Roman populace had seen the popular performances of Plautus, a non-Roman, performing as part, and only part, of a festival sponsored by the senate or by some prominent man.

Roman literature saw its two most important ages as the early and the golden, those transformative periods of 240 to 160 B.C. and 70 B.C. to the death of Horace in 8 B.C. Native diachronic accounts of the worth of a literature are open to all measure of dispute; what is important is the status granted the early authors and, of course, the linguistic resources recycled and replayed by later authors. I have tried to stress the uses Roman authors made of the original anxieties about literary production and worth, for Roman literature did not shed its ambivalence to literature as a latecomer, a foreigner, a social parvenu. I have also tried to point out the fault-lines inherent in such protestations of continuity—the programs and particulars masked by a talk that maintains it is the same as the past's talk.

When the social aspect of literature has been seen as an issue in Roman literature, preeminently it has been understood as a question of patronage. Thus literary composition has been included in a social system known as *clientela* (a strong strain of apologetic criticism has sought to differentiate the practice of literature from the rest of Roman patronage so as to secure independence for literature and its geniuses). This Roman term, translated as "patronage" though its viewpoint is exactly opposite, has been seen (to oversimplify) as a system of vertical integration, appeasement by handout, or at best an unequal traffic in services, and hence as a foil to social revolution.[5] A typical technique of the criticism of Roman literary works notes the locus in the text where the patron is addressed. In a way, the critic is looking at the signature of the poet as we might look at the conventional farewells of Dr. Johnson's letters, "your most humble *etc.*," and read these as pained and truncated gestures and consequently draw conclusions about the great man's ambition, pride, and ambivalent feelings toward his social superiors. This practice makes for a piecemeal approach to the text, specifically to the construction of the persona of the author and to issues of the support and influence of literary production. In addition, such conclusions about literary society presuppose a model of literary production that is fundamentally anachronistic. The twilight critics bat Horace and Virgil across the net of their own literary propriety, recognizing the poets' team colors as now republican, now Augustan-imperial. Such positivist conclusions about literary dissent versus literary accommodation to a new master take one trope drawn from the vocabulary of Roman social relations, that of personal dependence, and relentlessly literalize this figure as the whole text and that text's relations. On the other hand, the notion of literary economy stresses not autonomy but the relation of parts of a system.[6] Of course, economy is too strong a term; like "literature" it leaps across the divides of time and culture. Economy is a useful metaphor for understanding how the social institution of literature sought to regulate its influence and influences upon it. Strictures about speech or literary style (again the term Latinity collapses the two) are then involved in other social protocols. Yet while participating in other systems of decorum, Latinity enjoyed a privileged place since language is a potent, perceptible means by which people tell and show who they are. So let economy serve a provisional program of interrogating categories of status and genre, society and literature.

Native writing about language is in part about identity. The questions where is the Roman? what is the Roman? arise under some stress. The contrasts drawn between proper and improper speech, whether in the prescriptions of rhetorical theorists or in the various speakers of a Roman drama, seek to influence and not simply mirror native concoctions of identity. In particular, issues of social mobility are bound up with issues of propriety of speech. Like sumptuary legislations—the legislated restrictions on costume and diet—talk about proper talk will defeat the scholar who is solely intent on objectifiable results or referents. Proper deportment may not be the intended aim of the author, but simply a medium for talking about, resisting, or enacting social change. Prescriptions about speech or dress seek to make identifiable a person's status, and attest to the increased difficulty of such knowledge. Sumptuary legislation is the most formal and only recorded vestige of one small segment of Roman society's attitude toward confusions of status, generations, and genders; it is the codification and extension of much small talk—griping and complaining about how the *arrivistes* or the young dress, of how women do in fact, if not in law, have disposable assets. Whereas these written behavioral prescriptions have been understood as reactionary moralism or as responses to individual or group deviancy, at a more fundamental level they are public gestures about the look of elite bodies. Such attempts at social prescription may well betray, somewhat after the fact, social changes that the legislators were powerless to affect. Equally, they can be weapons of social change. Stylistic prescriptions attest not to culture wars (an overblown term that does not recognize how essential to civic life such discourse is) but to social contest. It is important to recognize that such speech does not declare war on its society; rather, like that new man and arch-censor Cato, it masks its bid for status and seeks preeminently to pass. The allure of Latinity arises, at least in part, from this potential for transformation.

From Ennius, the father of Roman poetry, to the Renaissance

revivers of Latin style and culture, Latinity has been the cherished aim and declared accomplishment of *literati*. To write Latin—pure, proper Latin—has of course as many meanings as writers. At times a community of language users agrees on the authors who exemplify proper language use, yet just as often a new understanding of the language, the discovery of a long-lost manuscript, or external forces can sweep away the canon on which the experts themselves were nurtured. And of course, these are not independent processes. The authorities of language and culture play a role within their own society that is not exclusively of their making.

Despite abandoning the ambition to speak and write classically, the modern classicist echoes the rancorous claim of the Renaissance humanists that they alone were true Ciceronians. Today, the social sphere of such invective seems paltry. Perhaps we gain in congeniality and collegiality when our readership diminishes: book reviews in academic journals have neither the venomous wit of the poet and Latinist A. E. Housman nor the pontificating diatribe of Cardinal Bembo nor the eclectic anti-Ciceronianism of a canon reformer like Petrarch. Modern scholars indulge in imitating Ciceronian style chiefly in the last stages of language learning—the training of university and graduate students in Latin prose composition from late-nineteenth-century prescriptive grammars. But confident imitation of ancient style is still exhibited in the practice and publication of textual criticism.[7]

As the Renaissance had countercries to the zealous and exclusive Ciceronianist, so modern voices continue to set various "interpretive" modes against the professors of Latinity. Naively put, the question is: Are we to copy and replicate or to interpret? The issues that cling parasitically to these polar hosts make the debate about textual practices far more volatile and significant. Are the curriculum and professors and culture intact and adequate, or do they need revision? How shall we revise—by diligent imitation of the original rather than reliance on intermediary tradition? The divide of interpretive critics, on the one hand, and preservers or apologists for the classical texts, on the other, is but a modern manifestation of the struggle for what constitutes proper study, what culture these texts represent.[8] Of course, these polar polemics do not map the same social or intellectual problems again and again down through the ages. Such a reductive hermeneutic model of the problem of proper Latinity simply reformulates the ancient terms of high and low style, elite and vulgar. What does ally these oppositions, aside from the reuse of ancient polemical terms, is a social contest for disciplinary and curricular authority. Similarly, curricular reform can be presented as the strife between the reformer and the traditionalist, yet this insistently masks the deep social and institutional changes that education can effect and which debate about it enacts. The struggle over who properly interprets a perished language, who is a master of the elite style, necessarily involves contemporary social and institutional programs.

If we were concerned solely with the topic of European expertise in language, we would not touch upon classical scholarship after the nineteenth century. Modern linguistics has a separate, though derivative, history. Even here, especially in education and especially in America, we would have to grant that the linguist and the sociologist, not the classicist, have been society's experts for curriculum, child development, and national language standardization. The change in the constitution of language experts and their social roles can be traced, at least within the field of classical languages, to the development of comparative historical linguistics. This product of German scholarship challenged the powerful, traditional claims of prose composition to teach "language" (substituting "scientific" comparison and classification for imitation of the masters). A nationalist battle, with a German scholarship seeking linguistic expertise in historical linguistics (one of the chief early practitioners was Jacob Grimm, more famous for his collection of folktales, who exemplifies the interest in discovering a native antique that was preclassical and preliterary) against an English display of mastery through the adoption of a high style, shows two different routes to standardization. British students lost their regional dialects in favor of a Southern Standard English at the same time as they polished their Latin style. At university they moved from the schools' exercise, verse composition, to the adult or adolescent practice of prose composition, thus mirroring the ancient division between the *grammaticus*, who taught boys the poets, and the rhetorician, who was in charge of the last stage of education, prose speeches.[9] Expertise in a highly literate code was bound up with individual coming of age and with class and nationalist identity. All this was conducted and debated in terms of the proper recovery and pedagogy of Latin.

In the search for mastery of the ancient style, for the proper methods of language study and acquisition, German linguists sought a new scientific knowledge of the classical languages through study of their own vernacular and through a third classical language, Sanskrit, which stood outside the inherited dualisms of Greek and Latin, Latin and vernacular. In this they demonstrated a different practice but the same ambition as other European scholars trying to preserve a mastery of the classical languages in the face of the rise of science, the use and standardization of the vernaculars, vast social changes, and increasing academic compartmentalization. High style as an emblem of a single culture, if not the inherited high place of Latin and Greek, again seems to have seized Europe in today's social and nationalist polemics about standard, pure French or about German-speaking Turks. The vernacular sons, the freedmen who transgress and sully the birthright, are now the American media, multiculturalists, North Africans, or simply the political left. The social polemics of language seem only to increase with time.

All this may seem a most academic dispute among the now marginalized elite of speech instructors. *Latinitas* is all but lost (so the lament has often gone), replaced by the vernacular educational ideal of *humanitas*, and now with a more fragmented and particular ethnicity of identity, knowledge, and power. The study of Latin and Greek texts has led to the development of linguistics and has thus contributed to its own dispossession as a potent social authority on language. And further, faith in the power of language to shape the child and to civilize society has dwindled under the pressure of very different studies. I will not attempt to resuscitate arguments on behalf of literature nor cite the obvious: that interpretation of vernacular literatures occupies more people, produces more books, or is theoretically more advanced. Instead I will say that the ancient formulation and the continuing Western reformulations of arguments about education, culture, and language need to consider the source and history of their polemical debates. The university still represents the final stage in formal acculturation even if it has ceded much of its program of linguistic standardization. If Latinity has been (or has been paraded as) Western culture, a review of its contested origins is in order.

Literary Censors and Marble Latin

AT THE TURN OF THE THIRD CENTURY B.C. Rome's most iras-cible champion of Romanness, the elder Cato, faced aristocratic competitors in the law courts, in elections, and in the army who had every right to believe that they were the true Romans. The new man from Tusculum shifted the terms of definition of Roman identity in a move as revolutionary in its consequences for Roman public life and literature as it was conservative and nativist in its rhetoric.

Cato is of the utmost importance for the creation of the de-bate about language, personal style, and Romanness. He stood at a pivotal moment in history, but not in the melodramatic sense that he understood with Rome teetering on the verge of total cor-ruption. Returning from military service in Sicily by way of Sar-dinia, Cato brought the Hellenistic poet Ennius to Rome. Like his aristocratic contemporaries, Cato recognized the political and social potential of having Southern Italian Greeks write and, what is usually overlooked, educate in Latin.[1] Perhaps what most distin-guishes Cato from the other early patrons of literature is the fact that Ennius left his employ and Cato wrote for himself. A gen-eration later, gossip had it that his aristocratic rival, the younger Scipio, actually wrote the plays performed under the name of the African freedman Terence. But Cato put his own name on his Latin works; and when he came to history, the genre proper to aristocrats and which a Roman general, Fabius Pictor, had writ-ten (but in Greek), Cato dared at least a triple innovation. He wrote in Latin, did not restrict himself to campaigns in which he had participated, and excluded the names of the Roman officials.[2] All the family history, all mention of individual aristocrats and their great deeds, he stripped of particularity. The office held, be it general, consul, praetor—in short, function—supplanted aristocratic name.

In many respects the elder Cato prevailed in his struggles with his opponents: he is said to have defeated all those who took him to court; he was elected to the major offices; he succeeded in making his own family a leading political patron. The tradition of his uninterrupted legal victories may be as mythic as the notice that he ended his later speeches with "Carthage must be destroyed"—this too he finally, posthumously, accomplished. Cato the censor loomed large in Roman memory as the arbiter of Romanness who proposed and exemplified severity in all things, but especially in words. By Cicero's time his speeches were all but forgotten, but this amnesia did not eclipse his influence. He received the politician's reward: his slogans lived on. Indeed, a collection was later manufactured and attributed to him.[3]

Of Cato's genuine aphorisms perhaps the most famous is "rem tene, verba sequentur" ("stick to the matter at hand, words will come").[4] The disdain for ornament, which he so loudly proclaimed, has been reinforced by the accident of the survival of one-liners attributed to him. Cato was as close as any Roman came to being a self-made man, which is to say, he came not from the city itself but from an outlying village, had no claim to aristocratic birth but had to attract aristocratic friends, and did so by climbing up the sociopolitical ladder in a fashion stunningly innovative and professedly old-fashioned. According to Cato, all the trappings of office and social distinction naturally attended the man who himself embodied Roman things. In fact, Cato was adopting a Hellenistic commonplace about style and character ("as is the style, such is the man")[5] and using this truism, without acknowledgment, to communicate a view of the Roman self counter to the contemporary rhetoric of high birth and individual, aristocratic families. Subsequent generations would read as moral and Roman his rhetoric, which in fact polemically excluded aristocratic display, conspicuous consumption, and civic benefaction. Cato knew how the outsider must exploit Hellenophobia and anti-intellectualism to denigrate an elite who made a display of their culture; he also realized, like the consummate insider, that an honorific, extraordinary office—the censorship in his case—might contain more power than the regular posts of consul and praetor. And, paradoxically for a speaker who claimed that words followed directly from things, Cato recognized that he needed to learn Greek and to mask his acquaintance with Greek culture.

With his rigidly Roman posture, Cato deflected the aristocratic monopoly on literature and the arts by using these to create a visible life for himself, a public life that was unnotable. Scandal could not taint the life of one practicing a rigorous censorship. Throughout his writings—the letters and encyclopedia to his sons advising what to take from the Greeks;[6] the anachronistic project of the *De agri cultura*, which presented in great detail the way to manage a traditional farm as opposed to money grubbing from trade or banking (which the senators of his day were also pursuing); the historical work the *Origines*, which suppressed the names of the historical agents and left only the name of the author—a censorious author proposed to the reading public a self-effacing history, culture, and persona whose authority depended on the self as unremarkable, as generically Roman. Like his dictum that words attend things, his writings exhibit a transparent style that repeatedly marked its alleged equivalency of form and subjects as un-Greek and unrhetorical. In this pristine state of natural language, no rhetoric separates words from referents or a man's character from his words and visible life. Thus, at the outset of the work on agriculture, Cato asks rhetorically how the good old Romans praised a man and displaces the answers he could have heard in the urban, aristocratic family's self-laudatory funeral orations with the fiction of an agrarian past where "good farmer"— *bonus colonus*—was the most the Romans could manage.

We shall meet again in Roman cultural claims the fiction of a simple and earthy ancestral language. Here the deflation of laudatory terms changes the criteria of social worth, and this restriction on words of praise provides the author with a unique, censorious authority while stripping the aristocrat of his traditional terms of encomiastic propaganda, just as contemporary legislation attempted to restrict the displays of wealth and indeed the sources of wealth available to the class that had provided candidates for office. When a self-professed reformer calls for a return to a simple (idealized) economy, he may well be targeting the newly rich as well as the aristocrats. Although Cato asserts that there is only one, all but perished criterion of proper behavior, his strident rhetoric indicates the contemporary conflicts of classification and identity (Who is elite? Who is the Roman? What is tradition?) that lay at the heart of Roman social discourse about power and its display.

For generations Cato haunted the Roman imagination with his personification of an integrated literary, moral, and public censorship. Cato's self-censorship enrolled him into a tradition of noble heroes of the republic, although even this formulation may be anachronistic: Cato, like the first emperor, Augustus, had an interest in restricting the nobles' power and in constructing a new collective ideology. Where the aristocrat would have spoken, for instance in a funeral eulogy, of the signal service of his family, Cato's exclusionary, moral rhetoric, presented in a legal or political speech or in prose writing, provided an opening for social mobility above and beyond the narrow precedent of new men gaining office.[7] Precisely at this time literature was offering a new censorship, a new account of the identity of the true Roman. Ennius and Cato parted company, but both contributed to a literary language that claimed for its practitioners the kind of legitimacy and authority that had hitherto required high birth.

Various cultural forces from antiquity on have obscured the "interestedness" of the development of literature at Rome. The particular conditions of an emerging institution, especially its ambivalence about the status of its practitioners and its sense of "debt" or inferiority to Greek culture, came to be motifs in themselves. Roman literature continued to exploit a social function that arose in a complex and self-consciously transitional period of the late third and early second centuries B.C. In thinking about this period at Rome one should perhaps avoid all institutional and collective terms, the stock-in-trade of the historian: the aristocracy, the elite, indeed nationalism, are not simply foreign terms or anachronistic but reductive. It is from this period that Western historians have begun their histories of the "historical" (textually documented) Rome: Toynbee's famous term, "the legacy of Hannibal," memorably set the sweeping changes, the foundations of the far better documented late republican Rome, in terms of the consequences of the signal military victory of this period. We need not here take up more recent historians' replications or revisions of this dramatic causation and periodization, although we should see the hand of Cato and his historiographic reviver Sallust in this periodization. Though I try to resist the kind of diachronic association that terms such as "the aristocracy" and "literature" bring, I do replicate the emphasis on the period in which Hannibal invaded Italy, but not to make grand claims for how literature as one aspect of cultural contact changed Rome, and specifically its elite. The record changes all too conveniently at the very point when first we can read the disputes of the elites and their appropriations of the interests of the non-elites. Cato exploited and invented polemical techniques of identity. This is one signal instance of how Rome changed literature.

All literature practices a censorship more subtle and thoroughgoing than any emperor, magistrate, or school board. In the traditional terms of genre, diction, and style, literature declares what topics and words it will allow, what dialect or sociolect an individual may employ. The abstractions "literature," "genre," even "censorship" obscure the actual process by which a literary work comes to be written or recognized as literary. To speak of literature in such institutional terms participates in one of the grand strategies of its practitioners: the habit of presenting literature as a single unified discourse, a literature, a genre. What we miss is that particular practitioners or groups of practitioners, patrons, authors, readers, have interests in the various censorships of literature. In a modern instance, academic reading of Roman literature's ability to transform and transmit has been severely restricted by the habit of measuring as separate, and even antithetical, the Roman elements from the Greek tradition. The Roman development of genre must then be seen as a process of accommodation of the native to the culturally superior and anterior. In celebrating an alleged syncretism of the Greek and Roman in the brief flowering of the Ciceronian and Augustan classical period, modern scholars have seen the process of composition as a kind of elite censorship, selecting the best from the Greek tradition and moderating the linguistic resources of the Latin language in one unusual and inimitable moment. Both practitioners and later scholars abetted such a reading; but speech, and the specialized use of language known as literature, are not social constants: the social, political, legal, and cultural occasions and functions of speech vary from society to society and from class to class. Censors like Cato and the literary historian must feign that there is a code from which innovation departs.

In late-third and early-second-century B.C. Rome, literature could practice a far more open censorship than Cato would have us believe. The plays of the early poets distinguished their aristocratic patrons just as captured booty, including symbols of culture (statues and talented slaves), marched in triumph for all to see. With the Greek present as so much owned material, Cato's strident protests against things Greek can be understood as an effort to deflate these powerful symbols. Literature offered a different parade, one that could blur the interconnections of the Greek and the Roman. The production of a text by an educated slave or ex-slave under the patronage of an upper-class Roman was not the same as the procession of cultured slaves in a general's parade or a great man's daily entourage. As a novel social institution, literature was working out its roles and asserting its own autonomy, no doubt against the model of cultural and social ownership. Of course, the assertion of autonomy itself had a literary tradition and was a kind of social fiction. In practical terms, the mirage of independence could not always protect the artist. The poet Naevius would suffer for attacking the aristocratic rivals of his patron.

Here, perhaps literature, specifically the dramatic stage, tested the extension of the struggles of the elite. Future poets might learn a cautionary lesson from the story of the exiled playwright, but such transgressions created a space for literature at Rome.

The new venues for patrons and clients, for delegated intellectual and dramatic labor, brought with them a change in social relations and public life. We should not overestimate the immediate effect of this novelty: adding Latin plays to certain festivals and providing some Roman children with a Latin *Odyssey* for schoolwork does not imply the creation of a new public sphere or communicative medium; it does initiate a shift of censorial authority with new and changing capabilities to honor and to stigmatize. These performances also presented textual social orders—idealized, sometimes comic, mixed Greek and Roman versions of social relations. The author's personal display, the patron's display of his person, family, and office, and the audience's collective display intersect in what we might call somewhat blandly the founding moment of Roman literature. Under these pressures and public presences, with a patronage and resistance by a competitive elite, and in the performative hands of former slaves, who had once been free citizens of Southern Italian city-states, literature furnished the players in an innovative, polemical constitution of the Roman self and the Roman collective.

The first practitioners of Roman literature have directed readers' attention to the social posturing of authorial personae. In seeing a development from Greek to Roman, dependence to independence, servile to citizen, the literary critic follows a course dictated by the poets' self-notices. A social biography of Roman literature could trace a rise up the social scale from the freedman and Greek Livius Andronicus to the nearer (Oscan and Umbrian) Ennius, who became a Roman citizen.[8] Naevius upset such a neat genealogy: he was a Campanian and a citizen but a plebeian and the victim of patronage (the ancients say he was exiled for lampooning an aristocratic family, the Metelli).[9] Still, there follow those more adept at serving a Roman master, culminating in Terence, an African ex-slave whose work seemed so genuinely Latin that it was alleged to be the patron's own, the pseudepigraphical composition of the Scipionic circle.[10] His predecessor Plautus, with his funny stage names and huge Latin success, is seen as less Greek, more native Italic. A generation later, with Lucilius, whose niece would bear Pompey the Great, Roman literature had arrived at a grander social level.

Roman literature thus writes its own progressive narrative, from an act of translation in 240 B.C. to native satire, elite biting elite, at the close of the second century B.C. This process of naturalization has been taken literally as the diachronic history of writing at Rome, whereas in fact it is a social protocol about the emancipatory power of writing. The native history of Latin literature has a strong rhetorical color: writing frees the self, or writing reveals innate genius and native identity. Latin style Romanizes the self. The simplified teleology, from semi-Greek early poets through patronage to the domestication of literature, has partial truth; it writes literary history from the biographers of the poets, from the names of the poets, and from the poets' final salutations (genuine or fabricated). The epitaphs of Naevius and Ennius contend with each other, using epic language and aristocratic funerary display in order to find a place in Rome. Further, in their social and linguistic innovation they make preemptive claims to high status. As a consequence, their legacy is not simply fame for the poet, a literary language for Rome, but an opening for literature and men of letters to construct the Roman.

These two poets—or the fabricators of their words—present the poet as founder of Latin.[11] The epitaphs of the poets write a literary history where speaking Latin is not the birthright of a senator, or even a moral censor, but the inalienable possession of the poet. Linguistic purity depends on the poet's words and, paradoxically, living Latin depends on their marble words. The elder Cato had inscribed himself as the public arbiter of language and morals; but these poets lay claim to that high status for themselves in the lapidary medium of their art. Here the poet has the only speaking part, yet at the same time the funerary inscription issues a challenge to the living to speak with the same authority as the dead.

In reading the epitaphs of the poets we enter a long tradition, by no means inaugurated by the Romans, of poetry's attempts at final signification. Naevius left this as his epitaph, in a verse form markedly Roman, the Saturnian:

> Immortales mortales   si foret fas flere,
> flerent divae Camenae   Naevium poetam.
> itaque postquam est Orchi   traditus thesauro
> obliti sunt Romae   loquier lingua latina.

[If it were right for gods to weep for mortals,
the divine Camenae would be weeping for the poet Naevius.
Accordingly, after he was handed over to the treasury of
    Death,
at Rome they have forgotten how to speak Latin.]

Ennius addresses his fellow citizens:

> Aspicite, o cives! senis Enni imaginis formam:
>   Hic vestrum panxit maxima facta patrum.
> Nemo me lacrimis decoret nec funera fletu
>   Faxit. Cur? Volito vivos per ora virum.

[Behold, citizens, the shape of the image of old Ennius;
He rendered artistically the greatest deeds of your fathers.
Let no man honor me with lamentation or produce
A tearful funerary procession. Why? I live in my flight on
    the lips of men.]

Ennius's opening direct address announces his improvement on Naevius: his statue calls out to fellow citizens. In their final, alliterative half-lines, both poets represent the Roman as coterminous with Latin speech. Latin speech has died with Naevius, but it lives on in the oral quotation of Ennius. Ennius asks for no funerary procession, the ritual procession of the aristocratic family, but claims a different legacy. The later poet, he emphasizes the Roman context, the Latin speech community who are citizens and men, not the epic mortals of Naevius's first line or the unnamed subject of his last, but *cives* and *viri*. The agents named by Naevius are the weeping Italian Muses and the Italian Hades. The Latin speakers, the Romans, are unnamed, as they are silent. In this silence Ennius has placed the epitaph to his statue. The Romans, the audience, are here named citizens, and no gloss on Greek conventional names—Camenae for the Muses, Orchus for Hades—reminds us that a poet, needed for translation of culture, is now missed. The translation that Ennius does offer is "the greatest deeds of your fathers" for the epic κλέα ἀνδρῶν, a Latin periphrasis and not a single gloss. The more fluid Latin phrase escapes the rigid monumentality of Naevius's sepulchral note on Latin language and literature. The later poet thus inscribes himself into a living tradition—this constitutes the competitive response to Naevius's prior grand claim to have buried Latin with him.[12]

Roman authors continued to make proprietary claims to Latinity, which remained a contested ground. The social status of some of the first poets and, into the empire, of language teachers (the grammarians and rhetoricians who taught Roman schoolchildren) kept alive the problematic association of literature with the parvenu and the libertine. Curiously, the freedman (*libertus*) remained a prominent and significant figure in Latin literature in part because he had no legal father, and hence no patronymic in his name. At Rome, then, the identification of a writer with his works is more than a metonymic conceit by which we call a poem Homer. Without bloodline and ancestral name, the writer could be seen as self-sufficient and self-identifying. The freedman also embodied the emancipatory potential of literature, especially its ability to travel, to move from Greek to Roman, to concoct a new identity, a new society, even to move beyond certain censorious, traditional speech. In his acquisition of a Roman name, Roman language, Roman citizenship, in his pedagogic and professorial roles, and in his role as the first (Roman) legal father of his line, the freedman passed on Latin to the uninitiated.[13] Throughout this book the reader will encounter the freedman and other latecomers to Latin because such figures enjoyed a special status: socially mobile but at the same time despicable, latecomers to Latin but quite often teachers of Latin, these characters allowed Roman literature to refract its own problematic origins, functions, and ambitions.

The period of classical Latin has won its periodization from the search of subsequent generations for a standard literary language and a high culture, but also from the judgments of the Augustans themselves. Cicero, Virgil, and Horace were recognized in their lifetimes as having accomplished perfected work, something distinctly superior to prior efforts. Also at this time, vulgarity conspicuously worried those claiming to be cultural authorities. The Augustans recognized the claims of Ennius and succeeded in enrolling themselves as the new champions of an enduring and definitive Latin. Although this book is devoted to ancient Latinity, indeed to the generation customarily celebrated for its achievement of Latinity and to their first inheritors, I should like to conjure up before the reader a pair of epitaphs in opposition to those of Naevius and Ennius. These two epitaphs bear witness to two Renaissance rivals who laid claim to high Latinity.

In the poem "The Tomb at St. Praxed's" by the English poet Robert Browning, the chief characters, the dying bishop and his dead rival, figure well the anxiety of the author facing high style. I turn to a nineteenth-century meditation on the encounter of the self with the classical because Browning vividly illuminates the problem of facing Latinity. His poem complicates the picture of modern scholarship's yearning for mastery and reveals the potentials within the traditions of Latinity that one of the keenest readers of Latin poetry detected. In highlighting the clash of critic and poet and their different Latins, the English poet thematizes his own difficulty in writing a new, living, and yet enduring language. Browning picks up the two strands of linguistic and poetic mastery in a fashion that reveals the artifice of such self-authorizing tropes.

The poet dramatizes the problems of facing Latinity in the voices he gives to two who would revive the old language. These vernacular sons do not, however, belong solely to the sixteenth or the nineteenth centuries, the dramatic date and compositional date of the poem. Like Ennius and Naevius, these characters are unsure of their status and try to refound their identity on their mastery of Latin. Unlike the oldest of Latin poets, but like many of the texts from the first centuries B.C. and A.D., they fear that they will betray their belatedness through a vulgar error. The early poets suppressed their Greekness with a show of Latinity; this, too, collapsed ethnic and social identities. To a greater extent, the later texts foreground a perilous displacement from the old, authentic, and authenticating speech, but both Latinate and Latin authors employ the artificial (social) pole of Latinity and consequently try to exclude its antonyms.

Chief among the forces that oppose Latinity is vulgarity, which we may define in terms of each poet's context (Italian or Italianate Latin for the starchily educated Browning, the vernacular mixed Greek and Latin of the socially despised freedman for Petronius or Suetonius or the elder Seneca), but we cannot so easily reify the targets, the antipodes of high style. Vulgarity stands at the margin, and not only because of the historical fact that Latin literature went on repressing its connections to Greek culture and to the *semigraeci* who had been its first practitioners. Literature's census presents the other in almost Protean form—his language, like his name, shifts unsteadily from the classical to the vernacular —so as to align the socially pathological with the artistically inept.

For the secret is that, against or without these despised codes and figures (empty speech, hyper-rhetorical sophistry, impolite, deadly, or vulgar speech), there is no Latinity. The thoroughgoing simplifications of the ancient rhetoricians presented the proper grades of Latin, but there was no high, middle, and low style.[14] No simple system of autonomous codes and code switching can adequately describe rhetoric. Proper language is relational and oppressive, and identity, like language, is a mutating oppression. Protean and impotent (in the ambivalent Latin sense of powerless and not under control), Latinity inscribed its own oppositions—thus we meet with the critic in the text and the figures and languages that do not measure up, from the Latin forgotten at Rome, according to Naevius, to his Latin buried by Ennius' living speech, and on down through the efforts to define a proper place for the newcomer, social or literary, amid the censorious display of Roman public life. The qualities vernacular and vulgar are not the isolated attributes of those taking up the challenge to write Latin but are inherent in this culture of Latinity.

In Browning's poem, the anxious bishop views his rival's (Gandolf's) tomb and reads its words, searching for a flaw, for vengeance. The Roman church Browning visited and evokes for us seems in some ways a conflation of the Italian and the English, but this is not the first impression the poet-guide allows his reader-pilgrim. The excerpts below once again set the reader to reading the form of the image of an old man, himself judging Latinity and providing a niche for well-chiseled Latin. Reading stones is an apt exercise for this church, not simply because of the use of granite columns but for its mosaics of the New Jerusalem, and especially because of its relics: the stone slab on which Saint Praxedis slept, the well-top where the sister saints Praxedis and Pudentilla hid the bones of martyrs, and the stone sarcophagi of these saints. In place of these stones, Browning guides us to the bishop's stone, a monument mute or never erected.

> And I shall have St. Praxed's ear to pray
> Horses for ye, and brown Greek manuscripts,
> And mistresses with great smooth marbly limbs
> —That's if ye carve my epitaph aright,
> Choice Latin, picked phrase, Tully's every word,
> No gaudy ware like Gandolf's second line
> —Tully, my masters? Ulpian serves his need . . .
>   (73–79)

Your tall pale mother with her talking eyes,
And new-found agate urns as fresh as day,
And marble's language, Latin pure, discreet,
—Aha, ELUCESCEBAT, quoth our friend?
No Tully, said I, Ulpian at the best!
Evil and brief hath been my pilgrimage.

(96–101)

In our direct viewing of the poem, we overhear a father asking his sons for that which the living can never be sure of, a lasting memorial. The bishop instructs his sons on the building of his tomb, changing the directions in a voice that slips from paternal injunction to senile worry. We hear, too, the polemical voice of the cleric, and finally the (elegiac) voice begrudging through the ages the rival's superior spot. For Gandolf is already dead and buried, decked out with an inscription that prods along the anxious bishop. Of course, we hear by the mediated reading that the poet reconstructs. The only bits of speech left to us, those words the poem presents as archival and objective, are the fragment of the rival's inscription quoted to us by the bishop (ELUCESCEBAT). Now that Gandolf has pride of place, the not-so-good bishop wishes for the best he can get: better Latin. The bishop's resentment arises from the bitter sense that inferior ware and language have been inscribed in memory, in visible record. The poetic commonplace that genuine words, good poetry, will endure longer than the rival's marble holds out the possibility of redress. The poem would constitute this redress—if it were not a Protestant English poem displaying the ungodly Renaissance, Italian rancor of its subject.[15] An English reader sets the sons the bishop should not have and the pleasures he should not have pursued against the religious and linguistic legacy for which he longs. In this mediated reading, where we see his desire for stone as southern materialism and not immortal estheticism, Latin fails to arise as the poetic medium but instead lies dormant, given voice only as the language of the feuding past, of death, of monumentality.[16] The epitaph's lines, the archival Latin, once scrutinized, read as bitterness, pettiness, and worldliness; and the bishop's language, circuitous in its logic, redundant in its syntax, belies its quest for fine chiseled form.

Browning's monologue at first seems to picture two epitaphs in the church; in our own reconstruction of the scene of composition from a knowledge of the poet's Italian trips, we imagine the poet reading the two epitaphs. These readings lead to the dramatic monologue of the poem, which resurrects past voices where now only stone letters survive. And yet do we know there are two inscriptions?[17] We know Gandolf's name but not the bishop's. Reader and poet would know the latter's name had he succeeded in having his sons erect his tomb. In rereading we come to realize that there is no second inscription; the dying man's fear has been realized: his sons, slow to attend him, have substituted common travertine for the choice lapis lazuli and marble he coveted. His criticism and his worry endure: we know of but one epitaph, which reads the inceptive ELUCESCEBAT. What space, what poetic possibilities does the fault, detected by the English pilgrim-poet at the Roman church, open up? Gandolf had inscribed the inceptive verb for the plain form (*elucebat*, "he flourished"). Is he thus the Ulpian, the third-century academic lawyer, rather than the real orator Cicero (this is the charge the bishop makes)? The inceptive form is lively and late, like us or at least like Italian. The Ciceronian ELUCEBAT can be written but not voiced. So ran a strong Renaissance polemic counter to the ardent Ciceronians like Cardinal Bembo—Browning did not stand alone in portraying the imitation of Cicero as deadly. The bishop's proper Latin, however, would make his rival really dead, yet Gandolf's Latin survives and invites our criticism. If we engage in a scholarly tracking of error, we easily determine that the spoken Latin of the Renaissance, or an uncritical reading of the Vulgate Bible, where this form occurs, has caused the "mistake" in diction; but this is only a mistake from the partisan view of Bembo or the nineteenth-century English schoolmasters. If Browning were simply endorsing the criticism of vulgarity, then the reader would group the English poet with the Italian cleric: for such a poet, Rome seems to mean not his church, not the Latin he was taught to write in Ciceronian prose exercises at school. But to reinscribe an authorial name in monumental style, to respond to the linguistic, poetic, scribal rivalry of the past with proper, sterile Latin, without anachronism, is a deadly, name-effacing opus.

Browning has right not the "spirit" of the Renaissance and its contentious clerics, as Ruskin enthused, but the monumentality and linguistic torpor of Latinity facing the vernacular sons.[18] Latin continues to be celebrated for its hard, clean lines, for the rigor and clarity of thought and expression it allegedly instills in unruly young minds. Again and again, Latinity is conflated with education itself, with adulthood, and, in an allied move, with fixed and signifying language, not with the shifting medium of native speech. These are not simply latter-day constructs, for in high literary language the Romans themselves located anxieties about genuine and spurious language, about the authority of language to convey status and identity. Arguably, for the Romans, Latinity was a far less fixed notion. But to treat the past as fluid and the present as stilted inheritor simply recapitulates the polemical shape of notions about linguistic authority and change. Alternately, one could conjure up from the rich and varied Latin past not the lapidary language of the classical age,[19] the squared capital letters of classical architecture and the interlocked word order of the mason-poets, or the revivalist scripts of Charlemagne and the humanist-poets, but the analogous countervoices: the scrawl of Roman handwriting and the palaeographically opaque hands of the Middle Ages. In facing the past, Latinity has been both the medium for continuity and the reminder that our own Latinity constitutes an anachronism. In part, this dual phenomenon and the fact of bilingualism, with Latin as the learned and learnéd language, have succeeded in equating Latinity with classicism and have subordinated or suppressed the other Latins.

Browning's bishop subscribes, as do many postclassical poets, to the elevation of Ciceronian and Augustan Latin at the expense of others. Such a vision clusters together a number of themes (which are at the same time anxieties of composition) and thereby associates proper Latin with endurance, fame, and revenge. Even in Browning's day, Latinity offered material rewards: University examinations and scholarships, civil service positions, and academic posts were all prizes for the individual's public exhibition of Latinity, chiefly determined through composition in the language of Cicero or the Augustan poets or through textual criticism, the detection and remedy of linguistic and stylistic errors perpetrated by medieval and Renaissance scribes. The polemical contexts of this high estheticism need to be emphasized. Reputations continued to turn on judgments of whether a word or idiom was "good" Latin. Among Latin textual critics, such mastery and polemicism have continued to be virtues. The bishop and the textual critic compete for recognition in an economy of extreme scarcity: positions and praise are hard-won; enmities endure. Indeed, this bitter republic of letters sees itself as dwindling, its citizens the rare legitimate sons of the classical. This gendered and social construction of composition, with a strong emphasis on the difficulty of writing properly, hopes to exclude those who have come between the classical expression and the present self. Thus Latinity comes to represent arrival, self-vindication, and a return. It manages these moves only by fixing its own reading at the expense of others', and is consequently acutely aware of the difficulty of making its own reading and writing endure.

When we read "Gandolf," the name of the bishop's rival, do we, like Browning, insert ourselves as readers of the extant inscription and reconstruct the aggrieved, displaced alternative? Do we establish ourselves as champions of Latinity, the true returners, pilgrims to the classical as at the same time we English the scene by not saying Gandolfo? Thus we eschew Italian or vulgar Latin. Browning's poem offers insights into the general issues of this book, and specifically into the literary inscription of the vulgar. The Latin text that enjoys the distinction of barely being in the canon, Petronius's *Satyricon*, the most unmarblelike work of high Latin literature, invites and eventually discredits a similar reading, in part because the most memorable character of that work, the freedman and host Trimalchio, prefigures the bishop as sensualist, literary critic, and tomb orderer.[20] My final chapter considers his libertine language and linguistic relations.

In both Browning's and Petronius's works the reader over-hears a narrator citing a low voice. Never reading or hearing directly for himself, the reader receives a report or comment that orients his reading by censuring the utterance of the text's character. Browning's dramatic monologue, where the poet gives voice to the dead, accentuates the mediated status of our reading. The principal speaker hails the reader not with his epitaph, as was the tradition for some inscriptions and the elegiac poems modeled on these, but from the absence of his epitaph. The vulgarity, the slip of the extant inscription, opens a space for comment, for signature, criticism, and literature. In giving voices to the freedmen, Petronius employs a similar technique of indirect reporting, overhearing, and linguistic snobbery that thematizes the role of language and, as surely, misguides our reading. Characters in the novel do speak their own words, just as all of Browning's poem purports to be the bishop's letter, but linguistic censure and frustrated ambition direct the characters' attempts to inscribe their epitaphs as records of their genuine, Roman selves. And the presence of writer and narrator in the text places the reader in a position analogous to the censorious personae of poet and critic: we overhear the critical voice of the bishop disparaging his rival's Latin; we overhear the snickers of the freeborn protagonists at a vulgar dinner party and, in the first fragment of the narrative, over-hear Ascyltos, himself overhearing a declamation going on inside, complain of the bad speech and speech education of the present day. The critic within the text seems a classical figure, at hand to engage the author's and readers' sympathies.

Yet in reading these self-proclaimed censors, the reader develops a worrying sense of the context and indeed of the voice of the criticism; the speakers seem displaced or belated, like the bishop who has had the best place in the church usurped, anticipated by his rival. The *Satyricon*'s three freeborn heroes follow dimly and clumsily the epic footsteps of Odysseus and Aeneas; no epic hospitality warms them to declare their identity, to deliver epic tales as just recompense for epic treatment. Rather, they seek profit, dinner, sex for their every word. When these characters attempt to adopt a high, literary prejudice, it is as if bad speech were the only thing to move them to literary speech. High style becomes not a corrective or a return to the classical but a nervous tic disquieting all literary and artistic discussions of the *Satyricon*.

More generally, "The Bishop Orders His Tomb" reveals the difficult stance for the postclassical author of the linguistic sneer: the inclusion of bad Latin with criticism of this as vulgarity proves difficult to contain, as reader and author, like the characters, have come late to the banquet of Latin letters. While Petronius's, Varro's, Phaedrus's, Seneca's, and Browning's texts present for the reader's censure the linguistic failings of the socially despised— the Greekish freedmen, the hireling experts, or the Italian cleric— the critics within the text prove venal and rancorous. They commit linguistic sins of their own.[21] Their confidence that they are classical figures, speaking Cicero's language, championing Virgil's text, is eroded as the reader gleans the characters' anachronisms or other small slips that reveal mastery of speech as ambition, snobbery, and an ever-receding desideratum. By making arguments too partisan and complaints too strident, the author presents characters with only the pretense of being the same as the past. Petronius's ironic and ironizing text sullies the high stance of the inscribed critics on the greatest scale, with important consequences for the writing of fiction and the position of the narratorial voice. A reading of Browning's poem suggests how a literary technique of vulgar inscription implicates poet and reader in a shared but belated project.[22] At the same time, such a textual strategy redirects the writing of fiction, leading away from a sterile recapitulation of past language and past genres. For the Roman world, Petronius offered a fundamentally different kind of reading, one that in its postclassical posturings, in its play upon the reader's sympathies and anxieties, has proved inescapable.[23]

When the text does not offer Latinity as something fixed and clear to read, Latium itself becomes a foreign land, a shifting landscape, or a masquerade. With Browning, Italy might be the site of latter-day, contentious claims to dead speech rather than the bucolic, Virgilian land of the poet who is both natural and classical.[24] For the Roman author, mother tongue should distinguish the native of Latium from the *peregrini*, the foreigners and pilgrims who come to Rome and adopt her language. Roman literature, especially in the hands of Phaedrus, for example, exploited for its own ambitious ends this presumption of linguistic identity and legitimation. Mastery of Roman speech replaces mother tongue as blazon of Romanness. The fables of Phaedrus try to keep distinct the polemical, polar lands of Latium and Greece, the places of Latinity and, through a chauvinistic reversal, barbarity. The reader who would find where Latium lies must credit speech, high literary style, as the significant criterion of Roman identity.

Thus Cato has succeeded in erecting a rhetoric of style. His own rhetorical style had masked a reliance on Greek culture and his own innovations under a strong public censorship of all things un-Roman. Just as the drafters of sumptuary legislation hoped to restrict the outward signs of what they took to be vice and extravagance, so the practitioners of Roman letters helped to create a new medium of identity that eschewed the signs of excessive display (any too patent signs of Greekness in style or origin or status). A writer of the first imperial generation employed a topos about the transformative power of literary language not because he was bound by a tradition, but because this topos in its peculiarly Roman nativist guise had significant possibilities for his writing and his culture. Cato, Naevius, and Ennius had helped to develop a rhetoric of stylistic purity on which depended the authority and identity of the writer. The next chapters consider the lines of reproduction of these rhetorical techniques not to chart a progressive development from nativism to marble language (the boast of Ennius and a customary literary history of the difference between early Latin poetry and the Augustans), but to indicate the interconnections of linguistic protocols and the social ambitions of Roman literature.

2

Latin Experts and Roman Masters

Quare mihi non invenuste dici videtur aliud esse
Latine, aliud grammatice loqui.

[And so I think it well said that it is one thing
to speak Latin, quite another to speak pedanti-
cally.]

—Quintilian 1.6.27

ONCE UPON A TIME a Greek diplomat came to Rome, fell into a
sewer, and broke his leg. In fact, the accident victim was a famous
scholar, Crates of Mallos (a small coastal city in Cilicia), who was
visiting Rome in 168 B.C. to represent the king of Pergamum.[1]
Suetonius tells us this story not to illustrate the perils of Roman
streets or the virtues of her sewers but to indicate the beginning of
Latin scholarship. This inaugural story for Western philology reveals a bizarre founding moment of learning, rhetoric, and learned
literature. In place of the libraries of Alexandria and Pergamum,
overflowing with busy editors, old papyri, and royal funding, the
transmission of culture to Rome was a dubious epiphany. The
Greek who captured Rome was an envoy, a king's delegate whose
words captivated the republican Romans.

Stephanie Jed has well exposed the founding anecdotes of
Florentine humanistic philology. These stories self-consciously
bear the marks of dynastic founding stories: they invoke Lucre-
tia and Brutus. Under the pressure of supposed Milanese expan-
sion, the Florentine humanists sought a connection with repub-

lican Rome and founded their philology and political identity on a practice of the restoration of violated texts. Livy provided the story of violation and liberator, and the humanists replicated this plot in their textual practices. By restoring integrity to the text they replayed Brutus's role.[2] But there is nothing dynastic about a stumble in the gutter.

Indeed, chance is present not to mark the hand of the divine, as in some story of an unrecognized heir or the beginning of empire; instead, the Roman story of the dawning of philology codes philology as a late and accidental happening. The Greek who swayed the senate one day has his body maimed the next, and this accident, by definition nonsignificant for the philosophical man, is turned to good use by the practice of the mind: the recuperating patient gave lectures, to which all the youth of Rome flocked. Like the Renaissance humanists, the Romans represented their newfound textual expertise in terms of violation and national identity: an accidental tainting by the sewer and its injury, and recovery, forced recuperation, provide the first cause for scholarship. In these essentials the anecdote mirrors the first exemplum of literature in Rome: Livius Andronicus, the prisoner of war who staged the first play there. Both stories are etiologies of sorts, first accounts of cultural contact and debt, with all the distortion that accompanies such neat genealogies.[3] The Romans receive literature and learning through an accidental, compulsory visitation.

This anecdotal understanding elides cultural contact, cultural continuity, and also the dynamic context of 168 B.C., the year that saw the defeat of the Macedonians and the dedication of a statue group in celebration by the victor Aemilius Paullus in Delphi, the first time a Roman followed the lead of so many kings in remunerating the great religious site of Greece. And as a prize of triumph Paullus brought the great Macedonian library to Rome. This seems a significant, pivotal moment in aristocratic display and in a public valuation of Greek art and artists. Perhaps Crates was simply the first name or anecdote Suetonius had, or he had special relevance as the teacher of Stilo, in turn the teacher of Rome's greatest (noble) scholar, Varro. Crates was also the champion of anomalism, an aspect of a theory of language that Varro would put to such peculiar use. Suetonius has made a significant choice that expresses an anxious ambivalence about the control of speech and expertise. The story of Crates figures very large in the native apologetics about Greek cultural influence and Roman practice. In the biographical accounts of the first practitioners of Roman literature and scholarship, the Greek played the maimed body with a genuine voice. This strain of apologetics and polemics shaped the Romans' intellectual genealogy.

In this chapter I scrutinize the scholar in service, the expert of Latin who served a Roman master. This requires reconsidering the history of philology at Rome. I do so by rereading stories such as that of Crates which, along with a work such as Cicero's *Brutus*, made up Roman thinking about the transfer of cultural expertise. The main focus of the chapter, however, is on the encounter of two elite texts with the figure of the linguistic teacher and expert. Varro's treatise on the Latin language, the *De lingua latina*, like Suetonius's work on grammarians and rhetoricians, affords us a glimpse of the threatening philologue, that figure suspect and masterly in his Greek training and Latin display. However, like Crates's accident, Varro's work is no pivotal moment in the story of philology. Rome abounded in cultural experts and teachers of all sorts. The orator Cicero was publishing dialogues that both performed and laid down prescriptions for an urbane Latin. Within late republican cultural life these two well-published authors had an aristocratic rival expert in Caesar. In trying to construct and exhibit model Latinity, Varro and Cicero were fighting the same battle—they were both vying for cultural authority against, but with the help of, Hellenistic science and Hellenistic experts.[4] Whereas Cicero welcomed a moderated Greek theory, Varro asserted a paradoxical claim to authority. He put forward a strong nativist claim: Latin could be known by Romans and from Romans, without blind reliance on the *semigraeci* poets (and the *grammatici* who taught from their texts). The *De lingua latina* promised to let the reader overhear and understand the speakers of old, those nobles who had handed down their words and left their imprint on the names of Roman places, rites, things.

Varro is important, then, for the trajectory of thinking about Latinity and identity, not because he was more influential than Cicero or because anybody in the subsequent generations preferred reading his massive book to a brief dialogue or sample speech, but because it is through the juxtaposition of his text with those of Cicero and Caesar, and the works of antiquarians and the practices of teaching, that we can see the cultural discourse about Latinity. Varro makes the claim that there can be a Latin more native than the old poet Ennius, that by his authority the recovery and preservation of language—and with it culture—are possible. In his engagement with Cicero and in his preferred methods and statement of authority, Varro emerges as an author working in an ostensibly Hellenistic mode, the technical linguistic treatise, without ceding any authority to the Hellenistic experts.

This chapter treats Varro's technique of etymologizing as a kind of intervention into the cultural discourse about the role and shape of Latin. This necessarily involves a broad account of the context of Varro's work—its intervention in the discourse and practice of the Roman antiquarians and of Cicero and Caesar. To understand Varro's position or posturing in this polemical practice of culture making, I also consider how he etymologizes his own authority. From this account of his advocacy of the words of the eponymous heroes he crowns, Latinus and Romulus, a sense of his target emerges. Varro attempts to displace or suppress the scholars in service, and this silencing of the authorities pushes him to a theoretical difficulty—a misstatement of the categories analogy and anomaly.[5] This theoretical failing shares with the story of Crates the effort to inaugurate a Roman philology; it is in fact a suppression of the continuity of culture and of the role played by the Greek expert serving a Roman master.

In particular terms, Varro advances the practice of etymology as a corrective to declining language, social decay, and the socially inferior teacher. Etymology is a process of intervention.[6] For the most part scholars have dismissed this practice as haphazard and unscientific. Ancient theoretical explanations of etymologizing offer only partial insight into the intellectual and cultural affinities Varro marshaled in selecting and publicizing such a method of expert inquiry. As with Crates's accident, the portrayal of cultural expertise as haphazard conceals significant polemical contexts and practices.[7] Indeed, what needs to be stressed is the seriousness of Varro's endeavor. He was fixing language, as his very definition-etymology of "speak" indicates: "loqui ab loco dictum. . . . Igitur is loquitur, qui suo loco quodque verbum sciens ponit" (6.56). Varro makes the etymology that to speak is from place, but continues to define not what speech is but who is the genuine speaker. This is the conclusion of his paragraph on speech (*loqui*): "Therefore a speaker is one who puts each word in its proper place on the basis of scientific knowledge" (*sciens* meaning "with *scientia*"). Proper speech is not accidental but self-conscious and expert. The passage, like the book, promises a word for every place and a place for every word. Indeed, Varro had begun his books on etymology from the word "place" and then "place-names" (5.14).

Linguistic order and the sites of nature and of Rome are being mapped alongside a social hierarchy. Cicero might agree that only the expert can speak whereas the laity must keep its silence. Varro is assigning words their rightful places,[8] against the practice of metaphor, against the poets and their diction. For metaphor, as Quintilian says, confuses a word's proper and improper place: "transfertur ergo nomen aut verbum ex eo loco, in quo proprium est, in eum, in quo aut proprium deest aut translatum proprio melius est" (8.6.5: "metaphor transfers a name or word from its proper place to a place where there is no proper word or where the transferred word is better than the proper word"). Etymology is thus a kind of anti-figure, a straightening of tropes back into speech. Of course, etymology does make use of analogy, another Greek word for metaphor, as it depends on the drawing of similarities. Varro's science refuses to grant the poets the high authority for constituting language. His work will anchor semantic motion and verbal drift with a proper, moderated analogy.[9]

At the end of this chapter I return to Suetonius's account

of grammarians and rhetoricians for some bad examples—a more direct encoding of the socially pathological teacher. These denigrated lives of teachers make transparent the Roman masters' worry about Latin experts.[10] But a chapter devoted to experts in Roman speech and scholarship begins with the author of the *De lingua latina*, the heir to Crates who substituted a vast Roman encyclopedia for the accidental transmission of Greek learning.

Why did Varro write a major work on the Latin language in the last decade of the Roman republic? Not many have found this a question worth asking. Varro was the greatest Roman antiquarian and scholar. He had had a great philologist as a teacher. He had written on language before. And so scholars have delineated the strains of Hellenistic scholarship allegedly shaping his work. We might look ahead and celebrate Varro for inaugurating a great tradition of writing about Latin. I do not mean the innumerable dissertations on the Latinity of every and any author from Plautus to Dante, but the grander Renaissance tradition of Erasmus or the translator of Thucydides, the fifteenth-century Lorenzo de Valla who, when Italy was agog with the introduction of Greek texts and Greek scholars from a fallen Byzantium, wrote six books on the elegance of the Latin language where he perversely declared that Latin was better suited to philosophy than Greek. There were staunch advocates for the revision of written Latin on the strict model of Ciceronian practice, like Cardinal Bembo, and vigorous opponents, from Erasmus, who disdained to ape Cicero, to the great poet himself, Dante, whose *On Vulgar Eloquence* made the arguments for writing in the vernacular. On the Italian peninsula and in the Renaissance more generally, beneath issues of mastery of speech there fermented such divisive topics as scriptural authority, the status of pagan literature, the authority to interpret both, and, along with these, social codes of aristocratic and middle-class culture, and regional disputes. All those who dared to enter this fray chose their authorities carefully; chief among these were Cicero's thinking and practice on Latinity and Varro's great response, the massive, allegedly systematic and encyclopedic account of the *De lingua latina*. We should not be taken in by the basic strategies of most of these texts: the confident assertion that there is one Latin, and that language choice and use resides in an autonomous realm of rules and propriety.

If we stick to the high plane of intellectual history, we miss what is distinctively polemical about the *De lingua latina* and risk making Varro into a caricature of the unscrupulous antiquarian muddying the clear fonts of Hellenic knowledge. Intellectual history practiced on a Roman author falls all too easily into a canonical form: the Latin text symbolizes weak intermediary, with the passage from Greek to Latin explained as intellectually and chronologically a divertimento in the journey from Greek to modern. The scholar discovers the Roman misprison and traces the ramifications for the errant science of the Middle Ages before restoring his readers to the Greek contribution. Again we see the anxieties of the vernacular son, with the twist that, for the philosopher or the physicist, the Greek represents the quondam genuine, transparent knowledge.

In the years that saw the assassinations of Julius Caesar and Marcus Tullius Cicero, no inevitable logic compelled an author to stuff twenty-five books with etymologies and obsolete words. Perhaps there was nothing inevitable about other great Roman projects: the various fora and public buildings of Pompey and Julius and Augustus Caesar or the textual megaliths of Livy's 126 books of Roman history or the more readable twelve of Virgil's *Aeneid*. From the Theater of Pompey of 55 B.C. to the death of Virgil in 19 may be yet another arbitrary periodization, but I evoke these public, unifying works of culture as much for their rhetorics of a single Romanness as for their historical context, the bitter, sometimes violent contests among the elite for power, the changing social conditions, and cultural and political involvement of the peoples of the Italian peninsula and to a lesser degree of the provincial elites.[11]

As an endpoint for all the literary production of the forties B.C., the decade in which Caesar, Cicero, and Varro wrote on the Latin language, one might fix upon the redistribution of land in Italy in 41 B.C. and Virgil's *Eclogues* arising from and influencing this arrangement of Octavian. But to imagine the range of textual projects we should include the writings of men like the upper-class partisan of Pompey and writer on Latin grammar, Nigidius Figulus, who died in 45. It is hazardous to think of Roman cultural and national context solely in terms of Virgil, the dispossessed landowner born a Paduan and made an Italian with the rest of upper Italy in 42.[12] No doubt we should remember those who did not win the support of the new regime, like the former praetor, Cicero's friend and informant, the learned Figulus. Varro eclipsed that scholar, his fellow Pompeian, and managed to escape his fate and win a new life under or alongside Augustus. Was Varro a political chameleon, more suspect than the esthetic Virgil (for Varro had strong ties to Pompey and Cicero)? Virgil would be introduced into the schools, and schoolmasters then set upon his and Horace's poems to inculcate Latinity. But we must forget the *Aeneid* for a while and think of other definitions of Rome, Italy, and Latin, including the works of antiquarians such as Nigidius Figulus. Thereby we read afresh these texts not as discrete fore-runners of Virgil or of Renaissance social and esthetic codes but as organizations and inventions of knowledge.

In many ways, Varro lost the culture wars until the Renaissance required a monumental model for linguistic and cultural hegemony.[13] More to the point, Varro's works were not the disinterested creation of a scholar at leisure. His success and program can be glimpsed from the overwrought praise that Cicero would pay him (as prepayment, arranged by Atticus, for Varro's dedication of his magnum opus to Cicero himself, the well-published authority and Varro's opponent in many spheres—political, social, and intellectual—especially as Cicero was the recognized authority on rhetoric and proper Latin style).[14] Cicero wrote a dedicatory letter to Varro, assigned him a leading role in the dialogue the *Academica*, and exuberantly declared, in the course of the work:

Tum ego "Sunt" inquam "ista Varronis. nam nos in nostra urbe pere-grinantis errantisque tamquam hospites tui libri quasi domum deduxe-runt, ut possemus aliquando qui et ubi essemus agnoscere. tu aetatem patriae tu descriptiones temporum, tu sacrorum iura tu sacerdotum, tu domesticam tu bellicam disciplinam, tu sedum regionum locorum tu omnium divinarum humanarumque rerum nomina genera officia causas aperuisti." (*Acad*. 1.9)

[At this point I said, "Those are the achievements of Varro. For we were wandering in our own city like foreign tourists when your books brought us back to our home, as it were, so that now at last we can see who and where we are. It was you who discovered the antiquity of our fatherland, the periods of our chronology, the laws of our rites and priests, our practices at home and at war, you restored the names, distinctions, rites, and origins of the sites, locales, and places of all our human and sacred affairs."]

Varro had given "us" back a Rome formerly so murky that she had been unknown. Cicero's simile of readers as foreigners in their own native land grants the written text great authority. The reader is a pilgrim recovering lost rites and seeing shrines for the first time. No doubt Varro thought he was improving on Cicero, who peopled his dialogues with Roman historical characters but acknowledged a certain looseness with history.[15] In fact, Varro's provision of a Roman homecoming anticipates Augustus's "restoring" the republic, refurbishing temples, and resurrecting lost rites, and, like the future emperor, he does so against the counterclaims of others to represent the true republic. Furthermore, he is hailed with perhaps mock solemnity as a god (the repeated familiar "you's" [*tu*] characterize the opening of a prayer),[16] a conceit which amplifies that of reader as pilgrim. Of course, the revivers of culture had much to invent and looked back on an ancestral language and customs they could not understand. By hailing Varro as a bringer of light, Cicero means that old Rome was unknown and that the new Rome is inhabited by Caesarians who make a mockery of the old institutions. The literary congratulation of another author can subtly deflect the course of the original's work.

Rather than seeing Rome restored, as Cicero would have it, we should see claim and counterclaim for cultural authority. The decade of the forties is not the birth of history or historical self-awareness but one sophisticated moment in Romans' use of history, originary thinking, and primitivist versus modernist rhetorics, all of which should remind us not just of Virgil but of old Cato and his—the first Latin—Roman history, the *Origines*. Varro is not quite the bold innovator or disinterested scholar but the inheritor of a strong polemical tradition of Roman native writings about their recovered past. By probing the animus of Varro's *De lingua latina*, I shall describe some of the social and cultural forces behind the rise of Roman antiquarianism and illustrate why and how theorizing about the Latin language was a potent form of cultural discourse. For, like many of the texts discussed in this book, Varro's *De lingua latina* includes its own flawed critics. It inscribes linguistic authorities who oppose the author and insistently marks these as deviant. Varro, however, has succeeded in convincing readers that his is the authoritative account and that his text represents nonpartisan theory or, a little worse, slightly haphazard but wide-ranging note taking.

Roman Antiquarianism

Varro, Cicero, and Caesar wrote about language in a world overflowing with expertise. We cannot survey the Roman literate classes on their scholarly interests or chart the movements of all the journeymen rhetoricians, philosophers, and physicians drawn to Rome. But just after our period we can see Augustus taking a strong interest in Hellenistic experts, and he was exploiting, not inventing, an increased interest in Rome's past.[17] The symbiosis of Roman national self-consciousness and Roman literate expertise demands volumes in its own right, again over familiar territory, beginning with philological interest in the early poets and extending to world histories, such as that of the Greek Dionysius of Halicarnassus who wrote under Augustus, and beyond to the library of culture offered by Plutarch and the general recension of republican history and culture in the early empire.

Our focus must be far narrower: Varro, Cicero, and Caesar had contemporary Roman experts to consider. These include

those who suffer the name of "antiquarians," probably an unjust appellation. The term embraces such contemporaries as Varro
and Nigidius Figulus, whose works set themselves at a distance
from narrative history. The word *antiquarian* in English distinguishes from the historian a researcher into the past whose work
is essentially pointless. Such refined scholarship is pursued for its
own sake, directed by the eccentric and idiosyncratic taste of the
scholar. As a professional term of abuse, it marks a scholarship
that refuses to attempt synthesis and interpretation.[18] This understanding of the term does not suit Varro, except that it accurately
captures two aspects of the scholar's project: a distance from narrative history and the allied stance that the work is free of ideology and partisan spirit. Apparently, the antiquarian, like some
sense-impaired bee, gathers from every flower; his archival study
replays the record of history more accurately than does the work
of the avowed historian. In more exact, literary terms, the antiquarian's writings present a shift in genre and in the claims of the
text's authority. Here we see the past directly and fully, whereas
the annalistic historians had followed the fiction that they were
commemorating the kind of highwater marks in public life that
the priest's annals had listed year by year or where the panegyri-
cal poet or eulogist had overcelebrated a family's role in Roman
history. In particular, Varro offered a totalizing work, not tied
to chronology, one family, or even one period or event (like Sallust's monographs). Thus, whereas many authors in Rome would
use etymology or perhaps comment on some old-fashioned spelling, Varro devoted unique books to etymology and orthography.
Similarly, Nigidius Figulus wrote individual works on Roman
grammar and religion; he did not simply recount early practice, as
Livy did, where appropriate in his narrative, and Figulus was the
acknowledged expert.

What has been missed in accounts of the scholarly activity of
the 60s to 40s B.C. is the social pressure and use of such knowledge.
Cicero provides two clues: he refers to the utility of Atticus's little
book of comparative chronology and in the *Brutus* tries to connect
his young dedicatee with the founding consul, L. Brutus.[19] Atticus

had written genealogical works.[20] The custom of false genealogies, which Atticus's works made less possible, aroused the aristocrats' indignation.[21] But the real innovator and propagandist of genealogy had been Caesar, whose funeral laudation for his aunt made the boast of divine ancestry for the Julian clan.[22] Varro's *De familiis troianis* was no doubt in part a response to Caesar's *laudatio*, but one that the freedman of Augustus, the learned C. Julius Hyginus, saw fit to redo in his *De familiis troianis*.[23] Essentially, Caesar constructed genealogy through etymology: he derived his clan name (his *nomen* or *nomen gentilicium*), Julius, from Julus, the son of Aeneas, the son of Venus. Roman family names (*cognomina*) lent themselves to this kind of history from nomenclature, as many family names seemed originally to have been nicknames, describing a personal attribute, often a physical oddity—so the Caesars could have invented a story that their founder was born by cesarian section.

Some names and the stories derived from them are better for politics than others. No doubt it helped old Cato that his name meant "shrewd." But Caesar's great etymologizing claim was bolder, and perhaps spurred Varro to realize the social and political dimensions of etymology. For it is one thing to write etymologies of the words found in an old and difficult text, and quite another to etymologize an entire culture. Of course, Varro did not write in the modern tradition of the alphabetized, complete dictionary. In the *Antiquities*, he raised etymology to a method for the reconstruction of the history of the institutions and customs of the Romans from the earliest, most nebulous period. And his etymologizing depended on inference about connections of words with other words, of words with institutions, of Roman words or practices with Greek words and practices. Etymology thus practices a comparative culture making, working backwards from the present word to explain the reasons for its original *impositio* and explaining its formal *declinatio* from this original state. The past is recovered at the same time as the present ruin is explained.

The skills and habits of mind of the etymologist have seemed arbitrary or peculiar to modern linguists whose credo is simply

that no ancient hunter for the original could have tracked anything, for we need the keen nineteenth-century hounds of phonology just to discern the appropriate *comparanda*. Thus the old
etymologizers have been abandoned as manifesting an alien thinking. But both the last republican and the nineteenth centuries
may have fetishized the individual word. Certainly, Varro's generation wrote widely on the proper etymology, spelling, and use
of Latin words. No doubt there was greater concern over the pronunciation of the Latin word than the isolated references from
ancient literature provide.[24] Like these other prescriptions on the
individual word, etymologizing presents language expertise as a
diachronic mode. Synchrony along with syntax is displaced. This
allows a fixity of culture, a restoration of a pristine state.

The practice of etymology does not constitute a primitivist,
early stage in language inquiry. Etymologizing is an ideological reflex that allows associations backwards, elides contemporary connections (partisanship), and substitutes a universal deviancy for
complex causation.[25] Plato had ridiculed in the *Cratylus* the kind
of etymologizing now practiced by Varro. To its critics, etymologizing has always seemed capricious; but the caprice was always
one of association. Socrates playfully derives οὐρανός (heaven)
from ὁρῶ τὰ ἄνω (seeing the things above)—this was too much
for Plato, who knew from the science of the day plenty about the
heavens and had his own ideas about vision, naming, and knowledge.[26] Etymology's great allure is its ability to trespass, to make
the connections that ordinary parlance has forgotten, and to suggest an authority that a proper discipline like astronomy or religion cannot glimpse. Etymologizing presents oblivion, historical
deformation, and human error as linguistic phenomena. Thus the
exact speaker or researcher can gather unto himself all correction
—social, national, moral. In etymologizing, Varro practiced not
just a recovery or invention of the Roman but a model in identity
making and, in the judgments of rival experts like Palaemon, in
false identities.[27]

The modern critic may see only the error, his own distance,
from all this ancient, contentious expertise. More charitably, in

thinking about Atticus writing his censorious account of Roman genealogies, we might have characterized both his own "true" and his opponents' "false" time lines as simple progress in the dawning of Western historical consciousness. Romans were examining their past in a spirit of inquiry made possible by a more perfect acquaintance with Hellenistic scholarship under the pressure of the late republican and Augustan emulation of the Greeks in particular and past great empires in general. Cicero's notices do attest to the fogginess of the Roman past, to the difficulty of knowing Rome's early history and her many like-named citizens—topics that twentieth-century archaeology and prosopography claim as their signal contributions. But here we would be arguing again for a progressive narrative, this time about historiography.

The difficulty of historical investigation did not stop the Romans; surely it provided them an opening to write themselves into history. The progressive argument maintains that they were simply doing what they could do: applying a simplifying word-based science to a difficult area. In fact, the antiquarians were making choices; they were practicing a form of revisionism that aimed to recover the past from those who would put it to different purposes. Those include the historians who were writing grand narratives, and also the men who claimed noble (or divine) ancestors not their own. We might understand Rome's antiquarian program not as fixed version of truth regained but as authoritative legislation: a comprehensive rule-making is published so as to check the poaching of partisans. Varro's and Atticus's efforts can then be seen as an effort toward social fixity—declaring who has genuine Roman blood. Varro's method is far more devastating than any census list, because he takes up the symbolic subjects of cultural authority. Caesar's emphasis on state religion, which I suggest Varro appropriated and perhaps rerouted in his own treatment, may not seem innovative, as it anticipates the familiar developments of Augustus and the empire; but it was essentially anti-antiquarian. "Religion" becomes an academic subject as it becomes a state, collective phenomenon whose revival is jointly a state and a literary function.[28]

In the abstract these views do not overlap: the antiquarian view would locate practices in individual settings and families. Antiquarianism is a reflex of a dispossessed nobility, but it is also a collective, textual practice. At the same time, it marks the end of its possessors' exclusive rights, for the rites of the aristocratic priestly colleges, once known by oral tradition, can now be read, as surely as the old words of Latium will live on not in the mouths of old Latin nobles but in the readers of Varro's pages. Both the dictator's laws and the scholar's text assimilate and institutionalize heterogeneous practices, rites, and socially marked traditions.

The past of the antiquarian's pages remains foreign in a way that the past evoked by Caesar, Cicero, and Augustus did not. That is, a certain kind of scholarship is interested in leaving murk to the past. The gap between it and the present can be strongly marked and even lamented. Varro would be conscripted into the Caesarian sharing of the past: he was saved, ostensibly, after the dismantling of his own library, to administer Caesar's public library. Varro's work the *Imagines* may have been a textual analogue to the collection of *imagines* with which Augustus lined his own forum. The characters need not have been the same; the technique of excerption, illustration, and epigram was. The *De lingua latina* makes a similar museum or picture-gallery display of Romanness. The reader is more a tourist than he ever imagined: his language, like his generals, stretches back in an uninterrupted line to the virtuous founding time of the state. The two Caesars, Cicero, and Varro, among others, were engaged in a contest of *imagines*, in reconstituting who the Roman heroes were.[29] Cicero and Julius Caesar were more consciously engaged in a form of leveling: Caesar in his chosen style of egalitarian but aristocratic *commentarii* (the general's unscripted notes overread by the public) and, I believe, in his linguistic writing *On Analogy*; Cicero in his dialogues, whose triumphant union of conflicting viewpoints performed the very *concordia ordinum* the author repeatedly called for in Roman society.[30] Varro fragments these teleological histories: far more learning is needed than the simplifying evocations of the rhetorician and politician admit.

Relations with Cicero:
Responsion and Appropriation

Cicero and Varro produced very different, though intersecting, major texts in a politically tumultuous period. It is not the case that Cicero was a towering intellectual presence who had to be reckoned with, a literary force who could not be ignored, nor simply that their mutual friend Atticus had brought about the reconciliation of the two leading literary beneficiaries of Caesar's *clementia*. As authors, Cicero and Varro came close to ignoring each other, that is to say, not naming one another. But in the end they did submit to that gesture of literary deference, the inclusion of the other author's name either as dedicatee or as interlocutor. Cicero's correspondence with Atticus provides the following chronology of the social and literary relations between Cicero and Varro: Cicero hoped Varro's influence would move Pompey to shield him from exile at the hands of Clodius (*Ad Att.* 2.20.1; 2.21.6). Varro disappointed Cicero. Atticus pressed Cicero to include Varro as a character in one of his dialogues (*Ad Att.* 4.16.2). (Varro dedicates the second half of the *Antiquities*, on state religion, to Caesar. Caesar removes Varro from the list of the proscribed and names him as curator of the public library he promised to establish.) The spared Cicero and Varro enjoy a reconciliation. Varro visits Cicero at Tusculum where they have a friendly, high-minded discussion (on philosophy, *Ad fam.* 9.6.4). The alliance between them began to cool after Caesar's return.[31] Varro failed to fulfill his promise to dedicate a work to Cicero, who, for his part, insulted Varro by not including him among the orators in the *Brutus*. Atticus renewed his suggestion that Cicero include Varro in a dialogue. Cicero rewrote the *Academica* with Varro as a main speaker representing the views of Antiochus of Ascalon. After much hesitation, because he had better defended his own philosophical position in the dialogue (representing the view of Philo of Larissa), Cicero had Atticus present a copy of it to Varro. The *Academica* achieved its goal, as Varro dedicated the *De lingua latina* (in part) to Cicero.[32]

Biographical histories of the figures of the late Republic tend to depict every occurrence as opportunistic reaction to political events. As do the biographers of Cicero, the Varronian scholar measures his man against the pop-up figures of supreme power. Allegiance to and disaffection from Pompey, Caesar, or Octavian are tortuously traced.[33] Through a course of political events impinging on authorial production, we come to the *De lingua latina*, the magnum opus. The connections of Varro's text are more subtle and deep than either the historical readings of political biography or progressive intellectual history allow.

Both Cicero and Varro were writing Roman constitutions —far more textual and concrete utopian writings than Caesar planned or the great nineteenth-century scholar Mommsen imagined. Cicero's philosophical writings form something of a counter-Rome during the disrupted and divisive times of the 50s and 40s B.C. These Latin dialogues with Roman characters, however anachronistic, are complex texts, the publication of a professed, not legal, exile. The dialogues and the texts on rhetoric and oratory abound with visions of Rome, Roman language, and society even as they transmit versions of Hellenistic philosophy and learning. Both Varro and Cicero were involved in unifying and totalizing projects, at times in competition or in complicity with Julius Caesar's own literary, legislative, and architectural plottings of the new Rome. Along with his other works, Varro's *Antiquities* described what the genuine Roman world was, in a time when such a claim had the highest political and social importance; for the discourse of the civil struggles centered around who the true Roman was.

The rancorous propaganda of this time presented Caesar as ambitious autocrat or as republican noble and champion of the people with wounded dignity, Caesar as pontifex and general or Caesar as the pathic homosexual.[34] So, too, the partisans cast Pompey in the roles of republican champion or as the Eastern devotee and betrayer of his friend and father-in-law, Caesar. All this political biography, the slanderous and the euphemistic, turned on an exclusivist claim: the political figure is alleged to be the arch-Roman or the arch–anti-Roman. Whereas Varro's *Antiquities* accepted Caesar and inscribed him and his view of state religion into a massive text, so his partial dedication of the *De lingua latina* to Cicero included Cicero's project—the dialogues, which, though set off generically as more Greek and biographically as the work of his retirement, in fact continue, like his speeches, to create a new consensus of what constituted proper Roman style and behavior. Cicero's dialogues stressed a new readerly Romanness not on the basis of birth or military distinction but on the authority of proper Roman speech and culture.

Of course, Varro's gestures toward his addressees have appropriated both ways: he adopts Caesar's ideology and yet, by imbuing it with scholarly authority, attempts to shift its basis of authority, to deradicalize it. And Caesar's vision of religion is only a part of the *Antiquities*. Finally, despite its totalizing aims, the *Antiquities* would be revised by Cicero's dialogues the *De divinatione* (published in the wake of Caesar's assassination) and the *De fato*. Thus, the contest for literary capital has resonances beyond personal or even party animosities. The writing of these large works presented a Roman reader with synthesizing efforts that mirrored and rivaled the political, social, and military cohesion of Caesar and his generation. Cicero's and Varro's relationship should thus be seen as a trading and jockeying of status and authority that do not simply devolve from Caesar or his victory but are a shaping element of contemporary forces.

Varro's Etymologizing

In the *De lingua latina* Varro seeks to redirect the manner and substance of these great rivals in constituting Latinity. As an antiquarian work and a moderated champion of anomaly, the long work departs significantly from the self-consciously rhetorical and political "historical" dialogues of Cicero and the *De analogia* of Caesar, with its leveling, easy, egalitarian language. The length of Varro's work, its use of abstract terminology, and its conflation of methodologies defeat any reader looking for a manual of

Latinity. And yet the *De lingua latina* makes way for both Caesar
and Cicero, devoting a book to Caesar's position (book 9 is *pro
analogia*), following Cicero's dialogic division (one book contra,
one pro, one practical Roman synthesis, although without allowing the voices of these books the authority of a historical mouthpiece).[35] The scope of Varro's work testifies to its author's leisure
and demands a great deal of its reader's patience. Its method has
none of the economy of a handbook. For instance, he explains
that the Palatine Hill received its name

quod Pallantes cum Evandro venerunt, qui et Palantini; <alii quod Pala-
tini>, aborigines ex agro Reatino, qui appellatur Palatium, ibi conse-
<de>runt; sed hoc alii a Palanto uxore Latini putarunt. Eundum hunc
locum a pecore dictum putant quidam; itaque Naevius Balatium appel-
lat. (5.53)

[because the Pallantes came there with Evander (they were also known
as the Palatines); others explain that the Palatine received its name because the Palatines, a native people from a plain of Reate, which is called
Palatium, settled there; still others attribute the name to Palanto the wife
of Latinus. There are even those who think the place was named from the
flocks; so Naevius calls it the Bleatine Hill.]

This passage nicely shows the state of the text, the near ab-
surdity of some of the information, and its uselessness. More to
the point, it reveals the categories of inclusion and analysis. Within
the broad categories of his subject matter, place-names, Varro is
conducting a tour of the city of Rome. Despite his polemic elsewhere, here Varro employs a more than Herodotean tendency to
report variants. He lumps together mythic material, a corresponding place-name that we may imagine only a citizen of Reate like
Varro would know, and poetic exegesis. The poet's *figura etymologica* comes last, disparaged perhaps by the final *quidam* (people
whose names do not matter).[36] No one will find this an easy
tourist guide or a synthesis of the Greek and Roman. It may seem
a kind of free association, a morphological drift from Palatium
to Pallantes to Palantini and on to Palatini via Palatium, then

to Palanto, and last and least Balatium. In fact, he derives place-name from inhabitants and vice versa in a move from Greek gloss (the Greek companions of Evander) to sympathetic, resounding nature (the baaing sheep). One could try to describe admissible phonetic parameters: voiced for voiceless stop, reduction of syllabic length through reduction of double consonant, insertion of nasal. None of these, however, needs to be so categorized, for the set of authorities is a more important criterion than any system of sound variations.

Varro ranges through languages but not in a random fashion. The origins he imagines for Rome itself guide his choice of language. Etiology and etymology are one and the same: transplanted Greek, aboriginal Italic, natural Sheep are the potential sources for the Latin word. Virgil understood this technique of identity when he came to write an Italic topography in his founding poem. In the *Aeneid*, Evander and Latinus would figure as rival founders, against and alongside the native wolf that had traditionally suckled Romulus and Remus. In the native concoction of identity, the autochthonous and the Greek are recurrent rivals. But Virgil is not the only literary parallel. The first text known to the Romans that dealt with linguistic investigation was Herodotus's *Histories*. At the beginning of the second book, the pharaoh Psammetikos seeks to discover who is the oldest people and founds this quest for human origins on a linguistic experiment. Isolating some children from all human contact, he carefully waits for their speech. The first word ($\beta\epsilon\kappa\acute{o}s$) he then finds to be Phrygian. Herodotus records the savvy anxiety that perhaps the children were imitating the sheep that were their only companions.

Although his mininarratives do not so clearly rely on naming from nature and animal speech, Varro too is tracking first words. He admits the concern that his science may simply be mistaking the asinine or ovine for the rational and human. The etymologizer returns to dumb animals, for he is always close to the complaint that his science interprets the ass's braying as significant expression. At the same time, Varro shares with Herodotus a fascination with linguistic inquiry as a process of ethnic or collective identity

making. In his hesitant and self-conscious search for an explanatory model—for what the connection of place, name, and people
is—the range of authorities represents the permissible fields of
explanation: Evander, Reate, Latinus, the poet Naevius with his
version of Herodotus's old etymology. The criteria of Hellenistic
textual practice—analogy and anomaly—are no guide here. Instead of seeing Varro's method as a tepid conduit of Hellenistic
theory, we should ask where the search for origins leads the late
republican Roman. Who and what practice are authoritative?

The striking fact is that Varro is not rigorously exclusive. He
does not communicate an easily imitable science, a technique of
analysis, but rather a field of possibilities: his work holds out the
promise of his and his reader's mastery of a Roman landscape,
a cultural and historical layered landscape where names gather
for their exegesis other texts—Greek and Latin, written and oral.
Poets and historical figures have the same epistemological weight
as the Italic landscape itself, so too the all but lost ways in which
Italic ancestors spoke, words and places that only a noble Roman,
with his contacts of patronage throughout the Italic peninsula,
could bring to bear on the text of Latinity.

In his sense that his words and places are of literary importance, in his moderated disdain for the poet, and in his contempt
for the expert's single explanation and the exclusivist claim of
analogy, Varro displays an aristocratic inclusiveness with affinities closer to the poet and satirist Lucilius than to the new man
Cicero. In fact, Varro's etymologizing maps a Roman culture at
odds with Cicero, especially in its resistance to Greek culture and
to various figures of expertise. At times he seems to evoke and
even surpass Cicero's technique in the philosophical and rhetorical
dialogues to construct an anachronistic, almost utopian Roman
world. Varro, however, refuses a facile textual synthesis of Greek
and Roman culture. According to him, there are not three schools
of philosophy but 288 kinds. Whereas Cicero delights in quoting
the old Roman poets, Varro shows a hostility to these figures as
cultural authorities.[37] Like the old heroes of Cicero's exempla, the
early poets added a Roman flavor to the decidedly Greek subject

and form of Cicero's dialogues. Like Plato's quotations from the poets, Cicero's citations of early drama and epic help to create an *urbanitas*, which is both a style of Latin and a more general intellectual, social, and political outlook. Varro's text constantly brings his reader back to Latinus and the early Roman shepherds.[38] For the poets, and especially for those who would rely on them for establishing *Latinitas*, Varro has special barbs.[39]

Undoubtedly, Varro did continue the polemics and principles of some of his teachers. Stilo's interest in the Twelve Tables and the *carmina Saliorum* may have contributed to Varro's more eclectic definition of Latin and anticipates his emphasis on recovering the language of the *prisci Latini*. But this can be only a partial explanation for Varro's antipathy to the *grammatici* and his polemical championing of *rusticitas*. He breaks with his teacher Stilo, who had claimed, according to Varro (Quintilian says, at 10.1.99), that the Muses would have spoken in Plautine style, had they wanted to speak Latin.[40] Like Cato's work on farming, Varro's *De re rustica* trumpeted the author's simple country ways. Tertullian called Varro the Roman Diogenes for his spare, sever life-style (*Ad nat.* 1.10), which would have delighted the cosmopolitan scholar; but he was fantastically wealthy, as were his relatives: Marcus, the brother of L. Licinius Lucullus, was adopted by an M. Terentius Varro.

Varro preserves Rome in the *De lingua latina*, but a Rome whose reconstitution time, memory, usage, and the *grammatici* threaten. He delayed the publication of the work, apparently on the impulse of a different sort of threat. Written between 47 and 45 B.C., the text appeared between the deaths of Caesar and Cicero (the Ides of March 44 and December 7, 43 B.C.). Perhaps a fear that the optimate cause was lost held Varro back, and then in the hopeful days of Brutus and Cassius he brought it out. In some sense, like Cicero's account of the Roman orators in the *Brutus*, the publication can be thought of as a revival of the author's conservative program addressed to a young generation who were both aristocratic and onetime Caesarians, men susceptible to a rhetorical call for reconciliation and synthesis. Such an explanation of the mo-

tives of composition and publication remains fixed in the political
sphere. In addition, the text posits other sorts of threats and im-
pulses, which provide an index to its wider and deeper anxieties.

Varro's readership is as vague as Cicero's *boni omnes*, the consensus of good men who, the text assures the reader, would respond properly to the text. Varro and Cicero indulge a technique
that levels the literate into one approved, Roman political class. In
the *De lingua latina* this idealized leveling of the readers depends
on a number of antitheses: slaves and gods do one thing, we free
men another;[41] the people lapse in their speech, we should not
(we read Varro);[42] the *grammatici* turn to the poets for their construction of proper Latinity, we have a better source; analogists
and anomalists pursue their extreme courses, we a Roman middle
ground. Thus, from a contrast of national, social, and philosophical differences, the true Roman emerges. In Varro's pages the genuinely Roman exists as much by the contrast with these categories
as by any archival investigation into old Latin. The *grammatici*
constitute a particularly important antithetical pole, as they professed the rival authority and the rival methodology to the declared subject of the text. In searching for authorities, for names
of old-time Romans like the interlocutors of Cicero's dialogues,
Varro conjures up the vaguest of Rome's historical exempla, the
eponymous heroes Romulus and Latinus:

Non enim videbatur consentaneum quaerere me in eo verbo quod finxisset Ennius causam, neglegere quod ante rex Latinus finxisset, cum poeti-
cis multis verbis magis delecter quam utar, antiquis magis utar quam
delecter. An non potius mea verba illa quae hereditate a Romulo rege
venerunt quam quae a poeta Livio relicta? (5.9)

[For it does not seem consistent for me to investigate the etymology of a
word which Ennius invented and to eschew a word which King Latinus
had invented long before, since I enjoy far more than I use many poetic
words and I use far more than I enjoy ancient words. Really, aren't those
words more my own which have come to me as a legacy of Romulus than
those left by the poet Livius?]

Latinus and Romulus stand in for tradition, but what or whose tradition? How are their words to be known? How will Varro respond to the experts who cite the early poets? He represents the poets' words as belonging to the world of pleasure, whereas utility characterizes the kings' words. The commonplace of pleasure and utility does not promise much. Varro is conflating a number of antitheses, and the forced bridging of their differences reveals an insistent concern with defining who, and not simply what, constitutes Latin. The vagueness of his appeal to the old kings has a certain rhetorical point; the contrast of the literally Roman-named (Romulus and Latinus) with the poets who assumed Roman names suggests that the needed supplement for establishing Roman and Latin identity rests in the spheres of nature and tradition. In addition, this passage's appealing call for moderation and synthesis replays a contemporary construct of thought, speech, and action. The shadowy, mythical figures establish Varro's singular authority. The passage pleads that no single, exclusive means will suffice to describe and communicate Latinity. If it did, anyone could adopt that method. In fact, we cannot even depend on the authority of the unknowable Latinus and Romulus, but must rely on the native interpreter who has access to that tradition.

In the semimythic kings Varro has etymologized his own authority. He has provided us with signifying ethnic names rather than the individual Messapic and Greek-hybrid names of Quintus Ennius and Livius Andronicus. Perhaps, too, with some humor he has turned from the poets to his own metaphor for the resuscitation of the past. Nonetheless, he draws attention to the obscurity of the past, that muddled state from which Cicero had said Varro had rescued us all. If Varro was illuminating the shadow world of Latinus and Romulus, why present his authority and results in such a discursive, inconclusive form? Why should a work of Hellenistic science seek authority in an obscure past? By resurrecting Latinus and Romulus, Varro indulges in a rhetoric of a markedly nationalist cast. He here makes use of a rhetoric familiar to us all:

commonsense, inherited tradition, not innovative theory, must guide us.

The application of such arguments to debates about language can propound particularly exclusivist and reactionary programs. Thus, arguments about the purity of French perforce ignore the expertise of linguists who would think of linguistic change as typical, and this modern nativist rhetoric harkens back both to an idealized past of purity and to a less theoretical and more pre-scriptive, normative linguistics. In the modern debate, the gram-marians are ranged against the linguists, the teachers of children against the professors of adolescents and youths, the idealized school world of rules and fixity against the more open experimen-tation associated with the university, young adulthood, and mod-ern society. Common sense is inextricably bound up with national sense against an internationalist or European science. Of course, in trying to exorcise the foreign, and more specifically the Ameri-can, this obscurantist program works its own oblivion: the role of French linguists and intellectual history is conveniently ignored. Quite clearly, the Roman grammarians figured influences and social anxieties different from the French. I cite this contentious issue as a reminder of the spheres of polemic that debate about language carries and because, within these social and national con-tentions, the teacher of language enjoys a unique status. Far more than father or mother, he signals access to an authoritative past and its high language. Parents may speak the standard language at home, but the schoolteacher spreads it to the newcomer. He alone validates change or makes the arriviste indistinguishable from the native son.

Schools, Schoolmen, and Scholastic Practice

Varro makes a grand display of the proper access to ancestral speech. By its very size his book precludes other investigations; the task of reassembling Latin is done; no theory, no expert need compete. Varro discusses his technique as a corrective: he will uncover the old prose words so as to make whole the partial treatments of the Latin language fabricated by the *grammatici*. In practice, then, Varro outdoes his professional rivals in the scope of his work, which he defines as adding the words of aristocratic tradition to the poets' diction and which he displayed in the twenty-five rolls of the *De lingua latina*.[43]

Varro found the *grammatici* a convenient target.[44] He does not assail them by name (though Suetonius would), for this would be beneath him and not in keeping with the high literary inter-salutations of the works of Caesar, Cicero, and Varro on language. But the target is clear: it was the *grammatici* who taught Latin from exegesis of the old poets. And they applied analogy, especially with Greek, to justify regularizing the language. Analogy, however, rather than the conservative anomaly, would have produced a literary Latin modeled on a normalized Greek.[45] (Of course, any regularizing of Latin cannot be laid to the sole credit of the schoolteachers; an empire's need for standardization of all sorts, the increasing economic and social importance of provincials and freedmen, and the breakdown of aristocratic control do not suggest themselves to Varro, although the second was to provide the elite from Cicero to Petronius with convenient targets for linguistic satire.) Varro did not recommend the course of the Atticists, although this might have produced a high literary language to rival Greek.

Just what Varro was doing with the subject of analogy and what he was recommending have puzzled scholars. Briefly put, anomalism has nothing to do with Varro's subject (etymology).[46] The concept of analogy developed from the Alexandrian editors who determined the correctness of a form by comparison with other words; thus nouns were grouped into declensions, for example. Analogy thus tended to regularize morphology: not "mouse, mice" but "mouse, mouses" (although of course the editors knew about archaisms and did not expel a word on such simplistic grounds as my English examples suggest, and the search for *comparanda* led to scholarly word lists foreign to the spoken Greek of the day).[47] Anomaly might be thought of as the opposite, conservative editorial practice: "brethren" in an old text need not be emended to "brothers." But this is not what anomaly meant. The Stoics used this term to signify the noncorrespondence of the form of a word to its meaning. (They did not celebrate the arbitrariness of the sign, but treated it as yet another indication of the decline from the natural order of things.) Anomaly thus could not direct editorial practice or etymologizing.[48] However, if we recognize in his representation of an analogy–anomaly opposition a technique of constructing consensus by conflating opposites, then Varro emerges as outdoing Cicero in the orator's own strategy, and thereby rescuing Latin from its great publicizers: the teachers, Caesar, even Cicero.[49] Varro found in an exaggerated contrast of the modes of analogy and anomaly a theoretical weapon with which to decry the influence of the theorists. I have already suggested that the structure of the books on this topic followed Cicero's model, and that Varro uniquely appreciated Cicero's rhetorical strategy of constructing consensus by conflating opposites. Perhaps, too, he realized the virtue of conflating positions that were in fact not opposite.

Varro's model of language and linguistic change explains in part why he has so elevated anomaly. *Impositio* was the original state of language (some person or persons originally gave names to things); thus language even at its most distant is not divinely or naturally given. Romulus and Latinus, it would seem, enfigure this pristine state. Real historical figures like Naevius and Ennius, or like the people in general, represent a *declinatio* from this state. The poets, however, make freer use of analogy to enrich the language (so analogy also covers such phenomena as word coinage and the use and spelling of loanwords). *Declinatio* is something of an umbrella term, for Varro at times means by this the people's *consuetudo* (which explains why analogy is not an accurate model for language reconstruction). Here Varro seems trapped; he might reasonably have asserted a reactionary and restorative *impositio* by applying a rigorous analogy so as to redress the declination from old Latin, but the people's custom introduces anomaly; that is to say, Varro locates the irrational and irreducible element of language in the people's usage. Why does he not condemn this? Why are the people necessary? They aren't, or not for the theory of etymology, as Dahlmann's objection to the inclusion of anomaly indicates. But if Varro is to map Roman society, historical, contemporary, and linguistic, all at once, the people's authority must be appropriated.

Varro does not assert a restorative analogy because he wishes to defend tradition against the professors of analogy. These were essentially teachers like his own, Accius, who on the analogy of Greek wrote *Hectora* for *Hectōrem* and was attacked by Lucilius for this innovation (in book 9; Accius's innovation was to transliterate the name Hector rather than assimilate it to the Latin third declension, which in masculine nouns of this type has a long *o* [where the Greek name has a short *o*] and, like all Latin masculine singular accusatives, an ending in *-m*; a modern Accius would substitute Beijing for Peking). Varro is aligning himself with the Roman aristocrat and satirist against a Hellenistic practice that would make Latin regular, Greek-like, easier for all to govern. However, it is easier for the satirist than the linguistic theorist to dispense with analogy, and so Varro modifies it.

In the following passage from the beginning of book 9, Varro is further explaining the actual instances of analogy, the degree of regularity that varies by type of speaker. This is at the end of his introduction to the subjects of analogy and anomaly, just before he argues for analogy. In the succeeding paragraph, the end of the introduction, he expands on the potency of the people's usage. But here he stratifies language into a tripartite society, ranked and divided by the degree of application of *ratio*.

Alia enim populi universi, alia singulorum, et de ieis non eadem oratoris et poetae, quod eorum non idem ius. Itaque populus universus debet in omnibus verbis uti analogia et, si perperam est consuetus, corrigere se ipsum, cum orator non debeat in omnibus uti, quod sine offensione non potest facere, cum poeta transilire lineas impune possit. (9.5)

[For the people as a whole have one practice and individuals another. Of the individuals the poet and the orator do not have the same practice since they do not have the same privilege or license. Consequently, the people as a whole ought to extend analogy (use regularized forms) to all words and correct itself wherever its use is in error. The orator, however, ought not to extend analogy to all words because he cannot do so without offense. But the poet can cross the lines without fear of punishment.]

This makes a most curious union of the natural and the artificial. The rhetorical (generic) division naturalizes the inconsistencies of Varro's linguistic scheme: a natural order structures Roman society and hence Latin speech, which will not allow of total regularization. Of individuals or groups such as teachers or speakers, only the poet can transgress. Varro does not distinguish here between what we do say and what we ought to say, as he had just been doing; provided we understand ourselves as the orator, no ungrammaticality will taint us. In the place of propriety and impropiety, he distinguishes between individual and collective behavior: the orator mediates between the poet and the people; in him the inconsistency of analogy and anomaly lives.

The orator's split speech, his failure to apply *ratio* completely, is presented as a rhetorical necessity; the orator has *officia* to two realms (*debet* characterizes the social and political obligations of a Roman's duty, *officium*), and so his use of popular forms is not irrational or submissive, craven behavior. Again, Cicero's dialogues offer a parallel: Varro centers the genuine Roman, the synthesis of the new and the old, in the figure of the orator; he echoes both tradition and Cicero in the high valorization of the Roman orator and, like Cicero, transforms this figure for an age when the old republican practice of conducting personal and public business through the attack or defense of individuals in the law courts, the senate, or the assemblies had waned significantly. Cicero's practice had been perilous; his redefinition in the *Brutus*, with Brutus as the new orator, and his revived practice in the *Philippics* would be fatal. The orator of Varro's passage does not even correct speech. Rather, the poets cross lines; their capricious blend of what is and what ought to be places them outside of society. The people are said to be self-correcting, and the orator by definition makes no mistakes, he lives and speaks within the lines.[50]

Why did the poets so offend Varro? In the aftermath of Caesar's death, no poet led a conspiracy or sought the overthrow of the senatorial elite. The significant change seems to be that the poets are at the center of instruction. Cicero wrote that as a boy he read the Twelve Tables at school, which no one does today.[51] Q. Caecilius Epirota, a freedman of Atticus, introduced the study of contemporary poets into grammar school.[52] Thus, whereas Varro's teachers had produced learned books on Plautus and the old poets, in his old age grammar-school teachers were teaching the boys of Rome's elite to read and write by expounding Virgil and Horace. This is more than a shift in curriculum. With the slow fading of the orator as emblem of an age and an elite, an ambitious young man now sought distinction within the declamatory schools and might tarry there rather than serve an apprenticeship with a leading patron. Teachers would be more important in the empire, and Varro's strictures reflect a resentment toward their numbers and influence.[53] In Roman society, with its slave pedagogues and ex-slave teachers and where the slave was a highly trained expert (doctor, cook, pottery maker, surveyor), resentment of their economically potent skills and their transmission of these must have been a constant, and one periodically inflamed by anxieties about foreigners, social subordinates, rival men within the house.

In the early empire, the teacher's importance makes a more dramatic appearance in literature.[54] Seneca the elder and Suetonius wrote collections that catalogued and displayed famous and infamous teachers. Pliny the Younger will be recruited to find a suitable teacher and will make a literary letter of this mission.[55] Learning promised access to imperial office and ultimately, hope of hopes, to the emperor's attention. To this point and under this pressure, Rome's educational institutions would develop. But in the late republic we find the antecedents that would make such a universal imperial program possible. Schoolteachers, often ex-slaves, taught throughout the empire; they and their students represented the potential for standardization of the language more formidably and really than any conjury of Asianists and Atticists. In fact, in the literary polemics of the day, these schools of high style mask the actual social and linguistic changes that would bring, in the next generation, Rome's leading poet and philosopher-councillor from one Spanish family. Chapter 4 explores this family's, the Senecas', concerns with education and with literary and social Romanization. The grammarians and rhetoricians both offered and standardized access to Romanness of speech, subject, and style. In the provinces, the old poets continued to be taught (Suetonius, *De gramm.* 24); thus Varro may in his criticism be castigating Cicero's habit of quoting old verse, the grammarians' teaching of the old poets, and the provincial's knowledge of them. Latium is in danger of redefinition (as the imperial freedman-poet Phaedrus would attempt; see Chapter 3), and Varro tries to reclaim the *patria* for the natives.

The *grammatici* embody the potential and the peril of Latin letters. Education can be liberal; this claim is a basic tenet of the literate class's self-mandate to rule. Only the educated are free—from passion, irrationality, partisanship. Letters promise a larger society, including communion with the past. The pressure of social change directs the need and the display for including oneself in the past. And, in the professional teacher, we can see Roman culture's ambivalent ideology of letters, one essentially and inextricably bound to issues of social identity. The fragments of the remarkable work *De viris illustribus* (*Famous Men*) of Suetonius, writing circa A.D. 110 reveal patterns of cultural understanding of the *grammatici*; here we glimpse how these teachers saw themselves and were seen. Suetonius's biographies of the grammarians and of the rhetoricians provide a counterpoint to Varro.[56] He has graced each group with a book, two-sixths of his study, which included poets, orators, historians, and philosophers. The parallel presentation of these genres of very different status marks Suetonius's attitude as imperial; he attests to the devaluation of the orator and the inflation of the paid teacher that Varro had resented.

All writers are becoming simply *litterati*, whereas in the republic aristocrats had reserved history and oratory for themselves.

The title and arrangement of Suetonius's work, then, level traditional distinctions, but the individual treatment of figures retains traditional social attitudes. He surveys Rome's teachers down to his own time; the anecdotes and elements of a life he finds significant chart the resistance to, as well as the achievement of, the schools. From the start, the author treats schools as a foreign graft on Rome; they have increased greatly in number. In fact, his first words recognize that grammar is not original to Rome. For it is here that the reader meets as the founder of Roman grammar the Greek visitor Crates of Mallos (2) and notes that the first teacher were *semigraeci* (Suetonius explains that he means Ennius and Livius). The chronological development of schooling at Rome he sidesteps. Clearly he did not know much about the first stages (other than the names of prominent teachers and poets). He marks development by mentioning that there were "at certain times" over twenty schools (3) and that very distinguished men deigned to write on the subject of grammar ("ne clarissimi quidem viri abstinuerint quominus et ipsi aliquid de ea scriberent"). One further proof follows this litotes and the reference to the number of schools: Suetonius gives the purchase price of a famous teacher and the salary of another. From the outset Suetonius displays an ambivalence and an economic literalness about the value of letters at Rome. His opening sketch of the history of grammar study in Rome stops short of calling education an alien infection but successfully communicates a national diffidence about the value of grammar and liberal studies in general, through an emphasis on the almost indifferent participation of the elite, the monetarization of the professional teacher, and the further denigration of the professional as Greek or half-Greek. These elements return in the body of the text almost as literary themes or plot elements of a literary life, in the sketches of individual teachers. In sum, these concerns try to fix the troubling status of letters and the *litterati*.

In Suetonius's portraits several recurring elements, positive and negative, suggest the outlines of an ideology of Roman education and educators. What is most remarkable is that the *grammaticus* needs to be slandered, for doubtful birth, double naming, plagiarism, and punishing penury often attend Suetonius's characters.[57] I do not deny that a certain freedman grammarian died in squalor but merely stress that Suetonius repeatedly finds such information worthy of record in his rather brief biographies. The included anecdotes present an aristocrat (or a recognizable superior, e.g., Horace, the canonical poet and freedman's son whose poems proclaim his happiness with his allegedly humble status) slandering a teacher on the following occasions: Messala Corvinus disdains the *litterator* Cato (4); L. Orbilius is attacked by Horace's, Domitius Marsus's, and Bibaculus's verses (9; he had dared to attack Varro); L. Ateius Philologus suffers Ateius Capito's witticism; Pollio blamed him for assisting Sallust in the pursuit of archaism (10); some called P. Valerius Cato *libertus* (11; Ticidas's and Cinna's verses attest to his expertise, Bibaculus's reveals that he died in poverty); Curtius Nicias is released from Pompey's service for bringing Memmius's love note to Pompey's wife; Suetonius also quotes from two letters of Cicero that do not show Nicias in a positive light (Cicero has to resolve a dispute between Nicias and a Vidius; Cicero declines to have Nicias visit him and cites his *imbecillitatem, mollitiam, consuetudinem victus*, 14); Lenaeus attacked Sallust for defaming his patron, Pompey (15; Lenaeus is not directly slandered, but his presumption is clear); Q. Caecilius Epirota was suspected of seducing his charge (16); Scribonius Aphrodisius attacked Verrius's *De orthographia*, his scholarship, and morals (19); M. Pomponius Marcellus, *sermonis Latini exactor molestissimus*, complained of his opponent's solecism in court—Cassius Severus delivered a withering reply; Pomponius also criticized a word of Tiberius that had been defended as good Latin, by Ateius Capito, and was abused as a former boxer in a verse by Asinius Gallus (22); Q. Remmius Palaemon, *infamis omnibus vitiis*, censured by Tiberius and Claudius, called Varro a pig (23).[58] The battlelines are so clearly drawn that Suetonius seems to be communicating a social pathology and eulogy.[59]

The caustic witticism of a Pollio or the anecdotes of Suetonius could not dismiss the troubling freedman and his role in Latin letters and society; heaped with the charges of plagiarism, social ambition, and the seduction of the Roman wife and heir, the literary freedman draws to his persona the troubling anxieties of speech and social mobility. Varro was wrong: Ennius and Livius could not so easily be replaced by Romulus and Latinus; and, if Latinus was to take a leading part in the reconstitution of the Roman, it would be under the shaping hand of the Italian poet Virgil, master of deference to the old poets and ideology, master of appropriation and transformation. But the aristocrat Varro chose to align himself against the *libertinus* and so handed down to Suetonius a pose to set against the teachers smeared with charges of venality, sexuality, mobility. The irony is that all might read about proper Latin and the proper deference to be assumed by an aspirant teacher. When from within a written text linguistic issues frame questions of identity, status, and social change, a change in orthography can include as surely as a provincial accent once excluded.

The following chapters investigate the textual and social issues of owned speech in Latin literature. The attitudes are not consistent or discrete: talk and writing about language within the special language of literature figures and refigures social, political, and cultural anxieties. As in Suetonius, the *grammaticus*, the social inferior mastering Latin, can be a positive exemplum. Like letters themselves, he is consistently allied with the Roman noble; and provided he die in poverty, he proves a worthy Roman client or minor friend.[60] Indeed, the profitless pursuit of learning marks the good teacher, according both to himself (Orbilius wrote of his poverty) and to the elite. The consular historian Clodius Licinus wrote of his impecunious friend, the freedman of Augustus and his librarian, the scholar Hyginus (*De gramm.* 20). Suetonius writes with evident approval that Staberius Eros bought his own freedom and took in the children of the proscribed, tuition free (13).

The positive pattern of literary life, the social protocol communicated through writing, shows the freedman as self-sufficient (buying his own freedom), properly loyal and dependent on his patron, and finally self-failing in an impecunious death. The litrary man makes no cash demands; he is no threat to aristocratic capital. And in the overdetermined notices of his submission and subjugation, the reader recognizes that letters are here only to serve. The *litterati* do not constitute a clan in themselves, self-naming and self-sustaining; they are not *nobiles*. But of course, this is a contested claim. Like Seneca the Elder, Suetonius is making the socially new and mobile into Roman anecdotes, examples of literary lives, but also Roman lives. In itself this is a form of literary and linguistic control, appropriating the language controllers, disputing and assuming literature's power to render its readers and practitioners Roman. Suetonius's work thus contextualizes Varro's antipathies, and those of Pollio and Messalla, in a deeper, wider cultural construct.

Despite the shifts in political breeze to which scholars have related Varro's every work, he is always beating his way back toward Pompey, the champion of *mos maiorum*: that is, deeper structures of understanding and concern animated this individual and the high literary discourse about Roman language, society, and identity. Thus Caesar and Cicero are rivals, not the enemy; for society with them is possible, given the proper gestures of mutual deference. But there are those Varro will not abide, onto whom he will displace a number of antipathies and anxieties. The excluded and the appropriated masters and authorities, and their dynamic, ambitious speech, contest who and what the Roman will be.

3

The Rhetoric of Freedmen:
The Fables of Phaedrus

THE ROMAN POET PHAEDRUS wrote five books of verse fables from late in the reign of Augustus until after the fall of Tiberius's minister Sejanus. These poems have been mined for autobiographical details and metrical peculiarities. As a result, Phaedrus has been deemed a poet of the second or third order, writing fables—some Aesop's, some his own—in a Latin of correct, that is, unobjectionable style.[1] Phaedrus is thus spied forecasting, at the turn of the Roman literary tide, the flood of Silver Age authors slim on content, adept at form, though his school fare has not their difficulty. I am not here interested in reordering the poets. I am concerned with the social and cultural world Phaedrus portrays, which I shall argue his poems fabulize.[2]

This chapter begins by considering how Phaedrus made the role of speech within the plots of his fables significant and problematic. The worthy characters know their own voice and station; the fables' victims fall prey to overestimation of their own voice or to a kindred excess of social ambition.[3] Speech and station are both problematic and programmatic, for the poet boasts in his prologues and epilogues that despite the envy of his critics, his poems constitute a Roman genre.[4] The poet sets himself against the misspeakers; their speech runs on, crossing boundaries; here he avows that he takes Aesop's chastening lead (see 3.19, *Aesopus Respondet Garrulo*). First-person pronouncements circumscribe Phaedrus's own controlled speech, for example, in the epilogue to book 3 ("Supersunt mihi quae scribam, sed parco sciens"), where the poet's speech will earn a promised reward:

brevitatis nostrae praemium ut reddas peto
quod es pollicitus: exhibe vocis fidem.

(8–9)

[I ask you to grant the reward for our conciseness
as you promised; display the proof of your word.]

Proper speech, credible speech, *fides* made manifest in words, is most important in perilous times, as 4.13, "The Monkey King," opens: "Utilius homini nil est quam recte loqui" ("Correct speech is a man's most valuable asset"). I treat below the particular peril of the speech of a duplicitous adviser, a character who occurs as false *laudator* and *fraudator*. Are rulers or simply those freedmen higher up in the imperial service to take heed from poems like "The Monkey King" and the "Lion's Rule"? In the latter we are advised "Tacere ubi tormentum, par poenast loqui" (*De leone regnante*, 4.14.3: "Where keeping silence brings torture, a like punishment attends speech"). In this fabulous world the lion seeks not the substance but the reputation for justice (*aequitatis . . . famam*) and thus gives the ape *laudator* the chance to practice fraud. Amid the false praise and proper virtue repeatedly invoked by the poems' framing statements and enacted within the fables' plots (see the ant and the fly of 4.25), place for the poet emerges distinctly. The poet Simonides can repair his shipwrecked fortune by the truly valuable and abiding treasure of his voice (4.23).[5] The tyrant Demetrius, whom the mob and the leading men (*principes*) of Athens come to flatter, turns himself into a flatterer when he learns that the effeminate dandy he has been making fun of is the poet Menander (5.1). Poets undo flattery and make the tyrant into a flatterer. The mob and popular entertainment are not to be trusted. The critics whom he would silence would have him a Greek, a mechanical imitator of Aesop. In critics' and readers' responses to the voice of the poet, we come to play out one real freedman's life, a corpus of poems, and our own reception of both as a Roman fable. A successful reading depends on the reader's granting the poet his due status.

The particular difficulty of this poet's status is that he is a freedman writing to include himself in the high society of Latin letters. The status itself is marked as servile or libertine in at least five ways: generically and programmatically, Phaedrus associates himself with the ex-slave Aesop, the founder of fable, and describes fable as the slave's medium; the title of the work declares Phaedrus a freedman of Augustus; the addressees of the prologues are freedmen (one is recognizably an imperial freedman); freedmen are included as (vicious and self-seeking) characters in the poems; the poet presents himself as victimized, specifically in the lack of credit granted his voice. Throughout the poems Phaedrus equates proper behavior with individuals who speak and act according to their station. Somewhat inconsistently, the freedman poet presents the persona of one who has mastered the art of knowing his station and of using language in proper accordance with societal hierarchies, but he claims for himself as a poet what he could not claim for himself as a freedman. He seems to break his own rule by suggesting that social mobility is possible and not dangerous for one type of freedman alone. The link, he would have us believe, is that voice is the only genuine possession of the freedman and the poet. This alone is native to both, and as proper, faithful voice is essential to society, he deserves special recognition. I wish to treat, first, the two elements that most closely concern the persona of the poet and also communicate the libertine status of that persona: the book's title and the concern with the credit of the poet's voice. My treatment of the second topic leads to a general consideration of the role of voice in the poems.

We know that Phaedrus belonged to the emperor's household from the *titulus* to his manuscript: PHAEDRI AUGUSTI LIBERTI FABULARUM AESOPIARUM LIBER PRIMUS.[6] The first half of this title is familiar from contemporary epitaphs. Freedmen and freedwomen of the emperor took particular pride in drawing attention to their status on their gravestones.[7] The Latin funerary inscription of an ex-slave advertises the Roman citizenship of the dead and the descendants.[8] Such epitaphs create their own traditions even as they strive to emulate the functions of the epitaphs of the freeborn, which have a different course of honor to record.[9] The freedmen's *tituli* intended to be traditional so as to assert the Romanness of the dead man or woman. The transfer from tomb to title page of this tie to the emperor and to Romanness publicizes the poet's ambition.[10] Beneath the title lies a Roman legacy. In the prologue to the fourth book the poet characterizes the potential fabulist as one "talis . . . tituli appetens" (4). The resistance to the presumption of such title seeking is palpable.[11]

Phaedrus writes the critics into his own text. Prologues and epilogues tell of the slanderous ill-treatment he has suffered, and the poet repeatedly constructs a plot or draws a moral about the proper estimation of voice. He instructs the reader in the epilogue to book 3 to display the credibility of his voice. The language here, "exhibe vocis fidem," has specific resonances for a freedman and for this poet.[12] Within the context of the poems such advice is especially pertinent, for oath breaking is pernicious, and yet produces the plot; it provides the violence central to a number of the fables. In Roman society the oath of a freedman established the relationship between former owner and the newly manumitted. In this oath consequent to freedom, the freedman pledged his loyalty to his patron and swore to perform certain services. This is the legal, contractual aspect of what was known as *iusiurandum liberti*; but the same freedman had sworn just before, when he was a slave and his oath could not constitute a contract, to perform the same duties. For a freedman to show his faithfulness meant displaying his allegiance and his newfound ability to make a contract, to be a freeman.[13]

In oath keeping and breaking, in speaking in one's voice or appropriating the voice of another, the fables present a boundary being crossed, one couched in terms and contexts that a Roman reader would have readily understood as the poles of free and slave, citizen and foreigner. In so positioning his poetic persona and reader, Phaedrus makes special claims about the social and literary power of his verse.[14]

False Witness: *Contumelia* and *Calumnia*

Phaedrus's fables teem with insult and injury; indeed, verbal violence marks critics, animals, and the poet himself so that injury and insult seem inextricable. A social context unites the two, for the language of insult, that particular species of verbal violence, is a tool of social injury, especially in the mouths of the self-praiser and the false witness, the *laudator* who is in fact an evil counselor. The language and structures of the poems oppose the benefits won by the *fraudator* and *laudator* on the one hand with the perils of the creditor on the other. Violence does not simply occur; it is made possible by the complicity of the victim or the powerful whom words deceive. Declarations in the poet's voice about his own detractors, intimations about his enemies' successful slander, and parallel speech acts and attendant catastrophes in the plots of the fables establish an anxiety about criticism, verbal abuse, and false testimony and so constitute thematic and structural resonances that blend social and literary concerns. For the social context of the harm worked and the social position of the slanderers, slandered, and potential redressers distinguish between verbal insult and real injury, *calumnia* and *contumelia*.

In analyzing the concerns of voice and social violence that animate poems and poetic persona, I have not found allegory to be a significant technique for the fables of Phaedrus. Critics, characters, protectors, and addressees are far too structural and literary. When we ask who are these critics or who are the animals, we do not see individuals lurking behind cloaked lampoon but recurrent situations. When the reader meets the most generic element of the fables, the animal characters, it does not seem terribly important that the animals are members of animal species, or indeed animals at all. In Aesop the fox acts in foxlike ways: Aesop has an interest in nature. The animals of Phaedrus are more sche-

matic, and are so marked, as undeveloped dramatic masks for the
rhetoric they speak, by Phaedrus's inclusions of proper interpretation. The poet emerges as one acutely conscious of his readers'
potential responses, which in turn he tries to direct, on a small
scale, with these interpretations, the promythia and epimythia [15]—
gnomic statements that frame the fable proper.

On a larger and dramatic scale, the presence of the readers
and other listeners in the fables vividly enacts a concern with the
problems of reading and speaking, of correct discourse and its recognition and appreciation. This concern comes to direct the text
so insistently that a new set of characters, the critics (who appear
from the start and are the special subjects of the books' prologues
and epilogues), almost upstages the animals as the focus of the
poems.[16] As a result of the critics' presence in the poems, the Latin
fables shift their interpretive realm increasingly from the ethical
to the social. Critics have been provided with a society. Instead
of universal human criticism—the egalitarian chastising voice of
Aesop—criticism occurs at many levels. The critic internal to the
fables' plots would level society; the poet's criticism, that of the
interpretive frames and at times that of the victims, would hold
society in its structured order. But there is a further shift in the
fabulous moral universe, not simply from the ethically to the
socially good, but from ethical behavior to social speech.

Phaedrus has not called up his *senarii* to castigate the critics, as Catullus had threatened with his hendecasyllables to right a
wrong worked by a *moecha putida*. No Lesbia or Clodia, no single
poetic person or Roman individual, lurks behind his unnamed
detractors. Sejanus is named once,[17] but even he is neither the
source of the poems' anxieties nor their single target. The critics
of Phaedrus are thrust into the reader's presence throughout the
five books.[18] Phaedrus names them *calumniatores* and tries to banish them from the start: the initial poem instructs us that if anyone
wishes to carp or criticize (*calumniari*) remember we are but jest-
ing in fictional fables. Phaedrus's poetry constantly keeps them at
bay and invites the reader to distinguish his own reading from the
critics' calumny. As the comic poets Menander and Terence did
to the misanthrope, Phaedrus has placed the *calumniator* outside

the community of exchange, but Phaedrus protests too much: the poet's directives about his critics appear so often that the addressee of book 3 in the final poem of that book wonders whether they really do exist. He is assured they do; they will make themselves known upon the publication of Phaedrus's work.[19]

The humor of Phaedrus's lament stems not only from his put-upon addressee but from the characters and plots he subjects to a pattern of calumny and the related contumely, for verbal abuse (*calumnia*) and the violent harm that is the outward manifestation of contempt (*contumelia*) afflict more characters than the poet. Picking up the overtly programmatic reference to calumny of 1.1, the second poem links the Latin terms *calumnia* and *contumelia* and thus establishes the grounds for the interpretation and structures of the later fables. The second fable of Phaedrus's work tells the story of the frogs who asked Jupiter for a king, didn't like what they got, asked for another, and very much regretted the viper sent to preside. The interesting element in this familiar fable is the frogs' treatment of one another and of their first king (a piece of timber). Neither of these elements is essential to the plot, which needs only the foolhardy request, its repetition, and the dire consequences. The pond citizens parallel the Athenians under the sixth-century tyrant Peisistratus (Phaedrus tells us at the beginning of the fable that this was the context for Aesop's telling the story). The first three lines establish the situation:

Athenae cum florerent aequis legibus,
procax libertas civitatem miscuit
frenumque solvit pristinum licentia.

[When Athens flourished in democratic equality,
bold liberty threw the citizens into confusion
and license let loose traditional restraints.]

In the actual fable Phaedrus alludes to the parallel situation of the frogs with a simple reference to their *dissolutos mores* (12). A "mixture of morals" attends the leveling of social strata, and

this, like similar moments in Phaedrus's plots where social distinctions are forgotten, occasions real harm (not just *contumelia*
but *malum*).[20] Once social difference is muddied, not equality or
democracy but injury follows.[21] But the second blunder of the
once democratic frogs, the treatment of their king, is even more
distinctive and characteristic of the fables. The first slip toward
disaster was occasioned by social confusion; the next, which pre-
cipitates the final, deadly stage, is abuse of the high (mistaking the
status of the powerful, especially through verbal insult). The frogs
treat their log-king thus:

> illae timore posito certatim adnatant
> lignumque supra turba petulans insilit.
> quod cum inquinassent omni contumelia
>   (19–21)

> [With fear set aside they fight with each other to swim up
> and in a crowd dance upon the wood impudently.
> Once they have smeared it with every insult. . . .]

The frogs have leapt above their station and so smeared their
divinely sent superior. The log-king is, upon examination, not
much of a superior, but it is the quality of the subjects, not the superior, that is at issue. Setting the inanimate over the animate precludes any animal hierarchy. Jupiter's arbitrariness in this appointment answers both the presumption and the noise of the request.
The whole of 1.2 depends on voice and its silencing: the frogs in
their disruptive state call to Jove *clamore magno* (11); the timber
impresses by its sound (15); the one frog silently (17) explores the
new deity; the frogs' subsequent insult and violence suggests verbal insult (*omni contumelia*, 21, and *petulans*, 20—*petulantia* can
be insolent language, e.g., what got the poet Naevius in trouble,
see Gellius 3.3.15); fear of the viper takes away their voices (26),
so they send Mercury; Jupiter, who earlier laughed at the frogs'
clamor, now thunders (28); Aesop then speaks to stem the Athe-

nians' complaint. So the fable silences speech of complaint and would forestall *contumelia* and *malum*. With this second fable Phaedrus has set a pattern, which will prove invariant, of disaster attending *contumelia*, itself the result of confusion of social boundaries.[22] The noise of complaint fills the poems from the start, or perhaps the reader can learn to distinguish noise from voice.

The succeeding poem ensures that the reader will understand in just what *contumelia* consists. Phaedrus tells the story of the jackdaw and the peacock in such a fashion that *contumelia* is no mere plot element. In fact, the fable of the plain bird who tried to pass himself off as a peacock and was abused by those birds and his own kind defines this term:

1.3 Graculus Superbus et Pavo

Ne gloriari libeat alienis bonis
suoque potius habitu vitam degere,
Aesopus nobis hoc exemplum prodidit.
Tumens inani graculus superbia
5   pennas pavoni quae deciderant sustulit
seque exornavit. deinde *contemnens* suos
immiscet se pavonum formoso gregi.
illi impudenti pennas eripiunt avi
fugantque rostris. male mulcatus graculus
10   redire maerens coepit ad proprium genus,
a quo repulsus tristem sustinuit notam.
tum quidam ex illis quos prius despexerat:
"Contentus nostris si fuisses sedibus
et quod Natura dederat voluisses pati,
15   nec illam expertus esses *contumeliam*
nec hanc repulsam tua sentiret calamitas."
(Italics mine)

[To take no pleasure in glorying in another's possessions and to live our life in our own attire,

Aesop has given us this example.
Puffing himself up with empty pride, a jackdaw
5   picked up feathers fallen from a peacock
and dressed himself in them. Then, disdaining his own flock,
he mingled with the fashionable set of peafowl.
Those birds stripped the feathers from the impudent fellow
and pecked him away. Badly beaten, the jackdaw
10   tried to return grief-stricken to his own kind,
who drove him off with stern censure.
Then said one of those he had earlier despised,
"Had you been happy with our station
and willingly suffered what Nature provided,
15   you would neither have experienced that insult
nor would your misfortune feel now this exclusion."]

Just as the frogs with their big noise had thought themselves superior to their log-king and so worked every violence on it only
to meet with disaster in the end, so the jackdaw puffs himself up,
falsely and disastrously despising his own station and kind.[23] The
violence of the jackdaw's fable is of two causally related kinds: his
disparagement of his peers leads to physical attack by his superiors
and then the social disparagement (*notam*, 11) from his peers. The
social and political character of his punishment is unmistakable:
the poem here humorously transfers to the society of jackdaws
the mark (*nota*) the Roman censor made to demote a senator; in
addition, *repulsus* is drawn from the language of electoral defeat.[24]
These are the social injuries that the victim suffers from his equals.
The injury from his superiors is named as *contumelia* (15).[25] And
yet the two are related, not simply as the double punishment of
the jackdaw's error about his self but by a double *figura etymologica* that links the puffery and pride with the punishment: the
participles *tumens . . . contemnens* provide the etymology and cause
for what the epimythium, spoken by the fellow jackdaw, names
as *contumelia*.[26] Unlike much of fable (Hesiod's nightingale and
hawk, for instance), Phaedrus does not focus on the injustice of

might but on the improvidence of social confusion, itself a consequence of self-delusion about status. To figure social injustice as a
result of personal moral error is hardly novel. Peculiarly, Phaedrus
aligns failed society with overarching speech. Attempts to pass for
a higher order, through speech not one's own, wreck society.

In Phaedrus's fables such confusion about one's status, about
what is proper behavior, is ruinous. In insulting their king the
frogs misjudged themselves, that is, their own status relative to
their king, as the jackdaw did his fellows, his betters, and his true,
unswollen self. A related misjudgment is *calumnia*, which means
the bearing of false witness or, in a less technical sense, verbal
abuse. *Calumnia* and *contumelia* confuse mine and thine, *proprium*
and *alienum*, through a miscalculation of *genus*. The individual is
known and should know himself by estimation of his *genus*—the
group to which he belongs and which determines his status and
hence his relation to others. In their working of *contumelia*, the
frogs exceed their station by showing disdain for their divinely
sent king. Both false witness and arrogant speech work fraud, the
theft of real and social capital, respectively.

There are differences between the frogs' and birds' poems:
working on his own and only dressing up, the jackdaw represents *superbia*; the frogs' collective croaking develops to *contumelia*. Phaedrus, however, has not presented particularized fables
of different vices; rather, he has fragmented what his Greek source
would have called hybris. Though this word's two notions of violent excess and violent retribution cannot be contained by either
tumens/contumelia or *calamitas*, *vis* might have done; but Phaedrus
fragmented the Greek term. His translation of Greek fable does
not systematize vices but aligns them as self-deception and points
to the greater vice as that which involves voice, and so injures
society. A single term would have blurred this hierarchy.

In the poems of Phaedrus the *calumniator*, the insulter and
defrauder, succeeds by imposing and having credited false distinctions about the *genus* of his victim. The poet makes this figure of
the abuser of words the recurrent target of the poet's own animus. In the fables discussed so far, the abuser is simply an upstart

member of a lower order (the frog who first pokes his head out of the mud, the jackdaw proud above his station) who mistakes social divisions. But more frequently the abuser is a sort of middleman, standing between the high and the low, between two animal species. For instance, Phaedrus names as a *calumniator* the dog of 1.17, who falsely accuses a sheep of owing him a loaf of bread. The dog summons a wolf as witness who falsely and rather rapaciously claims the sheep owes ten loaves. The sheep loses her lawsuit. What is peculiar to Phaedrus, besides the emphasis on litigation, is the special emphasis on fraud and the defrauder working a kind of social harm.[27] This social framing of the genre of fables is as distinctive as the formal frame of the promythium and epimythium.

Phaedrus thus steers his genre away from its antecedents, or perhaps he fuses two literary forms tied to the figure of Aesop. Common to fables of all sorts is the violence of the mighty and the victimization of the lower orders. The biography of Aesop takes this natural violence and applies it to the life of the teller of fables: Aesop emerges as the wily fox; that is, in the literary life of Aesop, the ex-slave, when threatened, uses fable as his own deliverance and so redresses this violence. The slave's cleverness is pitted against the learning of his master (in the *Life of Aesop*, the philosopher Xanthos).[28] In this biography Aesop is depicted as extraordinarily ugly—sympathetic nature mirrors his social station, his status as a slave, whereas his master's name (but of course not his deeds) means the blond, the fair one. The slave's beauty lies unrecognized in his cleverness, which wears a mask of ugliness just as his fables are a masquerade. Phaedrus has taken this literary offshoot of fable, the writing of a biographical context to the fables, and combined it within his fables. He presents himself in the prologues and epilogues and animal characters within the fables, instead of the maligned or threatened Aesop, as the victim of abuse. The ugliness, which his critics see and he denies, lies behind the calumny and contumely of his characters. Whereas the mob or the learned master was Aesop's critic, the *fraudator* fails to appreciate Phaedrus, his poems, and proper social relations.

In the world of Phaedrus's fables there is a great deal of injury, and much *contumelia*. These need to be distinguished. *Contumelia*, as the ancient annotators report, is contempt atop of injury.[29] In the world of fable, injury is natural and almost unavoidable; it belongs to the realm of *Fortuna*. The wolf will eat the sheep or her loaves given a chance. *Contumelia*, on the other hand, is escapable. Perhaps it is to be associated with culture, not nature. The jackdaw's ugliness ("quod Natura dederat") was a natural condition, an unavoidable injury; his suffering from his own and the peacocks' flock was self-created and cultural.

A further example of *contumelia* clarifies this distinction. A woman about to give birth (1.18) refuses to rise from the ground to the comfort of a bed, for she does not trust the place that was the origin of her present evil condition. This would allow the bed and her husband opportunity for insult as well as injury. The woman refuses her husband's request to rise (3: "humi iacebat"), for, in her words, which conclude the poem, "By no means do I believe the spot which conceived an injury can bring it to an end" ("'Minime'" inquit "'illo posse confido loco / malum finiri quo conceptum est initium'"). Injury is unavoidable, but to misplace one's trust or to trust in a higher position than the "natural" is far worse, and avoidable.

Such fables stress the social quality of *contumelia*: superiors injure and do so with impunity; when subordinates injure a superior, they insult. On occasion, equals may injure. Thus in 1.21 an old lion suffers the attacks of a boar and a bull, but when an ass comes to kick him, he gives as his final words "bis videor mori" (12).[30] The lion, who, as the epimythium declares, has lost his social rank ("dignitatem pristinam"), still distinguishes between the blows of the "fortes" (10) and those of the "Naturae dedecus" (11). Injury from an *indignus* is double death, as life and status are imperiled. Calumny and contumely consist specifically in an attempt to level social strata; such confusions of the high and the low are insults in themselves. So at 1.29 an ass calls a boar "brother." This salutation is an insult and merits a rebuke.

The *calumniator* speaks falsely; his speech shows the contempt and malicious treatment of *contumelia*; his action we are to rate worse than natural violence. Who speaks truly? What voices are we to acknowledge and credit? Perhaps the victim at the moment of death, and the poet too, as he makes his critics into *calumniatores*. Those who deny the poet his due status and praise are akin to the *fraudatores* of the fables' plots.[31] The defrauder in life comes between the self and that self's property. Phaedrus intimates that he has suffered a literary or social defrauding, and fears a repetition. But what is the connection between such fraud and language? Is language, lies in particular, simply the vehicle for fraud? Phaedrus does not present language in such a simple fashion; it is not the case that his fables offer a straightforward moral about straight and crooked speech. Rather, speech offends and is marked as improper when it crosses and so confuses social boundaries.

The Language of Violence

The language of violence, the language of the victor and natural superior, does not offend in the same way as *contumelia*. Two kinds of characters speak so as to bring harm. The wolf and the lion may speak in triumph or lay claim to everything, life and property, as their own. Here, there is no prospect for redress, and the violent but not arrogant speech mimics the natural hierarchy. The fox and other interlopers speak so as to deceive, so as to muddy the hierarchy. There is no thoroughgoing, consistent allegory of bestial language in Phaedrus, for in some fables the lion is the hero and not the villain of the fable. Rather, particular animal character is not as important as the relative position of the character within the animal hierarchy, and the words they speak.

Two fables will serve to illustrate the language of the wolf, though in the second a lion speaks. The very first fable presents the great divide to the reader:

‖superior stabat lupus
longeque inferior agnus.

(1.1)

A wolf accuses a downstream sheep, who employs unimpeachable logic in each of his rebuttals: of muddying his water ("but I'm downstream"); of insulting him six months ago ("but I wasn't born yet"); of his father doing it—and so the wolf ate the sheep. False accusations all, but there is nothing to be done about this state of nature. The poem's sympathy is clear—the action begins (3–4) with "fauce improba / latro incitatus" and ends "lacerat iniusta nece" (13), but Phaedrus's epimythium instructs that the particular target is not the unjust, but those who work injustice through trumped-up charges (*fictis causis*). Even here, in a scene of natural violence, the poet presents the offense as deceptive language. In the first line of the first fable of the second book, the hierarchy of violence is again made clear by *super* and *stabat*: "super iuvencum stabat deiectum leo." No criticism of the lion follows for eating his prey. Indeed, the poet offers his division of the prey as a positive model.

These fables, then, do not so much lament injustice as depict it as natural violence. The poet's animus is reserved for the workers of fiction, those who, in the poet's words, feign causes, motives, and agreements. The poet himself is a feigner of words: "fictis . . . fabulis" is the defense he makes against the abusers of words at the end of his first prologue. But the common diction, the echo in this fable of the diction of the programmatic poem, delineates proper from improper fiction as declared in contrast to hidden. Both the initial poems of books 1 and 2 have two points of interest for the analysis of this proper and improper speech: the victor and victim stand in vertical arrangement, and the victim cannot speak with the victor—there is no possibility for exchange, suasion, and redress if the one higher stationed is *improbus*, wicked and violent, like the wolf.[32]

Fables of Social Hierarchy

The poet does object when the mid-stationed, the socially mobile, the adviser to the mighty who speaks for the lowly, are *improbi*. These fables display a concern with social relations both through their more developed, vertical societies and through their social language, the Roman language of social obligation. The poet's positioning of the various speakers represents, with some humor, an anxiety about status and specifically about the possibility and appropriateness of social mobility. Transfer between the strata is resisted; such movement is mimicked by the attempted communication and verbal pacts between members of different social strata. Like the vignettes discussed above, the more developed societies of the following fables (1.5, 2.4, 2.6, 3.13) present the same hierarchy but differ significantly because the mighty go astray. Social interlopers like the robber and ass are not rebuked; their *calumnia* remains unrecognized and so is effective; it passes to actual violence, *contumelia*, and fraud.

"The Eagle, the Cat, and the Sow" (2.4) presents a natural hierarchy like that of the first poems of books 1 and 2, with one addition.

1   Aquila in *sublimi* quercu nidum fecerat;
         feles cavernam nancta in *media* pepererat;
         sus nemoris cultrix ad *imam* posuerat.

         [An eagle made her nest in a lofty oak;
         a cat gave birth in the hollow she found in mid-tree;
         a sow, a tree dweller, took her spot at the base.]

The cat plays the accuser: as false informant, she tells the eagle that the sow is rooting around below so as to overturn the tree and eat the eagle's young, and then instructs the sow that the eagle is plotting to eat her little piglets. Consequently, both the sublime and the humble families starve to death, too afraid to leave their homes. Again, the contrast between the *humiles* and *sublimes* in status, virtue, and fortune is not lamented. The poet makes it quite clear who is his villainess. The middle figure plays the troublemaker who disrupts the concord of society. Phaedrus draws the moral for us in the epimythium:

25   Quantum homo bilinguis saepe concinnet mali,
        documentum habere hinc stulta credulitas potest.

        [Of the great load of harm that a two-tongued man can
            often work,
        those resistant to belief can find a proof in this.]

Again the classes of the characters guide interpretation: here the
stulti enable the bilingual or forked-tongued *improbus* through the
granting of belief. Phaedrus frequently puns on words of the root
cred-. Indeed, *credere* and its cognates are the same sort of charged
diction as, for instance, *celsus*. These signal and constitute important elements of the plot. *Celsus* (or *altus* or *sublimis*), which comes
early in the poems, signals what is worthy and what quite often
will not be credited as valuable. At times such notice seems generic and simply humorous: the fox sees grapes on high and in the
end will falsely disparage them (4.3). But, more frequently, social
evil attends such confusion about the high and the low. The eagle
residing on high in 2.4 or flying on high at 2.6 will err by lending
credence to the lower cat and crow. A false understanding of social
relations brings disaster to all but the pernicious intermediary.

    Phaedrus's use of the language of credit blurs the contractual,
the lending of services or capital, with the interpretive or epistemological, whom or what to believe.[33] For instance, Phaedrus uses
words from the root *cred-* to signal the moment of deceit at 1.31.10
(the doves entrust themselves to the rule of the kite) and at 3.10.33
(the father's *credulitas* caused him to kill his innocent son). The
epimythium of 2.4 points out that the evil worked by the *bilinguis*
arises from *credulitas*, while in 3.10 ("Poeta de credere et non credere") the promythium declares: "Periculosum est credere et non
credere." More humorously perhaps, the crane entrusts her head
to the wolf's throat (1.8.8). Quite clearly, Phaedrus uses and puns
with the meanings "believe" and "entrust," but the crane and the
kites, at least, believe they have entered into a relationship of trust;
they believe they are owed a return different from the natural vio-

lence they actually get. Their belief proves faulty, for they trusted the wrong party. They have not loaned services or made a contract; they have misunderstood *credere*. A similar misapprehension characterizes the animals who use the words *socius* and *societas*. The poet points out, again in an epimythium, that those who believe in the abstract noun *societas*, at 1.5, do so at their peril. In declaring that there is no abiding (*fidelis*) society with the powerful, the poet again puns resonantly. There is no social community; and there is no legal equality, for slave and free at Rome can make no contract. The reader must come to recognize the high and the low in order to learn where to place his trust.

Similar plots of easy credit are found in 2.6 and 3.13. In the first a crow comes between the eagle and her prey, a tortoise. The by now familiar *sublimis* signals the vertical alignment (4: "Aquila in sublime sustulit testudinem"), and again the villain (2: "consiliator maleficus") holds the middle (7: "venit *per auras* cornix et propter volans") and brings disaster through her speech. The eagle had been at a loss, the tortoise safe (6: "nec ullo pacto laedi posset condita") until the malicious adviser can invent a pact where none should be (Phaedrus may be punning from the legal-contractual sphere with *nec ullo pacto* as "by no agreement" and "in no way," i.e., *nullo modo*). As with the wolf and the dog who defrauded the sheep or the sow faced with cat and eagle, two enemies are irresistible and overthrow the concord of nature.[34]

The only recourse seems to be the proper judgment of those higher up in the hierarchy, as the positive outcome of 3.13 underscores. Here drones try to appropriate the honey that belongs to the worker bees. The wasp judge decides rightly, for he knows the *genus* of each (4) and is not misled by their similarity of appearance. Still, he sets a formula to test them (he provides hives for each litigant to fill with honey; the successful party will win the suit). The drones decline the challenge (12: "fuci recusant, apibus condicio placet"), for legal formula can only confirm nature's order (which was declared in line one: "Apes in *alta* fecerant quercu favos").

The conflation of natural, social, even legal, and poetic orders marks and excludes the false claimant. Phaedrus emerges as the Roman censor. The poet has structured his poems as he has organized his characters in a most transparent reading from high to low. The poems open with a notice of high and separate standing—the unmixed society of the frogs, the wolf upstream; plot and poem proceed by a notice of the mixture of these strata that leads to the final element of the narrated fable and the penultimate section of the poem: the fall of the high, catastrophe. The poet's final comment restores or aims to restore order. Closing sententia would contain or forestall the villain. Reading is for Phaedrus a descent and a reconstitution, with the stages clearly marked and well paralleled, and with intimations of the restorer of order.

Preventers of Fraud: Patriarch, Poet, and Audience

Phaedrus's natural hierarchy is upset to the detriment of the lower classes by the meddling of a speaker, one who confuses boundaries and thus works fraud, through his position as intermediary and through his verbal accusations. The workers of fraud fail to see their proper social boundaries; perhaps, they can range too far and are by nature unstable, as the freeborn thought of the freed at Rome. Phaedrus introduces one fable (1.5) with the warning "numquam est fidelis cum potente societas." Only equals (members of the same *genus*) can make agreements with one another, as at Rome only the free could make legal contracts. What, then, is proper behavior in a fundamentally hierarchical society? Phaedrus does tell of one wise sheep that refused to enter into a contract with a wolf and a stag for she knew their qualities (1.16: the sheep declines to take the wolf as *sponsor* for a loan to the stag). Nonparticipation may be good, cautious advice for the dispossessed, for those of low status, but Phaedrus has something more to offer. The poet may seem the conservative convert, the ex-slave who endorses society's structure and instructs slaves and perhaps freedmen not to rise, but he has a more radical program tied to his permanent status as a freedman.

Freedmen occupied a unique position at Rome.[35] The epigraphical record attests to the frequency in the urban *familiae* of slaves purchasing their freedom. In significant ways, though freed, the former slaves did not leave the household of their master: they still had obligations to him, and he remained their patron. Indeed, legally they were parentless. Imperial freedmen were a privileged subset of this order.[36] Although political office (the nobles' traditional career path) was barred to all freedmen, governmental service was not and became the bailiwick of the emperor's household.[37] Still, in terms of traditional, aristocratic status, the freedman was at a dead-end position, except for the accumulation of wealth, influence, and a certain religious office.[38] Though these are hardly to be slighted, it is perfectly understandable that a new, publicly active, and moneyed group would want recognition. Certainly, as Tacitus's account of Claudius's reliance on freedmen reveals, their recognition was resented.[39] And, as the exiled Seneca's letter to the imperial freedman Polybius attests (6.5), aristocrats sought their influence, even at the cost of flattery. One insight into what an aristocrat thought such freedman wanted comes from Petronius's infamous Trimalchio. The *Satyricon*'s freedman has succeeded in accumulating wealth and influence (or so he thinks), and makes proud boast of his priesthood. Of course, the nouveau riche is an abysmal failure at gaining the respect of the freeborn, or of the reader. This is Petronius's true ridicule. Trimalchio remains hopelessly uncultured, his speech ever derided by the freeborn characters even if they are penniless. Phaedrus is bent on avoiding such ridicule; he is intent on having his culture and status properly recognized.

The poet presents two alternative solutions for resistance to fraud, both of which—either appealing to the just patriarch or properly estimating one's own voice and station—integrate the poet and reader into Roman society as they banish the fraudulent. The second solution radically shifts the generic element of fable, cleverness and canniness, to a sort of confident linguistic self-knowledge. Two fables from the third book offer the solution we have already seen: proper judgment from on high, though the context is more specific. In the story of the ugly sister and handsome brother (3.8), the daughter, tired of her brother's insults, falsely accuses him of incest. Father knows best and presents each with a mirror. The girl will see her ugliness and remember to be virtuous; the boy will not corrupt his looks with base deeds. In the second example, Augustus himself must finally intervene to prevent the slander and false witness of a freedman against his master's family (3.10.42: the emperor "tenebras dispulit calumniae"). These events reveal the customary pattern: the head of the hierarchy, provided he is moral, acts to prevent fraud, to champion legitimacy. The master prevents the passage of *calumnia* to *crimen*. Such is the first solution to fraud.

The second solution is more potential, less positive: the plots of a number of fables show the perils of trusting one's own boasts or another's false claims. A solution to such fraud arises from the poet's directions, either in the framing morals of particular poems or the framing poems to the books, the prologues and epilogues (again, for this poet, who and what are first and last is most significant). The latter would write Phaedrus out of such plots by having the reader act the master and reject the claims of the critics. For the poet's directions to be effective, the reader must appreciate the identity and methods of the *fraudator*. In particular, the reader must come to be wary of the defrauder's linguistic strategies, the social quality of his lies. For it is in such speech acts as salutations, promises, agreements, and contracts, that the fraudulent would make his addressee into a victim.

Phaedrus's thoroughgoing transformation of fable, especially in diction, syntax, and plot structure, presents the genre of fable as preoccupied with the *genera* of its characters, their relations, and language. From a few examples of Phaedrus's departures from the Greek prose collection that he used, the focus of this insistent pattern will come clear. In the story of the lion and the ass/would-be huntsman (1.11), Phaedrus has omitted Aesop's "having pledged alliance/equality with one another." κοινωία becomes, not its obvious translation, *societas*, but *comite*. The ass is no Roman equal; he goes as a companion—a word that means dependent follower,

here technically of those who carry the nets, spears, and so on at
the hunt, but used at 2.5.16, for example, of the slave who tries
to impress Tiberius and similarly fails. The poet had announced
the absence of alliance/communion at the beginning of another
fable where a lion takes hunting companions: "numquam est fidelis cum potente societas" (1.5.1). Between social unequals, equality
is not possible and must not be relied upon. The Latin syntax
underscores this division as well. The Greek (*Aesopica* 151; Halm
259)[40] presents the characters paratactically: "The lion . . . and the
ass. . . ." Phaedrus has neither followed the Greek nor made the
opening sentence of the story hypotactic: "Venari asello comite
cum vellet leo" (3) dangles the ass in an ablative absolute.[41] In
such a world the isolated figure should expect no equal exchange
of words or services.

In 4.9, Phaedrus has similarly modified the Greek original
and shifted the emphasis of the plot and moral to draw his social
caveat. The epimythium introduces this story of the fox who fell
into a well, enticed a goat to come down, and climbed out on the
goat's horns as an instance of the clever man who escapes danger through harm done to another. The fox is the fraud worker
(7: "fraudem moliens") and, unlike his victim, understands fully
his vertical level.[42] As in so many of the fables, the victim starts
high and ends low, and true position is seen and destroyed by the
defrauder: at the start the fox "altiore clauderetur margine" (4:
"he was imprisoned by a too tall well top") and at the end, "evasit puteo nixa celsis cornibus / hircumque clauso liquit haerentem vado" (11–12: "with the aid of the high horns he escaped the
well and left the goat stuck in the imprisoned mud"). Initial positioning is important in Phaedrus's poems, as the phrasing "super
stabat" of 1.1 and 2.1, or the first three lines that locate the eagle,
cat, and sow of 2.4, suggest. In part, features such as the recurrent notices of relative position make possible Phaedrus's vaunted
brevity; in addition, he was reworking traditional fare, and so the
presentation of relation was more important and better appreciated than a full recounting of plot.

In a medium where narrative plot is already known or easily

discerned through title or allusion, diction is both highly charged and can in itself define character role and even interpretation of the entire fable. In this poem, the contrast of final positions is further emphasized by the straightforward word order and verticality of "evasit puteo nixa celsis cornibus" and the sticky, interlocked "hircumque clauso liquit haerentem vado." This poem presents the injury received and the fraud worked as a reversal of station. The poem's development and closure enact this epimythium. Fraud, the injury done another, consists in the fox's language, which can make a ford, a passageway, into a prison—the oxymoron of "clauso . . . vado." The goat descends from his proper level, convinced by "Descende, amice; tanta bonitas est aquae / Voluptas ut satiari non possit mea" ("Come down, my friend; the water is so sweet that I alone should not have the pleasure of it"). In Aesop (9) further conversation is needed to bamboozle the victim; the fox proposes his trick of standing upon the goat's horns. Phaedrus is not concerned with further exchange between the two, nor is he concerned with the misjudgment about pleasure which leads to the Greek goat's downfall. The Roman goat falls because he believes the salutation *amice*—which is Phaedrus's addition.[43] Phaedrus's fables do not show the equality wrought by wit but the perils of status confusion.

The failure to distinguish the high from the low consists in confusing false and true speech. The speech need not come from another; from the story of "The Stag at the Spring" (1.12) it would seem there is a *calumniator* within. Again, the worth of lofty horns is misjudged: gazing into the water, the stag praises (*laudat*) his antlers and denigrates (*vituperat*) his slender legs. Of course, his *vituperatio* and *laudatio* are exactly reversed: chased by hunters, it was his speed that almost saved the stag—had his antlers not become entangled. In Phaedrus's source (*Aesopica* 74; Halm 128), the stag had confused the *lepton* (his legs he faults as λεπτοῖς οὖσι καὶ ἀσθενέσιν) with that which has *megethos*. This diction, which in Greek easily admits literary resonance, has become even more pointed in the Latin. *Laudatio* and *vituperatio* belong not to soliloquies upon hooves and antlers but to the Roman schools of rhetoric and the performances of forensic oratory. Literary praise and censure are also the constituents of imperial panegyric, letters of recommendation and appointment,[44] and petitions of grievance. Quite simply, these rhetorical techniques were of the greatest importance for the administration of government and for catching the emperor's attention. The good and successful estimator of these modes distinguishes between the voices he hears, crediting the true and punishing the false. That is, the critic too enters into *laudatio* and *vituperatio*. Social order exists when the worthy are recognized. The difficulty is, of course, whom and what to credit, how to keep *laudatio* and *vituperatio* straight. The entangled deer warns us that function, the ability to render service, is to be preferred to form, but function is strictly circumscribed in the fables.

A crane sticks her neck down the throat of a wolf to remove a bone. She then asks the previously voiceless (throat-blocked) wolf for her fee. She thinks she stands on firm legal ground, for the wolf had come to hire her (1.8.6: "inlicere pretio")[45] and sworn an oath (7: "iure iurando"). Only then had she believed him (8: "gulaeque credens colli longitudinem").[46] Against her the wolf maintains their language was that of informal, social agreement: "'Ingrata es'" inquit "'ore quae nostro caput / incolume abstuleris et mercedem postules'" (11–12: "You are an ingrate, as you have removed your head in one piece from my jaws and demand a reward"). No contract had been made, and so the crane is but a client. To insist upon one's services was odious; so Cicero complains: "Odiosum sane genus hominum officia exprobrantium" (*De amic.* 71: "Really odious is that race of men who harp about their kind services").[47]

The declaimers found ingratitude a favorite theme. Phaedrus's contemporary Valerius Maximus, a collector of rhetorical exempla, devoted an entire chapter to this subject. The applicability of this school theme to Roman law has long been doubted,[48] but such legal exactness should be as unimportant to the Roman historian as it was to this wolf. Legal or pseudo-legal language is here but an intimation of social sentiment and practice.[49] Ingratitude was felt to be important and overrides any reality about the law. In the *Persa* (762), Plautus had defined the wicked as he who fails to return good for good: "Improbus est homo, qui beneficium scit accipere et reddere nescit." Phaedrus, too, defines wickedness: in 1.5 a cow, she-goat, and sheep go hunting with the lion as *socii*,[50] but in the end his speech does not entitle them to any part of the prey. Phaedrus's conclusion seems severe: "sic totam praedam sola improbitas abstulit." The crane got away with her neck; the lion with everything. This is not surprising simply because of the divide between the mighty and the weak. Phaedrus does not celebrate the rapacity of social superiors, nor does he try to invert society (as Aesop the slave made his master into a fool in the *Life of Aesop*). Instead, he contains the viciousness of society within the realm of the natural. Cow, she-goat, and ewe were partners with the lion (1.5.4: "socii fuere cum leone"). This arrangement falls short of contract, as the natural markers would warn any cautious reader. The female lined up with the male, the sheep "patiens . . . iniuriae," as she is introduced, with the lion in the wilderness ("cum leone in saltibus"), bear in their gender, *genera*, and epithets all the weight and orders of nature. Against which stands the ambiguous term *socii*: Are the lesser animals partners with legal rights or simply companions, lesser friends who can make no claims on the patron? Phaedrus does not rework Plautus's definition of the *improbus* so much as restrict its applicability. Among peers (between *amici*), failure to exchange *beneficia* is immoral, but for those who mistake their legal or social relation, the ability to serve has no automatic merit. That is, the crane's service cannot be a *beneficium*; she is not the superior and so, at most, can hope to have her services understood as an *officium*, which merits no necessary return.[51] In addition, the crane has erred by seeking monetary reward, which, as the *Digest* tells, is completely alien to *officium*.[52] Relationships between unequals should either be social, where gratitude will direct the parties, or legal, where contract stipulates behavior and portions, or natural, where violence rules. Mistakes about the self's role and status follow from misapprehensions of social relations and social language.

In a number of fables such errors involve a character being misled about his own role, status, or language. The plot does not always provide the external *calumniator* to assert false distinctions about what belongs and what is alien to the victim's self. And yet the speech of the *calumniatores*, including those who would deny the poet his due *fama* by misconstruing the *genus* and status of the poet-freedman, finds a parallel in the individual's confusion about self and other. At times, this confusion can seem folkloric, as with the stag who got wrong the relative virtues of his legs and horns.[53] In that fable the connections to issues of speech and status were metaphorical, and especially metonymic. The diction of the high antlers and the slender legs invoked themes of social and literary position and worth. In the fables to be considered below, the body part praised and misconstrued has a similar connection to the literary polemics of the poet, for it is their own voice the animals overestimate and come to rue. The crane with her neck down the bone-obstructed throat of the wolf, the stag praising his antlers, later imprisoned by them and eaten by the hounds, and the ass who believes his braying is a great boon to the lion present selves deceived about the value of speech. Though comical, voice verges on gullet; mistakes are perilous.

In his first poem Phaedrus had asked, much like the crane or the ass, for the *pretium meriti* (the reward for service); the addressees of the prologues, and ultimately of course the readers, must judge whether his *libellus* (1. prol. 3) is a legitimate petition, whether he is of a status to contract for fame, or, in social terms, whether he is a true *socius*, a legitimate citizen. In the fables, words have not always freed the animals from their awkward positions; and where they have, the *improbi* have emerged from the well. In these the reader recognizes the words and rhetorics of the social interloper. But the poet also provides models for judgment of one's own voice, and these poems constitute a developing link to the reader's understanding of true poetic voice.

Many miscalculate the worth of their voice; 1.11 is the loudest. The ass who went hunting with the lion thought his beast-terrifying braying a *beneficium*; he was rebuffed by the lion, who

had never forgotten his asinine *genus*. Only victims get confused,
or, as the epimythium puts it:

> Virtutis expers, verbis iactans gloriam,
> ignotos fallit, notis est derisui.
>
> (1–2)

> [The man without virtue who boasts of his excellence
> fools the ignorant and is a fool to the knowledgable.]

The reader's laughter is elicited as he is educated. Self-advertisement is not being faulted; the verbal appropriation of virtue and
glory not one's own is. The ass's false assumption lies clear for all
to see in the fable's humorous close:

> tunc ille insolens,
> "Qualis videtur opera tibi vocis meae?"
> "Insignis," inquit, "sic ut, nisi nossem tuum
> Animum genusque, simili fugissem metu."
>
> (12–15)

> [Then he said in all his impudence,
> "How do you like the good service of my voice?"
> "First rate," said he, "if I hadn't known
> your courage and kind, I would have fled terrified like
> them."]

The ass's faux pas was to think his action was an *opera*, which the
Romans used as a technical term for the service owed a master by
his manumitted slave and which the master stipulated (e.g., *Dig.*
38.24). No such social relationship exists, as the lion's response
makes clear.[54]

Only when properly used and appreciated (as, say, by Phaedrus's ideal reader), does language assert social identity and check

social ambition. Phaedrus makes this very observation in the epimythium to 1.27:

> Haec res avaris esse conveniens potest
> et qui humiles nati *dici* locupletes student.
>
> $(1-2)$

> [This tale can apply to the greedy
> and the lowborn who are keen to be *called* rich.]

The illustrative fable that follows tells of a dog so entranced with the treasure he has discovered that he refuses to move and finally dies of starvation. A vulture from on high reproves the corpse:

> "O canis, merito iaces,
> qui concupisti subito regales opes,
> trivio conceptus, educatus stercore."
>
> $(9-11)$

> ["O dog, you deserve to lie so,
> you, who wanted to be rich as a king on the spot,
> were conceived on a streetcorner and born in shit."]

The poem is thus sealed not by slander but by truth telling. The dog's error, the introductory moral has made clear, was wishing to be called (*dici*) wealthy.

Speech can confuse the high and the low, but this is not the natural or desirable order of things. Consider the cobbler who passed himself off as a physician: "verbosis adquisivit sibi famam strophis" (1.14.4). The quack confesses:

> non artis ulla medicum se prudentia,
> verum stupore vulgi factum nobilem.
>
> $(11-12)$

[not by any expertise in the physicians' art
made famous, but by the mob's stupidity.]

The use of the word *nobilis* is rare in Phaedrus: a famous vintage
Falernian wine has this epithet transferred to the wine jug.[55] Better
than old wine and quite unlike the quack is the poet Menander,
identified by Phaedrus as "nobilis comoediis" (5.1.9). Phaedrus
finds two poets worthy subjects for fables: Menander and Simonides, a rather odd canon perhaps, but their connection, in the fables
at any rate, is that very Roman equivalence fame/nobility. Menander is ennobled by his poetry; Simonides toured the famous cities
of Greece and is rewarded by being recognized as the cities' peer
(4.23).[56] The common theme with the fables as a whole is this issue
of the estimation of voice. These two poets provide a positive example of the recognition of literary status capital.[57] Collectively,
these poems about the boasts of one's own voice and true recognition of the poets' voices provide the paradigm for the second
solution to fraud. Against the mob, the quack, and the ass, the
figure of the poet has his voice properly recompensed.

In 4.26 Simonides knows the value of his voice, as do the
gods. Having contracted to write a poem in praise of an aristocratic patron, Simonides is defrauded, paid only a portion of his
fee. This is the famous story, usually told by rhetoricians as an instance of the power of memory (Cicero *De oratore* 2.86, followed
by Valerius Maximus 1.8.7), where Castor and Pollux call him out
from dinner with this fraudulent master. The house collapses; all
die. The bereaved relatives must turn to the poet, who remembers the seating order, to identify the squashed remains. Phaedrus
has changed the moral; he has made most prominent what was
simply an element of the plot (the gods' favor). Phaedrus's second
poem about this poet identifies Simonides as the one who wrote
lyric poetry to stave off poverty and so toured the famous cities
of Asia (4.23).[58] Abandoning a sinking ship, his fellow passengers
load themselves down with their possessions; some drown; the
rest are fleeced by robbers. The poet has taken nothing (to an in-
quiring shipmate he says [14], "Mecum . . . mea sunt cuncta") but

is saved from penury by an admiring reader, a wealthy citizen of Clazomenae. Simonides is not the only character in Phaedrus to confront Fortune; but he is the sole figure *pauper*, and hence seen by most as *impotens*, to confront and achieve nobility.[59]

Poetic Status

In the prologues and epilogues Phaedrus stakes his claim to be a *homo doctus*, to belong to the *genus* of Simonides. These poems, which have addressees and are the most directly programmatic (literally), are also concerned with *calumnia*. A literary polemic in the prologue introduced in the poet's character is patterned, like the *senarius* itself, on Terence. The Terentian connection is not accidental: the African ex-slave who wrote pure Latin, associated with a circle of Roman nobles, and gained literary immortality no doubt appealed to our poet. There are crucial differences in situation, and certainly in self-presentation. Phaedrus's work does not claim connection to a noble patron. He appeals instead to three addressees about whom we know nothing except what we find in these prologues, and that is little.

Of Eutychus, graced with the third prologue, we think we know the most: he may have been in charge of Tiberius's estate at Misenum.[60] The other addressees are Philetus (5. epil.) and Particulo. The first two are Greek names and, commonly, slave names. Managers of the imperial estates were freedmen. Phaedrus is in all probability addressing his fables, his petition for redress from calumny and for lasting fame, to high bureaucrats within the *familia Caesaris*.[61] The name Particulo may be something of a joke, for it is not a proper name. The grammarian Nonius is the only other source for this word; he derives it from *pars* and explains that it means co-heir (20.6). In addition, names like this ending in *-o* imply that the person has that quality in large measure: thus, some Naso originally had a large nose, Capito a large head. Particulo has a large little part, which may be a pun; he is the one well-endowed in his anatomy and his inheritance. Fellow freedmen,

colliberti, could expect to be named in their master's wills. Phaedrus with this nickname draws attention to the common origin
and status that links him to another of the emperor's freedmen.[62]
Indeed, Eutychus himself may be lurking behind "Particulo."

At the same time as the poet appeals to these freedmen, he
bases his claim for distinction and recognition on his Latinity,
his pure *sermo*. Indeed, in the first half of the epilogue to book 2
he phrases the criterion for literary success as a dependence on
whether Latium approves his poems:[63]

2.9 Auctor

Aesopi ingenio statuam posuere Attici,
servumque collocarunt aeterna in basi,
patere honoris scirent ut cuncti viam
nec generi tribui sed virtuti gloriam.
quoniam occuparat alter ut primus foret,
ne solus esset, studui, quod superfuit.
nec haec invidia, verum est aemulatio.
quodsi labori faverit Latium meo,
plures habebit quos opponat Graeciae.

[The Athenians dedicated a statue to the genius of Aesop
and placed a slave on an eternal pedestal,
that all might know the road to distinction lies open
and that good fame follows not rank but virtue.
Since this man has gained first place,
I have striven that he not be alone, which is what is left me.
This is not envy but emulation.
But if Latium approve my effort,
it will have more to compete with Greece.]

Latium is of course the original limit of *Latinitas*. What Phaedrus
strives to assert is that Latinity is no longer a birthright, that correctness and purity of discourse and not purity of lineage enroll

one in Latium.[64] This poem, then, is not simply an account of Phaedrus's source and originality. The Athenians have seen fit to recognize the genius and not the birth of a fabulist; the Romans should do the same.

In the prologue to the second book, also offered in the author's voice, Phaedrus had laid down his contract or alliance with the reader. Phaedrus presents himself as repudiating the *contumelia* of his critics with this, the non-noble's, plea

> quicumque fuerit ergo narrandi iocus,
> dum capiat aurem et servet propositum suum,
> re commendetur, non auctoris nomine.
> equidem omni cura morem servabo senis.
>
> (5–8)

> [Whatever the style of the humor of the subject,
> provided it please the audience and fulfill its intention,
> it should be approved for itself, not for its author's name.
> Indeed, with all diligence I shall follow the rule of the old
>   man.]

The conditions of reading are set down in terms that specify the reader-creditor's role. The author's epilogue to this book and the prologue to the next reaffirm this association for fame. In the epilogue especially, the abstractions of Latium and *Livor* (envy, begrudgment) distinguish the *lector* from the *calumniator*.[65] Still, the persona of the poet remains separate; as yet, he belongs to none of these categories, and these categories remain fluid. Latium and that poetic landscape Livor are coextensive. This is why Phaedrus can have Eutychus wonder, at the end of the epilogue to book 3 (3. epil. 32), who these detractors are. They are potential; any reader might slip from *Latium* if he allows the *calumniator* to exploit envy. Phaedrus, however, is concerned not simply with dividing the community of readers but with creating a new *genus*— both genre and literary community. And so he writes, in the prologue to book 3, of the origin of the *genus* of fable and urges his addressee Eutychus, preoccupied with business, to change not his way but his *genus* of life so as to pass within the threshold of the Muses (3. prol. 15–16: "mutandum tibi propositum est et vitae genus, / intrare si Musarum limen cogitas"). The Muses will include both freedmen in a *domus* of a different sort of authority and legitimacy. In this fashion, by the reading of Phaedrus's fables the freedman Eutychus, who like all Roman freedmen has no parents, will reoriginate himself.

This prologue continues to establish Phaedrus's own literary pedigree—we are told that his mother bore him on the very Pierian mountain where Memory bore to Jove the nine Muses, that he was all but born in a school. These "textual facts" have been used to conclude that Phaedrus was a Thracian abandoned on the doorstep of a schoolmaster who brought him up as a slave.[66] In addition to the general drawbacks of reading autobiography from Roman poetry, Phaedrus's hyperbole and vagueness should not have allowed any reconstruction of the poet's life. He protests too strongly of his abusers and his calamity. Even the mention of Sejanus (3 prol. 41) serves the Ovidian trope of condemnation for an ill-specified *crimen*.[67] Phaedrus continues his prologue by asserting that he has ever clung to the life of the poet and yet "fastidiose tamen in coetum recipior" (23: "The salon receives me with disdain"). There may have been an act or acts of social snobbery directed at the imperial freedman who wrote these poems. His status and epoch make this probable, but the acts of injustice remain irrecoverable and, far more important, have no significance for this poetry. The poems, however, are concerned to construct a poetic *coetus*, a literary *genus* independent of noble disdain and noble patronage.

In this prologue Phaedrus has said that he has achieved no fame and yet has stuck to the profitless life of learned labor. After relating his school birth and poor literary reception, Phaedrus returns to the theme of riches and poverty by reminding that man of the world, Eutychus, of the ultimate pointlessness of heaping up riches. This commonplace he calls up short by quoting what

Sinon said to Priam. No doubt, the reader wonders what the "it" of "whatever may come of it" (27: "quodcumque fuerit") is—accruing wealth, the coming book, the poet's plea to his addressee? Without pause he announces his third book and follows this with an account of the origin of the *genus* of fable. This origin actually antedates Aesop; indeed, it seems essential to slavery:

> Nunc, fabularum cur sit inventum genus,
> brevi docebo. servitus obnoxia,
> quia quae volebat non audebat dicere,
> affectus proprios in fabellas transtulit,
> calumniamque fictis elusit iocis.

> [Now why the genre of fable was invented
> I shall briefly tell. The hurt of a slave's condition,
> since it did not dare speak its true desire,
> translated its genuine emotions into little stories
> and gave the ruse to insult and abuse with its joking
>   fictions.]

Fable is the translation of the self's passions and emotions that through fiction avoids abuse and delivers the poet from the injuries of his station. The poet implies that speech manifests the true self and can redress his servile birth and libertine station.

Of all the characters in this poem (Phaedrus will reassert his Thracian literary connection, saying he is closer to lettered Greece than the Phrygian Aesop and then including Linus and Orpheus as Thracians) Sinon is the most peculiar. Phaedrus has taken Sinon's obscure words "whatever may happen" from Virgil (*Aeneid* 2.77). Sinon is essentially and symbolically *duplex* and *bilinguis*, like the *calumniator* and fable itself. As a fellow Greek captive of a Dardanian king who plays the role of *consiliator*—adviser—he is also like Phaedrus, advice-mongering freedman of Caesar. There is yet a further likeness, as both present themselves as men repudiated by their own *genus*. After such a symbol of speech and sign-giving, it is little wonder that Eutychus will (in the epilogue) doubt the existence of Phaedrus's detractors. The Greek-speaking Roman bureaucrat should, however, be ready to receive Phaedrus into the *genus doctorum* and will be disposed, as Phaedrus hopes at the prologue's end, to make a *sincerum iudicium* (62–63), to banish the critics and honor the genuine voice of the poet.

Epilogue

Reading the poems of Phaedrus elicits an uneasy feeling: Pindar's crows have grown into a zoo, and the reader, if he is not careful, may be one of those carping animals. Actually, the critics seem to be of two species: the poet's social peers, freedmen who would intervene between him and the mighty, and the poet's (self-styled) literary or cultural peers, the Romans who would dismiss him as a Greek ex-slave. Advancement for the literati depended on attracting the notice of the freedmen of the emperor's staff and of the Roman reading public. Perhaps the cleverness of Phaedrus, his plot structures and the identification with Sinon, appealed to freedmen of the imperial household. His archness of style and tone sought the approval of both audiences. The remarkable fact is that those hallmarks of Silver Latin, judgments of cultural vulgarity and self-conscious statements of literary decline, do not arise only from the dispossessed and aggrieved aristocracy. Such statements, whatever changes in literary esthetics they may imply, reflect an extension of literary culture. The pages of Suetonius are ample testimony that intellectual culture, the trade and profession of schooling and governmental careers for the schooled, was at a new height from the time of Augustus. Phaedrus is a product of that extension of culture and status and is fiercely proud and possessive of both. This connection of literary culture, public status, and economic opportunity finds a parallel not so much in courtly speech, where mastery of social conventions reflects and augments birth, as perhaps in the figure of an itinerant, marginal Renaissance scholar, trying to make his way by his learning, overly anxious not to betray his origins by an error of speech or gesture, or by respect improperly shown to a subordinate or not shown to a superior. This, too, is a world where the scholar is devoured for a faux pas and where arriviste and noble alike disdain "vulgarity" as dangerous.

Phaedrus has presented a poetic persona of the Roman freedman threatened by his peers and insulted by his fellow citizens in order to make his claim for a better status based on literary criteria. The poems do provide another equally confrontational clue as to how they are to be imagined. The important, programmatic quality of this directive is signaled by its initial placement and its peculiar dialogue or polemic with Phaedrus's precursor in Roman satire and fable, Horace. In the third line of Phaedrus's first prologue a dramatic metaphor locates reader, poet, and poem: "duplex libelli dos est: quod risum movet, / et quod prudenti vitam consilio monet" ("This slender book has a double dowry: the means to raise a laugh and to guide life with savvy advice"). All but the first half of the third line of this seven-line poem has received critical attention (Phaedrus's relation to Aesop, the double point of his poetry as a modification of or allusion to Horace, the trees—not just animals—who are said to talk; I have emphasized the fiction and importance of *calumniari*). The feature of the prologue that has not received comment is the metaphor and personification of the book's double dowry. Critics are right to recognize the echo of Horace,[68] but Phaedrus's allusion is far more significant, his revision of Horace more drastic than the repetition of the commonplace of poetry as *utile* and *dulce*.

Phaedrus's book of poems has a dowry, in stark contrast to Horace's work, which is keen to leave the poet's *familia* and prostitute itself: "Vertumnun Ianumque, liber, spectare videris, / scilicet ut prostes Sosiorum pumice mundus" (*Epist.* 1.20.1–2: "Book, you seem intent on the Vertumnus and the Janus [a neighborhood of Rome], no doubt to troll for men, decked out with the polish of the booksellers"). Horace pretends that his book is an illegitimate slave, sleek and ready to be bought. In contrast, Phaedrus's *libellus* is a proper bride, the *ingenua* of New Comedy, to be recognized by her tokens of citizenship. Phaedrus's trope of marriage is more than a response to Horace. Every dowry is *duplex*, as on marriage it falls under the control of the husband but can revert to the wife. To the reader who would appropriate these poems, the double dowry warns that use but not ownership is possible. The poems cannot be owned any more than the freedman himself. *Duplex*, like *bilinguis*, is a highly charged term for Phaedrus because it characterizes fable itself and fable telling. The fabulist can never simply advertise the sweet and the instructive to entice his readers; he expects and preempts a certain hostility.

But marriage was inappropriate for Horace, or so the persona of the *Odes* insists: "virtute me involvo probamque / pauperiem sine dote quaero" (*Carm.* 3.29.55–56: "I cloak myself with virtue and seek an upright poverty without dowry"). Phaedrus has learned much from Horace, including this technique of targeting the reader. For in Horace a longing for a dowered bride characterizes the censured object of the poet's satire: those who worry about dowry are the noble adulteress (*Sat.* 1.2.131); the *pater ardens* of comedy, whose high-living son turns down a well-dowered bride (*Sat.* 1.4.49–50); the husband ruled by his moneyed wife (*Carm.* 3.24.19–20); and the lowborn Mutus of *Epistle* 1.6 (especially line 21, where he is anxious about his profit from his wife's fields). As Horace rejects *dos* and prefers the *liberta* to the noble-born adulteress, so he stands at a safer remove from Catullus and the Roman noble's sphere. He remains the unambitious, childless son of a freedman. Phaedrus declines to represent his self, family, and genre as self-sufficient and closed. Horace's marriage to poverty is not for the imperial freedman. The reader is expected to accept Phaedrus's poems as legitimate Roman offspring whose native Romanness shows their father a true citizen. To question this legitimacy is to purloin another's capital. The reader shrinks from such willful, criminal *calumnia* and *contumelia*.

4

Declamatory Pleading: A New Literary History

THIS CHAPTER CONSIDERS ONE TEXT that is prescriptive of Roman culture and speech. The elder Seneca's treatment of declamation seeks to display a very Roman world, where proper Latinity and Roman nobles censure the upstart and the Greek. The various speakers in Seneca's book pose as the successors to Ciceronian Latin and republican oratory; they compete to demonstrate proper speech, one that is neither craven Caesarian flattery nor Ciceronian pastiche but a reworking of traditional topics which, if properly handled, reveals those defining characteristics of a traditional Roman-speaking male citizen: *ingenuitas* and *libertas*, free birth and free speech.

At the same time, declamatory oratory was *oratio* displaced. It was school speech, a ludic version of forensic conflict, performed under the eye and sometimes the punishing hand of a schoolmaster by those at a distant remove in time and even origin from Cicero and Antony or the Catos and Scipios of the republic. Thus worries about political and social inferiority overlay a sense of linguistic inferiority. Praise of the past is nothing new in Roman society, but this new medium of school exercises burgeoning into literature engaged in a fundamental and contradictory fiction. The boy could be fashioned into a man, a Roman man, by this play-speaking on behalf of prostitute-priestesses, ungrateful sons, villainous stepmothers, and harsh fathers. Cultural and social categories are here being defined and contested within that peculiarly liminal site, the school with its fantasies of adult speech and life. For the cultural historian, declamation is most interesting as the site of these mythmaking processes.[1] In this quasi-Greek world, a schoolteacher, who might well be an ex-slave, taught an originally Greek academic subject, still filled with pirates and tyrants, to Roman boys. From this world Seneca the Elder fashioned his history of contemporary speech.

The crabbed expression, bizarre situations, and the very weight of all the names of individual speakers in a text stitched together by the elder Seneca, purportedly the reminiscences of his old age, and excerpted and abused by the scribes have made the *Oratorum et Rhetorum Divisiones Colores et Sententiae*[2] the most difficult of Latin rhetorical texts. Works of theory or pedagogy can be more easily considered by the scholar: they have allowed themselves analysis by reference to prior sources and theories.[3] Seneca has resisted such treatment and so was labeled an indiscriminate or descriptive, not a prescriptive, critic.[4] His work then appealed all the more as an objective account of Roman declamation, provided one credited the veracity of his memory.[5] But little should be taken as objective reporting in his history of declamation. The difficulty of the text has obscured an ambitious program.

This work shares a characteristic of much of Julio-Claudian literature, which, at the same time pedagogic and novel, avoids the subject matter and treatment of the prior generations' classical achievement. If we are to maintain the divisions of genre, which authors of this generation collapse, the historical works have turned from the grand narrative of Livy and the antiquarianism that runs from Varro to Fenestella to works of encyclopedic culture and schoolboy learning: Asconius, Celsus, Valerius Maximus, and Seneca. The exploitation of a form drawn from, and perhaps for, the schools is seen again in Phaedrus's elevation into a Roman poetic medium of that school exercise, the translation of Greek fable. Seneca shares the connection with the schools and also Asconius's gesture of address to sons. He departs in essaying a new topic and in that topic's scope: unlike Valerius Maximus and Asconius, his prose sources and models are not the canonical Cicero. One other Tiberian author offers a parallel: the poet Manilius's appropriation of a Greek subject, the intricacies of astrology, illustrates well the extremity the Latin writer felt in his quest for an untreated topic. Didacticism and a search for the novel, however, fail to explain the early imperial historians' choice of the German Wars (for example, Aufidius Bassus) or the poets' choice of fable and astrology.

Amid the topics of Julio-Claudian authors, declamation may have been the most unlikely and unworthy for a developed history and apology—unworthy because, like fable, declamation was a school exercise. Literature need not purport to be serious, but when written from the avowed stance of the *pater familias*, it makes itself out to be so. The Roman father wrote of what he participated in: most traditionally, war (history) and agriculture, or memoirs of a consulship when there was not much war tó write about. Cicero's publication of his speeches conforms; the letters do not. Or the letters offer a different tone and persona, the *amicus* writing to his equals. When he writes to his son Marcus for all the world to read, a different tone and topic prevail. Seneca's address to his sons mixes the seriousness of paternal instruction with a suggestion of the unimportance, the novelty of his subject. "Women's literature" offers a parallel: the author both dignifies and apologizes for his subject through notice of the audience. The persona of *pater* maintains the text's serious stance while the young women addressees enable the author to write on a new topic—a handbook of etiquette, for example. Like a literature of instruction in behavior addressed to girls, a collection of Roman pedagogic exercises frees the author to write of what had been parental, domestic, and oral. Thus the book presents itself as traditional while hiding its innovation under the guise of being practical and informational. The author communicates, ostensibly to a new audience, one without familial connection to the material, a subject avowedly traditional.

Seneca's volumes were a sort of handbook of the etiquette of the new speech; he is greatly concerned with proper and improper style, especially with avoiding the vulgarism or Grecism that vitiates the Romanness of declamation. In neither Seneca's book nor in manuals for feminine improvement need we believe that the addressee is the sole or indeed the real readership. In part, Seneca adopted the locus of paternal injunction because declamation was much criticized: beneath the recurrent rhetoric of its unreality and impracticality we must remember that in Seneca's lifetime declamation had become the final course of training for educated Romans—the medium for the dissemination and modification of speech training. But in Augustus's and Tiberius's day it was no more a traditional topic of reading than was a collection of rhetorical exempla or the exegesis of a Roman political speech.[6] If Seneca's work does demonstrate the aspects of a serviceable work on a topic previously oral, why has the author chosen to add this particular subject to the course of young men's reading? Why has what properly belongs to the schools and to oral instruction become literature?

The established answer opines that old-style speech has perished with old-style politics, a conclusion that effaces both the changes in literature and their reasons. Indeed, the causal link between political and literary change only establishes the possibility, not the quality, of change and innovation. Further, a rationale based on the lament for the fallen republic simply replicates the rhetoric of the participants and represents, in keeping with that rhetoric, that nothing else has changed. But to say that Rome is the same with the single change of the Caesars, and a series of attendant consequences, is to accept the ideology of the day.

Another answer lies beneath Seneca's assertion that he writes so that his sons, who have not heard the early declaimers, may know the genuine and approved from the spurious and spurned. Seneca and his approved circle of critics, including Latro and Pollio and Messala, are preoccupied with issues of taste, of what constitutes proper and improper Latin, of vulgarity, license, *copia*, and control. The declaimers serve up a public Latin demonstrably alien to the forensic and legal speech of Cicero's day. Seneca hopes to bridge this difference by a history of declamation that extols the proper Roman style of his favorite practitioners. Only thus can declamation be a subject worthy of study, a pursuit allied in setting (the schools) and style and purpose to the now so venerated and academic model of Cicero.

Seneca thus makes two crucial junctures. The first refutes the charge of impracticality: declamation is the proper training for law (public speech and public life), philosophy, history, the gentleman's life.[7] The second, allied aspect of his program connects this innovation in style and pedagogy to the canonical past. The declaimer Latro emerges as a new Cicero while emulation of Cicero is carefully delineated: neither aping nor censuring the old orator will do.

Seneca's work creates and contains its own origins. Arguably, any history of public speech includes itself. Seneca had available an authoritative history of Roman speech: Cicero's *Brutus* presented a chronological series of Roman orators, each with a particular virtue, culminating in the unstated but obvious apex of Cicero himself, most versed in Greek culture and the most perfect Latin orator. To write a new history of Roman speech or to add an appendix, Seneca must inscribe himself, his circle, and declamation into this authoritative genealogy.

This chapter describes the structures, motives, and allegiances of Seneca's history of declamation. After a discussion of the ambitions, social and literary, of Seneca and his collection, the central portion of the chapter considers the allegiances of the declaimers. This treatment reveals the particular biases and distortions of the elder Seneca. The final section reconsiders Seneca's and declamation's rhetorical program. The questions asked are quite simple: Why did Seneca collect declamatory purple passages and dedicate these to his sons? Which speakers does he grace with prefaces and why? What did declamation teach, or what in declamation appealed to Seneca, his sons, and his circle? A constant hypothesis is that there is nothing inevitable about declamation—either as a stage in Roman literary, social, or cultural history or as a topic of consuming interest for Romans living under the first emperors. In fact, the recurrent criticism of declamation reveals the difficulty and ambition of Seneca's program: impractical, perhaps vulgar, and suspected of being Greek, declamation may not belong to the Roman curriculum.

The Ambitions of Seneca *pater*

The elder Seneca was misnamed by later scholars *rhetor*—an affront to the equestrian, who uses this term only of professionals (although he defends the practice of such teaching at 2. pr. 5). He was an ambitious man, and one who succeeded in his ambitions. We have simply to look at his sons. The eldest, Novatus, was adopted by Junius Gallio, Tiberius's senator and later victim, who was the leading practitioner of the new style. Novatus himself reached the consulship and judged Saint Paul while he was proconsul of Achaea (c. A.D. 52). The middle son, after an adulterous intrigue resulting in exile, repaired his fortunes by tutoring Nero (or, perhaps more accurately, Agrippina had the philosopher Seneca recalled and made praetor in A.D. 49, eight years after his affair with Caligula's sister Julia Livilla).[8] Tacitus should not be believed when he describes Mela, the youngest son and father of the poet Lucan, as a financier who eschewed public life; he tried the route, in his case more lucrative and more closely allied with the emperor, of the equestrian governmental posts.[9]

The success of father and sons was not simply the reward due a literary family. The elder Seneca's grandson, the failed conspirator Lucan, similarly mixed politics and literature. The account of declamation and the lost histories of the elder Seneca did not in themselves launch this provincial family into Roman letters and public life, but the extant collection reveals this program: Seneca dedicates his work to the public and moralizes throughout the work in ways that associate questions of taste with the health of Roman society. The philosopher son seems to express the ambition of the father when he writes that his father's writings, if published, would have lifted him to social prominence, to clarity, and perhaps nobility.[10] Perhaps it took the highhanded recognition of Nero (and the adoption of Novatus by Junius Gallio, whereby, as the son of a consular, Novatus could be a *nobilis*) and not simply the pen of the philosopher to make the family noble.[11] The elder Seneca expands the orbit of the word "noble" by applying it on number of occasions to those not of a consular line but of literary merit.[12]

The father has masked his ambitions as successfully as he has written himself out of declamation. In a preface the reader hears of some of his judgments or his questions to Cassius Severus, but the extant account would have us believe that this habitué of the schools said nothing. Surely, if he did not perform like his friends Gallio and Latro, this judge of *sententiae*, *divisiones*, and *colores* did not refrain from the witticisms and analyses he so loves. Whatever his actual role in the training of his children and attendance on his friends, the father's devotion to schooling, like that of Horace's father, had a clear social aim. Fortunately, Tacitus communicates a recognition of this ambition from two points of view. The condemned freespoken aristocrat Publius Suillius taunts Seneca *filius* with two charges (in addition to his hatred for the friends of Claudius and his adultery): Seneca has preferred impractical, academic speech to real oratory, and he is an arriviste. Suillius refuses to submit his ancestral familial rank and station to the nouveau riche Seneca.[13] Syme points out that Tacitus uses *felicitas* only here and at 14.53 and so draws attention to the novelty of the *homo novus*.[14] In a second passage from the *Annals* of Tacitus, Seneca proposes his own retirement to Nero, using the words of his aristocratic critic. Significantly, the historical exempla he chooses to mirror his state are the ambitious high climbers Marcus Agrippa, reviled for his supposedly low origins, and Maecenas. Horace, the freedman's son who claimed to have no social ambitions, when playing Maecenas's encomiast, made his non-noble birth into the virtue of self-sufficiency: Maecenas, the *clarus eques* who aims no higher; the mythological Etruscan royal ancestry is no substitute for *nobilitas*. Suillius and Tacitus seem to speak through Seneca's confession: "Born from an equestrian provincial family am I to be counted among the chiefs of state? Has my recent arrival outshone the nobles and their long records of distinction?" (14.53: "egone equestri et provinciali loco ortus proceribus civitatis adnumeror? inter nobilis et longa decora praeferentis novitas mea enituit?").

A history of style should ignore (or displace?) distinctions of class. Candidates for stylistic excellence line up either in a series through history, as in Cicero's *Brutus*, or, with a different anachronism, as rival speakers at the same *controversia*. The discussion below of the identities and backgrounds of the subjects of the prefaces, and the reconstruction of the circles of the declaimers, show that Seneca is not so "objective." The very notion of being objective in a literary ranking smacks of an egalitarian canonization whereby *nobilis* can be applied not in its technical sense to the families of magistrates but, as Phaedrus does with Menander and as Seneca *filius* proposed to do with his father, to literati. The Senecas reveal a concern with engrafted nobility rather like Latro's when he used this unfortunate phrase before Maecenas, Augustus, and Agrippa just when Agrippa had succeeded in marrying into the imperial family.[15] Like the senatorial historians who were new men, the elder Seneca professes an ardent, upper-class Romanness by castigating vice as effeminate, vulgar, and Greek. The felicity, the great good fortune that elevated a *homo novus* to the consulship, the "luck" of the son, may be of the father's making.[16] The inscription of the sons into a history of oratory recommends the three young men to the community as surely as did Cato's dedication of his encyclopedia to his first son or Cicero's instruction of young Marcus in the *De Officiis*.[17] A conservative, moralizing pedagogy publicizes the promise of all these Romans sons and was just part of the fathers' promotional activities. The readership of these works includes the sons, their Roman peers who are to take the writers' sons as models, and the older men who are to recognize the father's virtues in the new generation. Like their polemic, the circles of Cato and Cicero are far better known than those of Seneca *pater*. In the case of Seneca, the characters and critics within the work present a model, imperial circle: Pollio, Gallio, Latro, Messala, and perhaps beyond them the emperor form the panel whose judgment must be satisfied.[18] Seneca also may have had a connection with the ladies of the court;[19] the son's familiarity with Julia Livilla would then be part of his patrimony.

Seneca's work has the simplest pretensions: an old man reminisces so as to instruct his sons. In fact, the pretensions are much grander: a selective memory drops important names and recollects as a single phenomenon what was inherently composite. By uniting speakers of different occasions, ages, and places in a single declamation, he has produced a cultural, social, and generational reduction.[20] The old man's protestations of a failing memory help him to exclude the more recent declaimers so he can focus on Latro and his own circle. So too, perhaps, he can skirt the written sources of Otho and Cestius.[21] For Seneca, "declamation" seems to mean a series of competitive performances on a topic apparently set by a schoolmaster and conducted in his school.[22] Students and master speak.[23] At times it seems outsiders could speak too. Certainly they can give their opinions. For Seneca has reported much comment upon the declamations; the epitomator recognized this and gave such criticism an independent section, labeled "extra." Speakers seem to have given their *divisiones* first; then came the developed treatment. Applause might interrupt the speakers. Spectators came and went. Some interrupted, even shouted impertinently.[24] Criticisms followed the performance. The instructor certainly must have had the first say, but Seneca reports what sounds like discussion of the experts, as if, as at an academic conference, a select subset of the audience discussed the speech at its conclusion or perhaps rehashed it later in private.

Yet this composite picture misleads. We can average the performances and reduce them to something like the picture of declamation as later described by Quintilian, part of the curriculum that a good schoolteacher practiced and recommended. But in doing so we repeat Seneca's blurring of the variety of declamation. Are we sure that we are witnessing the same event, the same sorts of people, the same locale? Seneca himself was playing historian and orator, and such a self-interested native witness hardly wins credibility. Quintilian was describing a later, simpler phenomenon. The occasional notices of performance suggest that speech training and performance were in far greater flux under the early Julio-Claudian emperors. Latro spoke alone. Albucius spoke in public only five or six times a year. In private performance, idiosyncratically, he remained seated, only rising if he got excited, and he rarely finished the *controversia*. It seems he once declaimed for six to nine hours straight, in public, his better medium.[25] In all probability, a number of the speakers never engaged in scholastic-competitive declamation (Cassius Severus, Asinius Pollio, Votienus Montanus). Other passages indicate a contest of professionals.[26] What is most clear is the effect of Seneca's presentation: he has reduced all these forms of speech to the most academic type, the brand of declamation known from Quintilian's treatise and the declamations attributed to him, where the master offers preliminary analysis and a model speech.[27] On one occasion Seneca reveals the surprise, the novelty of a Latin declamation followed by a Greek. There were separate Greek and Latin schools, but Seneca's text presents each topic as treated first in Latin then in Greek. The Greek is given short shrift, at least in part because Seneca makes the Greeks, rather than provincial Romans, the antitype for good Latin.[28]

Seneca stumbles when giving the early history of declamation.[29] He severs Cicero from the practice of "declamation" and, in a related disjunction, replaces the Greek *scholastica* with the Latin *controversia*. Thereby, declamation becomes a new phenomenon whose correct biography mirrors the author's. The old man himself connects declamation to the old orator and the venerated style. Our own histories of declamation have been written from the perspective of Seneca and the very academic Quintilian, who represents a later stage in which public performance had waned in importance. If we are to reconstruct the range of expression and diversity of the intellectual life of Rome at the outset of the empire, the schoolmaster's prescriptions are not the place to start. Declamation's range of subjects and concerns, along with fully developed excerpts, can be more reliably gleaned from Valerius Maximus than from the elder Seneca. Yet Seneca offers greater insight into the practice and practitioners of declamation, provided the critic recognizes his criteria of selection and presentation. In particular, the prefaces of the collection pirate our reading, forestalling criticism of declamation and, while looting the treasury of the Greek tradition and the practice of Roman declaimers, boldly making the newcomers' claim to what was not their birthright, oratory. Consequently, the reader moves from declamation's critics to its advocates, and from its petty practitioners to those Seneca would have us number among the old and the future orators.

The Ambition of the Prefaces

The prefaces are the most ambitious part of Seneca's work.[30] They constitute a juncture both in the technical, rhetorical sense of transition from one section to another, one set theme to another, and formally as letters of dedication, recommendation, and paternal injunction. Father, sons, patrons, Cicero, Spanish advocates, teachers, emperors, and aristocrats all meet here. The subjects joined are also self-consciously and problematically divided: the old practice of republican oratory does not square with the new styles and performances, and this great generational, stylistic, and moral gap has supposedly moved the father in all his disapproval to present the proper new models, the possible and not the distant style. Thus, in the prefaces Seneca juxtaposes criticism of declamation with criticism of free speech, actual lawyers with academic instructors, the aristocrats' verdicts and the newmen's blunders. These poles of discourse enable Seneca to align his project and provide it with a middle ground. His work is thereby set at a respectable distance from the genre of the technical treatise and proclaims his own amateur and superior status.

   The ten subjects of the original prefaces, and perhaps the subjects of a lost preface to the *Suasoriae*, constitute a circle not of professional schoolmen but of upper-class Romans. A rhetorician could have written a technical treatise and addressed it to his socially superior patron, but the form chosen by Seneca, a pater-

nal epistle recommending models to his sons, asserts the equality
or potential equality of all addressed. The prefaces, then, constitute textual, generational, and social juncture. Their canon of recommended declaimers subjoins disparate occasions and different
speakers while, in an anachronism fit for declamation, men long
dead plead alongside the peers and teachers of Seneca's sons. As
the prefaces elevate the subject to be narrated, and the particular
controversia, and more generally the role and importance of declamation, they, like any rhetorical juncture, elide distinctive differences, here especially those of time, place, and status.

The peculiar distortion that Seneca has worked on Roman
literary history is not all of his making. When modern handbooks
treat either declamation or the span of prose between Cicero and
Tacitus, their reliance on the names and characterizations penned
by the elder Seneca has as much to do with the fragmentary condition of the record as the program of Seneca's prefaces. In fact,
however, the Roman tradition of literary history broke from the
view of Seneca's prefaces. Tacitus, in his notices of some of the
figures praised in Seneca's prefaces, and Suetonius, in his biographies of speakers and teachers, present a significantly different account of the activities of some of Seneca's "declaimers," and consequently of declamation.

Tacitus treats men of equestrian status such as Cassius Severus
and Romanius Hispo with considerable disdain. In part he differs
from Seneca because of the notable excesses of prosecution perpetrated by such ambitious men (Seneca, too, has some censure for
the harshness of these two speakers). Tacitus considers such lawyers toadies of the emperor and social upstarts, two intrinsically
entwined and resonant aspects of imperial depravity, in this historian's view. But Seneca's list of the leading speakers does not agree
with Tacitus's occasional mention of individuals for social reasons
as well. The systematic divisions of Suetonius's biographies make
this social distinction most vivid. Unlike Seneca's mixture, Suetonius relegated individuals to their proper place: he grants a book
each to orator-lawyers, rhetoricians, grammar-school teachers.

Even in its lacunose state, Suetonius's work seems a more

objective account, primarily because his net is wider. He treats actual teachers, resisting the Ciceronian manner of the *Brutus*, which fastens upon one aristocrat, attributes to him a virtue, and progresses to the culmination of these Roman virtues. After its endpoint, such a history of speech cannot be repeated. Suetonius distinguished between professional teachers of grammar, teachers of rhetoric, and actual orators—those who spoke in the courts or in the senate. Seneca banishes the Greek professionals to the very end of each *controversia* or *suasoria*. The modern social or cultural or literary historian would want to know, no less for the republican period than for the imperial, who was teaching, for whom, and for what pay or benefit. What was the career of a schoolman? What were his languages, origin, training? Of course, these are not necessarily Cicero's or Seneca's or Suetonius's questions. But these questions do demonstrate the eclectic and exclusive focus of Cicero and Seneca. For in his prefaces Seneca offers as models of emulation figures Suetonius for the most part did not and would not have listed as practitioners of declamation. The speakers who do appear in cameo treatment in the prefaces make an unusual collection, for significantly and strikingly present are nondeclaimers or nonprofessionals.

A review of the status and activities of the men recommended in the prefaces shows their extraordinary affinities. To treat the subjects of the prefaces in order: Latro is a professional, but through a number of techniques that elevate his fellow Spaniard, Seneca succeeds in suggesting that Latro is a new Cicero. His friend is no teacher in the ordinary sense but a performer, who offers no instruction, but like the advocate of old or the canonical text is at hand only to be heard, perused, imitated. Fabianus is not a declaimer but a philosopher. As with Latro, Seneca is concerned to elevate the topic of declamation; Fabianus offers the first connection of declamation to philosophy. The thematic and familial importance of this connection needs to be emphasized. Cicero had, of course, treated the relation of philosophy and oratory not to resolve the Platonists' indictment of rhetoric but to assert and restrict the role of philosophical training in the Roman orator's curriculum. The young Fabianus and his philosophical declamation, then, exemplify Cicero's prescriptions, and perhaps too his practice in publishing Roman philosophy. Here, Seneca's approved circle follows Cicero. Perhaps, too, praise for his son's teacher is merely an oblique gesture: for it is the younger Seneca who most famously represented declamatory and epistolary (and not dialogic, as Cicero) Roman philosophy. To represent Fabianus, the friend and teacher of his son, as a declaimer requires quite a trick of memory: Seneca must recall Fabianus's school performances. Fabianus was, from the report of Quintilian, no great speaker, and may have been a Spaniard.[31]

Cassius Severus, subject of the third preface, likewise was no professional or frequent declaimer. Indeed, this embarrassing reality demands some apology, and so, in trying to connect the world of the forum with that of the schoolroom, Seneca represents himself asking the lawyer why he declaimed so poorly. Asinius Pollio, whom Syme believed to be the leading literary force at Rome after Augustus and perhaps alongside Maecenas, was no declaimer. What Seneca recalled of him in the lost book 4 (excerpted) we do not know; elsewhere in Seneca's work he speaks in a declamation only three times. The case of Quintus Haterius is similar. Here too Seneca elevates him by association.[32] Haterius was a prominent orator. The subject of the seventh preface, C. Albucius Silus, is the exception, for he was a famous, professional teacher.

Votienus Montanus, the subject of the ninth preface, who published his first speech before the centumviral court and who left other writings (C. 9.5.15 and 9.6.18), like Cassius Severus was a lawyer not a declaimer. Seneca says that he declaimed neither publicly nor privately: "Votienus Montanus so completely avoided performing show declamation that he never even declaimed for practice" (9 pr. 1: "Montanus Votienus adeo numquam ostentationis declamavit causa ut ne exercitationis quidem declamaverit"). Montanus shares another similarity with Cassius Severus: Seneca has Montanus explain in his preface why his declamation was inferior to his legal pleading. Montanus's answer stresses the unreality of declamation, its remove from the bar, and uses Latro's

actual pleading as an example. Seneca maintains that his sons had
suggested Montanus's name—clearly he is not a declaimer—and
this difficulty with finding suitable subjects for the prefaces re-
surfaces in the final book (Seneca apparently wanted prominent
equestrians, or better, from the capital).

At the work's end, in a developed *praeteritio*, Seneca lists
those who will not qualify for his prefaces; here too he ranks the
declaimers: the first tetrad (Latro, Fuscus, Albucius, Gallio) and
the second? He refuses to stoop: "Let those lesser-known nobles
go their own way, Paternus and Moderatus, Fabius and anyone
else midway between fame and oblivion" (10. pr. 13: "Hos minus
nobiles sinite in partem abire, Paternum et Moderatum, Fabium
et si quis est nec clari nominis nec ignoti"). The names proposed
by his sons he has rejected. The "nobles" who are included come
as a surprise; Seneca proposes his fellow Spaniards Clodius Turrinus and Gavius Silo (whose provincial name might have raised a
hoot of laughter). Silo's sole claim to fame was that Augustus, on
hearing him plead on several occasions in Tarraco, had called him
the most eloquent *pater familias* he had ever heard (10. pr. 14).
Seneca even allows that Silo lacked force and independence: he
was a devotee of Apollodorus and invariably founded his declamation on Latro's *color* (10. pr. 15: "Numquam non de colore Latroni
controversiam fecit"). Seneca mentions one other salient feature:
Clodius Turrinus's grandfather had entertained Julius Caesar (10.
pr. 16). Membership in the provincial gentry and a connection,
however tenuous, to the Caesars validate the Spaniards.

We shall return to the peculiar qualities of these subjects and
of the prefaces as a whole, but first, to recapitulate: of the nine
subjects of the seven extant prefaces only two were declaimers:
Latro, who performed but did not teach, and Albucius Silus, one
of the professional declaimer-instructors of Seneca's day. In addition, the leading teacher of declamation, Cestius, is excluded from
a preface, although Seneca very frequently quotes him in the body
of the text. Conspicuously absent from the prefaces and relegated
to second position in the text,[33] the Greeks who seem to have constituted the majority of rhetorical teachers are further slighted, for

Seneca makes them the target of much invective centered around the new style, its corruption and degeneracy from the old Roman. One might object that the partial record has exaggerated the bias of Seneca. Three prefaces are lost; what themes and declaimers might they have treated? I do not speculate so as to fill up the lacunae of the text. Rather, the extant prefaces, once their partiality is noted, reveal patterns of treatment and theme that in turn suggest conclusions about Seneca's work as a whole. The attempt to inquire what the lost prefaces might hide involves analysis of all the remaining speakers in the declamatory extracts—the candidates for the subjects of the lost prefaces. We must be quite clear about presuppositions. Had book 10's preface been lost, we could only have reconstructed the names Gavius and Turrinus from their appearance as speakers in book 10. Had the book survived only in excerpted form, we would never have come up with the names of two Spanish gentlemen. Nonetheless, we would have had a few clues and considerable reason to believe that professional declaimers were not the subjects.

Reconstructing the Lost Prefaces

The subjects of the prefaces tend not to appear as speakers in earlier books. Clearly, this practice causes great difficulty, as Seneca is constrained to bring up something new each round (the metaphor is his own). A survey demonstrates this point. Latro appears throughout the collection. Fabianus (subject of book 2) never speaks outside of his book (he is mentioned once in book 7). Cassius Severus appears eleven times outside of his book, only once before his book. Asinius Pollio does not appear before his preface. His matched pair, Quintus Haterius, has one appearance in book 1 (1.6.12), after his book, fifteen appearances. Albucius Silus is again exceptional; like Latro, his sayings are distributed throughout Seneca's work. Votienus Montanus is mentioned once before his preface (Seneca is here, 7.5.11, quoting what Vinicius had to say about a particular epigram of Saenianus and one of Votienus); his speech is reserved for his own and later books. Clodius Turrinus and Gavius Silo appear only in their, the final book. Who were the subjects of the lost prefaces? If they adhere to the general pattern, they should appear only after their book. At the least, the frequent declaimers of the early books will not have been the subjects and speakers of the lost prefaces of the excerpted books 5, 6, and 8.

There is good reason, however, to believe that two cases followed the exceptional pattern of Albucius Silus. When Seneca ranked the declaimers, he listed Latro, Fuscus, Albucius, and Gallio, of whom the first and third received prefaces. The sketch of the style and the man would not have been denied to any of these leading practitioners. And Fuscus is the third most common speaker (after Latro and Cestius and before Albucius). Like Albucius, he appears frequently in all the unexcerpted books. Cestius, who with these other three was the major source for Seneca, is disqualified as a subject for emulation, thus for a preface. Indeed, Seneca disqualifies many, either by slighting reference or characterization in passing or by direct exclusion in the preface to book 10. Fuscus, however, has been treated and dismissed. In his discussion of Fabianus, Seneca describes the philosopher's teacher, Fuscus, and characterizes the man and his style. Of course, he does so only to distinguish the development and improvement achieved by the philosopher who was the teacher of his own son. Of the candidates named in Seneca's notice in the tenth preface, the professional Arellius Fuscus received a subordinate treatment, but the Spanish consular Junius Gallio did not. Tacitus and Quintilian ranked Gallio among the leaders of the new style; Seneca's far more glowing references to the man who would adopt his son contrast strongly, just as the Latro of Seneca's pages does not square with Tacitus's and Quintilian's judgments.[34] That memorable reduction, Tacitus's *tinnitus Gallionis*,[35] has no antecedent in Seneca, except that his speech is described as *dulcis*, Seneca's slightly obfuscating, ameliorating term for new-style rhythmic parallelism. Gallio appears throughout the unexcerpted books. A declaimer recognized by subsequent ancient critics as a leader of declamation, who appears frequently, who has a strong personal connection, whom Seneca lists as among the first four declaimers, and whom he never disparages, makes a most likely candidate for the subject of a lost preface. Gallio, however, follows the pattern of distribution of Albucius Silus.

The tenth preface, itself an important juncture, bares Seneca's criteria. He has not granted prefaces to all those he has most used. The personal connections of those he has used little but to whom he has allocated prefaces (e.g., Fabianus) bear more inquiry. But those he perhaps should have included, the real declaimers, are dismissed. The techniques of his inclusion include antithetical labeling: Greeks versus Romans, new versus old, ours versus yours. At times he used only the negative of the pair: vulgar, insane, dry, scholastic. If one considers those who appear most frequently and contrast these to the nondeclaimers or rare performers he has graced with a preface, the pattern of his exclusion will come clear. Pompeius Silo has the same number of appearances as Gallio; after this pair come, in descending order, Triarius, Romanius Hispo, Cornelius Hispanus, Marullus, Mento, Vibius Rufus, Varius Geminus, and Rubellius Blandus, for all of whom except the last three Seneca has disparaging comment. Triarius, a popular schoolmaster, receives criticism from all the weighty: Seneca himself, Pollio, Latro, Cassius Severus, Cestius, Votienus, and Pompeius Silo.[36] That harsh accuser Romanius Hispo himself offers no positive model: Pollio criticizes him at 4.6.3; Seneca did admire him as an orator, but rather as one admires the weapons and skill of an enemy; he would eventually accuse the younger Seneca before Nero (Tac. *Ann.* 14.65). Of low birth, so Tacitus would maintain (*Ann.* 1.74), he began his career by accusation and, more remarkably, kept this up until he himself fell victim to *delatio* under Nero (Quint. 6.3.100). Cornelius Hispanus appears throughout the collection, but clearly as a minor declaimer; at 7.1.24 he uses a harsh *color*—lack of sympathy never pleases Seneca or those he considers adept critics ("Displiceat color hic prudentibus"). Seneca and Latro have harsh words for their teacher Marullus, and these ample criticisms leave no room for an additional characterization in a preface. About Mento, innovative in some of his *colores* and *divisiones*, Seneca simply has very little to say.

Of the remaining declaimers, no censure marks the suffect consul of A.D. 16, Vibius Rufus. Praised by Votienus, and indirectly by Seneca in the second *controversia* of the ninth book (Asinius Pollio approves his *sententia*, 9.2.25), he seems to belong to the set of noble orators or older practitioners. He actually figures very little in this *controversia*, for the most part has his speech reported, and in the last cited instance appears adjacent to a report of what Livy had said on another's use of vulgarism. Seneca's characterization—the justification of Vibius's everyday speech by reference to his old style of speaking—suggests that Vibius was a rare speaker, summoned here as an old-fashioned counterweight to certain new declaimers who overuse *verba sordida*. In Rubellius Blandus, the first Roman knight to direct a school of rhetoric, and Varius Geminus, orator and declaimer, we may not have convincingly found subjects of lost prefaces, but one clue does suggest that Varius Geminus was the subject of the preface of book 5 or 6. He appears once in book 4, once in 6, yet twenty times in book 7. In the excerpted text of book 4 he is named in the section "extra" (i.e., from the discussion and analysis, not from the initial sections, pro and contra, of *sententiae*); in book 6, as the section "extra," he is reported to have said something in the presence of Caesar— whether in a declamation is unclear. This distribution of appearances mirrors most of the other subjects of prefaces: he does not speak directly in the books prior to his preface, then appears with some frequency afterward (although his appearances are concentrated in book 7).

Varius Geminus, as a Roman orator in addition to a declaimer, and having some connection to Augustus, corresponds to the other figures of the prefaces.[37] Even if he did not receive more extended treatment in a preface (and it would be exceptional for such a frequent figure in Seneca's pages not to receive some sketch of style and character), at the least Varius shows Seneca's pattern of preference—the practicing orator is included and shows none of the insanity, ineptness, or dryness of the professional schoolman.

The Allegiances of the Declaimers

Amid the series of names, in a text excerpted and no doubt disjointed by its scribes as well as compressed by its author, the modern reader may miss the peculiar quality of the set of declaimers commemorated. To an ancient reader certain allegiances and patterns would have been far clearer. Nearly any freeborn Roman could have walked into the performances of the professional instructors and their students. The father with a boy in grammar school, the aspiring advocate, those curious and with enough income to be idle and not so rude as Cassius Severus to interrupt, could have overheard Cestius's tirades. Augustus and Maecenas did just this to Latro. But Seneca has given us no snapshot of public declamation. He presents a number of nondeclaimers so as to connect practical legal oratory with this public pedagogy and art form, and likewise he also blends declamation with *recitatio*, the prepublication of written works practiced by Pollio and by literati before him.[38]

The circle he has chosen to present, however, is even more intimate, for he purports to show his reader the private world, the domestic performances of leading nobles.[39] Most emphatically, he represents Asinius Pollio educating his grandson Marcellus. But his reference to Messala, who never declaims but simply judges, likewise offers a private vision. We see Messala at home, conversing with Seneca, Gallio, and Tiberius after a public performance of Nicetes (*S.* 3.6), and once hosting a recitation by a Spanish poet whose opening praise of Cicero and implied criticism of the sterility of the age so displeased Pollio that he left (*S.* 6.27).[40] Seneca says he knows that Cornelius Severus was there too, thus implying that he was an eyewitness. Seneca also presents himself as having been present when Pollio, three days after the death of his son, gave a private performance (*C.* 4 pr. 4). M. Lepidus, the "tutor of Nero" (*C.* 2.3.23), whom Seneca heard in Scaurus's house (*C.* 10 pr. 3), may have been the Lepidus who was the consul of A.D. 11. Like his mention of old-fashioned speakers and like his introductory history of declamation, the inclusion of noble patrons and critics connects what was a public, professional performance with both practical oratory and republican precedent. Asinius Pollio's criticisms legitimize and Romanize in the same way as allusion to Cicero or to Augustus's visiting the halls of declamation, what the critics called a Greek, scholastic exercise.

Of course, although declamation was far more Greek than Seneca would have us believe, it was also not traditionally Roman. I do not seek to argue that, for example, public performance emigrated from Spain but that Seneca, in proffering his own circle as the proper declaimers, promoted a group of Spanish *amici* to the most prominent position in Latin letters. Latro, Junius Gallio, Clodius Turrinus, Gavius Silo, and perhaps Fabianus, all subjects of the prefaces, were born in Spain. Asinius Pollio commanded the Caesarian forces in Spain in 44 B.C. This republican—who was, however, a friend of Caesar—was the best prospect for patron that a citizen from the Pompeian city of Cordoba could imagine.[41] Others of Seneca's speakers came from the Italian peninsula: Vibius Gallus was born in Perugia;[42] Albucius Silus in Novaria. Votienus came from Narbonne; Volcacius Moschus went to nearby Marseilles to open a school after Asinius Pollio and Torquatus failed to have him acquitted of a charge of poisoning (20 B.C.). So far will geography lead. I do not mean to suggest that these Western landowners were a tight-knit salon dependent on Pollio, but that lines of allegiance—of class, geography, and hence perhaps language[43]—not oratorical excellence alone, distinguished Seneca's preferred declaimers. Clearly there were other Spaniards who did not matter to Seneca: perhaps, like Marullus, the Seneca who was nicknamed Grandio and Quintilian *senex*, who may have been the famous rhetorician's father, were Spaniards whom Seneca chose not to promote.[44]

A Roman contemporary would have read other lines of allegiance in Seneca's text, for the author takes some trouble to make clear the bonds between disciple and master. As the notices of aristocratic patrons imply more than social intimacy, so too by publicly memorializing academic relationships Seneca elevates some circles and inscribes himself, his sons, and friends as the leading and most promising set. The references to teachers, students, and schools create a picture of rivalry and competition, within which sphere he would have us believe Latro preeminent. To reduce the plethora of names and characterizations found in Seneca's work to some polar scheme is to apply literally Seneca's rhetoric— to recapitulate his manner of describing speakers in polar terms that include or exclude. Indeed, Willamowitz erred in this positivist fashion in drawing his influential conclusions about Asianism and Atticism; but the leading Roman rhetorical and stylistic texts, especially those of Cicero and Seneca, also indulge in such oversimplifying labeling. In writing to his children to justify and construct the new style, Seneca constantly associates "us" with approved style and stylists; against "us" are ranged the Greeks, the Asiatics, the insane, the libertine. But his text offers the literary or cultural historian better indications of the variety of public speech and its instruction than does his reductive rhetoric. Certain circles can be reconstructed. Although much maligned (by Seneca, Latro, and their company), Cestius clearly exerted great influence. Among his students were Murredius[45] (harshly criticized by Seneca), Surdinus (praised as a brilliant young man), Triarius, Varius Geminus, the senator Aietius Pastor, Alfius Flavus, the younger Quinctilius Varus, and Argentarius, a professional whose student Fuscus himself had important students (Ovid, Papirius Fabianus, Vibius Gallus) and whose style Maecenas favored.[46]

In many respects the Greek-born teacher of Latin, Cestius, is the most intriguing declaimer. The criticisms of his rhetoric and declamation, especially those leveled at his fusion of Greek and Roman styles, at his allusiveness to and dependence on Greek culture, and his highly figured style, apply equally well to his student Ovid. His anti-Ciceronianism, which Seneca makes sound ridiculous and untimely, would have found a sympathetic listener in Asinius Pollio. Ovid's fellow student Fabianus met with Seneca's approval: the younger Seneca studied under Fabianus.[47] These family connections offer a glimpse into a clearly fluid world of Roman schooling and academic careers. Albucius Silus may have had a closer connection to Seneca than he suggests, for Albucius took notes, presumably along with Seneca's son, in the school of Fabianus. Seneca scoffs at the older man studying under the younger, but his vivid account represents himself as having been present.

In contrast, Seneca seems more careful in his delineation of Latro's students and influence. Ovid was his admirer and, as Seneca is sure to point out, imitated Latro in his poems. Latro's students included Pompeius Silo and Rubellius Blandus (in turn the teacher of Fabianus). Triarius may have attended his lectures— Seneca often does not distinguish Latro's paying student from the occasional auditor. This may have been difficult, for Latro did not have students whom he criticized but *auditores*, a term that came to supplant *discipuli*, no doubt as the schools grew more open, and perhaps more like Latro's. But perhaps, too, the inclusion of *auditores* allowed Seneca to make bolder claims about his friend's influence and importance. Florus came (9.2.23); perhaps Capito was a student.[48] Latro's actual students are no more distinguished than Cestius's, perhaps less so than those of Fuscus. The overlap and mobility of some students are even more striking. In addition to the peripatetic, eclectic Albucius, Argentarius broke from his master Cestius and set up a rival school. Cestius may have driven other students away: Seneca reports that Varius Geminus attended Cassius Severus.

Seneca's own allegiances are clearer than the lines of school affiliation; he writes of "our" Latro, "our" Gallio (where he studied we do not know, but he admired Cassius Severus and published his own declamations), "our" Passienus (who had his own school). He attends Pollio instructing his grandson and reports the private comments and conversation of Pollio and his fellow noble Messala. Seneca's sons must have attended the lectures of Musa, a freed Greek to whom father Seneca refers as "yours." The text provides some hints that Seneca's circle was in fact Pollio's circle. When Seneca refers to a real legal case, he is in one sense espousing the criticism that declamation pertains to an unreal world. When Latro fails, we see the failure of declamation; when Cassius Severus declaims poorly, we see the limitations of genius. But allusions to suits lost or won constituted clear signs to an ancient audience. Cicero reminded his auditors of past victories, his own and his clients'. In part, these add to a speaker's *auctoritas* and *dignitas*, for they display not only the speaker's rhetorical abilities but the inseparable lines of connection that sustain and augment his status. Such references in a Roman oratorical or rhetorical text proclaim *amicitia* and *inimicitia*.

In Seneca's work the proclamations have a recurrent bias. Three of the subjects of the prefaces (accepting my reconstruction for Gallio) had a common enemy: Seneca relates that T. Labienus spoke against Pollio; that Junius Gallio wrote a response to Labienus's speech against Bathyllus, the freedman of Maecenas; finally, that Labienus was an enemy of Cassius Severus. All this enmity is presented as having been conducted in a highly public, verbal medium, even if the vehicle ranged from the courts to the schools (Gallio's *laudatio* may have been a "school exercise" but this hardly means a private composition). The contest of individual declaimers or of their *sententiae* could thus appear as a synecdoche for other, larger, more "real" struggles. The performances and rosters of a schoolteacher could be important simply because this was another venue in which *amicitia* was exhibited and read. The orbits of minor friends were as important as the grander forensic battles of major friends, for both wielded the patron's power. This had been the practice of the republic: if a Greek poet had lost his case for Roman citizenship in 62 B.C. the ex-consul who defended him and the family who championed him would have been injured as certainly as when, four years later, this advocate, Cicero, was exiled, and four years before the patron, Lucullus, had lost his command. These contests had tried Pompey's power. Historians of Rome are by now accustomed to determine the course of politics from such legal losses, although we have not perhaps sufficiently valued the symbolic value of these clashes. Thus we should conclude that Pollio lost more than just the case, and his circle suffered when his client Volcacius Moschus was condemned and went to Marseilles to open a school. Of course, the family of Pollio encountered larger losses. Seneca does not tell us, but the declaimer Vallius Syriacus was exiled in A.D. 30 as a friend of Pollio's son, Asinius Gallus. Perhaps, in retelling the fate of one Greek satellite, Seneca employed an oblique technique that would have been far more resonant to an imperial audience, for the hazards of oratory extended from the republican exemplum of the mob of partisans of C. Porcius Cato who beat up their patron's prosecutor, Pollio (*C.* 7.4.7; in 54 B.C.) to Seneca's own cryptic warning to Mela (*C.* 2 pr. 3).

The naming of relationships and defections and the recording of compliments and insults has a strong symbolic force if the audience both of declamation and of Seneca's work knows who has educated whom and who champions whom. The symbolic contests for preeminence in nonforensic fora, then, are not the idle play of an upper class with little else to do. Rather, they constitute another mode for preeminence in speech and patronage, for social maneuvering and mobility through the dominant discourse. Perhaps, therefore, when we see a declaimer exiled, supposedly because he was a friend of Pollio's family, we should see the emperor's hand disciplining the display of a noble family as surely as we do when Tacitus so meticulously records Tiberius's reaction to various senators' speeches in the senate. The aristocrats' public and even published praise or disdain for imperial freedmen, for example, and the emperor's patronage or prosecution of the nobles' clients, are not exclusively acts of dissent or discipline, but kindred jockeying for power through exhibitions of influence and affiliation—all conducted in the linguistic mode of the free and equal. It is as if the genre provides speakers with a level playing field, and yet social relations puncture this fiction of linguistic and social equality. The emperor restores the republic and makes possible equal display. Anyone may write, anyone may speak. Yet we see played out in miniature the support and exclusion that are not the metaphor but the mode of careers, power, and success in this society. The Roman reader or auditor is like the Roman diner who comes to a table spread with the same fare for all and where allegedly all speak the same language; yet in this egalitarian gesture of hospitality he knows his worth and that of others from where they sit, how they are dressed, and whose friend they are. Like

Pliny serving the same wine to freedmen and freeborn, the aristocrat comes to the declamation to stoop; feigning to hear all, *he* is
the critic who counts. Seneca makes sure we know who sat where.

The Declaimers' Concerns

The reconstruction of Seneca's circle and the discussion of the
various subjects of the prefaces have revealed the social ambition
that lay beneath an ostensibly literary program. For Seneca at the
very outset of the empire, declamation held out the allure of literary prominence, a Romanness of speech and social identity, even
imperial recognition and patronage. Declamation was not, however, a neutral vehicle for the display and rivalry of particular literate classes at Rome under the Julio-Claudian emperors. Certainly,
while posing as old-time oratory, declamation served a new elite
as it pronounced their accommodation to the old literary order
and the new political one. But what did declamation teach? How
did its structures, situations, its process of forming and directing
speech, and not simply its contested delivery, serve its practitioners and audience? To the professional Latinist or Roman historian,
the ancient desire to be an orator, the high social value placed
on that skill, may seem so patent as not to need explanation. But
there is nothing natural or inevitable about the role of speech in
a society, and further, the naturalness of this belief hides a social
ideology about the fitness of the literate to rule. In the concluding
sections of this chapter I ask what particular social functions the
kind of speech and speech training known as declamation fulfilled.

Nietzsche set the supreme task of Greek society as εὖ λέγειν.[49]
Had Seneca been asked what he wanted for his sons or what was
the highest station in life for a citizen, like Cicero he might have
replied to be an orator, the *vir bonus dicendi peritus* that Cato no
doubt hoped his son would be and Quintilian would train his
students to be. Of course, neither Demosthenes nor Cicero nor
Nietzsche was solely concerned with questions of language and
style. Oratorical speech was one weapon of public life, one marker

of social distinction; and criticism of speech, behind the mask of purely esthetic concerns, strove to direct and control the acquisition and use of speech. But rhetorical precept, the register of and about speech training and performance, maintained the fiction that public prominence, power, and well-being depended on discovering and applying the apt expression for the particular audience. If rhetorical precepts are understood as reflections upon the process and possibility of social control and distinction, works of rhetoric need not be read exclusively in genealogical terms. In particular, the Roman writers need not be seen either as debased transmitters of Greek theory or as accommodaters of Greek theory to some compromising Roman reality.

The declaimers found in declamation a peculiar form of pedagogy. If declamation had been limited to a phase of school curriculum, it would still offer fascinating insights into ancient education, Roman speech training, and Roman acculturation. But given its added public prominence, the stature Latro and Seneca seem to have wished for it, declamation could be perceived as more than mere preparation. Speech on ridiculous topics is a fun and even profitable pursuit. A panegyric on salt advertises a product: in the ancient world, the versatile flexibility and resources of its composer. Even in such an exercise the selection of topic might be significant. Especially in Roman declamation, the point did not seem to be solely that public speech and hence public distinction could be achieved through this novel means, nor that, like the salt-praiser, another career awaited the virtuoso declaimer.

Nothing is more commonplace in ancient discussions of declamations, even within declamation itself, than complaint about the fatuity of declamation. Modern critics have taken seriously the ancient pedagogical lament that contrasts the scholastic world with the real—that is, legal—sphere. Both ancient and modern invectives posit preparation for the bar as the endpoint of declamatory training and then triumphantly demonstrate the noncorrespondence of the two types of public discourse, which differ, most notably, in pertinence (a criterion that, although it simply replicates the general complaint, does point to the differences of permissible subject); degree of ornamentation (i.e., excess versus restraint, figured versus straight speech); and relationship to audience (declamation allows the audience's interruption, indeed seeks applause, the positive form of interruption—no such relief is granted the lawyer, Votienus Montanus says [9 pr. 1]; the imperial lawyer had to move a judge). In ancient terms, *copia* characterizes declamation, whose abundance spills over to include the audience in its play. In fact, far greater points of contact link the practices of declamatory and legal speech, but to play the apologist within these limits simply replays the ancient division. To step out of the ancient rhetorical trope, at least for a moment, the critic must advance other purposes and contexts of declamation.

If we are still to treat declamation as preparatory, surely we should recognize Seneca's inclusive program—he would have us see declamation as the core curriculum prior to philosophy, public service, the literary life, perhaps too the business affairs of those landowners who, like his youngest son or himself, actively pursued the emperor's attentions and promotions through an equestrian career. But to return to the ancient antithesis of law and fancy, declamation did provide certain valuable tools to the future lawyer (and bureaucrat or administrator, I use "lawyer" loosely as a convenient term for all those Romans who administered the law, wrote and read petitions, recommendations, etc.). Bonner has shown, so as to close debate on the Romanness or Greekness of the laws within declamation, that frequently the law as it appears in a *controversia* never recurred in the student's professional experience.[50] Of course, the laws of declamation were convenient fictions; for had they been real Roman laws, the discourse about them would have been severely limited, and part of the pedagogic point of declamation was to get teenaged boys to speak freely. Had the laws been mined from Greek experience, then history, questions of fact, precedent, outcome, even legal practice, or some historian's version of these, would similarly have delimited what could be said.

The serviceability of declamation stems exactly from the fact that it is neither set nor open-ended discourse; it is not, as some have tried to make of Greek sophistry, the mechanical outcome of *dissoi logoi*, the practice of saying everything on a subject by speaking its extremes, and hence the morally neutral manifestation of speech severed from reality, context, social stratum. Declamatory speech may be double, pro and contra a set theme, but theme and treatment are not "value neutral," a *copia* run wild.

Even at its most fantastic, Roman declamation sets themes that examine a conflict of allegiances. Formally, this conflict depends from the *divisio* that splits the case in question into two headings. But even Hellenistic *stasis* theory does not adequately explain the actual set of recurrent themes. Law is not simply set against justice in some abstract consideration of the conflict of the spirit and the letter of the law. Nor is declamation reducible to a series of alternative lexical classifications: Is the present case an instance of homicide or manslaughter? A system of polar analysis and lexical classification describes the process by which the Roman or the Hellenistic Greek learned to speak of whether an oath to a pirate should be honored, but such systematic analysis does not explain the choice of themes. Repeatedly, the declaimers examine conflicts of social allegiance.

The subjects that have given critics the greatest difficulty, those cases of ingratitude and of lèse-majesté, which correspond neither to Greek precedent nor to Roman reality, illustrate well the tendentious preoccupations of declamation. In these features Roman declamation has far more in common with Roman comedy. The fantasy of declamation mirrors that of the stage: freedman and slave are so promoted that they are or have advocates. The son speaks against the father. Generational and social strife may be said to be surfacing, but, more concretely, Roman schoolboys were performing a sort of role-playing that did not directly advocate the dominant ideology. Indeed, declamation reads, like much of New Comedy, as a confrontation with paternal severity.[51] With father off the stage, in temporary exile, at sea, or away from school, the son seizes his liberty of speech and imagined action. Law, the embodiment of the *patres'* severity, does not rule adolescent speech but is instead elaborated, embellished, its unyielding verbal texture resisted. Thus arises a speech not bound by law, not answerable to the single judge, to the older judge, or even exclusively to the freedman schoolmaster or servile pedagogue but, to a degree, to peers.

The role-playing of declamation must have trained the rather insulated upper-class adolescent in a sort of situational ethics, for the speakers of declamation appropriate voices. This sort of transgression is no doubt fun, and much humor, not simply comedy, depends on the disjuncture of person and speech type (register), like the old man of the *Miles Gloriosus*, who speaks like the young lover, or those adepts of all the different registers of Roman society, the parasite and the plotting slave. In declamation the greatest challenge, the greatest training and virtuosity, lay with the adoption of the minor voices. To speak with paternal authority, to castigate, to act the *laudator temporis acti* had become trite; it took Fabianus's philosophical reflections to animate such tired work. The part that does offer some challenge is the speech of the father who would marry his daughter to his freedman.

Thus declamation trained its pupils intensively in the hard part of advocacy. More generally, declamation trained a young Roman in a sympathy of viewpoint, emotions, motivations, and speech that he would need in treating his future clients. The free-born official would need to write to and for freedmen; Pliny (10.85) and Fronto (*Ad M. Caesarem* 45) demonstrate the restraint with which to compose letters of recommendation for worthy freedmen. Declamation, then, versed the schoolboy in the appropriation of voices from below his station as well as the grand voices of past Roman heroes, the training he received from speaking historical exempla and from addressing the famous *maiores* in his *suasoriae*. To recommend or deprecate a course of action to the mighty, to speak as a traditional *nobilis*, to appreciate the voices and desires of the slave, the freedman, the woman, constituted the trinity of training for the early imperial schoolboy.

Even a brief tour of a few bizarre and unreal *controversiae* reveals some of the specific techniques that were useful for Roman social life and imperial administration. Most fundamentally,

once through rhetorical school, boys would sound like young
Romans, knowing not only epigram, division, or *prateritio* but
the cultural stock of historical exempla and the shared experience
of anachronistic, imaginative involvement with "the past," with
"history." The young master would also emerge drilled in speaking in socially awkward situations. No Roman in real life need
speak for and against a prostitute's application for the position of
priestess (1.2), and this declamation hardly explores the nature of
the sacred. Yet, in discerning the holy from the most profane, the
advocate must recommend the candidacy of one whose publicly
perceived station, whose dress and profession, disqualify the petition. The declaimers take up what might have been philosophical
investigation into interiority and exteriority, reality and appearance, as a question of a virtuoso letter or speech of recommendation. The recreated narrative rivals Cicero's technique in the ability
to imagine a set of circumstances altogether decent in the eyes of
the public that entirely mitigates the present awkward status of
the defendant. To speak the other part, to disqualify a candidate
for an office or a position, though also of great serviceability, does
not carry the same challenge; *vituperatio* and *delatio* seldom do.[52]

As a meditation on social utility and social roles, the case of
the aspirant priestess-prostitute sets social convention against the
letter of the law. Some of the declaimers, conceding the chastity
of her body, object to the chastity of her occupation and environment. The replotting of the set theme that the declaimers work
in their *colores* thus explores not so much linguistic or legal possibilities—what is the chaste? what was the intent of the law?—as
social responsibilities and allegiances. What should she have done
in these social circumstances? What is proper speech for such a
person? Indeed, should she be petitioning?[53] Her worth and candidacy concern the declaimers more than the law or its interpretation. Their innovations do not consider novel legal interpretation
but rival ways to evaluate her motives and behavior. Thus the
"dominant ideology" is not questioned; rather, exceptional sympathy is elicited as a rival public judgment is put forward.

What could a boy learn from the historically inaccurate and

legally impossible case of Callias's prosecution of his son-in-law Cimon for ingratitude? This case, similarly anachronistic or unreal, likewise turns on issues of behavior and allegiance. Again, social roles come into conflict. The speakers dispute an apparent or alleged state of dependence. The son-in-law who is tied through social debt to his elder acts independently: Callias has paid Cimon's debts and so delivered him from prison; Cimon has married Callias's daughter, whom now he has caught in adultery and wishes to execute. Cimon is accused of ingratitude. The declaimers contest who owes what and to whom, and so debate in terms of an economy of social debt and credit: Votienus Montanus: "Now you push me to say, 'I have received no good service, or I have paid it back. . . . Only if I am free [to punish the adulterers] do I owe anything to Callias'" (9.1.3: "Facis iam ut dicam: 'non accepi beneficium aut reddidi. . . . Nihil Calliae debeo nisi liber sum'"); Vibius Gallus: "You gave one good service, you ask for two in return" (9.1.4: "unum beneficium dedisti, duo petis"). To calculate *beneficia* openly and publicly is in itself impolite, a social transgression, but so is hauling one's son-in-law into court or, from Callias's point of view, Cimon's intended violence to his wife. The familial breach, the confusion of familial and social roles, occasions the novel speech of the declamation that performs rival calculations of *beneficia*, social payment and repayment, so as to restore order.[54]

The reductive vision of Seneca and his contemporaries, who treat a historical event or invention in terms of a conflict of familial and social allegiances, has not impressed the historians. Indeed, the historical quality of the material does not affect the declaimers' treatments, except that, like the unimaginable case of the prostitute who would be priestess, a certain distance from Roman reality better enables the speakers to estimate and rank social duties. Thus the old Athenian noble and the fictitious prostitute come to constitute an inquiry into social transgression, for this is what lies behind cases of ingratitude, and indeed those of lèse-majesté.[55]

Themes of social and societal injury reflect, then, the general interest of declamation in investigating *pietas*, in determining the stance to be taken toward father, paternal authority, and speech. The speakers' division attempts to isolate social roles that in fact are not separate, as, for instance, the *filius* can also be *sui iuris*, the woman can be daughter and wife. The liminal quality of both speakers and subject needs to be emphasized.[56] That of subject I have tried to demonstrate very briefly by the cases cited above: the defendant appears in the fictional court straddling two roles or modes of behavior; but the theme and structure for debate cannot be isolated from its speakers and audience. Those who took up the theme of *pater filium abdicans* or *uxorem repudians* were still *liberi*, a word likewise ambiguous—free and child, those still in the domestic domain of the women, slaves, and freedmen about whom so much declamation revolves. The schoolboys, in their confrontation with or appropriation of paternal severity and paternal speech, speak as men. But declamation was a broader social phenomenon: fathers themselves, even senators, chose to perform, to speak as adolescents imitating the serious speech of men.

Declamatory Impropriety

Declamation was thus teaching, along with advanced linguistic skills, particular attitudes and roles. Proper language could not be detached from the site of learning and performance, and from the set of practitioners. Educated Latinity, learned in a ludic setting, had serious social dimensions. I wish now to consider the qualities of declamation's seriousness of speech, in particular to look at what the declaimers thought was bad declamation, where they agreed social and linguistic transgression had occurred. The declaimers' esthetic strictures debate and define who belongs and why. Specifically, in the discussions of improper expressions and treatments, the declaimers strive to limit their own society, and their often caustic comments blur the grounds of error: linguistic mistake becomes a social failing. Paradoxically, the chief crime in this genre of speaking various parts is the appropriation of a voice not one's own. The speaker who tries to pass off others' words as his own is detected and humiliated. But plagiarism is narrowly defined.

Significantly, several declaimers are faulted for their harshness. All might criticize the freedman who denied his services to his patron; this is not harshness. But to speak so as to neglect the imagined jurors' sympathies does bring down the critics' censure.[57] More positively, speeches of reconciliation and arguments against formalism and literalism of the law or of paternal severity did appeal, in part because of the challenge inherent in speaking the freedman's or the repudiated son's part. Also, the Romans tended to value speech for the defense more highly. In this crucial matter of diagnosing and directing an audience's sympathies, forensic reality influenced declamation. Declamations, however, required a sympathy of viewpoint paralleled in Plautus and Petronius, and not for the most part in Cicero. The exploration of emotions and obligations that trained the future lawyer rehearsed the parts of stepmother, slave, freedman, son, daughter, and wife. These low voices marked declamation as speech quite manifestly distinct from actual oratory, whether that were Cicero or contemporary legal discourse.

Declamation demonstrates an anxiety about the appropriation of voice that corresponds as a negative extreme to its ubiquitous fiction of speaking in another's voice. It is as if the declaimers were trying to rein in this habit of speaking like someone else. Seneca and the speakers of his pages worry at some length about plagiarism in particular. At times Virgil, Ovid, and Cicero seem to have instilled in this generation a zealous vigor in preserving their words. In addition, Seneca says he writes to end the theft of the earlier declaimers' coinages and treatments: he will restore their legitimacy, much as Asinius Pollio, Messala, and others are keen to detect the unacknowledged borrowing from the canonical, written authors. The text of the *controversiae* draws attention to issues of criticism by bringing in discussions of the poets Virgil and Ovid, and in one case the historian Sallust. The declaimers do not simply turn to these poets; the poets break into Seneca's text, into the discussion of the declaimers, in a quite specific context: plagiarism by an individual declaimer goads the declaimers to mention Virgil and Ovid.

The detectors of plagiarism pride themselves in excavating the unacknowledged classical strata of one-liners. But how can there be plagiarism in a literary genre that requires a series of individuals to speak upon set themes? Originality of treatment is surely the critical issue, and the critical anxiety. For a declaimer's words or structure of argument to be recognizably different, they must be memorable. Memory seems to involve not a number of variants but one distinct treatment. That is, preeminence of treatment displaces prior treatments from the audience's collective memory. When what is forced out is not a prior declaimer's oral version but the Augustan poet's published verse, the critics make a display of their own memory. A line stolen from another declaimer might well have been deemed a plagiarism, but Seneca records no such theft. Perhaps, these could not have lasted long—the original speaker or his friends or a member of the audience was likely to decry the theft. Cestius convicts Alfius Flavus of plagiarizing a *sententia* taken from Ovid, *Metamorphoses* 8.877–78 (the excerpta of book 3 relate the criticism as "extra," i.e., neither in the speeches pro nor contra) and is himself censured, by Julius Montanus the *comes* <*Tiberii*> (*C.* 7.1.27), for his attempted imitation of Virgil. The line of imitation does not stop here: Virgil is said to have been imitating Varro. As seal on all this comes Ovid's suggested improvement of Varro. Again, at 10.4.25, a suggestion of plagiarism leads back to Ovid: P. Vinicius points out that the idea of the *sententia* in question had been best treated in the *Metamorphoses* (12.607–8).

Seneca seems interested not so much in tarring the reputation of individuals as in discouraging a more recent development; he overtly harkens back to a time when speech was transparent, when genuine speech was universally known: "Back then the audience was so attentive, perhaps I should say aggressive, that not a single syllable could be purloined; but now anybody at all can pass off the speeches against Verres as his own without fear of detection" (*Suas.* 2.19: "Tam diligentes tunc auditores erant, ne dicam tam

maligni, ut una syllaba surripi non posset; at nunc cuilibet oratio-
nes in Verrem tuto dicet pro suis"). The context of this comparison
is most striking, for it leads back not to the utopian, omniscient
audience of the republic but to the aristocrats Messala and Maecenas: Seneca observes that Latro's pupil Abronius Silo reused his
teacher's *sententia* ("si nihil aliud, erimus certe belli mora") in a
poem. Perhaps, however, Latro had been accused of plagiarism,
for Seneca continues to show how much better Virgil expressed
the idea of *belli mora concidit Hector*. Seneca then cites Messala's
opinion that Virgil should not have continued the line, an opinion with which Maecenas disagreed. Seneca manages to avoid any
censure of Latro by fastening upon his student and then turning
to Virgilian criticism. The subjects of Maecenas and the imitation
of Virgil recur in a rather extended account of the declaimer Fuscus, who, Seneca writes, often imitated Virgil to please Maecenas
(*Suas.* 3.5).

The course of borrowing continues: Gallio takes up the Virgilian phrase Fuscus said he was imitating and applies it as an epithet to Fuscus and enraptured declaimers of his ilk. Seneca then
mentions two occasions of Gallio's use of the tag: spoofing the
Greek rhetorician Nicetes at Messala's home and, once, the equestrian orator Haterius in the emperor's presence. Tiberius was told
the whole history of the witticism, which he thoroughly enjoyed.
Finally, Ovid again is brought in to have the last word: Seneca reports that Gallio said Ovid, too, liked the phrase (*plena deo*) and
used it in a tragedy. Fuscus himself did not wish imitation to go
beyond his own treatment: he reproved with another quotation
from Virgil (*S.* 4.4), a student who used a line of Virgil that had
brought great applause to the master in an earlier declamation.

Criticism seems to be waged in a *cento*-like dialogue, much as
the declaimers' treatment of Cicero's death is a pastiche of Ciceronian quotation. Notably, imitation of the poets Virgil and Ovid
in itself does not offend; indeed, it is marked as particularly ambitious in the case of Fuscus.[58] Maecenas, and later Tiberius, are
pleased with the elegant reuse of Virgil, even though, or perhaps
especially when, the allusion closes off the line of imitation. Virgil

and Ovid are invoked to end or cap a trend of poetic declamation. Plagiarism crosses boundaries—mine and thine; but its crossing of generic boundaries, verse and prose, violates propriety of speech and so elicits the verbal reproof of the masters of speech when the speaker does not intend his echo of the poets to be recognized. This false speech leads ultimately to Messala, Maecenas, and Tiberius as the champions of the classical. This is a curious phenomenon. The aristocrats' memory of the poets corrects the deficient memory of the audience and rescues the poets' patrimony from the clutches of the parvenus.

Seneca and his fellows locate proper appropriation in the recognizable and restrained rehandling of poetry. Throughout the instances in which the declaimers purloin each other's words, the unrecognized borrowing, the duping of this modern audience, riles Seneca. And so he writes to reclaim Latro's genuine words and to sequester the forgeries passed off as his.[59] The declaimers' discussions of their own plagiarism, the reuse of each other's *sententiae*, provide the crucial insight into their notion of imitation and plagiarism, in a way that supplements and explains their habit of bringing the poets in to accuse and chastise one another. Caught out in manifest borrowing from another declaimer, Adaeus (9.1.12: "rhetor ex Asianis non proiecti nominis"), Fuscus defends his Latin version of Adaeus's *sententia* as practice; he had no wish to steal or praise the Greek. He describes his exercise of translating Greek into Latin in a way that has been taken as emblematic of the Silver Age's literary aesthetic of *aemulatio*: "He said, 'I concern myself with competing against the best aphorisms, and I do not try to mar them but to vanquish them'" ("'Do,' inquit, 'operam ut cum optimis sententiis certem, nec illas corrumpere conor sed vincere'").[60] To justify this practice, he quotes Sallust's version of a *sententia* (which he attributes to Thucydides, although in fact it comes from pseudo-Demosthenes). Fuscus continues to tell of Livy's mean-spirited criticism of Sallust's translation of the *sententia*—Livy is motivated by the same desire that drives the speaker Fuscus; he wishes to overcome (*vinci*) Sallust. This genealogy of imitation again displaces the declaimer's alleged plagiarism onto the higher, more authoritative realm of classical literary practice. Thereby, the declaimer's speech is validated as Latin and original, decidedly not Greek.

What, then, was proper rivalry among the coiners of *sententiae*? To a great degree, the positive examples go unremarked: Latro is not accused of plagiarism, and so we have no notice of his borrowings or of his influences except when he speaks in a series and his treatment is said to be superior. Fuscus, in imitating Virgil to curry favor with Maecenas, seems to represent an extreme in his allusion and refashioning of the poet. To emulate the master too closely seems a fault. Those too slavish in their imitation of Latro now have their words credited as his (at 9.2.23 Seneca re-attributes a *sententia* to Latro's auditor Florus, for the facile word-play is not in the master's manner). Cestius, angry with his former student Argentarius for so often borrowing and twisting his epigrams, called him ὁ πίθηκός μου (the very use of Greek is part of the abuse: Argentarius, the man who never declaimed in Greek despite being a Greek [9.3.13] is thereby a *scholasticus* or rhetor and a Greek, not the good Roman orator or *magister*), and Argentarius spoke of Cestius as *cinerem* and *manes*, the sort of state to which Fuscus wished his *sententiae* had reduced the prior declaimers.

If overimitation reduced the declaimer to the status of Greek ape, underimitation (a lack of reworking) similarly seems to have reflected a lack of independence. Neither habit constituted genuine discourse. In fact, Seneca seems interested not so much in the fault or phenomenon of plagiarism as in the social qualities of the transgressers. He consistently garnishes the moral failing of plagiarism with social polemic about those men he catches trespassing. The plagiarists are damned not so much as thieves of others' capital but as Greeks, freedmen, the socially ambitious and dangerous. Seneca's observations of plagiarism include a specific set of examples that come closest to what we would call plagiarism: not imitation of the manner of a teacher or an unrecognized allusion to a line of published verse, but the small-scale purloining of other declaimers' lines.

For example, in a series of similar *sententiae*, Cassius Severus censured as plagiarism the sort of minor refashioning that only substitutes, removes, or adds a single word to an earlier *sententia*. This series censures the sort of *sententia*-making that is verbatim translation. Glycon had offered a Greek line, which Triarius stole (*subriperet*) by translating it into Latin and so incurred Severus's disapproval. The line of plagiarism was not so easily cut off, for Seneca continues with a series of Greek *sententiae* that stole Triarius's line (10.5.21: "Sed et Graeci illam subrupuerunt"), which he interrupts with a significant digression identifying one of these Greek purloiners, Craton, an excessively free-spoken and independent Asianist who refused the emperor's recommendation to Passienus's service; for, in his ambition, he wanted only imperial patronage and, so Seneca says, was in the habit of disputing the freedman Timagenes, a social-climbing cook turned imperial panegyrist who finally fell out of imperial favor. The concurrence of motifs (freedmen, Greeks, freedom of speech, plagiarism, the presence of Caesar or Caesar as final judge, plagiarism as unacknowledged translation) serves to damn this petty plagiarism as Greek, but also underscores the fact that plagiarism never involves equals. The thief is always a social inferior, predominantly a Greek and a freedman.

Seneca has refracted a double anxiety of speech—that of the aristocrats who no longer had the same control over it[61] and that of the new generation's sense of linguistic inferiority. The peculiar aspect of the well-publicized, self-conscious sense of the postclassical's failure to write and speak like the classical is that both the traditionally literate and the new practitioner benefited from the attention drawn to the difficulty of good writing and speaking. The concept of a creeping, burgeoning vulgarity isolated both as proper practitioners. Stylistic prescriptions and a sense of linguistic inferiority restricted the access to literary practice and provided the published techniques and motives for such activity. In Seneca's discussion of plagiarism, the combatants can appear as a Greek cook and a Greek rhetor, united in their transgressions of media and social strata. Seneca indicts plagiarists only partly to set the record straight and thus restore or create a preeminent place for Latro; his indictment displaces censure as surely as it inscribes Caesar as the final arbiter of Latinity.

These notices of plagiarism do not by any means decide the complex issues of linguistic authenticity and transgression in Seneca's text. Indeed, the preoccupations of the discussions of falsified speech suggest that the willful detractors of his friend Latro were not Seneca's chief or sole target. Seneca reserves his longest discussion and his personal worry for a related instance of literary misappropriation: the various accounts of Cicero's death. The connection of this theme to plagiarism may need some explanation, but the common bonds center around the author's presentation of himself as the champion of genuine Roman discourse. Cicero is, of course, the Roman canon, the rule whose words Latro and ultimately Seneca's sons must take as their pattern. Seneca does not advocate direct mimicry of the old orator's language or life, but he does present Cicero as the model orator, that distant yet animating form for the new style that intends to be properly and exclusively Roman.

Seneca relates that the differing accounts of the death of the old republican and his dying words have driven him to the texts of historians. Thus he departs from his proposed scheme, the history of declamation allegedly recalled from an old man's memory, to write a section that includes the written texts of the historians. An entire *suasoria* explores the various accounts of Cicero's demise (*S.* 6), including that of the hostile and polemical Pollio, who would falsely ascribe to the orator a cowardly speech of supplication before Antony. Here Cicero's own text, the *Philippics*, seems threatened. Seneca sees fit to bring in the nondeclamatory—the treatments of historians—to recover the genuine Cicero, just as the declaimers on the pressure of plagiarism digress from their criticism of the declamation by discussing the poets. The unfixed, oral genre of declamation invokes poetry and history as the index of genuine speech.

Seneca thus makes his most overt irruption into declamation, shattering its fictions, in defense of the true orator. What has the alleged cowardice of Cicero to do with plagiarism? Seneca enters his text on both occasions in order to champion authentic words. Cicero's dying words must be defended as surely as in a separate declamation his recantation is to be denied: Cicero did not agree to burn his speeches so that Antony would spare his life. In both these declamations Seneca is the advocate of the republican texts. In a similar fashion, he had ridiculed Cestius for preferring and teaching his response to Cicero's *Pro Milone*. Seneca's generation introduced Cicero and Virgil to the schools, but the generation of Seneca's sons really canonized the classical authors.[62] They treated them not as contemporaries but as exclusive models. They declined to innovate again; they retaught these authors; they wrote commentaries. Seneca is as concerned as Cicero's commentator Asconius to champion the words and life of Cicero. There must be a fixed canon from which to mark deviance. Indeed, by presenting his authorial persona as champion of the classical, Seneca establishes his own authority. For his purposes and circle, it is of no importance that his Latin is not Cicero's: mimesis is not the point, deference to the old master and the posture of restorer of the true Latin voice are.

In arguing about declamation, as in Seneca's ranking of the declaimers, the speakers engage in a sort of self-policing. In reality, the audience applauded or, like Cassius Severus in the house of Cestius, interrupted and was asked to leave. But rather like Cicero in the *Brutus*, Seneca is interested in the conjunction of the praise of the audience and the approbation of the critics. At the same time, he disparages the new generation's taste by championing Latro and by presenting the reader with the select judgments of an inner circle, much as Atticus and Brutus, the interlocutors of Cicero's dialogue, revise some of the narrator's judgments and focus the debate. Cicero's interlocutors helped produce criteria crucial to the development and apogee of Latin oratory as Cicero would have his reader see it—in particular, the growth of *Latinitas*, the subject of *urbanitas*, and the criterion of an increasing acquaintance with Greek culture. Such topics, raised in "digressions"—which in dialogue are highly charged with meaning—

provide the grounds for proper judgment of style. Seneca's strategies for creating *Latinitas*, for inscribing himself and his circle into the narrative of Latin prose style, involve a similar technique of irruptions into the facile movement of the narrative. In his text, issues of propriety of speech emerge in comment upon declaimers, made for the most part by other declaimers and by an elite subset of the audience.

Significantly, the declaimers take up the subject of improper speech by contrasting what has just been spoken to the authority of Latin poetic texts and poetic practice. All esthetic argument, it seems, is grounded in the poets, especially Virgil. But, when they do not reflect so grandly, the declaimers express their worries, their disputes, in a finite set of categories. First, both in its position in the text and perhaps in the declaimers' minds, the division of the set theme was hotly disputed, for there seems to have been great innovation in this sphere, perhaps a real change in declamatory practice. Again, in the larger sphere of content and its arrangement, harshness was censured, for, as I have discussed, this neglected the sympathy of viewpoint crucial to the pleader's success and to the social economy.[63] In particular, the expression of declaimers is damned as vulgar or foolish—as belonging to those of low class or few years.[64] Solecism as well indicates that the speaker does not belong.[65] Finally, anachronism reveals a confusion of time, of history and culture, which, like the linguistic confusion of proper and improper diction, points up ignorance.[66] Again and again, the declaimer must exercise discrimination.[67]

Although he writes his part out of the written record, Seneca is of course the arch-declaimer because it is he who makes the most significant and abiding *divisio*. Good and bad, Latin and Greek, original and fake he distinguishes in an embracing rhetorical project of a scope not to be contained by oral medium, indeed, that spills over into ten books and the *suasoriae*. In the end, rhetorical *copia* is best attested in his mastery of theme, division, *sententiae*, and *colores*. Seneca stands as the final censor of vulgarity and champion of proper Latin, just as it is he who connects the

new generation with the old, his sons with Latro, Latro and declamation in general, through his introduction of the poets and of
Cicero, to the old republicans.

In writing to his sons Seneca champions manly taste. On a
number of occasions, and most importantly in the first preface,
he sets the approved virile style, to be learned from his collection,
against the reigning effeminacy of the day.[68] This highly useful
topos delivered by an old man helps to elevate Seneca's circle
from the general opprobrium directed against declamation. The
persona of the narrator introduced in this first preface allows a re-
luctance to write to be overcome by the entreaties of curious sons
and by an antipathy for the new direction in education and in style
generally. The opening words of his first two sentences had been
exigitis and *iubetis*. When the father concedes to his sons' demands
ten paragraphs later, he echoes the opening word and at the same
time moves from the private service granted his sons to some sort
of public munificence: "For this reason [the widespread plagia-
rism] I am all the happier to do as you ask, and I shall dedicate
to the people, so they may not be the exclusive possessions
of an individual, all the eloquent expressions of famous men that
I remember" (*C.* 1 pr. 10: "Eo libentius quod exigitis faciam, et
quaecumque a celeberrimis viris facunde dicta teneo, ne ad quem-
quam privatim pertineant, populo dedicabo").

Seneca thus styles himself a dedicating magistrate. He sidesteps the issue of naming a patron and continues in the loftier vein
of the censorious magistrate: today's young are no genuine men,
he erupts in this preface: "a perverse addiction to song and dance
captivates the effeminate. . . . Among your set who is a real, I don't
dare say genius or scholar, but man? Who wins popular approval,
I won't say by great, but by his own talent and effort?" (*C.* 1 pr. 8–
10: "cantandi saltandique obscena studia effeminatos tenent. . . .
Quis aequalium vestrorum quid dicam satis ingeniosus, satis stu-
diosus, immo quis satis vir est? . . . Quis est qui non dico magnis
virtutibus sed suis placeat?"). He repeatedly assumes this stance of
restoring virtues to their proper men and combating contemporary vulgarity.[69] Indeed, Seneca emerges as the champion of taste

in a text that so rambles that it might seem vulgar if its *copia* were not controlled and punctuated by the consummate orator. The style of his first preface borrows heavily from Roman satire; its description of adulterous and effeminate youth, its denunciation of contemporary speech as effeminate adulterer, makes Seneca the Roman satirist, master of Roman *sermo*, displaying his own control and restraint, his allegiance to the *imperium* of *Latinitas*.

The elder Seneca has fashioned this empire of Roman speech by presenting the declamatory display of his fellow Spaniard Latro and the education of his full-grown sons as manifestations of Romanness allied to republican oratory, to contemporary poetry recitations, to the leading orators' styles, and to the conversational criticism of noble literary patrons. Thus, for Seneca "literature" was a social institution, one that negotiates questions of identity and allegiance.[70] Rather like the poet Phaedrus, Seneca has moved the target of criticism into the literary work: individual declaimers, not the institution, offend. But, like fable, the very genre shows an anxiety about its status; in origin non-Roman, its practitioners ranging from Greeks and freedmen to landed provincials, and a vehicle of social mobility, declamation, in Seneca's skillful presentation, combines Roman dialogue and Roman satire with paternal epistle to recommend declamation and Seneca's circle as the new old Romans.

5

The Imperial Mask of Rhetoric:
Animus and *Vultus* in the
Annals of Tacitus

AMID HIS COMMEMORATION OF declamation and declaimers, the elder Seneca had carefully marshaled scenes of *correctio*—a rhetorical figure in which a speaker corrects himself by restatement. Seneca's restatement was not of the simple type where a speaker pretends to substitute a better term, as Cicero had corrected himself for calling Clodius Clodia's lover rather than her brother. In the controversies Seneca has interwoven whole scenes of correction that chastise as linguistically and socially despicable those who would falsely pass for the true Roman. The author includes declaimers who improve earlier statements and aristocratic critics who correct the excesses and thefts of the declaimers. And, of course, Seneca's whole project may be seen as a *correctio*—a restoring of genuine words to their original speakers and a chastisement of the interlopers. Thus the new rhetoric could represent itself as a return, even though it was censured as being an innovation so overblown that it could never be genuine.

In the *Dialogus*, Tacitus provides spokesmen to consider the new rhetoric, which by his time had been much influenced by the more famous Seneca, the son who was tutor and adviser to Nero. But it is in his history of the first emperors, the *Annals*, that Tacitus develops the social polemics and possibilities of linguistic representations. The imperial historian has figured a pathology of empire as a conflict of linguistic and rhetorical styles. In the emperor Tiberius he locates a kind of aphasia, a speech and style disorder, that gradually infects all reachers of the empire. Tacitus figures social disorder as a state of the language, and his *correctio* has more connections to the literary riot of the novelist Petronius than to the stylistic regulators whom Seneca or the critics summoned to deliberate, the aristocrats Pollio and Messalla, in the pages of the declamations.

Tacitus writes about the language of state, the high official speeches of the senate and the emperor; and of course he writes in the language of state, as an aristocratic historian who was once himself consul and now writing of public affairs to which he has a natural claim. The language of state may be oratory at its grandest, or it may simply be despotic command. Tacitus exploits this antithesis of civic republican speech and imperial rhetoric into a pathology of government.

In great measure, Tacitus hangs the thematic patterning of language and imperial control in the *Annals* upon two words, *vultus* and *animus*. This polar pair are, at first, face and thought, form and content/intent. Classical rhetoric dictated that a speaker's face, like other gestures, could be a trained, signifying aid to persuasion. A rhetorical commonplace maintained that a man's character could be read from his speech.[1] Thus rhetoric responded to the charge that it was histrionic, feigned, and fake. In the historian's depictions of individuals' speeches, there is far more at stake than a sense that an individual's language is bound up with his identity. A protocol of elite speech training, from Cato to Quintilian, insisted that the orator was a good man, that his words and body were transparent indices to his character. There is, then, no social deception in the elite command of language. Tacitus takes up these classical postures about the natural legibility of speech. Of course, there had been harsh criticism of rhetoric as deceptive and even some recognition of it as a system of social control. In Roman social practice, the rule of civic speech could be contested by demagogic speech, by sloganeering, by political doggerel, by the subliterary media of the mime, the fable, or the proverb. Tacitus is not content to replay traditional diatribe about the qualities of trained speech and speakers. His meditation on rhetoric is exceptional for its recognition of the emperor as arch-rhetor—the anxious controller of signs—and for its descriptive pathology of speech and society. He presents as the *arche* of his history and this development the emperor Tiberius, the first heir to empire and to imperial speech.

On a number of occasions Tacitus suggests that Tiberius's mind was difficult of access, resistant both to expression and to influence, especially to criticism and rumor. The historian presents an emperor of a most un- or anti-oratorical cast. The classical orator was supposed to aim at *copia*, both fullness of expression and the readiness to speak on all subjects in all circumstances, and had to be responsive to his audience. Thanks to Tacitus, Tiberius's speech is notorious for its rhetorical quality, for an opaqueness and indirection that are at times synonymous with rhetoric, not oratory. The second emperor thus stands to the old orator, Cicero, perhaps, or Cato, as rhetoric, both the scholastic system of speech training and an overly elaborated style, stands to the perished free oratory. In Tacitus's *Annals*, Tiberius embodies (almost as a synecdoche) a debilitating development of imperial language. He has so sundered the classical harmony of *vultus* and *animus*, form and thought, that words lose not only credibility but their very permanence and power. In his greatest treatise on oratory Cicero had Crassus warn that these were not to be divided.[2] Tiberius is not alone responsible, for Augustus had, in his "restored republic" and resuscitation of republican practices, set the precedent for a sort of imperial nominalism, where, as Tacitus would put it, only the names from the republic endure.

Once Tiberius has adulterated language so as to split *nomina* from *res*, signifiers from signified, proper language will be as difficult to achieve as proper behavior. For the latter subject much scholarly attention has considered the case of the career of Agricola —the historian's father-in-law, whose biography Tacitus wrote— as well as Tacitus's own rise under Domitian and his accounts of imperial victims. In appraising senators' actions under the evil emperors, historians have replayed Tacitus's categories. Even for the historian more concerned with nonelites, Tacitus's reflections upon an elite's struggle with a new political reality are significant because they have become an essential aspect of the historiographer's self-presentation. Perhaps Tacitus's greatest contribution to historiography is not psychological history or court history but the narrative persona of the historian as the recoverer of names who unworks the silencing revisionism of the autocrat.

In writing about the course of Tacitus's speech in the *Annals* I do not mean to restrict historical problems of class, governmental administration, and elite behavior to issues of linguistic discourse. But our contemporary appreciation of discourse mimics that of early imperial Rome, whose faith in the powers of rhetoric seems no more naive or thoroughgoing. Nonetheless, modern academic valorization of the powers of discourse is not the same as the ancient attachment to rhetoric. The roles of elite speech were different, but from the imperial historian as much as from any earlier rhetorician or philosopher, the modern academy has inherited both a reliance on the power of rhetoric and on the problematics of this political and historical mode. For the Roman senator, public speech, in the senate, in the courts, to his clients, was, like other apparently individual actions—invitations to dinner, the choice of companions while walking to the forum or while governing a province—a genre of social gestures and public behavior. Thus, for a certain class, to speak and to choose with whom one spoke were to act. Proper speech, the equation of *nomina* and *res*, has a more fundamental importance for our historian who declares the recovery of the names of imperial victims and their informers as an essential part of his historiographical project. Tacitus's writing of history is a rhetorical counter, a *correctio*, to the obfuscation created by *adulatio* and *delatio*. Such seems to me the strong rhetoric of Tacitus's own writing—against the imperial style of sycophants, Stoic martyrs, and emperors.

Tacitus has not located all problematization of language and its interpretation in one personage. The characterization of Tiberius and of his style are not discrete, objective formulations.[3] Indeed, the foils to his rhetoric are many. Germanicus is one, but so are his ancestors Augustus and Julius Caesar. Indeed, certain moments both in the narrative frame and in the narrative proper promise a classical or natural language, a discourse without fissure between form and content. These scenes of transparent rhetoric, however, are undercut in a number of significant ways, most fundamentally because they transpire during the breakdown, limitation, or failure of empire in confrontations with the mutinous soldiery, with the barbarian, and with hostile nature. This chapter traces some of the complex ways in which language is thematized and, quite unlike the views of the elder Seneca or Phaedrus, problematized as an index of social order and of Romanness.

The Mirror of Tiberius

I have suggested that Tacitus portrays an un- or anti-oratorical Tiberius: the late-appointed emperor is a speaker alienated from the fluency and clarity of expression of the idealized republican orator. This speech characterization has been taken so seriously as to elicit laments on the part of historians. Tacitus's verbally impaired Tiberius is read as an emblem of an age; the characterization of Tiberius has shaped our reading not simply of the *Annals* but of Julio-Claudian history and perhaps beyond.[4] Similar complaints distort the understanding of other writers of the early Silver Age as essentially hyper-rhetorical.[5] Perhaps readers of a non-rhetorical age have projected their difficulty in interpreting onto the compositional history of the Roman texts. Thus the difficulties of interpretation rewrite the conditions of composition. Be that as it may, the importance for the present argument is simply to underscore how persuasive Tacitus's picture of Tiberius is. If instead we relate his depiction of Tiberius to some other narrative techniques, especially those which foreground a contrast of genuine and artificial or spurious language and, in parallel fashion, a transparent and opaque hermeneutics, then the portraits of Tiberius as speaker, writer, and auditor emerge as dramatic scenes directing the reading of Tacitus's work.

My argument does not pretend to recapture how the learned and rhetorically trained second emperor spoke to his family, senators, or advisers.[6] An ingenious attempt has been made to delineate what diction is actually Tiberian in the speeches attributed to him.[7] No doubt Syme was right: Tacitus did consult the *acta senatus*, and, as Tacitus tells, perhaps read the speeches of Tiberius. What is important, what he saw and gleaned from those sources, and what he has most memorably and effectively conveyed is a pathology of rhetorical speech which, because of the status of its speaker, because of its initial, seminal position in the *Annals*, and because of its thematic resonances with other scenes, speakers, and formulas, informs the rest of the *Annals*.

Most simply put, Tiberius strives never to make his *vultus* match his *animus*. He does have difficulty with this obstruction—in Tiberius Rome has not yet witnessed the serene, sculptural, and near-divine mask with which the emperor Constantius II of Ammianus Marcellinus's pages entered the city, turning neither to the left nor to the right, impassive toward the crowd, a serene soul in tumultuous times.[8] There are even indications that the blocked and blocking figure of the *Annals* is not the "real" Tiberius, for two passages attest to the emperor's fluency: "[Tiberius] nusquam cunctabundus nisi cum in senatu loqueretur" (1.7: "only in the senate was he at a loss for words"). Even this statement prejudices Tiberius's speech, for Tacitus has not simply said that Tiberius hesitated; such would be the force of a finite verb or the simple participle. In Roman historiography, at least, the adjective in *-bundus* has an ominous ring. Perhaps Claudius Quadrigarius would seem a distant influence for the diction of the *Annals*; his disreputable Gaul, naked and chanting—*cantabundus*—so barbarously contrasted with the Roman Torquatus. But just a few paragraphs after this qualification of Tiberius's speech, *contionabundus* (1.17) disgraces the improper speech of Percennius, the chief mutineer.[9]

Similarly slighting praise comes in the second mention of the emperor's *copia*: "It was quite clear whether support for the emperors' actions were sincere or feigned. Even Tiberius, elsewhere a rehearsed and careful speaker, spoke easily and at length whenever he came to someone's aid" (4.31: "nec occultum est, quando ex veritate, quando adumbrata laetitia facta imperatorum celebrentur. quin ipse, compositus alias et velut eluctantium verborum, solutius promptiusque eloquebatur quotiens subveniret"). In assisting individuals and anywhere but the senate, Tiberius spoke freely —when speaking in the traditional defensive role of the advocate for his client (i.e., as a *privatus*), he displayed an old republican fluency. Tacitus had, however, condemned Tiberius's language from the start of the *Annals*: "Even when he did not want to mask his thought, Tiberius used an elliptical and obscure style, either out of habit or because it was natural to him; when he wanted to conceal his own views, his style descended to obscurity and ambiguity" (1.11: "Tiberioque etiam in rebus quas non occuleret, seu natura sive adsuetudine, suspensa semper et obscura verba; tunc vero nitenti ut sensus suos penitus abderet, in incertum et ambiguum magis implicabantur"). A minimalist and positivist conclusion is that Tacitus has distorted Tiberius's speech by exclusion. More significantly, Tacitus focuses on the emperor's public speech and its curious, contagious effect on speech and language in Rome.

But before we consider his effect as speaker, the remaining descriptions of Tiberius's private speech reveal through their rarity and their tortured form just how far the private man and genuine expression have receded.[10] On two occasions Tiberius speaks Greek. The shift to the language of his *secessio* (and rhetorical training in Rhodes) reveals the emperor's *animus*. (It should be noted as well that, for the educated Roman, Greek was a domestic, private language, spoken within the home to learned dependents or spilling over into letters to one's friends, as in Cicero's correspondence.) On leaving the senate house, having failed as usual to effect a transparent Latin expression from the senate, Tiberius used to say in exasperation, "Men trained for slavery" (in Greek, though Tacitus gives just a Latin version, "O homines ad servitutem paratos," 3.65). To Agrippina, who interrupts his sacrifice to upbraid him for attacking her through prosecution of her cousin, Tiberius responds in Greek: "her words wrested from him the unusual expression of his innermost thought, and he warned her with a Greek verse that she was not on trial because she was not on the throne" [i.e., the fact that she was not empress was no injury] (4.52: "audita haec raram occulti pectoris vocem elicuere, correptamque Graeco versu admonuit non ideo laedi quia non regnaret").[11] Agrippina does what the senators will not: she strips away the pretext and elicits Tiberius's naked expression—a Greek, verse litotes. Agrippina is a peculiar case; she will goad Tiberius into speech again; but for the present this episode, like Tiberius's aside to himself on leaving the senate, reveals a character not so much incapable of direct expression as incapable of such in Latin, in the senate, in public.

Tiberius never manages to speak fluent Latin. He walks to the forum to speak on behalf of the notorious Urgulania, the chief Vestal and intimate friend of the empress Livia, who has refused to respond to a summons to court from the free-speaking Piso. The emperor goes, we are told, *civile ratus* (2.34). But this is just what Tiberius is incapable of: *animus civilis, comitas*, the ability to act *comiter*, as Augustus did in attending the games, eludes the man who cannot reveal his *animus*.[12]

Tiberius's Silencing Effect as Speaker: The Uncivil Mind

Just as Tacitus pronounces on the quality of Tiberius's language, so the historian also calls attention to the effect of Tiberius's speech, in direct characterization and by the outcome of particular episodes. The accusation of Libo for conspiracy, for example, had come to an impasse because the law did not allow the torture of the defendant's slaves (without his consent). This scene, like others of Tiberius's judicial activity, establishes him as a subverter of the intent of republican law, but his instrument is prima facie not force or his authority but a change in words and their interpretation. Tacitus here (2.30) calls him "callidus et novi iuris repertor,"[13] for Tiberius had the slaves sold to the state and then tortured. At the very point where verbal formula seems to have controlled interpretation, Tiberius intervenes with a new, perverse legal formula.

Tiberius's own pronouncements subvert verbal formula. Even in the case of his own laws, words cannot or are not credited.[14] At 1.75, Tiberius refers cases of those seeking *veniam ordinis* to the senate. The effect is typical: "this was the precedent for the rest to prefer silence and penury to confession and charity" ("unde ceteri silentium et paupertatem confessioni et beneficio praeposuere"). Tiberius's expression brings not credit but silence, as if the power of words had been undermined.[15]

A final instance of Tiberius's legal style reveals his characteristic resistance to expression and his anxious control of words. To chart the reaction of audiences to Tiberius's words is every reader's course in the first books of the *Annals*. Worse perhaps than the demise of free speech, we witness senators struck dumb—this is the immediate narrative or narrated effect. The *Annals'* writer and reader must negotiate those twisted, silence-inducing words: Tacitus, in working with his sources; the reader, with the dramatic speeches that one reads with the help of the narrator's comments. The author himself can be touched by the hesitancy and ambiguity of his chief character: Tacitus declares himself in difficulty at 1.81 ("vix quicquam firmare ausim"). Trying to fathom Tiberius's policy on consular elections, Tacitus engages in a historiographical commonplace: the narrator reports the difficulty of discerning the truth and hence his own policy of reproducing the conflicting sources, a Herodotean mannerism that collapses the distance between reader and historian by purporting to put us in direct contact with the *res* of history. The opportunity to read and interpret the conflicting material with the guide removed initiates the reader into historiography.

The matter under dispute complicates this commonplace, as the narrated subject is an attempt at interpretation—the senators or Rome as a whole attempting to penetrate imperial policy, to learn who could or would be consul. Tacitus reports three variations of imperial policy: Either Tiberius would not name the candidates ("subtractis candidatorum nominibus") but instead described their qualifications; sometimes he offered no such signification but simply urged against bribery; finally, most often he gave to the consuls only the names of those who had declared themselves to him ("apud se professos"). Others might name themselves, if they had confidence in their own influence and qualifications. This passage, which ends the first book, seals the uncertainty of Tiberius's expression: "a show of words but in substance empty or duplicitous, the more a film of liberty covered them, the swifter they would erupt into abject servitude" ("speciosa verbis, re inania aut subdola, quantoque maiore libertatis imagine tegebantur, tanto eruptura ad infensius servitium").

By now the reader readily recognizes the divide between Tiberius's thought and his expression. In addition, the technique of selection, the electoral system that Tacitus attributes to Tiberius, bears striking similarities to Tiberius's speech disability. The first policy simply reflects Tiberius's language: it removes (subverts) names. In fact, this might have, like the second proposal, weakened aristocratic factions and factionalism, but Tacitus offers no such explanation from contemporary political realities. Instead, the reader again finds Tiberius the nominalist, one who refuses to credit names and words in general and who instead offers a vision or language that is anti-idealist, resistant to the equation of names and things. The irony, of course, is that the emperor who keeps up a charade of republican language, preserving republican laws and titles, distrusts and undermines this very idealism.

Tiberius as Reader and Auditor

Tacitus's complex depiction of the emperor's relations to thought and expression includes scenes of Tiberius as a reader, a receiver of words. At the outset of the *Annals*, aside from the interpretations put on Augustus's death and career, which, like Tiberius's threefold policy on consular elections, exercises the author and reader in historiographical method, Tiberius as auditor and judge constitutes the dominant textual paradigm of rhetoric and interpretation. No doubt these scenes resulted from Tacitus's reading of the senate's proceedings, but to champion source as explanation first ignores Tacitus's consistent and thematic concern with Tiberius's peculiar relation to language and, most fundamentally, radically simplifies the process of reading the text. Herodotus reports that Histiaeus tattooed his slave's head, waited for the hair to grow, and then sent along his secret message for Aristagoras. This is an independent constituent of Herodotus's depiction of the historical Ionian revolt (5.35); clearly, it has other affinities, as it is but one example of the stories' concern with code, secret reading, and interpreting. The *Annals* of Tacitus and the *Histories* of Herodotus, albeit in far different ways, foreground their own reading and hermeneutics. There is, then, nothing necessarily discrete in Tacitus's technique with Tiberius; that is, once again "speech characterization" will not suffice to account for the problematic text of Tiberius's language. Finally, if Tacitus has learned the thematic and structural importance of a series of speeches from Thucydides, he has also learned the dynamic value of scenes of signs, trusted dependents, and betrayal from Herodotus.

To read the narrative backwards, one could say that in the early accounts of Tiberius as auditor Tacitus seeks the latent signs, the moments the imperial mask slips, of the emperor responsible for that consuming blight: treason trials and the false oratory of the informers.[16] Thus he develops a technique of thematic anticipation through characterization or character unmasking. But a more comprehensive reading would not limit these episodes to discussions of character—the concern with characterization has misled criticism to erect a heroic Germanicus and thus to see Tacitean history as the psychological play of character. Simply put, characters in the *Annals* are not so independent as characterization suggests. For instance, Sallustius Crispus and Petronius seem to mimic the dissipated litterateur Maecenas; against this Epicurean relief, informers and Stoic martyrs replay a Stoic drama, until the author gives notice of this sickening and pointless exemplification. If the narrative makes lives into exempla (by recovering their names and memorializing their deaths), one must pay all the more attention to the pattern and rhetoric of those lives. Especially with successive scenes of the emperor, as with the series of deaths, the process of reading and interpretation cannot have the sort of organic and isolated completion that "characterization" suggests. Instead, a common rhetoric of the uncertain, turbulent relation of appearance and reality links many scenes.

Despite all dissimulation Tiberius can at times be read. Asinius Gallus realizes he has offended Tiberius (1.12: "etenim vultu offensionem coniectaverat").[17] This marks the second occurrence of the word *vultus* in the *Annals* and the second reading from physical expression, for upon Augustus's death Tiberius had practiced a similar reading of inner thoughts: the emperor noted and remembered the expressions of the chiefs of state (1.7: "nam verba vultus in crimen detorquens recondebat"). Such transparent reading, this chance to interpret physiognomy, wanes quickly as Tiberius's speech elicits silence or adulation.

The first book of the *Annals* casts the series of Tiberius's reactions to pleas, appeals, and other men's proposed legislation as a gradual movement away from the freedom of speech that characterizes death scenes in general and has, in the case of the funeral of Augustus, added thematic importance through a course that results not so much in flattery as in an indirect, opaque style mirroring the emperor's.[18] In great measure, speakers like Asinius Gallus, who has four significant verbal confrontations with the emperor in the first book, and Romanius Hispo, who founds the practice of prosecution for treason, chart the direction for senatorial speech for all the *Annals*.[19]

The literalism of Gallus and Hispo startles, especially the emperor. Gallus takes literally the rhetorical *dubitatio* of Tiberius by asking him what portion of empire he would like. This transparent reading of his own words shakes Tiberius's composure so that Gallus can see he has offended (1.12). Hispo's similarity to Gallus rests both in his effect upon Tiberius (his denunciation of Marcellus breaks Tiberius's composure — "rupta taciturnitate," at 1.74) and in his naive, transparent signification.[20] This latter quality makes his charges seem ridiculous to the reader. In his accusation of Marcellus, Romanius Hispo treats language and meaning as transparent. The narrator labels the central charge of this prosecution for defaming Tiberius inescapable, not because it was true, but because it was believable. An essential of ancient rhetoric was to make the verisimilitudinous (here, criticism of Tiberius) believed. In this particular trial the commonplace rhetorical technique has been pushed to the extreme, so that truth-seeming displaces the true. In a city of hostile accusations that the emperor deserves, occasion and context cannot now be judged—no particular knowledge is possible. Indeed, as *vultus* (outward expression) is no guarantor of *animus* (inner disposition), *vultus* is discarded. Control of appearance no longer guards the self in the age of Tiberius, just as evidence does not save one from condemnation. The Age of Rumor has arrived.

Hispo's charge employs transparent language not quite in the manner of Gallus, who had taken literally what was rhetorical indirection, the *dubitatio* of assuming empire, but by attributing spurious words that are believed to be genuine because they are reasonable. In fact, given some narrative progress, the reader of the *Annals* may come to distrust the possibility of genuine language; but for now we are concerned with the interrelation of such scenes with their linguistic claims to verity and ties to the emperor. Hispo's first charge (that Marcellus composed verses critical of the emperor) wins his auditors' belief; the second ruptures Tiberius's composure. Here, too, the literal, naive reading has been most effective. Hispo adds as a charge that Marcellus had his own statue placed higher than one of the Caesars. If it were true, Marcellus would have been acting as a classical signifier: form mirrors content and intent. The third charge displays the same naive symbolism: Marcellus had allegedly affixed the head of Tiberius to a truncated statue of Augustus. Here, the point at which Tiberius can contain himself no longer, Marcellus has indulged in literal representation of reality. Tiberius is an artificial graft, not a true son. The former artistic crime is the representation of future reality (of wish fulfillment). The prospect of clear, future signification (as troubling to Tiberius as the words of the astrologers whom he would expel), and an unrhetorical or classical expression of reality, strip off the mask of composure with which Tiberius purports to let the senate try its own case. Just as verbal criticism of Tiberius was credible to the senators, so graphic accounts of imperial succession are believed by the emperor. Tiberius overreacts, declaring that he will vote first and in public.[21] There follows one of the few instances where speech changes imperial policy. Gnaeus Piso deflects the emperor's proposal by asking when Tiberius will vote and expresses the pretext that he wishes to follow the emperor's example. If Tiberius votes last, Piso fears his earlier vote might offend. This rhetorical *dubitatio* prompts Tiberius to desist, and Marcellus is acquitted.

Tiberius behaves extraordinarily, even uncharacteristically, in these scenes from book 1, where verbal confrontations threaten his control of signs and signification. Significantly, the classical gesture—freedom of speech in the senate, an alleged use of portraiture as factional propaganda—perturbs the imperial *vultus*. In such scenes as the trials of Marcellus and Libo, the narrative allows a glimpse of the fiction of social concord, of harmonious relations between senate and emperor. Bound up inextricably with these subjects too, is the phantom of genuine, proper language, one that says what it means. For as the law and the role of the senate are subverted, so too is the power of words. Piso succeeds in one of classical rhetoric's aims. He seems to move Tiberius; but in fact his own expression, Tiberian in its division between narrative surface and intent, simply silences the emperor for the moment, that is, restores the imperial mask. Other attempts to move the emperor by oratory are not so effective. When Tiberius changes his stated policy, for example, in reversing his denial of relief to M. Hortalus, Hortensius's grandson, he is moved by the silence and murmuring of the audience (2.37).[22]

He tolerates that emblem of senatorial speech, Asinius Gallus, for the most part with silence.[23] Upon a flood of the Tiber, with consequent destruction of life and property (1.76: "relabentem secuta est aedificiorum et hominum strages"), Asinius Gallus suggests that the Sibylline books be consulted. In fact, the senator appeals to an authority other than the imperial. Prophetic authority, like astrology or the Sibylline books, could serve the ambitious individual senator; certainly these media threatened the emperor's control of signs. Tacitus does not reflect upon Asinius Gallus's motive; instead he explains the emperor's denial of Gallus's proposal in terms that echo his characterizations of Tiberius's style: "Tiberius refused, covering with equal murk divine and human affairs" ("renuit Tiberius, perinde divina humanaque obtegens"). Tiberius himself is like the muddy Tiber, sweeping over and obliterating all. As I shall argue below, scenes of hostile nature do not transform the emperor into some kindred hostile, natural force; rather, Tacitus evokes a nature sympathetic to the confusion of imperial language and the attendant social turbulence.[24] Gallus cannot get any exegesis: he can't gain access to a text that would alleviate human suffering; he can't sway Tiberius; instead he is caught up in the obliteration of Tiberian silence. The efforts to read Tiberius or to achieve any transparency of text are becoming more and more perilous.

At 1.77 Asinius Gallus speaks against the tribune of the people who blocked the senate's legislation to empower the praetors with the right to discipline actors ("ius virgarum in histriones"). Tiberius listens in silence. In quick succession, then, Tiberius has broken silence regarding Marcellus, *renuit* — "denied" but, etymologically, "given the nod against" (Tacitus cloaks the emperor's opposition as nonverbal signification) the proposal of Gallus — and now listens to his speech in silence. The senate's thwarted legislation comes as a seal, of sorts, on a confluence of themes and ideas: the muddy Tiber, Tiberius breaking the banks of his composed silence, actors (both the mimes, whose license the senate now seeks to control through discussion, and Asinius Gallus) being checked in their show of free speech through nonverbal means, and finally the license of the theater mob curtailed. Now the senate threatens the actors with corporal punishment and adds conditions meant to increase social division: no senator may visit a pantomimist's house; no equestrian can be accompanied in public by the mimists; they may only be seen in the theater. This is a most uncertain seal on social and linguistic turbulence. Again the emperor emerges as the controller of signs — there will be no

public or theatrical display of support for or attack on an aristocrat, but a hostile nature has been told to keep its boundaries by
speakers whose words, inaccessible and duplicitous, do not correspond to their intentions.

Imperial Speech

That blocked figure, the emperor himself, who dominated the development of scenes whether by silence or speech, obstructed the
course of characters, historian, narrative, and reader to clear and
final signification. His own language is thus not so much a recurrent motif as a contagious mode of expression and an element
of narrative or scene structure. Among the moments of unen-
cumbered expression, the deaths of Porcia, Petronius, and Seneca
stand out; these obituaries have as a typical structural element tes-
tamentary freedom of speech. The interplay of these final gestures
clearly is of great importance for the interpretation of the *Annals*,
but I wish to focus on those figures closest and most relevant to
Tiberius, his avowed precedent Augustus, and Germanicus, who
very much fails to follow his exemplar of speech. The rationale of
this focus is not exclusively familial, generational, or personal: the
funeral of Augustus and the confrontations of Germanicus with
mutinous speech and with an obfuscating nature share a narrative
technique that links social turbulence with ineffective language.
The link, in fact, is the speech and effect on speech of the imperial controller of signs, the almost sterile Tiberius. First I recall
the barren, debilitating quality of Tiberius from one scene in particular. Then the analysis of speech and speech, rather than speech
and action, at the funeral of Augustus will demonstrate the initial
frame Tacitus has created, which in turn guides the interpretation
of subsequent scenes of verbal and social confusion. Finally, I turn
to the broadest canvases of these scenes of confusions, the signs
Tiberius would control: Germanicus and Agrippina.

Tacitus suggests that Tiberius's resistant nature was sterile
and barren. His mind had to be raped for any natural reaction

to come to light. So Tacitus describes Asinius Gallus's attempt to reform the selection of candidates as an attempt to penetrate (2.36: "altius penetrare") imperial policy. This diction in itself is slight evidence, but two other moments that produce his natural feeling have an unmistakably gendered construction. During Germanicus's funeral the people's fondness and partisanship for Agrippina penetrate him (3.4: "nihil tamen Tiberius magis penetravit quam studia hominum accensa in Agrippinam"). Women, or more exactly public displays of or for women, rouse the emperor. Agrippina's speech to the returning soldiery disturbs him.[25] Germanicus's mother, Antonia, he prevents, Tacitus leads us to believe, from attending her son's funeral, just as he and Livia fear to reveal their faces. Here he works to prevent feminine signification—the display of a woman's *vultus*—as surely as when he dictates that there should be an end to lamentation.

Similarly, according to Tacitus's reckoning, an inscription Livia set up to Augustus with her name on top may have been the cause for Tiberius's antipathy to his own mother.[26] Porcia, it is true, is allowed her display: her funeral is celebrated, but without the *imagines* of Cassius and Brutus. Perhaps even more notably absent from this feminine display is Tiberius himself, left out of her will. Tiberius, of course, was forced to divorce the woman he loved and to marry the ever-shifting Julia. Tacitus seems to literalize this event in Tiberius's relations to the feminine, as perhaps he also literalized his secession, both to Rhodes and to Capri, in the emperor's inaccessible speech and manner. These homologies of language and life color the biography, yet Tiberius is not simply a divorced or alienated character. Tacitus has exploited contrasts of language and reality in many scenes that pit form against thought, classical harmony against postclassical discord. The attempts to close these divides concern reader and historian, not simply Tiberius or Germanicus (seeking, in his vengeance for Teutoburg, to restore the classical). The narrative charts the nuanced development of these, whether it be in the split life of a Petronius or the failed integrative life of Germanicus or perhaps, to step outside of the *Annals*, in the exemplary if tragic life of Agricola.

Nominalism and Idealism in the Funeral of Augustus

The funeral of Augustus has shaped subsequent interpretations of speech because of its position, its structuring about *fama*, and the interpretations of speech and a life that it provides in problematic variety. The historiographical technique of reporting conflicting versions, discussed above in relation to Tiberian election policies, first appears in the reports of men's estimations of Augustus. This instance shares an emphasis on the spoken word. The reader is not presented with three differing accounts of the facts; as so often in Tacitus, it is report itself—judgment and the reception of that judgment—that appears in variety. Whereas the names of candidates had been explored and suppressed, the outset of the *Annals* considers what epithets to apply to the life of Augustus. The *nomina* offered have, however, a narrative ranking—their authorship is noted in a most subjective and self-conscious fashion: Tacitus recounts first the words of the mob (1.9: "plerisque vana mirantibus"), impressed (like some historians—the historiographical point of these notices of source should not be overlooked) by synchronisms (Augustus assuming power and dying on the same day of the year, and, like his father, dying at Nola). A most minimal identification introduces the contrasting group: "at apud prudentis."

The opening of the *Annals* has often been received as a subjective—even cavalier—summary of Roman history, immediately devolving to rumor. Such criticism implies a naive or incompetent historian or, among Tacitus's defenders, elicits comment that the ancient historian was more rhetorician or simply had different standards than the modern. To dispense with these commonplaces, a reconsideration of the opening reveals a number of techniques of thematic anticipation and narrative direction—in sum, the means to open the greater narrative of history. These techniques include an initial and arbitrary compression of time and the eschewal of historical particularity that brings the present to the fore as a reproduction of the issues of the past.

Rumor is not alone in disrupting a neat historical or chronological connection. Speech does not lead to action but to counter-speech, and this is not rebuttal but alternate, subjective version. The extreme and apparently arbitrary compression of time in 1.1 is willful, dramatic, simplistic; replacing all of Livy, it grabs attention. In combination with the abstract nouns for power domination, the opening suggests that temporality will not be a strong or dominant consideration. Despite the annalistic frame, narrative will not flow as the reader of history expects. The text is broken by accusations, by the ruptures and silences of the emperor Tiberius, by his very impeding speech. The opening paragraph prepares for a text that offers very little unfolding. Instead, the reader has to rely on a technique of nominalism that does not inspire belief. Despite the best efforts of commentators, the changes of name for power in the first paragraph are immaterial: the kings' hold over Rome, the series of abstract nouns for subsequent potentates (*potestas, consulare ius, dominatio, potentia*), themselves changes in name, are subsumed in another change of name, the blanketing *nomine principis* of Augustus. Tiberius's own nominalism, his rhetorical practice of employing the same names for different, opposed realities, arises from here, but clearly the dynastic line is not the only connection. Tiberius's relation to words mirrors the opening account of Rome's history. His rupture of history, itself the latest term in the swiftly moving, chronologically ordered succession of abstract nouns for power, attempts to keep names the same.

The first sections of the *Annals* rely self-consciously on the theme of nominalism. When at the end of 1.3 Tacitus has finished the highly compressed account of Augustus's rise to dominance, he calls the Augustan peace not peace but "Domi res tranquillae, eadem magistratuum vocabula." This is a strained antithesis of names and things, for their relation is neither transparent nor opposed. As in Tiberius's speeches, they seem sundered. At this point of restoration Tacitus introduces rumor. His subject is ostensibly Augustus's potential successors, but the reader simply overhears what names, what epithets, Agrippa and Tiberius were called (1.4: "trucem . . . maturum"). In place of the archeology of Thucydides, the historian's compressed and thematically dense revision of the history he will not narrate, the reader has met a shifting series of abstract nouns. In addition, the μετὰ τοῦτο of Thucydides (the chronological suggestion of causation) [27] does not prevail here. Instead, a change of the *nomina* of dominion gives way to the discordant words of the people (1.4: "variis rumoribus differebant"). Upon the death of Augustus rumor runs rampant, despite Livia's orchestration of report. When Tiberius enters, speech is everywhere. He refers (1.6: "vocando") all to the senate. The beginning of 1.7 seems to promise a return to the compressed and swift-moving style of the opening sections ("At Romae ruere in servitium consules patres eques"), but a wealth of turbulent signification upsets such clarity: "lacrimas gaudium questus adulationem miscebant." The preoccupation with words and with words as signs of behavior and intent builds, for what follows is an account of who first swore allegiance ("primi in verba Tiberii Caesaris iuravere"); *vocabat* is again used of Tiberius; then the *verba* of his edict are described.

It might be argued that the rehearsal of the initial, inextricable connection of Tiberius and words results inevitably from an ancient historian working from speeches, from written sources. But the ancient historian removes the signs of his source; Livy reports what he read in an annalist but only infrequently cites his source and, more to the point, represents as action what he has read. Tacitus instead centers on Tiberius and his manipulation of speech and signs: 1.7 continues to tell that he gave the *signum* to the praetorians, wrote letters to the armies, spoke haltingly only in the senate; finally, that he wished to appear to have been called (*vocatus*) to empire. The imperial adulants get this connection immediately: L. Arruntius proposed that the *tituli* of laws and the *vocabula* of conquered peoples be carried in Augustus's funeral procession. The imperial propagandist adds the march of names to the solemn and traditional procession of republican *imagines*. As a narrative of history this would be as misleading as an imperial speech, for the real historian would have to read Marc Antony and civil war for the placard "Egypt." The early use of *nomina* to recount historical development creates a sort of historical nominalism rather than functionalism or essentialism/realism. Names are divorced straightway from their old significance, and the reader becomes wary of their procession. Finally, there is introduced not simply rumor as a historical agent or force but, in the place of chronological sequence and cause, the interplay of speech.

Repeatedly in Tacitus, and especially in these early sections of book 1, paragraphs begin with a notice of speech; what follows is not a movement to action, the expected historical exegesis, but a doubling back to speech. Words bring notice of more words—for example, 1.11 begins "Versae inde ad Tiberium preces"; then comes Tiberius's speech; then the senators' words, tears, prayers (notably Tacitus does not use the words *nomina* or *verba*—Tiberius has his customary effect upon verbal signification). Although the text means that some senators did speak, Tacitus has cloaked this with *adulationem*. This passage comes between Tiberius's summons of the senate to speech and the swearing of the oath of allegiance. The next paragraph (1.8) ranks the beneficiaries of Augustus's will before resuming with various proposals for the funeral.

The conflicting voices of the opening of book 1 gradually fall under the sway of the single character who summons, and often silences, speakers. When the senators approach Tiberius, they have already composed their looks (1.7: "vultuque composito"). Tiberius molds speech and countenance from the start; only future victims fail to control their expressions ("nam verba vultus in crimen detorquens recondebat"). Along with several others, this passage reveals a new ordering or census of Roman society. Like a *decimatio* destroying every tenth soldier, Roman numbers are being reduced, but not by execution of the cowardly. The reader comes to "The nobler they were, the faster they came to prevarications, and duly composed to avoid the show of glee for the death of a prince or regret at the accession of another, they piled together tears and joy, lamentation and flattery" (1.7: "Quanto quis inlustrior, tanto magis falsi ac festinantes, vultuque composito ne laeti excessu principis neu tristiores primordio, lacrimas gaudium, questus adulationem miscebant") after two other rankings: "the readier anyone was for slavery, the more they were rewarded and honored until, enriched under the new arrangement, they preferred the present security to the old perils" (1.2: "quanto quis servitio promptior, opibus et honoribus extollerentur ac novis ex rebus aucti tuta et praesentia quam vetera et periculosa mallent"), and "rare indeed was the man who had seen the republic" (1.3: "quotus quisque reliquus qui rem publicam vidisset"). With their proposals of honors the senators vie for leadership in this new society, which Tiberius directs and rewards. The announcement of the beneficiaries of Augustus's will, with its ranking of heirs (1.8) and the notice of graded payment to the various soldiery, constructs an imperial census. So too Tacitus reads, at 1.11, Augustus's *libellus* of the public resources that likewise quantifies and orders the empire. The narrative notices of 1.2, 4, and 7 express a counterordering, a narratorial voice that works against the narrated, dramatic voices.

The voices that Tacitus lets us overhear at the funeral of Augustus, the interplay of speech that constitutes a means of narrative structure and not simply individual characterization, link speech with the new order of society. A new nominalism forms the *vultus* of that society, as abstract nouns and republican terms cloud the intent and violence of the emperor. But just as naked expression can be wrung from Tiberius under certain peculiar circumstances, so scenes of naked, natural speech rupture the narrative of this new nominalism. Most literally, the words of Cremutius Cordus or the prudent estimation of the critics of Augustus puncture the opaque, imperial fiction. Narrative judgments, too, break through the flattery and difficulty of sources and scenes; they bridge matter and interpretation. The collocation of the themes and rhetorics of speech constitute the particular *animus* of Tacitus. The words of dissenters are well known and wind their way from Cremutius Cordus down to Thrasea Paetus, Seneca, and Petronius—though the last is a special case who points up, if not quite the pomposity, certainly the vanity of the Stoic gestures of withdrawal, silence, and protest. For Tacitus especially, speech constructs society as well as narrative. Opaque and unclassical speech does not simply reflect society; but, because it is exemplary, directs action and behavior. The nominalism of the opening prepares for the strange new society created by imperial speech.

Societies of Speech

Tiberius himself enacts the breakdown of persuasive speech, but other moments in the narrative attempt to use speech to create a rival society. The mutinous speech of the legions illustrates this well: in mutiny, the conflict of natural speech and the artifice of some commanders' speech causes mercurial changes in allegiance. At the extreme remove from Rome and the emperor, Germanicus's speech and interpretation of speech strive to return to classical signification and to the old allegiance and society of his ancestors' armies. Germanicus's style of speech and the effect of speech upon him, like so many of his actions, provide a strong contrast with the immediately preceding Tiberius. But the linguistic contrast will not make him a hero to Tiberius's villain. He is more like a foil to developments of speech and society beyond his ken and control. The movement of speech in Germanicus's case is a striking attempt to remedy the divide created or personified by Tiberius, for Germanicus is a naive reader and speaker. What some have thought, from the point of view again of characterization, to be emotionalism or melodrama is rather a literalism of signs, speech, and symbolism markedly anti-Tiberian, in sympathy however with the naive signification of the informers against Marcellus. The barbarian complicates any easy antithesis, for the painted, duplicitous German speaks genuinely. When he sees the desolation worked by the Romans, he undermines their nominalism by calling it desolation not peace. Evocative of Roman primitivism and yet enemy, Arminius and the barbarians do not pit Germanicus against Tiberius: like Germanicus, they indicate that the changed (overturned) status of Rome (which the narrative has declared in its various censuses) is internal, a problem of *vultus* and *animus*.

Tacitus presents the mutiny of the Pannonian legions as a process of words that contrasts with the preceding scenes of the senate. Simple parallel or parody it cannot be, for the soldiers' camp acts differently. The words of Tiberius, both the letters we read he had sent and his envoys' quotations, do not have the same effect as they did on the senators. Nonetheless, the process of sedition is one of words, first those of Percennius, "dux olim theatralium operarum" (1.16), who personifies the theatrical license that had troubled the senate. The echoes of the senatorial speech on social control, and of Tiberius as director of that speech, center upon this figure: he is "contionabundus" (1.17), whereas Tiberius had been "nusquam cunctabundus nisi cum in senatu loqueretur" (1.7). The narrator similarly provides the corrective census by relating the social ordering of the revolt; it attracted "deterrimum quemque" (1.16).[28]

In the verbal course of the mutiny, speech leads to more speech while contesting earlier speech. Percennius's opening speech takes up the issue of nominalism as defined in the opening scenes of the *Annals*. Mutinous speech recognizes the unclassical divide between words and referents. He complains of continued service and scant rewards, but his language would call Tiberius and Augustus to proper accounts: unremitting service hides beneath a change of names (1.17: "alio vocabulo eosdem labores perferre"); the veterans' discharge is rewarded with an empty word (here, a swamp *per nomen agrorum*). In contrast to the *aestimatio* of Augustus's will, they have a cheap price set on them: "denis in diem assibus animam et corpus aestimari." Percennius wants names to mean what they declare: the pay of a denarius should be precisely that and not the much reduced bronze coin the soldier actually receives after the subtraction for various fees.[29] This protest against counterfeit language has an effect as remarkable and unanimous as Tiberius's masked speech had had on the senators. Significantly, nonverbal display[30] follows immediately (1.18: "Adstrepebat vulgus, diversis incitamentis, hi verberum notas, illi canitiem . . ."). The mixed tears and joy of the senators contrasts with the signals of the soldiers. They offer transparent signs of their motivations.

Such natural moments do not last long in the *Annals*. The natural, unanimous, and anonymous society soon feels its first division: "then their fury drove them to propose to mix three legions into one. Driven apart by rivalry, because each man sought the distinction [of the name for the new legion] for his own legion" ("postremo eo furoris venere ut tres legiones miscere in unam agitaverint. depulsi aemulatione, quia suae quisque legioni eum honorem quaerebant"). Social distinction (*aemulatio*) perturbs their natural egalitarianism; but while they are forming a rival society, their commander Blaesus's eloquence (1.19: "multa dicendi arte") arrests their construction of a tribunal. Eloquence restores society. Like some verbal ebb tide, the mutiny recoils on its most ardent members: those dragged off to punishment call out the *nomina singulorum* (1.21) and then the names of their units; but at this point, with the return of obedience and Roman society, such name calling has lost its power. When the mutiny breaks out again, on the instigation of Vibulenus's melodramatic speech, the soldiers kill one centurion, whom they have named from his own words and action: Lucilius, "whom they had named with soldierly humor 'Strike-again'" (1.23: "cui militaribus facetiis vocabulum 'cedo alterum' indiderant"). A simple reciprocity graces the mutinous' soldiers speech and action. Their *vultus* reflects true emotion; names match the person, and the words *cedo alterum* are literalized, as this centurion alone receives the final blow. So, too, the legions go to meet Drusus advertising their sorry state (1.24: "inluvie deformi et vultu"). Most famously in their reading of the lunar eclipse, the soldiers act as naive, positivist readers: for them a *signum* is a *res*, and their reading is absolutely linear and literal. Whenever the moon's light wanes, they fear all the more and make noise; when it waxes they rejoice. The manipulators of signs and names, the imperial envoys, can divide such readers again into their units. Indeed, now the rhetoric of the centurion Clemens works; *amor obsequii* returns, and the *signa* are divided.

The two audiences for imperial rhetoric have yielded to its effect, although only the second, the soldiery, wears on its *vultus* admission of the nominalism. Tacitus's presentation of mutiny as a verbal, even readerly, process strongly connects social order to speech order. Imperial rhetoric and social division have thwarted an attempt at natural speech and natural society. In the most overt fashion yet, Germanicus and the contemporary mutiny in Germany will associate imperial speech with imperial society. Tacitus has reserved this development of the theme for the climactic position. The Germans revolt at the same time, but Tacitus's disdain for chronology is important. By saying that the German mutiny arose at about the same time and for the same general reasons, the historian strips historical event of particular motivation. Indeed, although he says the reasons for the outbreak were the same (1.31: "Isdem fere diebus isdem causis Germanicae legiones turbatae"), his narrative of cause differs. Tacitus maintains that no single individual caused the mutiny—there will be no analogue to Percennius.

The effect of writing out any individual players is heightened by the narrative's stated surprise that the mutiny occurred anonymously, collectively. Mob action, social turbulence, is becoming even more natural. Collective voices have replaced Percennius's single, lying voice.[31] This mutiny moves straight to violence and then to the creation of its own society: "the soldiers themselves divided the watch, posts, and all the other duties the present circumstances required. For those intent on discerning the motives of the soldiers, this was a special indication of the scope and seriousness of the mutiny: the troops were not split by factions or led by a minority but all together they railed and fell silent, so unanimously and resolutely that one would believe they were being commanded" (1.32: "vigilias, stationes, et si qua alia praesens usus indixerat, ipsi partiebantur. id militaris animos altius coniectantibus praecipuum indicium magni atque inplacabilis motus, quod neque disiecti nec paucorum instinctu, set pariter ardescerent, pariter silerent, tanta aequalitate et constantia ut regi crederes"). The reader is here inscribed in the text in terms that declare the transparency of the soldiers' *animus*. Their words and signs have the same transparency as the mutinous Pannonian legionnaires; on Germanicus's arrival they express a dissonant noise (1.34: "dissoni questus"—like the senators before Tiberius or their Pannonian peers);[32] their signification, even if it deceives Germanicus, is literal, corporal, and naive: feigning to kiss his hand, they stick his fingers in their toothless mouths (1.34).

The speeches of the army and the general will eventually move to a rapport. Indeed, Germanicus's speech tries to shape his soldiery, but for the present, it is as mixed as the legions themselves. Although the narrator's judgment has just established Germanicus's speech, and specifically his relation of *animus* and *vultus*, as polar opposite to that of Tiberius (1.33: "nam iuveni civile ingenium, mira comitas et diversa ab Tiberii sermone vultu"), he elicits from his audience the same response Tiberius had: silence or a slight murmur greets his talk of Augustus's and Tiberius's German victories.[33] The troops' responses again parallel those of the Pannonians; when Germanicus spoke of the mutiny and asked where was their former discipline, "they strip off their clothes and complain of their scars won in war and the marks of the whip; then in mass clamor and with particular terms they reproach [their various tasks]" (1.35: "nudant universi corpora, cicatrices ex vulneribus, verberum notas exprobrant; mox indiscretis vocibus . . . ac propriis nominibus incusant vallum"). Their signification makes the metaphorical literal—like thrusting the commander's hand into their mouths, these men distrust the verbal and enact the metaphorical. Given voice, they would say "Our condition is like our toothless gums, our discipline like our scourged backs"; likewise, they make literal the rhetorical and so call things by their proper names.[34] Germanicus thus faces deconstructers of rhetoric, naive in their signification, who, unlike good speech and good society, will not divide and so remain uncomposed (1.34: "permixta").

In his greatest speech, and the turning point in his relations with the legions, Germanicus succeeds in dividing his audience and returning it to Roman society. In part, the melodramatic parade of his family leaving the camp moves his audience, and this theater is consummated by a speech that employs rhetoric to engage the listeners with the past. Germanicus begins with a rhetorical question, a *dubitatio* over how properly to address the troops,

whose possible solutions are then formulated by a series of historical exempla: "What name shall I give this gathering? The deified
Julius checked a mutiny with a single word, . . . the deified Augustus stared down the legions at Actium" (1.42: "Quod nomen
huic coetui dabo? . . . Divus Iulius seditionem exercitus verbo
uno compescuit, . . . divus Augustus vultu et aspectu Actiacas
legiones exterruit"). At speech's end Germanicus too will transform his audience through direct address; he reads and writes that
his audience has changed its look and intentions (1.43: "Vos, quoque, quorum alia nunc ora, alia pectora contueor . . . dividite").
In the move from hesitation to command, the speaker strives to
attach his audience to the past; this move toward social reintegra-
tion and control asserts the transparent coincidence of thought
and expression. At the outset, according to the speaker, words are
in flux, lacking correspondence to reality. The nominalism and signification of the past were altogether different. Once the troops
have their *vultus* and *animus* changed ("alia . . . ora, alia pectora"),
rhetoric and the Caesars again hold sway.[35] Germanicus has been
given back his ancestral voice, which now determines the soldiers'
actions and emotions: on the return march from the exculpatory
attack upon the enemy, Germanicus loudly and repeatedly declares
that the name of sedition can now be replaced by another—such is
the force of *oblitterandae*, in "voce magna hoc illud tempus oblitterandae seditionis clamitabat" (1.51).

Germanicus has thus succeeded in renaming the legions: their
signa are divided and visible, their *vultus* and *animus* individually
recognizable and malleable. The ambitions of the general's speech
do not stop here. As Tacitus develops the theme of Germanicus's
speech, it becomes more than a reflection of Tiberius's or an evo-
cation of Germanicus's ancestors Augustus and Julius Caesar. In
the scenes that follow his successful speaking and rewriting of the
legions' loyalty, Germanicus becomes a good reader, yet his reading and sign-giving share something of the troubling aspect of
his emperor's. Unquestionably, he is capable of good reading—
Tacitus portrays him in terms that depict his action as a successful readerly process. At times this seems perfectly natural: seeing

eight eagles, Germanicus offers a propitious interpretation; Tacitus repeatedly associates good reading and signification in general with this first stage of Germanicus's career.[36] A slightly epic or classical quality tinges Germanicus's speaking and interpreting: to the *voce magna* of 1.50 should be compared the equally epic *mirumque dictu* which follows shortly on Germanicus's prediction from the sight of the eagles at 2.17. This positive, transparent action attendant upon speech, a rare event in the Tiberian narrative, helps to depict Germanicus as a speaker in search of a classical fusion of form and content and at the same time seems to embolden him in this search, as if this actor begins to believe his lines.

Not content to have men alone obey his words, Germanicus attempts in his further campaigns a rhetorical control not so much of the Germans as of nature. In this narrative the role of countervoice, no longer tenable by an army that has written off mutiny, is taken up by the barbarians. The German Arminius assumes the position of counter-rhetoric, of protest against nominalism, since the German-named Germanicus has now adopted imperial speech. While restless in his use of such nominalism (wherein names reshape things), he does not grasp the essentialism advocated by Arminius (where names transparently arise from and equal things). So the Roman general counsels that, as the land (whose characterizations as swampy, thick, and duplicitous recalls earlier descriptions of speech) favors the Germans, the Romans must take to the sea. This division will bring tempest and confusion to the Romans. But Germanicus seeks a transparent medium; the sea, however, will prove no more legible than the swamp.

In the speeches in which Germanicus tries to convince his troops to adapt themselves to an unfamiliar or even alien medium, a subtext undercuts the rhetoric of Germanicus's policy. Tacitus has used a famous passage of the annalist Claudius Quadrigarius as the inspiration for the structuring rhetoric of these passages, and for specific scenes in more direct detail (in particular, the verbal duel between Arminius and his brother, the Roman legionnaire). Quadrigarius had narrated the duel of a giant Celt with the David-like Manlius Torquatus (*fr.* 10b, Gellius 9.13.4). The Roman succeeds, despite the naked, chanting (*cantabundus*) "Gaul," by using to strategic end his medium stature and especially his short sword. The barbarian, encumbered with massive shield, is never allowed room to station himself.

This passage, classically reworked by Livy, provides arguments and diction for Germanicus's speech to the troops at 2.14. The general is concerned with an argument from terrain; so the speech begins, "Open fields are not the only terrain for the Roman soldier; if reason is brought to bear, he will excel in forest and thicket as well" ("Non campos modo militi Romano ad proelium bonos, sed si ratio adsit, silvas et saltus"). The application of reason that bolsters this thesis is description straight from the prior historians: "there are to be found no immense shields of the enemy or unwieldy spears among the limbs of trees" ("nec enim immensa barborum scuta, enormis hastas inter truncos arborum"). This argument reverses both the natural, traditional attributes of the Germans and Germanicus's own tactics. When he had resolved to go by sea, he had conceded the Germans' advantages: "the forests, swamps, short summer, and early winter aid the Germans. . . . But if we take to the sea, we shall possess it quickly without the enemy's knowledge, at the same time we shall begin the campaign early and convey troops and provisions together" (2.5: "Germanos . . . iuvari silvis, paludibus, brevi aestate et praematura hieme. . . . At si mare intretur, promptam ipsis possessionem et hostibus ignotam, simul bellum maturius incipi legionesque et commeatus pariter vehi").

Germanicus pursues a nonliteral reading here: instead of equating a particular climate and locale with a people, his rhetoric argues that reason can bring all under the Romans' sway. He seems to have forgotten that he thought the sea was fit for Romans (*promptam*). Now he directs reason against nature, not simply the Germans. Varus and his three legions had fallen to the fallacious fields of Teutoburg (1.61: "fallacibus campis . . . visuque ac memoria deformis"); faced with obscurity, Varus perished. Germanicus thinks that obscurity can aid the Romans. Thus he does not simply engage in Tiberian double-speak; he has begun to think rhetorically, postclassically: form need not mirror content, nor rule behavior. Just as Silver epic can now accommodate many genres, so the Roman heavy-armed foot soldier masters all media. Thus the battle depends not on character or fortune but on genre: "and the Germans were no less brave, but they were overcome by the type of battle and of equipment" (2.21: "nec minor Germanis animus, sed genere pugnae et armorum superabantur").

Germanicus's effort to extend Rome fails on several levels; nature, and in particular the ocean, prove implacable and resistant. He fails to revive the exemplum of Torquatus. Despite his characterization as a good reader in 2.20 (the Germans' deceptions are impotent—Caesar knew all, the text declares), three sections later the tempest destroys the fleet; and the scene is one of those whose confusion of media mirrors the murk and mutability of fortune. In addition to enacting this trite locus of the declamatory schools, the natural confusion decocts the general's rationalist rhetoric. Germanicus seems to have been caught up in schoolboy rhetoric —believing he could play Torquatus as he had imitated the words of the Caesars, going one better than Alexander, who was content to stop when he found ocean, although schoolboys delivered *suasoriae* to urge him on. Germanicus has reified these rhetorical exempla and *suasoriae*. But Tacitus has modeled his nature on the state of language and rhetoric at Rome. There may be attempts at classical closure, at formal division and discernment, but ultimately these are unsuccessful. The few who had spoken classically now know better. I reserve the discussion of another classicizing intrusion into the text, the epic gesture of night. For now it is important to understand how Tacitus's descriptions of mob scenes both recreate the obscurity of imperial language and destabilize any assumptions of orderly reading, of transparent signification.

Germanicus's journey to Teutoburg, whose motives and significance Tiberius found dangerous or obscure, is not a mission of expiation, but an exemplar of Germanicus's naive reading. Essentially, the general wishes to read the past. The narrator draws attention to a certain emotionalism behind the curiosity of the general and the soldiers: "Thereupon a longing to discharge the last rites for the commander and his troops took hold of Caesar, the entire army on the scene deeply moved to a state of pity because of their relatives, friends, and finally because of the fortunes of war and the fate of men" (1.61: "Igitur cupido Caesarem invadit solvendi suprema militibus ducique, permoto ad miserationem omni qui aderat exercitu ob propinquos, amicos, denique ob casus bellorum et sortem hominum").[37] Undoubtedly, the psychological temper of the army is significant here. Tacitus had portrayed the army in its slaughter of the Germans as incapable of the gentler emotions. The army's actions swing between pity and pitilessness, the pathetic and the active; sedition, the recall of Agrippina and her entourage, the slaughter likened to civil war, the slaughter of the Germans, and Teutoburg display an alternation of emotionalism and emotionlessness as the army responds or fails to respond to words and signs.

The description of Teutoburg, however, presents itself as a readerly encounter. Instead of objective description, the narrative joins item and interpretation, as for example in 1.61: "bleaching bones were lying in the middle of the field, scattered about or heaped together where men had run or stood together" ("medio campi albentia ossa, ut fugerant, ut restiterant, disiecta vel aggerata"). The reader is supplied with an interpretative narrator. To revisit Teutoburg is to read signs, and in this first passage the signs unmistakably correspond to the actions of the past. Yet the final reading of Teutoburg obscures the certainty of signs, for the soldiers who so accurately read the positions of the camp and the groupings of their predecessors are not allowed a final, transparent reading; their own emotions, the product of this reading, are similarly, sympathetically confused. The contrast with the scene of reading the whitening bones is the starker for the echo of the repeated *ut* and participle, but this time no separate reading is possible: "no one knew whether he buried foe or friend; they entombed all as if they were friends or relatives; though passion rose now against the enemy, at the same time they grieved and were angry" (1.62: "nullo noscente alienas reliquias an suorum humo tegeret, omnes ut coniunctos, ut consanguineos, aucta in hostem

ira, maesti simul et infensi condebant"). Especially in this moment
of closure, the narrator emphasizes emotional confusion. Scenes
to come will replay Teutoburg, both in the attempted distinct
reading of a scene and in the ensuing unclassical confusion. A turbulent reality resists the naive reading of Germanicus, as Germany
seems returned to its natural murk.

Germanicus's rhetorical policy is first put to the test in Caecina's battle in the swamp-plain. Here the Roman soldiers have
to adapt themselves to different terrain (1.63); in Caecina's second battle, after a march through slippery country, the soldiers
must learn to perform different tasks: they will have to fight and
construct bridges at the same time. Tacitus describes the first encounter as another scene of confusion: "Then the cavalry was
thrown into confusion by the new battleline; auxiliary cohorts
were dispatched but were overwhelmed by the retreating column and added to the melee; they were being driven into a
swamp, known ground for the enemy, unfavorable for the unac-
quainted, until Caesar brought up his extended legions" ("Tunc
nova acie turbatus eques, missaeque subsidiariae cohortes et fu-
gientium agmine impulsae auxerant consternationem; trudeban-
turque in paludem gnaram vincentibus, iniquam nesciis, ni Caesar
productas legiones instruxisset").

In the second battle (1.64) terrain again favors the weapons,
bodies, and tactics of the Cherusci. The Romans try to fix a camp
in the swamp, but every item of the scene, Roman and enemy, the
fight and the construction, water and land, even noise (1.64: "mis-
cetur operantium bellantiumque clamor") are confused. Indeed,
the barbarians adapt nature to their needs. Night had intervened
to save the Romans, when by working and diverting water upon
their foe, the Germans turn night into day, camp into swamp. The
legions have returned to the confused noise and uncertain light of
night and day, in short, to that state that marked their mutiny and
from which they were hastening to flee.[38]

Clear and penetrating knowledge does not characterize any
of these parties for long; those who drove Caecina's men into
the swamp took advantage of their knowledge of the country,

but Germanicus's policy, his intelligence, will on later occasions prevail. Confusion and knowledge are a recurrent, structuring antithesis, a thematic undercurrent common to Tacitus's descriptive mob scenes, but these are linked to and through Germanicus. They radically revise his particular reading and interpretation. The storm that overtakes Vitellius marching the second and fourteenth legions from campaign has an appearance as mixed and indistinguishable as the war dead of Teutoburg:

eadem freto litori campis facies, neque discerni poterant incerta ab solidis, brevia a profundis. sternuntur fluctibus, hauriuntur gurgitibus; iumenta sarcinae corpora exanima interfluunt, occursant. permiscentur inter se manipli, modo pectore, modo ore tenus exstantes, aliquando subtracto solo disiecti aut obruti. non vox et mutui hortatus iuvabant adversante unda; nihil strennus ab ignavo, sapiens ab imprudenti, consilia a casu differre; cuncta pari violentia involvebantur. (1.70)

[The plains of sea and shore had the same outlook, flux could not be distinguished from the sure and steady, shallows from the deep. Waves tossed all about and all was plunged into swirling depths; cattle, pack animals, human bodies intermingled lifeless, collided. The companies were all mixed together, now chest deep, now up to their mouths in water, sometimes thrown apart or overrun without any footing at all. Words and mutual encouragement were no avail against the adverse flood. No difference between the brave and the coward, the skilled and the rash, plan and chance. All was swept along with an undiscriminating violence.]

Night intervenes here too, and light will restore the land. The parallelisms of diction, especially of verbs signifying confusion or mixture, and of narrative elements such as the unavailing role of speech, the intervention of night, and the final social ordering (here a nonordering, as *quisque strenuissimus* cannot be known and is immaterial) establish this scene as one of social and not just natural breakdown. Where in mutiny the troops lacked their *signa* and bared their bodies, here they pass a night unclothed and weaponless ("magna pars nudo aut mulcato corpore").

Despite its natural confusion, the storm of the *Aeneid*, like the huge natural barbarian in Livy and Quadrigarius, delineates the foe from the Roman. Indeed, Virgil can have his reader see the fate of individuals. Tacitus has clouded both classical models; the classical subtext creates an expectation of order restored that the *Annals* never produces.[39] The tempest affects Germanicus's own interpretative faculties; he swings to an opposite extreme of interpretation. Faced with the signs of the misfortune, he disbelieves words. The reports that some have been saved do not move him; Tacitus reports that Caesar did not believe the troops delivered ("nec fides salutis") until he saw them. The imperial speaker, here simply called "Caesar," just as Tacitus had identified him when praising his insight into the German's plans, now resorts to nonverbal signification, like his troops at the beginning of his command who thrust his fingers into their mouths.

The course of Germanicus's reading charts a move from naive signification to the assertion of imperial rhetoric and to its own undoing. But just as the native and the Roman are categories that shift in these sections about mutiny and German resistance, Germanicus's speech and hermeneutics do not progress in a linear fashion. On occasion, Arminius and the Germans in general act and sound like old Romans—this is part of the Romans' peculiar fascination for a people they judged to be martial, primitive, and ethnically simple. The mirror that Tacitus brings to bear on the foe is essentially a linguistic and rhetorical one. That is, Tacitus offers a rhetorical understanding of social, natural, and personal conflict. Thus he is not, as he has been characterized, a weak military historian or a psychological historian: the author is not "interested" primarily in particular types of people, minds, or emotions, but rather his text presents a vision of conflict enmeshed and reflected in the distance of words from meaning.

Arminius, for example, when contrasted to Segestes, who would lead his people back to obedience to Rome, is the "turbator Germaniae" (1.55) and speaks a most inflammatory rhetoric (1.59.4: he is not conducting war *adversus feminas gravidas*). By contrast, Segestes longs for the ways of old and speaks a simple Latin: "vetera novis et quieta turbidis antehabeo" (1.58). But when Arminius, having begun conversation from the subject of his brother's loss of an eye (2.9: "deformitas oris"), calls the Roman soldier's rewards for merit (*praemium*) a cheap payoff for slavery ("vilia servituti pretia") and counters his brother's list of pay and military insignia with native, family virtues (2.10: "fas patriae, libertatem avitam, penetralis Germaniae deos, matrem precum sociam"), the German loyalist speaks a natural not mercantile and social language. Whose is the deformity of speech? Arminius's speech does agitate, but it strips away the nominalism of the emperors.

In the *Annals*, language itself appears transparent and natural, classical in its fusion of form and content, precisely at moments of greatest social discord that verge on anonymity and even unanimity. *Animus* can be revealed by the foe, but the Roman must wait for mob scenes, mutiny or funeral, to speak classically. Germanicus's attempt to speak like Julius Caesar or to glare like Augustus reveals the limits of classical speech and gesture. So, too, his wife elicits classical signification upon her mourning procession from Brindisi to Rome. This scene reunites speaker and audience —in particular, the line of Germanicus with its naive signification and the Roman audience, and, by conspicuous absence, Tiberius.

Upon the news of Germanicus's death, before the magistrates or the senate can speak their will, the people take a holiday: "everywhere was silence and mourning, artificial show of grief was nowhere to be found; and while people indulged in the marks and costume of mourning, they grieved even more bitterly in their hearts" (2.82: "passim silentia et gemitus, nihil compositum in ostentationem; et quamquam neque insignibus lugentium abstinerent, altius animis maerebant"). The mixture of silence and noise (Tacitus's oxymoron)—familiar from, among other scenes, the senators' reaction to Tiberius's indifference to Hortensius's plea— the lack of "composition," and the coincident if not proportional relation of expression and intent, characterize this as anti-Tiberian signification. At this point rumor intervenes: Germanicus is believed to be alive, "iuvat credulitatem nox." Tiberius does nothing. Finally, the people grieve even more bitterly on the dispersion of the false rumor. There is something strange in the proportionality of the people's grief.[40] While manifestly anti-Tiberian, their emotions have been affected by his speech and manner; they do not achieve a classical harmony; rather, their unaffected (natural) and customary signs of grief do not match their actual bitter emotion ("altius animis maerebant").[41]

At the funeral of Augustus, that prelude to the *Annals*, free and emotional speech was heard. Throughout the works of Tacitus, imminent death or the funeral itself can occasion free and spontaneous speech. But both here in this scene of the news of Germanicus's death and at the people's reception of the widowed Agrippina, spontaneous expression does not correspond to true emotion. This is even more startling as Tacitus reports a graded, proportional response to the death of Germanicus: individuals decreed him honors in proportion to their love for him (2.83) — one of the few occasions when public expressions of friendship and thanks reflect genuine *animus*. Tacitus locates in Tiberius the change in men's speech, for between the city's reception of Germanicus's death and of Agrippina, the historian relates that Tiberius declined honors proposed for himself. He refused to be called "parens patriae, dominus," or to have his actions called divine: "this led to a straitened and slippery speech under the leadership of one who feared freedom of speech and hated flattery" (2.87: "unde angusta et lubrica oratio sub principe qui libertatem metuebat adulationem oderat"). Individuals' *amor* for Germanicus has had its medium; feigned or real, passion for Tiberius will find no straightforward expression.

This uncertainty about expression seems to have infected the people: upon Agrippina's arrival the grieving knew not whether to weep or keep silence (3.1). The audience has adopted a rhetorical figure, a *dubitatio* that impedes while it considers the alternation of groans and silence at Germanicus's death. Spontaneous expression is being checked. A Tiberian composition marks the party of Agrippina. Her fleet arrives, not swiftly, but "cunctis ad tristitiam compositis" (3.1), and Agrippina herself had delayed at Corcyra, "componendo animo" (3.1). On the other hand, the audience reacts individually, spontaneously, and proportionately. Along the road to Rome each town sacrifices in accord with its resources; individuals weep "as each desired, without pretense, for all knew Tiberius could not hide his joy at the demise of Germanicus" ("3.2: ut cuiquam libitum flentes; aberat quippe adulatio, gnaris omnibus laetam Tiberio Germanici mortem male dissimulari"). Death provides the single moment of genuineness and insight. Even here Tiberius's *vultus* cannot be read directly; the crowd sees through his disguise, and so just later (3.3) Tiberius and Livia fear to show their *vultus*. But the uncomposed crowd makes the day of burial, like the army's long nights in Germany, now quiet now noisy (3.4).

Before the mask of Tiberius, the crowd's confused, nonverbal signification has become genuine, spontaneous expression. Tacitus depicts nature as sympathetic to this divorce of *animus* and *vultus*. Once the historian has established that words do not correspond to thoughts or deeds, he seems to displace this schism onto the realm of nature. Germanicus's longing to extend Rome figures the effort to find Rome, to have the word "Roman" correspond to its old significance. This longing for a reordering of society recurs both in those overt constitutions of natural (mutinous) societies and in the commander's own attempts to make Germany Roman. The nature of Germany proves as resistant to Germanicus's rhetorical policy as it had to Quinctilius Varus's legions. Tacitus's coloring of Germanicus and his campaign as a readerly and rhetorical process has particular resonances: the reader of the *Annals* sees one character attempting to rewrite classical historiography, here the subtexts of Livy and the *Aeneid*, of the Caesars' speeches to their armies, and also the historical exempla of Quinctilius Varus and Manlius Torquatus. But despite his efforts at classical speech and gesture, Germanicus succumbs to Tiberius's vice. Rather somewhat worse, as a naive reader he believes the nominalism with which the emperor shrouds reality. Searching for a word to recall his troops to loyalty and to classical precedent, his *dubitatio* becomes a sort of *aporia*—rhetorical doubt passes to real inability. In his efforts to hold nature to his verbal policy, Germanicus only demonstrates anew the rift between imperial speech and reality.

Tacitus uses a technique of classical gestures that arouse an expectation of order, of concordant form and thought. Germanicus himself plays a classical *imperator*, but he has only the name and not the power or triumph of the long-gone republican *imperator*. By such techniques Tacitus makes of Germanicus something of a tease for the reader. Both readers' enthusiasm for Germanicus as an antidote to Tiberius and critics' subsequent revision of this melodramatic actor are then both half-right, for Tacitus associates Germanicus's journey through the narrative with the reader's. But Germanicus goes awry, misled by his own classical rhetoric. Similarly, the text has other classical gestures that create the expectation of epic and orderly outcome. Chief among these is night, for on many occasions night appears to punctuate the narrative and to save the Romans. There is a classical, epic, formulaic quality to these notices. *Nox* appears early in the sentence, delivering the narrative from despair or openly assisting: on the exculpatory attack upon the Germans' "Iuvit nox" (1.50); to the tired commander after he had slipped out (2.13: "Nocte coepta . . .") in disguise to learn the sentiments of his troops, "Nox eadem laetam Germanico quietem tulit" (2.14); for Caecina slipping beneath the attack of the Cherusci, "Nox demum inclinantis iam legiones adversae pugnae exemit" (1.64). Night seems the time not simply of rest but of relief from conflicting signs: Germanicus can learn the *animus* of his men, Caecina rests on what he thinks is the firm land of his camp. But the Cherusci will flood his camp, whereas nature itself will upset Germanicus's clear reading of his troops and his clear knowledge of his enemy (2.20). Night becomes a misleading marker in the text, for it does not deliver Caecina.[42] Instead, an unclassical night and dream succeed: "Nox per diversa inquies . . . apud Romanos . . . interruptae voces. . . . ducemque terruit dira inquies" (1.65). Night, like nature, becomes more difficult of interpretation, for some. The soldiers mistake the confused night of the eclipse; the Roman mob mistakes rumor for truth in the night after the report of Germanicus's death (2.82: "iuvat credulitatem nox").

Night is a small textual gesture but one resonant with sympathetic nature and with classicism (epicism). Tiberius and his agent Sejanus subvert that intimate and direct time; due to Sejanus's enmity, Nero finds no refuge in night (4.60: "[Nero] seu loqueretur seu taceret iuvenis, crimen ex silentio, ex voce. ne nox quidem secura")—as his wife reported all. Nero himself literally adopts the attack upon a classical, harmonious symbol when he roves the night in servile disguise; others imitate him, until "in modum captivitatis nox agebatur" (13.25). Only exceptionally can night signify directly: upon Nero's bidding, Britannicus sings, but a song signifying his expulsion from his father's seat. Night assists this freedom of speech (13.15: "unde orta miseratio manifestior, quia dissimulationem nox et lascivia exemerat"). Under Nero, however, night becomes the occasion for crime. Paris, for example, enters the imperial dining hall "compositus ad maestitiam" and far in the night (13.20: "Provecta nox erat") to denounce Agrippina. The night of her shipwreck wears a serene face (14.5: "Noctem sideribus inlustrem et placido mari quietam quasi convincendum ad scelus dii praebuere"). The Neronian narrative's equation of *nox* and *dolus* or disaster inverts the interpretability of signs. The reader of epic finds a narrative auspicy in the formulaic appearance of night. The reader of the *Annals* learns to distrust such classical markings; night and classical gestures in general only fool the credulous.

Tacitus does not call for the return of the republic, and his own style does not model classical simplicity or transparency of signification. To sense the distance of the past is not, however, to lament the loss of the past. Tacitean style, like the narrative of which it is a part, draws attention to the alienation of thought and expression in the imperial age. This is polemical but not nostalgic. One more Tacitean formula illuminates here. Whereas Thucydides depends on the chronologically and causally ordering μετὰ τοῦτο,

Tacitus violates his ostensibly annalistically ordered narrative with the imprecise introductory and transitional phrase *per idem tempus*. The narrative does not allow events to hang upon chronology as explanation. Cause, event, and their expression are far more enmeshed. Augustus, Tiberius, and their successors have sundered the unity of reality. Tacitus takes their imperial and imperialistic language as a synecdoche for the historical process, the changed society that is Rome.

Tacitus's appeal as a historian stems from this synthetic account of change that enmeshes the linguistic and the social. Now it does not have many admirers, for of course it is elitist and partial in its strong foregrounding of the words and self-presentation of the capital's educated elite. And yet Tacitus has a rhetorical allure for the historian: the state of society can be glimpsed from texts, and from speeches within them, and especially from the propagandistic texts of the autocrat. Imperial language may have such power, but history is the rewriting of this doublespeak.

For Tacitus, who rose to prominence as an advocate and speaker in the courts under Domitian, Latinity of style did not mark quite the same issues as it had for Seneca or Phaedrus. The linguistic other, the threat to Latinity, is not the barbarian or the plebeian but the imperial speaker. Resuscitation of Cicero's style, or even the pretense that speakers and writers replay the classical, seems a vain pursuit to an inquirer who has come to question the power of speech and rhetoric as an orderly and ordering practice. In his representation of linguistic anxieties and pathologies, the historian has much in common with Petronius, and not simply a disdain for the overwrought complaints and stylistic pretensions of the Stoic senatorial martyrs and perhaps Seneca in particular. The historian's and the novelist's large literary projects explode the pretenses of speech—the longing for classicism, the easy diatribes against contemporary improprieties of speech, the persistent fiction that speech orders society. Both found their fiction in the disorder, the chaos, of language. In this regard they are profoundly antirhetorical writers, unlike Seneca or even his nephew the poet Lucan. Petronius has an even more fecund resistance to epic closure and rhetoric's claims to create society, and in his *Satyricon* the linguistically despised and critical are far more problematic characters.

6

The Rival in the Text

LIKE BROWNING'S POEM "The Tomb at St. Praxed's," Petronius's errant narrative presents plot and style as a pilgrimage.[1] The bishop of Browning's poem follows the lead of many aspirants to Latin culture: he tries to write himself into the inscribed record through censure of a rival's diction.[2] Similarly, Petronius's free but disreputable heroes, Encolpius, Giton, and Ascyltos, insistently deride the speech of the freedmen who are their dinner companions. This dispossessed trio hopes their speech will gain them a return of the freeborn's lost birthrights: power, property, office, and the voice of command. The reader mirrors the characters' placement as latecomers to classical Latin and as voyeurs in a slightly perplexed reading of scenes of removed hearing and writing. We seem to read, as Petronius's characters wander, to close the divide that separates us from the epic and the classical.

Petronius's narrator, narratorial voice, and narratological framing transit between *Latinitas* and *vernaculitas*, *libertas* and *libertinitas*. As in Tacitus's presentation of imperial speech, the classical recedes, as final signification and resolution become more and more enmeshed in a recurrent presentation of language itself as double and doubling. We read easily and surely the double of the classical that is the freedmen's vernacular, but the classical moments and gestures of Petronius's text—the allusions to epic, the high tone of criticism—cannot stand on their own. This compromising of the claims of Latinity is not the same as the linguistic anxiety of the characters, the wannabes of high culture. It is, however, kindred as the text fails to maintain linguistic partition.

The *Satyricon*'s complex thematizing of the types and roles of language involves far more than the "errors" of phonology, morphology, and syntax catalogued by scholars who were intent to characterize the speech of the freedmen as something distinct from the narrator's Latin.[3] This reductive reading had attempted to contain the errancy of the *Satyricon*: if the text contained the vulgar speech of its characters by means of its framing narrative comments, it too could be a classic. The novel thus would exhibit the split perception of the imperial age (and the universal age of postclassical scholarship): unable to maintain the high style of Virgil, it was at least a critical age, able to value the epic and self-conscious about the contemporary failure to meet this standard. However, the text's concerns with speech, its exegesis, and its imitation cannot be so strictly polarized into narrator and narrated, freeborn and freedman storytellers. In short, at its very beginnings, the imperial literary experience was not content to indict the contemporary and replay the classical. Whereas Pliny or the Senecas tried to present a seamless continuity with the past, for Tacitus and Petronius there was no return to the classical.

Undoubtedly, the text baits the reader with judgments of linguistic inferiority. The scorn of the freeborn is undisguised, for example, in episodes that cite and interpret inscriptions. In their loose syntax (e.g., *quisquis* for *si quis*), pedestrian subjects (the master's calendar, a guest's rental advertisement for his apartment), violation of genre (at the symposium, Trimalchio has his epitaph and even his will recited, whereas the proper genre for dinner is the drinking song or, since Plato, the quasi-philosophical discussion of love), and needless exegesis (the overlabeling of Trimalchio's pictures or his household utensils), linguistic transgression tempts us to read the whole work as parody of freedmen culture, itself an unselfconscious caricature of free culture. The contemporary social ambitions of Roman freedmen, visible especially in the funerary monuments they were erecting, have spilled over into the conversation of this text. But as we have seen in the cases of the freedman Phaedrus and of the *grammatici* who taught Latin, anxieties about Latinity cluster about but are not exhausted in the role of that peculiar Roman, the slave turned citizen whose difference from the freeborn was not visible, unlike the toga he now wore by right, and, more essentially, unlike the language in which he might well, with the help of Hellenistic scholarship, be more expert than the native.[4]

Roman culture saw the freedman as a linguistic bastard and as a scapegoat for other social transgressions. Critics of the *Satyricon* have focused on the freedmen because the dinner party of the arch-freedman Trimalchio is the longest extant fragment, because it is brilliant writing, and because this text and its linguistic artistry anticipate and represent the alleged "descent" from Latinity to Romance. By positing lacunae, by asserting two distinct levels of Latinity, and by seeking lost sources, scholars' readings of Petronius's scenes have duplicated the fragmentary quality of the manuscripts and overlooked the thematic and structural similarities of a number of scenes that foreground the conflict of different modes of speech and create affinities beyond integrity of plot or style. Further, all the speakers, not simply the ex-slaves, attempt to shift discourse, to speak like their betters, to appropriate the poetry of high culture, even to speak of education. All ape the classical, and ultimately all fail.

What emerges is not mock-epic but the mockery of the present belated age's desire to mimic epic. In addition, the power of the text itself to shift discourse, to keep sections, episodes, characters, registers, even diction separate, begins to slip. Most overtly, the freeborn narrator and his companions stand in for the classical. They present themselves as the champions of literature, proper speech, and nativist scorn, while in their wandering adventures, in their Virgilian diction, and even in the names of some of the characters they meet, they seem to play at epic roles. But in a work that declares and enacts the failings of speech ambitions and grows torpid and nauseating in scenes of the monumentality and sluggishness of an appropriated Latinity, the sense of distance from the classical comes to infect the narratorial voice as well. Characters and the text as a whole replay upper-class speech events—symposiastic, epic, scholarly speech—but both ruin this mimicry through contamination.

As in Browning's "The Tomb at St. Praxed's," a first reading reassures readers that we know exactly where we are, at an Italian church before the two rivals' tombs, or by chance at a vulgar dinner party, confident in our detection of the linguistic flaw that reveals ambition and improper origin. If we do not recognize the church's name, if we are not sure of the bishop's, nonetheless we can read wherein the prior writer has failed. From the rival's miswriting of his Latin epitaph and the bishop's and the poet's rewriting, we recognize the poem's composition. Similarly, the linguistic and social blunders of Trimalchio or any of his fellows scream out to the connoisseur of republican Latin, especially because the author has provided critic and critical audience within the text. The sordid purposes of the language of these freeborn critics, however, along with their inescapable errancy, destabilize their confident, superior, and central position.

On one level, the inscribed criticism of this text foils the characters' attempts to shift their discourse. The derision or ironic wonder that the text reports as the narrator's reaction to the diners' efforts at poetry or literary criticism deflates their ambitious language. Amid the ambitious efforts of the speakers—reciting poetry, disparaging contemporary education and its teachers—intrude monumental errors of genre: they speak riddles or sing tunes from the mime. In brief, they indulge in linguistic kleptomania, appropriating and sullying all levels of discourse, which amalgamation the text parallels in its mixture of the high and the low, and in the transgressions of the freeborn characters who scurry up and down the social ladder, as runaway slaves or, later, as wealthy travelers. Their efforts to rise are as unconvincing, at least to the reader, as their literary and social criticism. After all, we do not need mendicant rhetoricians to know that Trimalchio's verse is lousy.

In search of money or dinner, the free transgress by a change of dress or a show of educated speech while the speech acts of the freedmen spin on and on under the unrelenting stimulus of linguistic inferiority. It is an upper-class commonplace that one can read the hellish state of contemporary society from the novel, errant ways in which the lower classes speak and dress. They know

not their old station. In Petronius's text, however, the sociolect of
the lowborn gradually taints the freeborn. The forms, idiom, and
syntax of the freedmen are heard upon the lips of the free.[5] As they
don the dress of slaves, their language, too, suffers a descent. Of
course, when Trimalchio crosses alimentary and linguistic taboos,
constructing menus for both, he does not know what belongs
where. The menu that is the *Satyricon* does not straightforwardly
chart the irruption of the low or the colloquial or forecast the
first stirrings of Late Latin and Romance. Rather, Petronius self-
consciously presents the rupture of the classical by countervoices.
For all its proclamations of difference and distance, this text persis-
tently returns to the low. The fragmentary state of the manuscripts
has not produced literary disconnection; rather, numerous literary techniques highlight and thematize a sense of incompleteness.
This chapter describes some of the techniques by which Petronius
succeeds in redirecting the reading of bad taste. By interrogating
the categories of taste and tastelessness, Petronius himself escapes
the constraints of the genres of satire or mock-epic.

The intertwined types of passing in the text and of the text
perform various resistances, various evasions of what is better
termed upper-class silencing than simply the classical. The text
warily eludes threats of silence. High style would preclude the
very possibility of this text; the canonized heights of Augustan literary culture would seem to have left no place for epic, or perhaps
for satire. And so within the text we see the declaimers thrust out
of the performance hall and the nauseated and culture-shocked
silences of the free guests. The freedmen worry about saying the
wrong thing, but the free are as tongue-tied as Encolpius is impotent. The poet Eumolpus is stoned into silence. The rhetorician
Agamemnon is not allowed to say a word at dinner. Petronius associates repressive speech with the free and the classical; for it is
epic poetry and oratory that are blocked and blocking. Continu-
ous, unblocked speech, even though it is marked as lower-class
garrulity, comes from the freedmen. The speech of the free leads
to silences, whereas the freedmen traffic in speech.

This does not fit parody so much as deconstruction, which

is to say that the relations of speech are not one way. Satire may present deviance from the norm as the essentially derisible, but laughter and contempt taint the norms of the critical voices in Petronius's text. The fictions of the free are seen not as grand conventions but as unworkable repressions. In contemporary ancient terms, the form of the text is a mutation of *recusatio*—the alleged refusal by the Augustan poets to accept the grand manner, high style, and its genres. This too had been a ploy of evasion; the emperor's request politely refused and enacted. The silencing that doing the lord's bidding and replicating the past's generic dictates constitutes is rhetorically set against the autonomous genuine voice. The freedmen joust for the authority to speak in a sort of shadow fight, but the free emerge from a silent stupor only to be compromised by their speech.

This chapter has a threefold structure: it treats the pressures on the freedmen's stories (their collective drive to speak), the mercantilization of their language, and the mutation of the host from *magister bibendi* to *magister dicendi*. All three manifest *contaminatio*—I use an ancient term for literary or sexual staining, which the text uses once and which covers the blending and ruining of prior models. I conclude by considering the complex search for credibility, for material, and for closure that animates and connects the wanderings of this text and also deconstructs the classical fixity of linguistic, literary, and social censure. The frustrated, interrelated quests within the text (e.g., the speakers' for Latinity and credibility, the narrator's for virility) reinforce both the author's and the audience's sense of alienation from the classical.

The offensive character of the *Satyricon* widely felt but little discussed is its structure. Editors have sought to fix structural problems by alleging that the lacunae were once the transitions to the now disjointed sections. In addition, intertextual allusions and the notes of interrelation have been dismissed (some no doubt rightly) as the glosses of a dim-witted scribe. Whereas the text we have is a portion of a much larger work and has been excerpted (two manuscript traditions can be compared), these facts should not be projected onto the movement of the text. Scenes start abruptly, and so the editors posit lacunae. But the nuanced relations of the parts of a long literary work, signaled by transitions and formulae, belong especially to epic; epic gestures such as introductory formulae and typical scenes communicate an orderly, literary partition. The parts are easily deemed parts, easily separable and stratifiable; the interrelation of these parts in some ways equals the meaning of the whole. In Greek drama, for instance, speech and speeches are separable, making points of view discernible; arguably, the chorus attempts several collective readings before reaching the final synthesis of closure. This may well be a misleading account of how the chorus functions or how a drama means; but speech itself is identifiable, by actor, role, convention, meter, music, dialect, stylization. And whereas drama can invert all these easy identifications, the *Satyricon* confounds such literary partition and at the same time teases along expectations of literary opening and closure.[6]

In recompense for the "immorality" of the text, positive readings of Petronius have celebrated the work as literary showmanship combined with social indictment and have found as its virtue, when social indictment seemed unappealing snobbery, estheticism (a morality of taste). These readings essentially cordon off the language of the low characters as the recreation of a real, and hence vital, phenomenon. This study addresses the text's invitations to speak, to converse, to be silent, and the implications of these for the subjects, tone, registers, idiom, and syntax of different voices of the text. The linguistic prejudice that spurs on the characters could be reduced to the following ratios and metaphors: grammaticality:deviance::old:contemporary::socially high:socially low. Yet this proportion becomes more and more unstable as it gains more members and tries to structure other relations. The contemporary fails to divide into grammatical (learned) and semi- or illiterate, and perhaps, too, the proportion fails to be extended to audience:characters. I do not try to isolate or valorize the members of these proportions in some esthetic hierarchy, because the techniques of linguistic relations undermine the distinct vantage point necessary for snobbery. In the place of classical partition and subordination, there is a society of reading whose relations to texts, literary and social, transgress convention and expectation.

The Traffic of Libertine Speech

The questions of this chapter are, then: What samples of speech performance, speech acculturation, and speech criticism does the text present? How is speech about speech foregrounded? Ultimately, what society(ies) does speech construct in the *Satyricon*? I begin with a small set of linguistic items so as to demonstrate *contaminatio*—an effect and a series of techniques wherein the vulgar refuses to be contained. What is spoiled is the high stance of the narrator, the text's centering frame, from which censure devolves and which sets the narrator and the reader at a critical distance from the narrated.

In particular, features of vulgar style infect the narratorial voice.[7] Of course, narrative and frame will share a host of common items; the measure of their aberrations, the degree to which style is internally and perceptibly differentiated, is a commonplace technique of normative criticism, taken to extremes in Petronius's case with a disregard for problems such as sample size.[8] I chart instances where the narrator picks up some novel linguistic item introduced in a speech. This subtle technique could be spillover (an inadvertent repetition of diction in adjacent sentences or paragraphs, or the epitomator's reuse of a model's word in a different context). It may be in part a conversational technique in which a speaker responds to another speaker by adopting his or her terms. You say "subtext," and I abandon "model" so as to be conversant. But in narrative, especially in one that allegedly contrasts the sociolinguistic register of narrator with the narrated, this stylistic infection has other significances. Hugh Kenner noticed that the narrator in Joyce's *Ulysses* seems swayed by a proximate character's diction or syntax. Joyce shifts the focus, complicates the viewpoint of the narrator as the interior perspective and language

of Bloom or Molly temporarily becomes fused with the narrator (for example, in the Eumaeus episode [Bloom with Stephen
Dedalus] the narrator's use of polysyllables makes him sound like
Bloom).[9] Petronius also shifts perspective so as to play with narrative conventions of authority and objectivity, but not by such
a sympathetic, occasional seduction of the narratorial voice. Borrowings of diction and idiom ally the *Satyricon*'s narrator to the
narrated objects of his despite; thus the language of the freedmen
wanders and so sullies the self-alleged independence of the freeborn narrator.[10] *Contaminatio* is an appropriate term for that sullying of narrative distance that at the same time vitiates the stance
of the narrator and enacts the vital vulgarity of the language of the
freedmen storytellers.[11]

Petronius's textual strategy, of course, does not simply pit
the multiple narrators of the stories against the containing narrator of the entire text. In their ambitious speech the freedmen
appropriate their betters' conventions, roles, texts. In turn, their
betters cannot keep their inherited language free from the libertine. Most significantly, the narratorial voice does not sustain any
serene distance, just as the invoked Homeric names and accom-
panying structures (e.g., the beguiling lover named Circe, or the
epithet Polyaenus given to Encolpius, or the episodes of *katabasis*
and *ekphrasis*) do not contain the *Satyricon*'s characters and esca-
pades within an epic sphere.[12] The freedmen's transgressive speech
thus replays and reinforces the ubiquitous *error* of the *Satyricon* —
that wandering of language, genre, sources and subtexts, travel,
and characters' judgments and actions.[13]

The socially inferior, textually subordinated speech of the
freedmen affects the language of the narrator, and of each other.
Most noticeably, by borrowing and trumping each other's motifs, diction, and syntax, each speech becomes parody and parodying. The reuse of certain mannerisms renders these and their
speakers trite. The repeated attempt at polite speech and the repeated irruption of a low pronunciation, for example, makes
the faux pas collective; the usage is identified not as individual
aberration but as vulgarism or libertinism. By spilling over into

the narratorial voice, these items join the narrator to the un-
distinguished society. In addition, to the degree that the narratorial voice is Encolpius, his assumption of subservient roles—
pathic homosexual, freeloader-parasite, counterfeit branded fugi-
tive slave, legacy hunter—confuses his own identity and the authority of the narratorial voice. He wears so many clothes and
shares so many cloaks that it is little wonder he has succeeded in
staining his free birth.

The metaphor of *contaminatio* comes from the poet Eumolpus (the final literary guide, pedagogue, and freeloader of the
text), who says, ironically for the readers of the *Satyricon*, that he
will not allow the sailors to contaminate (stain/bugger) freeborn
men. Eumolpus makes no credible champion of the freeborn (and
those freeborn have disguised themselves as slaves to escape the
notice of the ship's owners, from whom they had stolen something, it's not clear what, in an earlier, lost episode).[14] Thief and
corrupter of the poet Lucan, corrupter of his free wards, lecherous
of Encolpius's Giton, and eventual impostor and legacy hunter,
the poet Eumolpus assumes a high tone that wins few adherents.
Just as his audiences forsake and attack him, few allies come to
help the advocate of the stowaways. As surely as with Eumolpus's
direct speech and with Encolpius's dress or sexuality, the speech
and narrative of the narrator Encolpius represents the failure of
this text to hold to a high style.

The repetitions of diction and syntax, traced below, suggest
how the various languages of the text interact. The reader can discover no absolute coherence of an individual's speech or of the
speech of social groups, for reported symposiastic speech must,
since Plato, be recognizably distinct and humorously partial. And,
most famously in Plato's *Symposium*, the incoherence of a series
of speakers' speeches (the incomplete accounts of love) creates an
opening for the next speaker and ultimately for the Socratic final
argument. Petronius's string of speeches ascends to no final resolution, but perhaps what does ally them is close to Plato's technique
of the frustration of closure. Socrates and his host Agathon, we
are told at the end of the dialogue, spoke on into the night, until

with the dawn the philosopher convinced the poet that tragedy and comedy were to be joined. When the *Satyricon*'s speeches do not seem to join, when resolution remains only potential, and the breaking of dawn allows no closure but only hurried escape, these thematic and dramatic disjunctures need not be reified in editorial fashion as lacunae in the text.[15] Rather, like the unreported conversation of Socrates and Agathon, the silences of the text may be deliberate, provocative if not protreptic, for one of the strongest threads binding the stories remains an attitude toward language that betrays anxiety about the mastery made manifest by speech. A fascination with ungovernable speech, both speech that leads nowhere and speech that will not be made to do its master's bidding, allies the speeches and the narrator.

The influence worked by the series of speeches upon one another helps to chart the course of language in the *Satyricon*. In particular, a few shared idioms reveal that Petronius has repeated certain emphatic kinds of speech: the speech acts of exhortation (the invitation to speak) and of threat (the command to be silent), and the lively assurance that the present speech is true (the command to assent). This speech about speech is but one manifestation of the *Satyricon*'s quest for stories and comment upon them. Only after describing the travel of these idioms do I consider the relation of the language of the freedman and the narrator.[16]

"'Oro te' inquit Echion centonarius 'melius loquere'" (45: "The rag seller Echion said, 'Please, talk better'")—so Echion interrupts the trite complaints of the freedman Ganymedes before starting his own speech with a rustic fable/commonplace. Later, Trimalchio similarly prods the silent Niceros into speech with "'Oro te, sic felicem me videas, narra illud quod tibi usu venit'" (61: "Please, as surely as you see me rich and prosperous, tell something that really happened"). Such solecism ushers in new stories. Now, *oro te* means little more than "please" and so has lost its ability to govern the rest of the sentence. Perhaps, like much of conversation, it is overly emphatic and emotional, not overly polite—"I beseech you, pass the salt," not "Would you please pass the salt." What is remarkable in this fragmentary text is that its language is not so very disparate. The characters share themes and linguistic errors. Indeed, Trimalchio's speech on this reading is but the culmination, pastiche, and exaggeration of that of the other diners—he seems more a *centonarius* than the rag seller/rag stitcher Echion. Trimalchio is the first to invoke death directly: in execrable verse inspired by the skeleton, the host explicates, "We'll all be like this after Death takes us away" (34.10: "sic erimus cuncti, postquam nos auferet Orcus"). Echion twice (45.9 and 46.7) says "nisi Orcus" at the end of a sentence (and the second use, "quod illi auferre non possit nisi Orcus," echoes the verb of Trimalchio's line). Niceros later concludes a sentence "fortis tamquam Orcus" (62.3)—using his own mannerism of metaphor but repeating Trimalchio's and Echion's *Orcus*.

Niceros intensifies the earlier language about death: he reuses the word *Orcus* by applying it as an intensifying modifier to his nocturnal companion, the soldier.[17] Of course, his whole speech literalizes the earlier phrases; his metaphor is not simply mannerist exaggeration (like *oro te*) but soon realized, for once among the tombstones, the brave as death soldier emerges as werewolf and will go on to butcher the sheep at the villa visited by Niceros. Niceros makes a story out of the earlier speakers' allusions to the imminence of death and with the license of metaphor presents this as the fulfillment of Trimalchio's request to tell something that really happened. Trimalchio continues the course of exaggeration as he must tell a death story to outdo Niceros's.

The complicated course of language and motifs and themes of death in the *Satyricon* grow from such small beginnings as Trimalchio's citation of Orcus. What begins as a feature of diction comes to dominate larger units of discourse so that, for instance, among the instances of emphatic speech of the freedmen, Hermeros will say, ridiculously, "spero, sic moriar, ut mortuus non erubescam" (57.6)—the confusion of this syntax I try to sort out below. But what at first seemed a throwaway half-line from Trimalchio the poetaster, a truism as commonplace as the silver skeleton brought out to dance before the guests, refuses to be contained in this parody and is soon on everyone's lips, eventually even the narrator's, whose diction makes the fishpond into the River Styx, the house of Trimalchio into the labyrinth of death.[18] The vital stories about death mediate this transfer of diction and thought.

On the small scale of diction and sentence type, *Orcus* placed last as if an afterthought comes to dominate certain aspects of the freedmen's speech; in particular, the freedmen mix reference to death with a highly and emphatic personal wish about the conduct or belief of others, about their effect upon others (Hermeros had just said [57.4], "et nunc spero me sic vivere, ut nemini iocus sim").[19] In an unusual sentence type, the freedmen (and once the profligate Quartilla) make a wish that has as a dependent clause what is in fact the topic of the sentence. The wish clause is no real wish for the future but an exclamatory, assertive mode meant to convince the listener.[20] The violent threats of Hermeros share similarities both to formulas such as *oro te*, as they seek to direct the speech of others, and to a smaller set of verbal threats meant to demonstrate the sincerity of the speaker's own words: "ita tutelam huius loci habeam propitiam, ut ego si secundum illum discumberem, iam illi balatum clusissem" (57.2) and "ita lucrum faciam et ita bene moriar aut populus per exitum meum iuret, nisi te ubique toga perversa fuero persecutus" (58.12). The violent aspect of this syntax is absent in only one case: Hermeros (58.3) humorously replaces the threat, "ita satur pane fiam, ut ego istud conliberto meo dono" (the speaker will stuff himself rather than his addressee).[21]

These threats posit a wish for the good health of the speaker as the validation for the coming threat; the happy state of the self assures the target of the seriousness of the intended violence. In the actual instances, the statement of that good health varies ludicrously, but not without point. Often a mercantile image contaminates the wish for continued health and life—the wish to turn a profit slips into the place of the wish to keep the gods propitious. In the transformative grammar of the freedmen, this transfer of themes suggests that profit and life or living well are the same thing (thus Trimalchio at 70.1, "ita crescam patrimonio, non corpore, ut ista cocus meus de porco fecit"). The violence may stand outside the actual sentence. Quartilla, for instance, responds to an objection that her maid is too young for intercourse, with "Iunonem meam iratam habeam, si umquam me meminerim virginem fuisse" (25.4).

One could see these various sentences as aberrations from a colloquial phrase "deos iratos/propitios habeam ut (si)," "as surely as I wish for good health and luck I will. . . ."[22] The phrase is little more than an intensifying expletive like "By God I will . . ." or "Believe you me I will. . . ." Quartilla, Hermeros, and Trimalchio then work their peculiar comic twists on both halves of the sentence. But the actual twisting cannot be unraveled in discrete strands—individual stories and speakers have colored this emphatic speech. Hermeros's threat to reverse his clothing, like his earlier threat to stop up Ascyltos's bleating, makes the speaker the sexual aggressor, the man who would sodomize the freeborn Ascyltos; yet it will take a reversal of dress on the part of the aggressor to bestialize the sheep Ascyltos.[23] Quartilla's exclamation, the first extant instance, made explicit the connection of sexual violence with this particular form of verbal threat. This element is present no matter how the various sentence components shift. So the passively named Ganymedes, complaining of the reigning corruption and decadence of the day, can exclaim, "ita meos fruniscar, ut ego puto omnia illa a diibus fieri" (44.16).

This sentence works violence of several types. Echion cannot abide the commonplace piety and so interrupts his fellow freedman's labored amplification of the theme. The vapid piety, truly the final inanity, rather than winning its hearer's credulity, prompts Echion's impolite closure. And the first clause, meant to reassure, has both violent syntax and violent thought. "May I enjoy my own as surely as . . ." locates its violence in the accusative *meos*, which "should be" *meis*, an ablative ambiguous in gender, but the masculinely marked accusative signals all the members of his household whom Ganymedes will enjoy fucking.[24] Trimalchio aims the same sort of threatening sentence type at Fortunata: "ita genium meum propitium habeam, curabo domata sit Cassandra caligaria" (74.14). Here, too, personal well-being validates the credibility of the violent sexual threat. The cross-dressed Fortu-nata (the Greek epic/dramatic heroine in Roman jackboots) will be mastered in the same way as the sheepish Ascyltos and Giton.[25] Trimalchio later repeats the same overgoverned syntax that links enjoyment and possessions but, somewhat typically, gets the ex-pression wrong:[26] the violence of his wish is aimed at himself, and this he predicates on a wish not for his own but for his speaker's continued "happiness": "non tenuit ultra lacrimas Trimalchio et 'rogo,' inquit, 'Habinna, sic peculium tuum fruniscaris: si quid perperam feci, in faciem meam inspue'" (75.3). Trimalchio reverses the sentence type: violence against the self is made to depend on the wish for the good health of another.

All these sentences purport to defend the speakers' actions and words; they would maintain or restore order: a character wishes that, as surely as he wants to keep the gods favorable, his luck or fortunes stable, he will silence Ascyltos, Giton, Fortunata. Of course, the two clauses are more directly connected than the syntax suggests: the maintenance of the wisher's good fortune de-pends on silencing his addressee. These statements that assert the dominant male's order are in themselves violent and ultimately destabilizing. They break out of civil speech and society, emanate from derisible freedmen, and display their faulty genealogy. Such ordering statements wish to tell the listener how to act; they col-lapse the difference between speaker and listener in much the same way as other of Trimalchio's speech acts: his bids for the diners to make the wine sweet, for example. Collectively, these attempted politenesses are flawed because they would direct and own the lis-tener. The threatening, often sexually aggressive language consti-tutes a speech characteristic shared among the freedmen as much as any phonological, morphological, lexical, or syntactic items. In addition, as the free mask their sexual aggression and trans-gression in linguistic expertise (a show of moralizing words gains them entry to a ward they will corrupt), the explicit language of the freed distinguishes them from the verbally restrained real tres-passers, the free. Petronius's reuse of a sentence type thus has far more to do with a connected, reinforcing presentation of attitudes toward language (and sex) than it does with the individual characterization of a single freedman.[27]

Politenesses assert or reassure a relationship; they define the boundaries of the speakers' relations. Precisely in the freedmen's gestures and formulas of civility, Petronius depicts an anxiety about speech, social relations, and identity. Ultimately, the diners' language fails to be polite, as it fails to win credence; it devolves to taller tales and more egregious tastelessness. Thus increasingly strong claims to verity and credibility accompany the growing excesses of the dinner; these signal the failure of language to affect the other, as do the involved wishes whose lack of restraint displays the insufficiency of ordinary speech. And so weeping, swearing, and naming abound. Conversational style fails to move Trimalchio in particular; the various offenders' postures of supplication, the diners' repeated prayers, speakers repeating his name instance his impassivity to restrained speech and his addiction to these more emotive speech acts. In sum, Trimalchio proves a particularly poor and naive reader and auditor. Ordinary speech has little effect on the freedmen, for unlike them it does not cross boundaries of personal space,[28] life and death, high and low style, free and slave.

Shared features of language are only part of the literary representation of the sociolect[29] in Petronius's dinner society. Attitudes toward language, and in particular a sense of linguistic inferiority, unite members of the same sociolect. The freedmen's use of language as a domineering, sexual instrument of social control constitutes one such unifying attitude to language. Those who must obey and those who command speak the same language with the great fissure of politeness dividing them. The freedmen's politenesses do not cover the violence they intend. The "come hither" boys[30] now freed men appropriate the power, though not the propriety, of the masters' speech. Their speech unveils politeness as a social fiction and lays bare the true hierarchy of language, as the order of the seating in the dining room reveals the hierarchy although the common food and discourse create the fiction of equality. It is little wonder that Trimalchio has so often staged acts of disobedience on the part of his slaves. This enables him to exhibit the theatrical show of that most powerful Roman speech act, manumission; but his liberating language is empty, all promise, the hierarchy still intact after the actors' mouth his lines. Speech fails of its effect; more to the point, politeness works in reverse fashion; rather than persuading it commands, rather than disguising it bares power relations. Trimalchio works like some of Alice's interlocutors in Wonderland, whose thoroughly literal interpretation of language demonstrates its inherent weakness and conventionality.

Linguistic Inferiority and the Value of Education

The fragments of the *Satyricon* begin with the three characters encountering their latest interlocutor on literary matters, the declamatory teacher Agamemnon. I suppose this meeting not to be a unique beginning as Eumolpus is later discovered in a scene of literary exegesis or ecphrasis: gazing at a picture, he becomes the object of Encolpius's gaze, a gaze that purports to be about art and its meaning and present unhappy reception but is in fact as tired and perverse as Eumolpus's interpretation and poetry.[31] The recurrent complaints of the venality of contemporary culture delivered by the most venal, if freeborn, characters of the text generate a suspicion in the reader that literary talk simply masks sexual or mercantile concerns. Both pairs of discussants behave so badly that the reader grows to distrust pronouncements about literature and literary expertise. In addition, these orienting scenes sound all the more trite after the silly "literary" readings of Trimalchio and his fellow freedmen.

The *Satyricon* does not allow straight readings of its accounts of literature both because of the dubious authority of the speakers and because of the recurrence of such scenes (often made more overtly comic than these beginnings). Talking about literature produces only complaint, and an invitation to dinner. The outcome of each introductory scene dissolves the pretense of high criticism: Giton in servile drag at a free dinner with his twin masters playing the role of literary parasites and, later, Eumolpus mouthing literary criticism as commonplace and hollow as Encolpius's bombastic complaints about bombast. Encolpius's complaints win him a new partner in the adventures, but the literary expert becomes as specious as the bad exegesis the text continually serves up. Also, within the scenes, complaint about contemporary style is strongly marked as commonplace carping: it reads not as the genuine expression of an individual but as a generic component of Roman satire, a traditional bias of social snobbery, and an overly loud protest typical of the series in this narrative that launches the narrator into more errancy under the guise of his and his companions' literary merits. For Encolpius goes to dinner under the wing, so to speak, of Agamemnon, as a learned man, a diligent student, much as he attaches himself as the sole, enthusiastic student of the bisexual poet (until the legacy-hunting mother bestows her two children on the old *magister*).[32] In turn, Eumolpus begins the Croton adventure from shipwreck and seeks to repair his fortunes in what is described as an antiliterary or antirhetorical world. Thus he replays the fortune-recovering, shipwrecked poet Simonides, but in a world as alien to high culture as Trimalchio's dinner society.[33] The even more errant Eumolpus succeeds Agamemnon and Trimalchio as *magister loquendi*.

The encounter of Encolpius and Agamemnon anticipates the interrogations of literary problems with abundantly wrong exegesis and the heavy diatribe of literary decline and social depravity.[34] The two speakers are outside a declamatory hall—we wonder if they have been thrown out and so their despair over contemporary standards is sour grapes. This scene of criticism from the margin highlights the characters' linguistic anxiety.[35] A beginning that seems accidental, the chance encounter of the ousted or silenced teacher, leads to a dinner at which this teacher is invited and silenced. For Agamemnon reappears, not again in lengthy declamation but as a presence worrying the Latinity of the freedmen; present but in the background with little to say, the rhetorician spurs the diners to talk of their own education and of the value of education. As a figure of their anxiety, he need say nothing in order to make them uneasy about the status of their speech.

Echion anticipates the schoolmaster's criticism and so turns from the story of Glyco's adulterous steward and the games at which the condemned freedman will battle beasts to his own veneration for education and his sons' progress in letters.[36] Petronius presents a speaker worried about the reception of his story: "Agamemnon, you seem to me to be saying, 'Why is that bore prattling on and on?' Because you who can discourse don't discourse. You're not of our stripe, and so sneer at the words of poor men. We know you're a fool for culture" (46.1: "videris mihi, Agamemnon, dicere: 'quid iste argutat molestus?' quia tu, qui potes loquere, non loquis. non es nostrae fasciae, et ideo pauperorum verba derides. scimus te prae litteras fatuum esse"). The proper speaker elicits from Echion imagined criticism and then the worst Latin of all his lines. Driven to solecisms, he tries to patronize Agamemnon by offering his hospitality.

The shadow of the rhetorician drives the speakers to talk of their own education out of fear that someone of better language will meet their stories with laughter.[37] Niceros picks up the diction and scorn of *derides*, dreaded by Echion, at 61: "'Omne me' inquit 'lucrum transeat, nisi iam dudum gaudimonio dissilio, quod te talem video. Itaque hilaria mera sint, etsi timeo istos scholasticos, ne me [de]rideant. Riserint [videri<n>t]; narrabo tamen: quid enim mihi aufert, qui ridet? Satius est rideri quam derideri'" ("'May all profit pass me by' he said, 'if I'm not now already splitting for joy 'cause I see you in such a state. So let's have fun, even though I fear those academics may sneer at me. Let them laugh. I'll tell the story anyway. How does the laughter hurt me? It's better to cause a laugh than a sneer'"). Niceros's worry returns at the end of his narrative: "'Let other men consider what they think about this; may I take on the wrath of your guardian spirits if I'm lying'" (62.14: "'viderint alii quid de hoc exopinissent; ego si mentior, genios vestros iratos habeam'"). The frame of emphatic wish and worry about critics (perhaps with the echo of *viderint*, as the Trau manuscript [H] almost reads) presents a speaker in search of respectability and credibility.[38]

Within the text Trimalchio makes good the freedman's fear: his disquisition on the fatal effects of constipation brings derision (47.7: "subinde castigamus crebris potiunculis risum").[39] After discussion of the menu and the wine, Trimalchio is ready for speech; the reader expects some developed story to follow these preliminaries. Instead, Trimalchio tries to get Agamemnon to speak, but Petronius will not allow it. Trimalchio questions Agamemnon but interrupts his guest and provides the answers himself (48).[40] The speakers search for a master's speech and a master's ear (cf. Encolpius at 49.7 "inclinatus ad aurem Agamemnonis"); the teacher of upper-class speech figures both and yet remains at a remove in this text. The reader is never allowed to hear him directly. For all the minute scrupulousness of the view of Trimalchio's home, we are never admitted into the declamatory hall, nor are we let in on its proceedings. Instead, we overhear a pseudo-declamatory complaint performed in the portico and, at the dinner table, a ludicrous account of the declamation's thesis. The characters seem to imagine the schoolroom as the arena of proper speech, from which they are excluded: their own, failing efforts attempt exegesis and imitation of the poets, or declamatory analysis, while they fear the teacher's derision.

Thus Echion addresses his accounts of the tutelage of his two boys to Agamemnon, although he ruins his search for legitimacy with such reassurance as "There's dough in this" (46: "Habet haec res panem"). Trimalchio also directs to the rhetorician his priamel of professions (at 56, where *litterae* are said to be the most difficult trade, *artificium*). Trimalchio had interrupted the general chatter of the guests (55: "vario sermone garrimus") with some verse. The narrator neatly suppresses the company's reaction ("ab hoc epigrammate coepit poetarum esse mentio diuque summa carminis penes Mopsum Thracem memorata est, donec Trimalchio 'rogo' inquit 'magister, quid putas inter Ciceronem et Publi<li>um interesse? ego . . .'") and now lets the domineering host have his way:

Trimalchio turns to ask Agamemnon a question that he again answers himself, with more verse. The host brings in poetry and shifts the level of discourse, on the prompting of a sense of linguistic inferiority that spills over to the narrator, as "vario sermone garrimus" indicates (*loqui* or the solecistic *loquere* was what Echion alleged Agamemnon could do but would not [46] and what Ganymedes had not and perhaps could not do [45]). Here Trimalchio declares the fine level of his discourse, although he tries to pass off his nonsense as the work of the famous mime writer Publilius: "quid enim his melius dici potest?"[41]

Against the background hum of freedmen chatter, rendered all but anonymous by the narrator's brief notices of what was said (cf. the impersonal *memorata est* at 55), individuals seek to distinguish themselves by speaking of letters, by nodding to the *litteratus*, and by introducing the higher discourse of verse. On these occasions and in this context, the freedmen speak of their children and their own biographies: to relate these private, familiar details is, in the freedmen's judgment, to speak better.

Agamemnon does not get to speak because Trimalchio appropriates his voice and role.[42] The one moment that he does speak, the declamation that Encolpius had witnessed, is about to be replayed in the dining room (48).[43] But Trimalchio will allow the speaker only to utter the first line of his thesis ("pauper et dives inimici erant") before breaking in. The narrator, however, here interrupts: "'Bravo,' said Agamemnon, and laid out some school exercise. Trimalchio immediately . . ." ("'urbane' inquit Agamemnon et nescio quam controversiam exposuit. statim Trimalchio"). In the dinner party the text itself will not abide free men speaking; it pushes Trimalchio and his fellow freedmen ahead, with the free man as prompter (although the Greek-named schoolteacher might be read as a freedman, he represents liberal studies and speech).[44] Trimalchio questions Agamemnon out of anxiety about his own speech and education. Thus he assures Agamemnon, on the occasion of his first question, that he has home schooling and, even better, two libraries ("ne me putes studia fastiditum").

The freedmen blunder blindly whenever they speak of education. They proliferate verbal faux pas in their proud testimonials about the acquisition of proper speech. In fact, the linguistic environment of slave and freeborn might not have differed in the most crucial early years of language acquisition, for Rome did not segregate within the *familia*. Slave and master-to-be could have spoken alike, indeed identically, as Plautus's *Captivi* imagines, with some worry. Segregation did come at a later stage of training, when the slave learned a trade and the free went to school to acquire a markedly different type of speech and at the same time new playmates or peers. Possibly, home-born slaves and freeborn women, who did not attend rhetorical school, could have spoken more alike than freeborn males and females. The idealized trope of Greek antiquity had imagined woman and slave in like linguistic condition: silent or at least reticent of speech, deferring to the freeborn male, who had plenty to say.[45] A more worrying prospect to Rome's elite was the possibility that the educated (male) slave might have received rhetorical training and thus might speak better than his betters.[46]

Petronius has overdetermined the freedmen's speech about education: the characters ridicule it; the text marks it, stylistically and conceptually, as low. The texts' viewpoints seem to converge: the voices of narrator, character, author, and, with the introduction of social norms, reader seem settled. The freedmen of Petronius's pages speak of their acquisition of education in two fundamentally socially flawed ways: they associate education with trade and with the home. The profitability of letters and the frugality and humility of autodidacticism or home training were not Roman virtues; they were, however, realities of many slaves' success, for manumission depended on the profits saved from a learned trade. Of course, education—by which we mean the peculiar literacy arising from and finally shaped by rhetorical training, however acquired—constituted a prime means of social mobility. Agamemnon himself complained of the ambitions of parents who ruined students (4); though not spoken of as a virtue, the profitability of letters and their social potential were clearly recognized. The freedmen only err in naming and trying to quantify this reality.

Nowhere is the text's scorn easier to read than when the freedmen rank education like their account books. Disturbed by the presence of Agamemnon, Echion gives an account of his two boys' progress in education. They are taught at home, and the father is quick to praise the sons and fault the masters.[47] To the second boy Echion has given law books ("Habet haec res panem," 46), as he explains before praising the *causidicus* Phileros to his son. Of course, Echion only blunders the more aristocratic and ambitious he tries to be. Law was learned by apprenticeship or in special schools. The purported aim of education was to become a *patronus*, an orator, not the paid hireling, *causidicus*. The comic error centering on education only burgeons as Trimalchio takes up the theme by offering a priamel on professions. Horace is no match: instead of working from the world's various opinions to the true opinion that poetry is the best life, as the poet had done at the outset of his *Odes*, Trimalchio baldly sets *litterae* as the most difficult *artificium* (trade not profession); then come medicine and money changing.[48] As in other respects, Trimalchio does not so much differ from the other *liberti* as inflate their thoughts and language out of all proportion.

Ascyltos cannot abide this speech, with its mercantile vision of education, and his laughter—again the freeborn get little verbal expression—prompts Hermeros to deliver a lengthy defense of libertine education. In all its hilarity, his self-accounting (58: "Non didici geometrias critica et alogias menias, sed lapidarias litteras scio, partes centum dico ad aes, ad pondus, ad nummum. . . . Iam scies patrem tuum mercedes perdidisse, quamvis et rhetoricam scis") asserts a counter-rhetoric, an education of real value to be set against the empty phrases taught in school.[49] He sets a riddle as the test of the competing systems and, just before introducing this subliterary genre, had challenged the freeborn critic to a wager of personal credit. Hermeros literalizes value: here his trump is simply that he is worth more in the marketplace. This self-appraisal forms the climax of his invective, in part by drawing on earlier monetary evaluations of persons. Hermeros had begun by describing the extent of his anger; hotheadedness is something of a minor motif among the freedmen (one of the ways in which they cannot contain themselves), but this freedman reifies his passion by declaring that, when angry, "I'd sell my mother for two bits" (58: "matrem meam dupundii non facio"). Freedmen are able to put a price on most anyone.[50] Hermeros may be an extreme, but the monetary calculation of human worth does distinguish the freedmen diners. Hermeros had called Ascyltos a "dominus dupunduarius" (58) and finishes his speech by quoting his old master: in the present age "nemo dupundii evadit."

In social terms, *aestimatio* was the publicly perceived value of a citizen or member of the opinion community. Although we are used to judging the Roman system in terms of the written "moral vocabulary" of *dignitas*, *pietas*, and *auctoritas* familiar from Cicero's speeches or Caesar's self-justifications, or as clearly read in the proper formulas of proper careers in inscriptions, judgments of this personal social worth circulated in many forms. *Aestimatio* was both a process of determining worth and the current calculation of that value, which involved all the things said about a person, the people seen to be one's friends, the access to power made visible in official costume, the size and number of one's houses, the poetry one could recite. All the visible and audible manifestations of power constituted the means for judgment. Money counted too, and not simply as the behind-the-scenes means to procure a retinue, a verdict, an office. In clothing, marriage, and hospitality, wealth was advertised, but not as wealth. This was not a monolithic, uncontested system. Call Crassus a banker or a profiteer and, provided your own *aestimatio* was high, you had defamed him.[51]

In addition, freedmen were developing, precisely at this time, an inscriptional and monumental vocabulary to articulate their status as Romans. And different members or groups would bitterly vie for a single traditional word of praise. Yet the mention of money mocks these fictions. Wealth and resources could be included in the *laudatio* of a Roman citizen, but social norms required depicting wealth as inherited, as the overflow of agrarian holdings, or as the bequests of grateful friends.[52] The conventions of Roman praise excluded attributing success to money making.

Seneca's critics pointed to his wealth; he himself would produce a philosophical oeuvre that stated, for all to read, the Roman way to philosophy and self-development. Petronius's freedmen do not observe these social proprieties; mercantilism inextricably sullies their references to literature, education, and personal worth.

The freedmen are quick to price others. Habinnas tells the price of one of his slaves (68) as the climax to his praise; his wife finishes the *aestimatio* by completing the list of the favored slave's trades: "Interpellavit loquentem Scintilla et 'plane' inquit 'non omnia artificia servi nequam narras. Agaga est; at curabo stigmam habeat'" ("Scintilla interrupted him as he spoke and said 'You really haven't told all the professions of this worthless slave. He's a pimp, and I'll make sure he's branded for it.'"[53] Niceros seems to love Melissa for her sexual and monetary generosity and reliability (61). The freedmen's assessment of human value mixes in capital (and often sex);[54] their bountiful transgressions take the practice of *aestimatio* literally, etymologically (as if from *aes*, bronze, a bronze coin, and τιμᾶν, to value). As if overhearing a will being read to the bereaved, we read what various people are worth. The freedmen mix media here, too, for they spoil the table talk by their inventories of worth.

Such naked calculations belong to the marketplace, where slaves for sale wore placards advertising their talents and price; the diners have not kept separate the dining room and the market—or the brothel, where prostitutes had similar signs (*tituli*). In the freedmen's utopian hierarchy ranging from the expensive to the cheap, those whom the dinner guests despise count as two-bit men, like the steward Glyco, *sestertiarius homo* (45), who incurs the diners' censure for executing his freedmen—a folly they rate as the loss of self, the loss of capital ("Hoc est se ipsum traducere"). When Echion prattles on to complain about a local magistrate, he characterizes the tightfisted game-giver as producing *gladiatores sestertiarios* (45). Trimalchio ironically calls himself a cheapskate when he remembers having passed up some capital: "And I, foolish cheapskate, passed up ten thousand sesterces. You know I'm telling the truth" (74: "Et ego, homo dupundiarius, sestertium

centies accipere potui. Scis tu me non mentiri"). Of course, Trimalchio is lying again; the young freedman had no prospect of a
dowered bride. Once again, the host tries to ensnare his hearers'
credit through a self-proclamation of his own truthfulness. All
these characterizations of the value of others and the value of
the speaker and his story constitute a curious system. Certainly,
money terms have displaced the mystifying terms of the elite (*op-
timas, vir bonus, nobilis, clarus, egregius, rei publicae amantissimus*
collapsed to *homo lucrans*).[55]

   In marked contrast to what the Roman elite said of themselves (high birth and landed wealth were presented as desider-
ata, although even the great mouther of such platitudes, Cato the
Elder, relied on neither), the origin of person or wealth receives no
such attention among the diners, who substitute for noble parent-
age the virtue of growing from nothing, of taking gold from a
shit-heap. As the culmination of their talk about proper careers,
Trimalchio boasts of his trade, which progresses from goods to
human credit (76: "libertos faenerare").[56] Trafficking in men had
threatened to stigmatize old Hegio in his effort to ransom his son
in Plautus's *Captivi*. The father's *aestimatio*, his peers' judgment
of his standing in the city and his audience's judgment of his persona as a sympathetic and generically comic father, fell into peril
when he veered too close to a slave mentality—to the confusion of
caput with capital. But whose mentality is this? A dominant voice
accuses the socially pretentious and the socially low of improper
appreciation of birth, rank, and elite doctrine (education).

   But in Rome the upper classes voiced the faux pas of putting
a price on human worth: under Roman law, the slave was not a
caput, a person, but capital, the famous *instrumentum vocale*. When
considering polemical, polar accounts of social value, we should
not expect to identify the viewpoints too strictly. A text so self-
conscious about social role and the power of language invites the
reader to ask, what is the social function of this bad taste, what is
its origin? Certainly, bad language and bad advice, the prattle of
the freedmen that has as a foil correct, traditional, or even pomp-
ous generalizing about social responsibility or the value of edu-

cation, while visibly and palpably wrong, have huge comic possibilities. Social and domestic confusion and role swapping become
possible when status is not observed, when all men are reckoned
in egalitarian coin. Roman comedy's concern with business does
not simply represent the intrusion of one Roman reality onto the
stage, nor is that stage simply an inversion of the quotidian. Roman literature more generally offered a safe viewing of such conflicts. Rather than seeing the appearance of the socially abject as
occasional, festal, or generic, and so relegating it to a Roman practice, institution, or class, we should consider the fool[57] and his
language in the text as a kind of social practice. The description
of who can talk right, of who belongs, of how social and familial
roles veer wrong, constitutes not just aristocratic sneer or servile
resentment but the negotiation for place and role that literature
itself, as social speech, continually enacts.

In the series of antonyms to the socially correct that articulate the libertine economy within the text, we witness on several
occasions a freedman attempting to deliver a sustained life story;
here too the text stoops to include the socially low view of the
socially correct and incorrect. Phileros, fresh from a funeral where
he could learn the final value of the dead Chrysanthus, displays the
libertine *aestimatio*: "He started with barely a dime to his name
and was ready to pick a penny from a shit-heap with his teeth"
(43: "Ab asse crevit et paratus fuit quadrantem de stercore mordi-
cus tollere"). Trimalchio's speech of his rags-to-riches rise and his
shameless resourcefulness picks up these earlier motifs and themes,
but, characteristically, Trimalchio appropriates to his own person
another man's characterization of yet another, without realizing
the transparency, humor, and bad taste of his theft. The comic antitheses spoof generic conventions for praise of the dead and, more
generally, the social language of public praise. In his mercantilist
laudatio funebris Phileros provides a positive model: Chrysanthus,
it seems, had a brother, distinguishable from the dead man in two
respects. Chrysanthus had a foul mouth (harsh or rough: "durae
buccae fuit, linguosus, discordia, non homo," and compare what

he was prepared to do with his mouth) and did not share his brother's generosity.

Petronius here parodies both the upper-class eulogy of the dead and the developing genre of Roman biography, especially the comparison of historical figures. Some forty years after the composition of our text, Plutarch would make famous the treatment of parallel lives, but strings of historical exempla within a speech or literary work had long done the same, and collections of lives existed, as did a long philosophical tradition mediating and debating the merits of different kinds of lives. As in Roman comedy, the author finds in the comparison of good and bad brother a technique to reflect on social roles. On such equal footing, without difference of status, what merits our collective praise; who will attain excellence, distinction? Of course, all around the table sit brothers of sorts, fellow freedmen whose "brotherliness" is suspect (as brothers in slavery, as natural sons, as homosexuals). Chrysanthus's career parallels that of Trimalchio: he grew from nothing and began his way up in the world by getting someone else's inheritance, with the suggestion that he ingratiated himself to his old master by means of sexual favors. He trespasses on his master's property: "named an heir, he took more than had been left him" (43: "hereditatem accepit, ex qua plus involavit, quam illi relictum est"). His sins in the eyes of the freedman assessor are linguistic, economic, and sexual.[58] His rough, uncontrolled speech mirrors his origin.[59] Likewise, even in birth and family relations, his error resides on the economic level, for he has no heir from his family; he has broken with his brother and is blamed for fleeing his kin and for trusting, and so falling prey to, his slaves.

The introduction of brother and of kin terms in general is important here. The truism "Longe fugit quisquis suos fugit" ("He flees far afield who flees his own") smacks of Hermeros's later riddle "I who come far from you, come broadly" (58: "Qui de nobis longe venio, late venio"). "Plane Fortunae filius," says Phileros of Chrysanthus, which means that he is both heaven's darling and a son of a bitch. I suspect that Hermeros's later riddle also pertains to doubtful paternity and legitimacy; uttered in a context that pits the birth of Ascyltos and perhaps of Giton against the native virtue of Hermeros, it reveals that the critics do not know their origins or the riddle's origin.[60] Be this as it may, Chrysanthus, for all his praise, falls down where all freedmen fail; they have no fathers, and so their entire legacy is suspect. The freeborn narrative, the dominant discourse, then attributes to them effeminacy, bisexuality, or hypersexuality. They are the roving D/dick of the riddle, the jack-of-all-trades,[61] and the freeborn who fail to solve this riddle do so at their sexual and economic peril. Like Chrysanthus, they ignore their brothers and leave their money to those outside their families. Caricature that he is, the freedman Phileros takes on the anxieties of the master.

Thus, even at their most ridiculous, the freedmen parody high culture.[62] Driven to speak by the silent or silenced rhetorician, they speak from their own anxieties; but in a text written by and for the free, which has as its plot the errancy of three professedly free though at times self-enslaving characters, the freedmen take up the anxieties of the masters they have become, with the difference that they strip naked the relations of power, the subjugation and ownership of social relations and categories. Their boorish calculation of the value of education and their allied, vulgar habit of pricing human worth are neither exclusively their own nor exclusively parody. There is too much overlap to allow such a stable, fixed reading. This *contaminatio* has trespassed, outside of the text, onto more orthodox Roman systems and languages of value; once appropriated and stripped of propriety, the master's language reveals its artifice and arbitrariness. As on the stage, the slave who plays master reminds us that social relations are roles, that power is not natural.

Petronius has overdetermined this *contaminatio* of slave and free narratives by including the freeborn critics Encolpius, Ascyltos, and Giton. Their presence impedes the *Cena* and the work as a whole from being read as parody. Situated as they are outside the text, the freeborn might define the freedmen's text as countertext, pure sham to the real speech and behavior of the free. However,

Petronius has placed within the party literary critics and interpreters (of the freedmen, their stories, their exegesis, their verse,
their appropriation of Virgil's verse). Further, the free Encolpius
repeatedly plays the naive reader and critic; Trimalchio and company enthrall, fool, and revolt him.

Admittedly, within the text, against the knavish coinages of
worth stands a rival judgment of the value of liberal education
and human essence that asserts its own correctness. Literature and
other niceties of social politeness are properly prized in the viewpoints delivered and implied by the freeborn, disreputable, homosexual trio, who manage to find figures of education, their shifting
companion the rhetorician Agamemnon and the poet-tutor Eumolpus.[63] Nonetheless, in talk of literature the free show as much
self-interest as the freed. In Eumolpus's case, literary speech masks
bodily desires: he speaks only as a feint, a come-on for someone
else's food, body, or property. When Encolpius and Ascyltos part,
Encolpius reminds his former friend that they can survive on their
own: "Et tu litteras scis et ego" (10).[64] In this text the return for
speech is highly suspect. The talk of the paid teacher Agamemnon,
like the diatribe of Encolpius delivered to him and for his benefit,
is flattery wangling a free dinner.[65] And Agamemnon knows it: he
explicitly compares declamatory teachers to comic parasites at the
outset of his disingenuous criticism of contemporary education
and speech (3).

Eumolpus's talk of literature has drawn more scholarly attention—witness the "issue" of the relation of his poem to Lucan's—what this notoriety misses is that Eumolpus's *Civil War*,
besides anticipating the internecine and self-consuming conflict of
the legacy (past) hunters of Croton at the novel's end, adheres to
recurrent principles of the irruption of high style into the *Satyricon*.[66] First, in this text's context even Virgil offends; no text succeeds in giving pleasure. In particular, poetry fails to elevate tone,
conversation, or the speakers, as the reported verse remains preeminently a transparent marker of social and cultural ambition.
Eumolpus's poem tries to capture a Roman past as vainly as the
ambitious inheritance hunters seek Eumolpus's fictive money, and

as hopelessly as the shrill-voiced freedmen and slaves pursue Virgilian or even Lucilian style. No voice, man, or verse remains unadulterated. Eumolpus's literary efforts are as contaminated as his appropriation and corruption of the freeborn students.

Trimalchio *Magister dicendi*

The most prominent appropriation of the master's manner is not Eumolpus's aim at Lucan and Virgil, but the literary efforts of Trimalchio himself.[67] With Agamemnon in the background, with the literary present only as a parasite, the upstart host can run riot, serving up a literary soup that has had scholars in a frenzy to recover the ingredients. The text sets the reader a task far more rewarding than the search for models: to read Trimalchio in his almost Protean roles as master of signs and speech, for the archfreedman performs not so much as *chef de lettres* as a libertine rhetor, a *magister dicendi* who silences, interrupts, and dominates speech. Whether or not Petronius took his inspiration from Plato's juxtaposition of cookery and rhetoric in the *Gorgias*, these two themes, adumbrated in the first extant fragment in Agamemnon's denunciation of the overspiced and overrich contemporary style of the schools, possess Trimalchio. He reads Plato's juxtaposition not as metaphor but as reality: incapable of distinguishing cooking from speaking, he tries to orchestrate both. In both realms, then, he conspires to be the controller of signs, and in him Petronius has highlighted the aspirations of freedmen (properly cooks and servants?) to traditional culture and, inescapably and inextricably, refracted the process of reading and interpretation.[68]

Trimalchio deadens speech. The guests had been speaking relatively freely; the turns of conversation, while not altogether polite, occurred at the ends of stories as one speaker gave way to the next: "Such stories were whizzing around when Trimalchio entered" (47: "Eiusmodi fabulae vibrabant, cum Trimalchio intravit"). He proceeds to give his bowel disquisition. At this point the host invites a number of guests to speak. He asks Agamemnon for his declamation and then delivers a solution to the thesis that silences all declamation and all fiction: "'If this is a fact,' he said, 'it's not a debate; if it's not a fact, it's nothing at all'" (48: "'Hoc' inquit 'si factum est, controversia non est; si factum non est, nihil est'"). Once conversation is stopped, Trimalchio manufactures it with his feigned interrogation of the absentminded cook and his own exegesis of Corinthian ware. The slave who has dropped a cup (at 52) no doubt received (in the lacuna) an arranged forgiveness, as does, we suspect, the boy who later falls on his master's arm (54). These scenes constitute speech acts in which the master displays his power of speech through formulas of entreaty, forgiveness, even manumission.

During Trimalchio's domination of the conversation, the naive Encolpius had tried to talk privately to Agamemnon, but the rhetorician is not allowed a word—the narrator has shut him out by filling up the scene with Trimalchio's histrionics.[69] The narrator's report subordinates the guests' discussion of poets; in sum, one clause reports the guests' conversation and then gives way to Trimalchio's lengthy discussion (in direct speech), which starts by asking Agamemnon (as *magister*) a question and then proceeds to answer it himself. This orchestrated nonsense is too much for the freeborn, and so Ascyltos snickers, pantomimes—but does not speak. Hermeros, identified in the text only as a surrogate for Trimalchio (57: "unus ex conlibertis Trimalchionis"), does speak, in the lengthy harangue to Ascyltos and Giton. Trimalchio stops Ascyltos from replying—we are to imagine him interrupted, for the narrator has again given the free men no words. The narrator simply reports that Ascyltos was beginning to speak (59). The effect of the host jars with the earlier freewheeling speech of the freedmen: after he sings a Latin translation of the Greek play of the *Homeristae* (59), silence overcomes all ("Mox silentio facto"). But Trimalchio fills up the silence with another literary exegesis. Finally, he asks Niceros to speak; but as soon as the werewolf story is over, Trimalchio must cap it, telling an equally implausible witch story. Niceros's story had reduced everybody but the host to silent wonder, or disbelief.[70] At this point Trimalchio issues another invitation to speak, but the freedman Plocamus declines and instead is reported to have produced some song (64.5: "taetrum exsibilavit"), which he maintained was Greek. After trying some hissing of his own ("tubicines esset imitatus"), Trimalchio turns to a dog-yelping contest, a performance of the same order as his contrived confrontations with his slaves. After freedmen, slave, and dog have all sounded on the master's nod, the party seems doomed. The deus ex machina of the drunken Habinnas enters to rejuvenate the conversation. The narrator can then recede; no longer reporting the nonverbal noise of the guests, he has found more libertine interlocutors. Let us not follow the courses of sound any further.

A catalogue of the host's linguistic roles has shown him to be in anxious control. He invites individuals to speak. He produces minimelodramas that prompt the guests to obsequious speech and whose solution depends on his sententia of absolution. He contrives enigmas and lemmata and then delivers masterly exegesis.[71] He sings a Latin translation of the Greek production of the *Homeristae*. He names, puns, and glosses at the same time. Only on his departure can the guests, like naughty schoolboys, speak freely.[72] He is the channeler and interpreter of speech and signs.

Nothing is so obtrusive in a text as a bad narrator. Like the peculiar, almost painful humor of chancing upon a very mixed-up tour guide or overhearing someone murdering a foreign language, reading with Trimalchio as *magister* provides a voyeuristic social-esthetic pleasure. The reader in his awareness stands superior. In the *Satyricon*, humor begins with the deviancy from the genuine thing, but Trimalchio wanders so far in his production of speech that he not only does not know how to imitate proper speech, he doesn't even know what to imitate. So he mixes media as recklessly as his cooks; imitation-fixation has taken over this character: he must appropriate all sounds and all voices (and genres)[73] as surely as he appropriates other signs not his own—emblems of office and dress and jewelry, for example. His trumpet imitation, just one example of his production of nonverbal noises and his preoccupation with sound (which runs the gamut from the *symphoniacus* who continually plays in his ear, to his operatic singing slaves and the crashing of dishes, to his own finger snapping), reflect Petronius's foregrounding of signs and signification in this character.[74] The reader sees and hears the imperatives, spoken, sounded, and visual, of the master—or are these just flatulence?

The freeborn characters, however, fail in their superiority. Their viewpoint soon collapses with that of the freedmen; and so the distance from which to measure the deviancy from the imperfect imitation of the freedman recedes, for they are caught up in the freedmen's school.[75] Nowhere are the three more stupid than at this dinner. Whereas Trimalchio makes a bad teacher, they are naive, unlearning students. In the recurrent narrative pattern of figuring, interpreting, and refiguring, Encolpius makes a poor reader.[76] Indeed, he seems like one caught in a bad dream. What can he not find? Why doesn't he see the pattern of his blundering? What can he hope to know of, or from, freedmen who tell their life stories in minute and sordid detail? The *Cena* concludes with more mistaken signs/voices/noises. Trimalchio gives a ridiculous exegesis of a cock crowing (74: "Qua voce confusus Trimalchio . . .") and tries to refound the dinner. A fire brigade, mistaking the clamor of the dinner for a cry of alarm, breaks in, perhaps more to restor social order than to quench any conflagration, for fire brigades were the only form of policing Rome knew.[77] The final textual sign then confirms both Trimalchio's ordering of society as riotous, uncivil, and seditious, and Encolpius's need for rescue.

The free have sat lower and silent—caught between the mime's chorus and the patriarch's table (Encolpius's initial doubt [31.7]: "Pantomimi chorum, non patris familiae triclinium crederes"). The text presents its own movement in terms of this shifting geography, where a characters' doubt doubles the scene and interprets at the same time—namely, takes on the role of narratorial comment. Like Croton, Trimalchio's dining room is a negative space—a textual place defined by its remove from expectation. It has taken rigorous modern scholarship to discover the real place of the *Satyricon*;[78] such effort is misplaced if we decide we know where we are. The *Satyricon* differs from Joyce's *Ulysses* in the latter's technique of making Dublin visible; the modern novel contains a map (however ironic, playful, or indirect), a key like the signaling of episodes as Homeric, to the reading of the text, or to Bloom's reading at any rate. The small indications of place and time may be assembled from the *Satyricon* to point to one South Italian city of Neronian date, but in reading, these marks are tiny irruptions into the larger geography of the *Satyricon*; the not Rome, not proper, not literary that, by ignoring boundaries of place and time and genre, flouts them, grossly inflating and popping them.

The place of the *Satyricon* emerges no more surely as one locale as Trimalchio succeeds in becoming the *pater familias* in a text in which the only named *pater familias* is a mirage, the dream-figure who turns out to be a john. So, too, medical interpretation, dream interpretation, astrology, and the recurrent narrative patterning of crux and farcical solution foreground the text's own interpretational needs (again, much as Joyce's suppressed subtitles had, and do, for *Ulysses*).[79] There is, of course, a dreamlike quality to these unending places of dimly glimpsed identity, where home becomes brothel, freemen become enslaved, sex does not climax, and where covers and cloths of all sorts abound. The closure that not death but awakening would constitute is put off. The text gives voice to the anonymous and marginal, but figures this process as the awakening of the lowly and nocturnal. Within the freedmen's stories the *nocturni* have been awakened in the tales of the skin-changer, the witches, and the widow, all of whom are allied as figures of the night who substitute an interloper for the genuine (beast for man, mannequin for male child, lover for husband), and against whom violent penetration is attempted. The text itself literalizes the connection of these characters to Encolpius by having him called *nocturnus* and by having him change his dress and sexuality.

In the hurried retreat from the dawning party, where a Roman detail, the fire brigade, breaks in, the trio's gaze and self-concern pass on. Even though the text is fragmentary, the structure in certain ways was clearly not episodic. In Homer's episodic epic Odysseus takes his leave, naming his name and concluding the story of his visit. Closure receives no such epic, formulaic marking in Petronius: the declaimers are droning on inside when Agamemnon and his itinerant friends go to dinner, and without leave-taking, without revelation of identity, and without Agamemnon, the trio slips out of the continuing ruckus of a party. Of course, such an ending ruptures closure just as any number of details had violated generic, seemly expectations. The text fails to impose its order, as Trimalchio has failed to govern his speech or had failed to be introduced. How could we meet this monstrosity? How would we greet him? To label the text's parts or the whole "parody" provides no solution to this negative closure, for scholarly genealogies of the target or the source simply replicate Trimalchio's habit of naming. Petronius's text resists such termination; to salute Trimalchio as *dominus* or *patronus* or *amicus* would be to situate Encolpius and company. But as uninvited interlopers they both replay the role of freedmen and, in refusing to fix social relations, contribute to the constant social and literary refiguring of the *Satyricon*. The text does, however, invite a criticism of the possibilities of speech, of what the pretensions and ambitions and not simply the origins of speech can be. It is humorous that Trimalchio cannot stop eating, talking, figuring, and refiguring, that he is captive in the text and narratives he would appropriate, but the rupture of closure has larger significances for the *Satyricon*. This playful text makes the collapse and resurrection of readerly expectation its focused play.

Latinity Lost?

It is easy, it pertains to the verbal surface of the text, to see the extremes to which the most problematic signifier, Trimalchio, is driven, but it is more interesting to consider to what he drives the text. The unfixed speech of the final stories, men telling of witches who will not be pinned down and of the widow thought most pious who is likewise sexually powerful and errant, are one reflex of Trimalchio's intended but ridiculous potency of speech. The sexually powerful women of the *Satyricon* resist the sort of ownership to which Trimalchio and his fellow freedmen aspire.

Within the framework of Latin literature, Horace in his *Epodes* offers a similar authorial and textual strategy. Amid recurrent motifs of loss and removal and the almost strident clamor of the poet's loss of virility and lyric potency, this work distances itself from the high lyricism of Catullus. Vulgarity distinguishes the author from the high Roman ambitions and persona of the *Odes* and allies him to the unthreatening and properly subservient acknowledgment of his libertine origins (that persona familiar from the *Satires*); but literary vulgarity is presented as an unseemly confrontation with the potent female, Canidia, who wilts his composition as she is its matter.[80] In their repetition and protest of impotency, both the *Epodes* and the *Satyricon* share a sophisticated, tongue-in-cheek sense of closure. The literary work presents its subject as the sexually threatening and classically distant. The *Satyricon* literalizes literary disconnection in its recurrent motif, situation, and even syntax of failed connection (failure to meet, understand, or recognize characters, origins, idiom, syntax).[81] And yet the sense of play is inescapable, just as the reader knows that no emasculating spell has caused Horace's literary problem in the *Epodes*.

The threat of vulgarity can forge or break alliances of reader and character and author. Vulgarity itself threatens the constraints of the text, its conventions, its estheticism. Always at the edge of the discourses within the Roman literary texts discussed in this book, vulgarity has threatened to dissolve the tenuous social fiction of the common ground of a common language. The boar's improper familiarity with his superior the lion or, on the Roman stage, the comic slave's mercantile account of human relations punctures the fiction of egalitarian speech and behavior. Beast and slave trespass by speaking a naked language—that unliterary tongue that does not respect convention but names things in the mundane language of money and power. The poet who makes a children's genre into a literary one, Phaedrus, versifier of fables, plays the master and celebrates his status of citizen and Latin poet by displaying his mastery of pure Latinity. The intrusion of the low into a high form is made as complex as in the *Satyricon*: the imperial freedman Phaedrus, a late-comer, assumes a canonical form as his own (the iambs of invective, the *senarii* of literary program); at the same time the poet writes what is a slave's genre and school matter. And the critic, lambasted in and by the text, accuses the poet of social and esthetic transgression. In its perilous outcome, the animal character's passage to a higher species or a higher ground reinforces an anxiety about the poet's detractors, and his progress. The insistence that the subject is not grand may have the Augustan and especially Horatian *recusatio* as model, but this deference to the high classical's mode of deference does not return the verse to child's play.

Both Phaedrus and Petronius associate the dangers of passage with the processes of composition and of reading: in particular, the texts create as an overt target a naive, obtuse reader. No doubt, Petronius makes a more sophisticated and devastating use of the potential associations of social ambition, the possibility of composition, the attainment of high style. Nonetheless, the inscribed critic and criticism within Phaedrus's text do not provide a stable, classical reading. Latinity emerges as a fictive, artificial process. Although a high estheticism may rescue the poet, the narrator mixes the serious and the comic: Phaedrus couches his bold claim to belong in conventional *senarii*, deferential to Terence, overtly seeking to assimilate, yet his programmatic poems call attention to the fables and their purpose as mere fun, fictive jokes. The stance that maintains the iambs will do no harm contrasts sharply with the actual harm wrought by speech within the fables—the transgressions of the middling animals, of freedmen, even of Sejanus. Phaedrus searches for a safe structure and context, a place from which to speak his double genre—the genre of a slave's lament, grievance, remedy, and redress.

In the speech between superiors and inferiors, Latin literature reflected upon its own roles: elevating the poet, doing the bidding of the patron, asserting its independent and potent status,

creating an alliance of the literate rival to the traditional map of
Latium. The choice of linguistic transgression as a vehicle for a
polemical literary and social identification reflects an inherited textual strategy and a contemporary worry about the prominence
and power of Roman freedmen. And yet the vulgar and the fictive
do not operate in identical fashion in these texts; like the imperial
magistrates and authors Petronius and Tacitus, Phaedrus burdens
his text with a sense of language's social potential. The refigur-
ings of Roman society presented in the fables, in the *Annals*, and
in the *Satyricon* depend on the appreciation of speech, and specifically on the reader's recognition of the literary representation
of speech as a synecdoche for social reality. In Tiberius's speech,
Tacitus plays out the fictions of the restored republic set against
an imperial mask, a figure of obtuseness, akin to the harsh critic
of Phaedrus, who does not and will not appreciate the poet's civil
speech, and also akin to the silenced rhetorician Agamemnon, the
invited guest who both propels the conversation and signals its
alienation from the classical, the republican, the civil.

These textual silences do not represent authorial disapproval
but the awkwardness and resistance that harry the text's narrative.
This resistance opens a space for our own reading. When the emperor speaks, for instance, no paradigm is created; narrative and
speech are not freed; his speech strikes its audience dumb, much as
the freedmen's tall tales produce silent wonder in the narrator. So
Tiberius's words stand, not for doublethink or doublespeak (no
such ease of reading is allowed), but for the blocked expression
that strangles genuineness. Through his appeals to the senators
to speak their minds and his posturing as a civil speaker, Tiberius
may maintain that his speech and action are classical or neoclassi-
cal, but an overly and overtly rhetorical expression refuses to allow
any classical reading.

The *Satyricon* also resists classical form or interpretation, but
this work appropriates, subverts, and ignores the classical on a
scale that the historian could not or would not allow himself. It
is not simply that the *Satyricon* is vulgar, and a rambling, mock
epic, which classicists might redeem for its linguistic anomalies,

the characterization of freedmen's speech taken as the hallmark of colloquial style and forerunner of Romance. It parades Roman vulgarity, as the *Annals* signals the republic alienated, through the representation of speech.[82] And the *Satyricon*'s vulgarity draws attention to its social quality, origins, and own belatedness. No aristocratic young rake, no Catullus or Caelius, distinguishes the aberrant behavior; scandalous behavior and speech have no high status to hide behind, at least not within the text.[83]

In our effort to map the shifting targets of improper speech, we have found that slave and master, Caesar and freedman, can transgress. But the imperial authors acknowledge a marked distance from socially correct speech—they declaim the loss of *comitas*, that ease of speech and manner that characterized the republican orator. Although Petronius marks the failed community of speech, he mocks the possibility of its return.[84] In Phaedrus and Seneca, egalitarian speech had seemed a permeable fiction—a code for speaking about and negotiating social relations. Petronius combines comedic strains of language with the imperial author's stance of alienation from citizens' speech. His was an exceptional response: the well-mannered Pliny and, to a lesser degree, the social climber Seneca the Younger in their careful styles disagreed.[85] Their letters seek and present a return, if not to the very words of Cicero, to a high style relentlessly advertising itself as Roman and correct.

This final chapter has described Petronius's ostensibly low-class speech not as isolated mockery—the literary representation of freedman's speech—but as an integral part of a system of language representation that disturbs norms and counternorms so as to achieve genuine, unowned speech. Purity and impurity of speech have, in Petronius, a special referentiality: they are not mirrors of reality but categories of analysis parodied in themselves. Ironically in a most ironic work, the foregrounding of speech and its evaluation results not exclusively in parody of the vulgar but in the rupture of normative judgment. In a work filled with language about literature and other language, language itself refuses to be contained by the set of contemporary terms: rhetorical, classical, or vulgar. Seneca's propriety and mastery of speech are not allowed. Speech bounds over labels and caste—the attraction of the stories and the popularity of Petronius display readers' reaction to this vernacular gesture. Scholars' efforts to label the styles, those involved genealogies of the critics, form something of a countermovement, discredited, I believe, by a text that serves up comic critics and ridiculous exegesis and, in these scenes and scenes of the free's failure to direct the narrative, replays the impossibility and implausibility of fixing linguistic taxonomies.

In contrast to Horace's *carmina*, the iambs of the freedman Phaedrus created a reading that fuses a social with an esthetic discourse (the classical poet had sought to elide a social reading by denying he had any ambition, or any power from his powerful friends).[86] In the fables, vulgar origin does not constrain the freedman: the real Latium is the literary Latium. In the *Epodes* and the *Satyricon*, however, the reader discovers topographies of *indecorum*, spaces that loudly proclaim themselves to be at a distant remove from the pure Roman. And yet all three writers present the subject and the possibility of writing Latin literature as a contested realm between the vulgar and the classical. Vulgarity is thoroughly, even excessively, stigmatized as the libertine—the sexually and socially errant. At the same time, classicism, aristocratic speech, is noted as old, unusable, itself impossible, if not perhaps impotent. In such a belated state, the reader is less and less sure how to read the freedman.

These techniques might be called rhetorics of composition provided one does not elide their social dimensions. The freedmen's sexual threats indicate a position of power; the text warily gives notice of the change in their position, their newfound ability to have a commanding voice. The freeborn's changes in position (lower at table, Encolpius impotent and sexually pathic) proclaim a social and esthetic displacement. Some have romanticized this depicted change, not lamenting the decline and corruption of Rome and her letters but heralding freshness, originality of speech and genre and voice. This is to misread Petronius' rhetoric by missing the ironic posture of the personae of such impotent narrators as those of the *Epodes* and the *Satyricon*. Certainly, the freed master is an owner, whereas to a degree (ideally, in the imagined republic of clan peers) the free master is owned by his *res*, having their care and disposition ordained, like his clothes and speech. The free's behavior then stands far more set; perhaps for this generation so too were the classical text and the life of senators living under the emperor. The freedman, however, even in an ideal stereotype, is no original owner, and so cannot be seen exclusively as originality (literary); he is an original with all the troubles of society, identity, and hence power that this entailed. Whereas shame directs the free, ownership continues to govern the freed (and so the ideal type of a freedman, the dead man praised by Phileros, had wished to fuck/own all his own)—this overstatement, the free's view of the freed as libertine, sexually errant and potent, directs Petronius's pages. The text recognizes the marginal as those capable of change; the center is stuck, unyielding, or hypocritical. Unlike the ambitious freedmen and the errant mis-hero Encolpius, the text does not search for a stable viewpoint, an objectifiable voice or register, because in part oppression, socialization, and acculturation demand contaminations of voice, identity, and behavior.

Encolpius's search for a *pater familias*—the search for a real man, for virile style—is doomed. None of the Greek-named (Ascyltos, Agamemnon, Eumolpus) or nameless (the john he meets when he has lost his way) will do. In these emphatic fashions the text declares the failure to meet the Roman. This literary disconnection has frustrated those searching for a final program in the *Satyricon*; such a recurrent text invites the query: what literary and social possibilities does the frustration of closure engender? The *Satyricon* closes off the family of Seneca and all the provincials playing at the Roman, much as Tacitus in his *Annals*, through a series of rehearsals and depredations of the grand Stoic death, makes the final words, perhaps all the words, of the pontificating younger Seneca sound hollow and trite. In its sexually and symbolically powerful females the *Cena* closes with errant signs, powerful unfixed signifiers. We have neither Latinity Lost nor Regained—and so Petronius postures at variance with Seneca and

Phaedrus; nor does he suggest the familiarity, the coexistence and contest of the Plautine stage. Instead, a symbolically charged linguistic anxiety accompanies a greater sense of loss and distance. But lest we see this as genuine sorrow, mourning for the passing of epic, we should ask which is more humorous and ridiculous, Trimalchio trying to speak like a consul and an author or Petronius like a freedman. The resuscitation of the old, that passing off the classical as one's own, brings spontaneous ridicule; laughter may be the censorious and spontaneous reaction that arises from a literature posing social roles and relations as questions of style. But literature cannot so neatly escape from its nonverbal effects, the laugh of derision, the silence of disbelief.

In the textual technique that has guided this book, Roman literary representations differentiate society, literary and real, through discourses that center around linguistic possession. In maneuvering between owned and genuine speech, Roman literature figures its own status and social ambitions, and also refracts certain specific cultural anxieties: it displaces paternal authority over the son and the slave, whose *peculia*—the property held by custom, not law—are both profitable and threatening. The recurrent manifestation of this anxiety advertises the fear of the *peculium* holder's sexual abandon: the failure to control his body parts that is a confession of both power and peril, legal formula and liability. The son can lose the father's money and status; the slave, although legally an *instrumentum vocale*, has a tool and voice not quite controllable. For the slave, too, is a man who can act as an independent agent with the master's property, son—perhaps even wife. *Peculium* and literature are similar displaced possessions of the patron; they figure a personal and social investment, representing both profitability and risk. Paternal rhetoric recurrently tries to return slave and son to the farm, to family, to infantile status; but this is simply a rhetoric of control: rustication or imprisonment are, like aphasia and aporia, a loss of self, the squandering or idling of capital.

I have not tried to trace the genealogy of Latin literature's self-reflection on Latinity, vulgarity, and servility; nor have I tried to itemize their roles. The debts of literary Latinity to its origins in public festival; its linguistic resources drawn from the native public traditions of law, oratory, and ritual; its own, original sense of debt to Greek language and culture and the Greek-speaking slaves or freedmen who transmitted these, easily come to mind for the genealogist intent on reconstructing contexts for the evolution of literature as a social institution. But such reconstruction smacks of the diachronic reductionism which asserts that Terence is an improvement over Plautus: because of such originary thinking the relationship of the best (preserved) two early authors, Plautus and Terence, has been interpreted as evolutionary; allegedly, literary sense is progressing, along with the sense of aristocratic identity, in response to and assisting an increasing differentiation of Roman society.

I do not wish to enter into such primitivizations of Rome and then expand them by synecdoche to all of Latin literature as a contest between the native and the Greek, the vulgar and the literary (aristocratic). What scholars have sundered as two rival dramatic techniques were two voices within one literature and conflicting voices within one society—one integrative, one segregative. Of course, this split cannot hold. Phaedrus, and perhaps Plautus, wrote as a vehicle of upper-class ideology and crated a servile or libertine literature deconstructing *officium* and *clientela*. Petronius associates the hypersexual, homosexual, and rhetorical not simply because a homophobic (at least in some public polemics) and conventionally Hellenophobic elite saw (and derided) its position being filled by different strata and different structures but because he is figuring intercourse between social classes (which could be portrayed as traditionally and ideologically unnatural). Latinity offers closure only by and in reading: all are written in the same text. Perhaps in the reduction of *realia* to *signa*, some sympathy of viewpoint emerges; but no single discourse holds. We hear and acknowledge the struggle for speech against the silence of oppression, against the total silence of secession.

The slave knew that only his future profitability prevented

the master from repossessing his capital. The slave had convention to rely on; perhaps he could use the master's language of obligation, service, justice, but the master had the language of law. Literature was another special, but not discrete, discourse serving and commanding an intermediary and mediating role. The very word *Latinitas* makes a claim for all society, but it is a claim made not *by* but *for* one stratum. Petronius and Tacitus, following Plautus, harry this fiction of a common style.

In tracing how Roman literature posed social relations as questions of style, we have not focused on the great, virile texts (with the exception of the *Annals*, and there we considered Tiberius's debilitating speech). The material of this book has included heterotopic texts and heterotopic loci within texts. The places of speech have great significance: characters and authors attempt to shift discourse in the mutinous assembly at the borders of the empire, in the freedmen's dining room, and in the declamatory hall or school, a freedman's house. Fable itself as another school genre, and one curiously posed between the Greek and the Roman, the childish and the adult, marks itself as not quite civil, still suspect in its move toward the Roman. In these texts especially, Roman literature does not present a utopia, a pastoral scene where differences of class and language are eclipsed and transformed by a natural or esthetic language.[87]

Our emphasis on the figures of the slave, the freedman, the arriviste may seem partial given the epic and lyric characters whose language Latinists usually celebrate, but the Roman text figures anxieties about Romanness and Romanization of speech in these more mobile characters and more marginal passages. From a question of social history—Whom did literature invest with status?—this study soon moved to issues of cultural representation—What society did literature represent? What alliances did speech produce? For textual evocations of Roman society, scholars have traditionally turned to Cicero's fictitious dialogues (*Friendship, Republic, Laws*) or to his speeches urging social concord, to Livy's spectacles complete with audiences, and to Aeneas in Italy—all of which are more critically understood when we have read texts driven by a worry that they do not measure up. Phaedrus and Petronius are not simply engaged in representing the low or mimicking linguistic relations; these they have thematized, with far-reaching significances for the processes of literary composition and reading. The society of reading may neither captivate nor repel, but it does create a fiction of understanding and sympathy that engages and refracts what the Romans took to be an essential social issue: Who will be the *magister loquendi* and what power of exclusion or inclusion does his mastery offer?

The question of who would have authorial authority and the possible answers (author, reader, teacher, freedman, long-dead aristocrat) remained in Rome resonant, vital, and bitter. In an empire with a learned language, with careers in the imperial bureaucracy, in education, in literature, there existed from the first literature a self-consciousness about language, language anxiety, and the concomitant, sometimes masked, concerns about identity and social change. This is one of the ways in which Roman literature is tied to its Hellenistic predecessors and first practitioners, and to its vernacular successors. And yet Roman literature is strikingly different from Greek in its complex figuring of the potentialities of a readerly society. We see the differences in small ways, too: Roman comedy includes greeting scenes with elaborate politenesses; not so the Greek New Comedy that was its model. Characters did not need more introduction to the "semiliterate" Romans; rather, the Roman author recognized and exploited the dynamic potential of literature to fashion social and familial relations. Whether or not social relations in Rome were more problematic, certainly they constituted a greater part of public discourse, which has shaped the West's notions about literary, civilizing speech.

Notes

Notes to Introduction

1. In origin "Hellenism" is a linguistic term, a virtue of style according to the rhetorical-philosophical tradition (see the references at *LS&J*, ἑλληνισμός II, including Diogenes Babylonius the Stoic 3.214 and the Epicurean Philodemus *Poet.* 2.18, and the list of individual ancient works devoted to and entitled "Hellenism"). In addition, the term would have been known to every schooled Greek and any Roman schooled in Greek, for the elementary school exercise, the *progymnasmata*, taught in the opening chapter that it was one of the virtues of any narrative (see Aphthonius, *Progymnasmata*, chap. 1).

2. For references to paideia in inscriptions as a marker of status, see Marc Kleijwegt, *Ancient Youth: The Ambiguity of Youth and the Absence of Adolescence in Greco-Roman Society* (Amsterdam: Gieben, 1991), 86.

3. Extant monographs range from, e.g., Probus (see Karl Barwick, "Die sogennante Appendix Probi," *Hermes* 54 [1919]: 409–22) to Bertil Axelson, *Unpoëtische Worter* (Lund: H. Ohlssons, 1945).

4. The symbolic value of Varro himself is not to be underrated. Asinius Pollio built his library where Caesar had been buying land for his; in *Ep. ad Att.* 4.16.8, Cicero says Caesar was buying land "*usque ad atrium Libertatis*" for his forum and library. Augustus built elsewhere and had the freedmen Melissus and Hyginus as librarians. But Pollio put Varro's statue in his library, thus appropriating Caesar's "friend" as well as his site and project.

5. I will not rehearse the bibliography of patronage and Latin literature. The historians, especially, do not see patronage as an integrated, rigid vertical system, but as a more fluid system of relationships dependent on the exchange and reciprocity of favors and services. The most illuminating general discussions of the social institution are Richard Saller, *Personal Patronage under the Early Empire* (Cambridge: Cambridge University Press, 1982) and P. A. Brunt, " 'Amicitia' in the late Roman Republic," in *The Crisis of the Roman Republic*, ed. R. Seager, 199–218 (Cambridge: Cambridge University Press, 1969). See now, for an account of

the poets' relations to patrons, Peter White, *Promised Verse* (Cambridge, Mass., and London: Harvard University Press, 1993), which belongs to the mainstream in its preoccupation with the Augustan poets and with its apologetics on behalf of the poets, concluding that Augustus was not orchestrating literary production.

6. See Pierre Bourdieu, *Distinction*, trans. Richard Nice (Cambridge, Mass.: Harvard University Press, 1984), 15.

7. To some, whether certain people choose to write in Latin poems, speeches, or translations of the day's editorial seems a matter of personal eccentricity, like speaking Urdu to a dog. The orbits of such eccentricity are important. Choices of language, register, or dialect are, of course, highly significant of personal and social identity, to note the obvious, as well as of the worth of various languages and peoples.

8. These extremes are strawmen, but that has not prevented scholars from identifying themselves with one or the other. Antitheoretical stances are celebrated, with varying polemic, in the "practical criticism" of Tony Woodman and David West, eds., *Quality and Pleasure in Latin Poetry* (Cambridge and New York: Cambridge University Press, 1974) or in some of the contributions to Jan Ziolkowski, ed., *On Philology* (University Park and London: Pennsylvania State University Press, 1990). Definitional studies continually bat about these polar positions, often with little sense of what ideologies their own readings entail. For a critique of practical criticism, see Ralph Hexter and Daniel Selden, eds., *Innovations of Antiquity* (New York and London: Routledge, 1992).

9. Of course, comparative grammar was not an exclusively German phenomenon, despite the title of IndoGermanisches and the nationality of the four (almost canonical) nineteenth-century pioneers: F. Schlegel, J. Grimm, F. Bopp, and W. von Humboldt. This genealogy would ignore the work of the Dane R. Rask. (For a description of the early historiography of European linguistics, see R. H. Robins, *A Short History of Linguistics*, 3d ed. [London: Longman's, 1967], 170–85.) But the innovative science drew its inspiration from the "discovery" of Sanskrit, which as a rival to the classical languages of Europe was said to exhibit a more transparent structure. (For a detailed query of the priority of claims to the founding of comparative grammar and incisive comments on the culturally determined vision or blindness of seeing Sanskrit as transparent and not analyzable, see A. Morpurgo Davies, "Language Classification in the Nineteenth Century," in *Current Trends in Linguistics*, ed. Thomas A. Sebeok, vol. 13 of *Historiography of Linguistics* [The Hague and Paris: Mouton, 1975], 618–22.) There were nationalist reactions to the German school and science: in England, Henry Sweet (1845–1912), a leader in the study of phonetics, was bitterly opposed to the historical linguistics he

associated with Germany. Although Sir William Jones had in 1786 delivered his famous lecture "On the Hindus" to the Asiatic Society of Calcutta, his influence was first felt on the continent; see Hans Aarlseff, *The Study of Language in England, 1780–1860* (Princeton, N.J.: Princeton University Press, 1967), 3–4. In the 1830s two English Anglo-Saxonists who visited Rask and Grimm brought the new philology to England, whose universities were slow to welcome the science (Aarsleff, *Language in England*, 165–66). For the similar indifference or hostility to comparative grammar in France, see Georges Mounin, *Histoire de la linguistique des origines au XXe siècle* (Paris: Presses universitaires de France, 1967), 186–87, and for the first important reception of Bopp's work in France (the 1866 translation of *Vergleichende Grammatik*), see idem, "Bréal vs. Schleicher: Linguistics and Philology during the Latter Half of the Nineteenth Century," in *The European Background of American Linguistics*, ed. H. M. Hoenigswald (Dordrecht: Foris Publications, 1979), 78. Such was the resistance from linguists; the classicists' outraged responses are described in Ludo Rocher, "Les philologues classiques et les debuts de la grammaire comparée," *RUB* 10 (1957–58): 251–86.

For comparative grammar's obscuring effect on the relation between linguistic and political order, see R. Howard Bloch, *Etymologies and Genealogies: A Literary Anthropology of the French Middle Ages* (Chicago: University of Chicago Press, 1983), 22.

Notes to Chapter One

1. Suetonius, *De gramm.* 1.1, reports that both Ennius and Livius Andronicus taught in Greek and Latin at home and in the homes of others or perhaps in a rented school ("utraque lingua domi forisque docuisse"); see Robert Kaster, *C. Suetonius Tranquillus, De grammaticis et rhetoribus* (Oxford: Clarendon Press, 1975), 51.

2. A. E. Astin's valuable and fundamental study of Cato, *Cato the Censor* (Oxford: Oxford University Press, 1978), downplays the innovation and influence of Cato's historiography (see p. 236, following F. Bömer, "Thematik und Krise der römischen Geschichtsschreibung im 2. Jahrhundert v. Chr.," *Historia* 2 [1953]: 196ff.); for the contrary assessment, see Erich Gruen, *Culture and National Identity in Republican Rome* (Ithaca, N.Y.: Cornell University Press, 1992), 59–60. Two issues especially concern us: the relation of the *Origines* to the Hellenistic genre of κτίσεις and Cato's omission of names in that work. As Astin points out (229), Cato, unlike Fabius Pictor, discussed the origins of Italy, not simply of Rome. Whatever the exact relation to Hellenistic historiogra-

phy, Cato had significantly shifted the focus of Roman historiography. He might not be followed again until Virgil and Livy, but this hardly means his innovation was not polemical and influential. Astin also does not view the omission of names as an anti-aristocratic gesture. In great measure, Astin has rescued Cato from the caricature Plutarch and classical scholars made of him; he interprets the omission as part of Cato's concept of duty and his outlook as a *novus homo*, although he views this as "a temporary enthusiasm, clumsy and extravagant." It seems to me to be an oratorical strategy that helps to champion the first-person narrator (e.g., by not naming, misnaming, or granting a common name to one's opponent or other agents).

On Cato's attitudes to Greek culture, see Astin, 177–81 and appendix 9, and Gruen, chap. 2, "Cato and Hellenism," 52–83.

3. Successful defenses: Plut. *Cat. Mai.* 15.4 and 29.5; on Cato's collection of *dicta* see Astin, *Cato*, 186 and Cicero *De off.* 1.104 and *De or.* 2.271; for sayings attributed to Cato, see Astin, 188.

4. Victor, 374, H.

5. Seneca translates this Greek proverb, οἷος ὁ τρόπος τοιοῦτον εἶναι καὶ τὸν λόγον (found in Aristides *Or.* 45, vol. 2, 133 Dind., but see further citations in A. D. Leeman, *Orationis Ratio* [Amsterdam: A. M. Hakkert, 1963], 448, n. 7) as "talis hominibus fuit oratio qualis vita" (Sen. *Epist.* 114.1).

6. Astin, 183, dissents from the older view that Cato wrote an encyclopedia (of medicine, agriculture, and rhetoric) for his son. In his view, the *Ad filium* was a collection of precepts.

7. See T. P. Wiseman, *New Men in the Roman Senate, 139 B.C.–A.D. 14* (Oxford: Oxford University Press, 1971).

8. Ennius was not enfranchised by the son of his patron Q. Fulvius Nobilior. Ernst Badian, "Ennius and His Friends," *Ennius, Entretiens sur l'antiquité classique* 17 (1972): 183, has demonstrated that the patron's son was only a child at the time of Ennius's enfranchisement (184 B.C.). For a corrective to the traditional account of the poet's receiving a Roman name, see Otto Skutsch, *The Annals of Quintus Ennius* (Oxford: Oxford University Press, 1985), 1, n. 1.

9. The issues are more complicated; see H. D. Jocelyn, "The Poet Cn. Naevius, P. Cornelius Scipio and Q. Caecilius Metellus," *Antichthon* 3 (1969): 32–47.

10. One should be quite clear that the Scipionic circle is a modern fiction; see Astin, 68–69. For another alleged literary circle, see David Ross, *Style and Tradition in Catullus* (Cambridge, Mass.: Harvard University Press, 1969), 142, n. 61.

11. For the epitaph of Naevius, see Edward Courtney, *The Fragmen-*

tary Latin Poets (Oxford: Oxford University Press, 1993), 47–48. Cicero quotes the lines of Ennius as separate couplets at *Tusculans* 1.34. See Courtney, 42–43.

12. In his proem to book three of the *Georgics* Virgil excavates Ennius's boast: "temptanda via est, qua me quoque possim / tollere humo victorque virum volitare per ora" (8–9).

13. On the manumission of literate slaves, see the discussion and bibliography at Kaster, *Suetonius*, 168.

14. The classical statement and illustration of a three-tiered system of style comes at 4.11–16 of the *Rhetorica ad Herennium*, a work that enjoyed great authority thanks in part to its wrongful ascription to Cicero.

15. For Browning's attitude to Catholicism, and specifically for his opposition to the contemporary Catholicizing movement to reform the Anglican church (the Tractarian controversy), see R. A. Greenberg, "Ruskin, Pugin, and the Contemporary Context of *The Bishop Orders His Tomb*," *PMLA* 84 (1960): 1588–94, quoted in John Woolford and Daniel Karlin, eds., *The Poems of Browning*, vol. 2 (Harlow, Essex, Eng., and New York: Longman, 1991): 260. Following K. I. D. Malsen, "Browning and Macaulay," *N & Q* 27 (1980): 525–27, Woolford and Karlin (p. 261) quote as a possible source for Browning a review by Macaulay in the October 1840 Edinburgh Review of Leopold von Ranke's *Ecclesiastical and Political History of the Popes of Rome*, translated by Sarah Austin. After much criticism of the decadence of the court of Rome, with enumeration of the popes' objects of passion, including "newly-discovered manuscripts of the classics," Macaulay offers as an argumentative crescendo: "it was felt that the Church could not be safely confided to chiefs whose highest praise was that they were good judges of Latin compositions." Browning did not follow the Latinate or neo-Latinate lead. He names Gandolfo "Gandolf" and, in Karlin and Woolford's words (p. 259): " 'Praxed' is the anglicized form of 'Prassede.' " Writing the Italian interloper out may be Browning's idea of reforming, restoring the English church and poem; but does he create a new Latin or is he embracing the vernacular, the spoken? The poem constructs such poles and at the same time marks them as polemical, finite, even sterile. Of course Browning was not going to publish in Latin; that was for schoolboys. But the classical and the English are being allied. He is denying the Italian as mediator and suggesting another sort of return, but one dependent on the error of the vernacular, the entrance of illicit passion that the Italian represents.

16. It is significant that the poet writes of stone; he imagines his predecessor as a statue. Peter Bing, *The Well-Read Muse: Present and Past in Callimachus and the Hellenistic Poets*, Hypomnemeta: Untersuchungen zur Antike und zu ihrem Nachleben 90 (Göttingen: Vandenhoeck &

Ruprecht, 1988), 56–57, writes of the Hellenistic poets' attitudes to their past: "The rupture with the literary past, which these poets so keenly felt, is manifested in a variety of ways. Theocritus, for instance, writes four epigrams that pose as inscriptions for the statues of ancient poets. . . . Theocritus is here casting the literary heritage in a very suggestive form—as a monument of stone or bronze, a literary fossil, envisioned by the poet and his reader. . . . the mute stones do not speak." Bing believes that the Alexandrian poets uniquely or especially felt the rupture with the Greek literary past. This Egyptian locus may be the wellspring for the West's literary combination of monumentality, linguistic anxiety, and displacement.

17. John Woolford and Daniel Karlin, eds., *The Poems of Browning*, 259: "Mrs. Orr (*Handbook* 247) states, probably on B.'s authority: 'The Bishop's tomb is entirely fictitious.'" The existence and site of the tomb developed into a scholarly controversy: the church has two monuments, but not in sight of each other; perhaps this provided the germ of the idea. Various models for the tomb have been canvassed (e.g., Ignatius Loyola's tomb, a deliberate anachronism); for a succinct account of the tomb bibliography, see Woolford and Karlin, eds., 259–60. The baroque tomb, as W. David Shaw (*The Dialectical Temper: The Rhetorical Art of Robert Browning* [Ithaca, N.Y.: Cornell University Press, 1968]), 105, states, was a metaphysical conceit. While Horace's *exegi monumentum* (*Odes* 3.30) is of course duly noted (the corpus of the poems is the poet's legacy), the connection between poets' tombs and fame is not developed. A spot at the crammed Westminster Abbey awaited the English seer (buried December 31, 1889). The press of this statuary rivals that of the Theater of Pompey, which seems to have provided a source for lines 15–16. Woolford and Karlin, eds., 265, quote from "a book B. knew well," Daniello Bartoli's *De' simboli trasportati al Morale*: "The living who seek refuge in the Theatre of Pompey are crowded out by the profusion of statuary." Their brief citation calls out for exegesis. The famous living who failed to find refuge in the theater was Julius Caesar, assassinated there before the statue of his dead rival Pompey on the Ides of March 44 B.C.—again, a contest of the dead and dying, with one piece of statuary as silent, provocative witness. This death scene, melodramatic after Plutarch and Shakespeare, should be added to the scholarly lists of deaths and statues in the poem. More to the point, it further complicates the longing for fame and for a classical tomb. It makes us see the poet's rivalry, and perhaps the poet's and the reader's place, as belated, fatal rivalry.

18. Ruskin lauded the poem for Browning's appreciation of the southern artist's veneration of stone and for his grasp of "the Renaissance spirit" (*Modern Painters* vol. 4 [1856], in *Works*, ed. Cook and Wedderburn [1913], vol. 6, 448). Ruskin treats the English poet as a lapidary

Latinist: all that the scholar had attempted to express in many prose pages Browning had got right in a few lines.

19. In damning Cicero as the obfuscator of that beautiful signifier Latin, Mommsen engaged in a recurrent prejudice (Theodor Mommsen, *The History of Rome*, vol. 5, trans. William Dickson [New York: Scribners, 1895], 504–7). Scholars come to their learned languages seeking clarity, an unmediated window on the past. The pioneers of Indo-European, the inaugurators of Western linguistic science, stated that Latin and Greek were more transparent in revealing their roots and structures (than the vernacular German and English). Of course, Europeans were gazing on their past, and on their school languages; Sanskrit stood outside their experience, but it was really this language which played the third, revealing the structures and correspondences that would allow the reconstruction of the original (see Chap. 1, n. 3 above for bibliography). Scholars seem to long for the sorts of tombs Herodotus reports of the long-lived Ethiopians. These most remote of men, closest to gods in their life span, buried their dead in crystal coffins.

20. The bishop has a complex literary past: Job, Trimalchio, Bembo, and Donne all have worked their various influence. For the parallels with Job, see bibliography cited by Woolford and Karlin, eds., 261. H. M. Richmond, "Personal Identity and Literary Persona: A Study in Historical Psychology," *PMLA* 90 (1975): 209–19, suggested Izaak Walton's *Life of Donne*, with its theatrical deathbed episode, and the similarly histrionic Trimalchio. Woolford and Karlin continue, "Dr. M. Halls has suggested to us a resemblance between the Bishop and Cardinal Pietro Bembo (1470–1547): advocacy of Cicero's Latin style, sexual profligacy before ordination, and interest in pagan antiquity and classical scholarship." Bembo advocated a strict Ciceronianism: spoken and written Latin must exhibit no word not exampled by Cicero. Trimalchio, Job, and Donne help Browning associate such a complete resuscitation of the classical with death.

21. Like Trimalchio, the bishop talks too much, employs dubious logic, recklessly mixes media, and may even use inappropriate syntax. Robert Langbaum, *The Poetry of Experience: The Dramatic Monologue in Modern Literary Experience* (London: Chatto & Windus, 1957), 182–83, points out in the superabundance of expression in the bishop's speech a gratuitousness "heightened by the fact that the speakers never accomplish anything by their utterance." See also Shaw, 107 ("All along the Bishop has shown himself to be garrulous and repetitive"). Shaw also describes (p. 105) how the bishop's argument and art break down: the inclusion of such pagan motifs as Pan, like other egregious juxtapositions, undermines any serious religiosity. Shaw notes that the bishop's paratactic syn-

tax becomes an index of his greed. It also undermines his argument and stylistic presumptions, for he here invokes marble's language (line 98), but his speech fails to exhibit a tight, lapidary, Latin elegiac style.

22. Michael André Bernstein, *Bitter Carnival*: Ressentiment *and the Abject Hero* (Princeton, N.J.: Princeton University Press, 1992), 17, asserts an almost generic connection between a sense of latecoming and the Saturnalian text: "Belatedness, the knowledge of coming after the festival has already been fragmented, is thus not limited as Bakhtin wants us to believe, to a post-Renaissance bourgeois culture; it is a condition of every Saturnalian text." The connection may be one common to any ritual that evokes integration and restoration. One attends necessarily hoping for recuperation. Be that as it may, the particular connections with inscription and a sense of linguistic inferiority seem germane and original to our Julio-Claudian text.

23. On the associations of literary error, repetition, and fiction, see Patricia Parker, *Inescapable Romance: Studies in the Poetics of a Mode* (Princeton, N.J.: Princeton University Press, 1979), and for the related nexus of change, fixity, and fiction, see A. Bartlett Giamatti, *Exile and Change in Renaissance Literature* (New Haven and London: Yale University Press, 1984), 115–50.

24. I use Virgil as a foil only. His bucolic poems themselves advertise an end to alienation and dispossession.

Notes to Chapter 2

1. Crates may also have been introducing parchment to Rome as a substitute for the papyrus of his king's enemy, Ptolemy VI; see Richard R. Johnson, "Ancient and Medieval Accounts of the 'Invention' of Parchment," *CSCA* 3 (1970): 115–22. For a redemption of Crates's scholarship, see Elizabeth Asmis, "Crates on Poetic Criticism," *Phoenix* 46 (1992): 138–69; and, more generally, Robert Kaster, ed. and trans., *Suetonius*, De Grammaticis et Rhetoribus (Oxford: Oxford University Press, 1995), 58–59 and 61.

2. Stephanie H. Jed, *Chaste Thinking* (Bloomington and Indianapolis: Indiana University Press, 1989), 1–50.

3. They are also epochal, apologetic pivotal stories like the accounts of the captured Athenians who survived by having something to teach their Syracusan captors. The old high culture is remembered as living on as a possession of the new empire.

4. For an illuminating analysis of Cicero's relation to Greek science

and to Roman cultural context, see Mary Beard, "Cicero and Divination: The Formation of a Latin Discourse," *JRS* 76 (1986): 33–46.

5. The analogy–anomaly debate has been much overstated, with the result that Varro's polemic has been reified into opposing schools. For a corrective, see David L. Blank, *Ancient Philosophy and Grammar: The Syntax of Apollonius Dyscolus* (Chico, Calif.: Scholars Press, 1982), 2–5 and 11–19.

6. See Mark Amsler, *Etymology and Grammatical Discourse in Late Antiquity and the Early Middle Ages*, Amsterdam Studies in the Theory and History of Linguistic Science, vol. 44 (Amsterdam and Philadelphia: John Benjamins, 1989), 19.

7. For acute comments on the anti-Roman prejudice of accounts of Rome as the accidental intermediary, see Luigi Romeo and Gaio E. Tiberio, "Historiography of Linguistics and Rome's Scholarship," *Language Sciences* 17 (1971): 32.

8. Haun Saussy reminds me of the contrast with metaphor.

9. On the transformation of etymology into a kind of signifying geography, see Bloch, *Etymologies and Genealogies*, 54–55.

10. Pierre Bourdieu (*Language and Symbolic Power*, ed. John B. Thompson, trans. Gino Raymond and Matthew Adamson [Cambridge, Mass.: Harvard University Press, 1991], 58–59) points out the role of grammarians and teachers in supplying explanations for particular uses of language in opposition to the practice of writers who claim an instinctive affinity or mastery of high style.

11. On the elite's competition for the topography of Rome, for putting their name and imprint on public places, see John Carter, "Civic and Other Buildings," in *Roman Public Buildings*, ed. I. M. Barton (Exeter: Exeter University Press, 1989), 44.

12. Katharine Toll, "The *Aeneid* as an Epic of National Identity: *Italiam laeto socii clamore salutant*," *Helios* 18 (1991): 3–14.

13. The scope of Varro, like that of Livy, was daunting even in the next generation. Contrast the long-winded Augustans to the succinct rhetorical age: Livy's 126 books were reduced to an epitome; Velleius Paterculus wrote a universal history in two books; Valerius Maximus's nine books collected from Cicero, Livy, and Pompeius Trogus the juicy anecdotes for declaimers and lawyers. The imperial reader could consult Celsus's six-volume encyclopedia in place of Varro, Cicero, and the medical writers.

14. The negotiations involved in the composition and dedication of Cicero's and Varro's works were complex. See especially Karl Barwick, "Widmung und Enstehungsgeschichte von Varros *De lingua latina*," *Philologus* 101 (1957): 298–304. The *De lingua latina* was written between

47 and Cicero's death on December 7, 43 B.C. Barwick concludes (p. 299), on the basis of notices of title in the fragments, that the entire work was dedicated to Cicero. This might not constitute a rededication or republication but the first publication of the entire work, for books 2, 3, and 4 are dedicated to Septumius. Cicero is addressed in all three books of the second triad. Barwick argues (pp. 301–2) that Varro did not originally plan to dedicate the whole work to Cicero; he decided this after the publication of books 2–4. Book 1 was then designed as an introduction to the whole and written last. The final argument from internal considerations is that book 5, in which the Latin word for camel is discussed (*camelus*, along with giraffe, *camelopardus*, at 5.100), may be dated after 46 B.C., in which year Pliny (*NH* 8.69) and Dio (43.23.1) record that a giraffe first appeared at Rome in the games given by Caesar. This composition history must be viewed in the context of Cicero's writing to Atticus and the publication of his own treatises. In his letter to Atticus of June 24, 45 (13.12.3) Cicero characterizes Varro's promise of dedication in mock solemn tones: "[Varro] denuntiaverat magnam sane et gravem προσφώνησιν" and then complains that two years had gone by without any progress (i.e., Varro had made his promise in 47 and, as Barwick suggests, had already written and dedicated books 2–4). Cicero may have been put out because Caesar's projects were preoccupying Varro. Cicero, too, had failed before in his letter writing to Varro. He had thought that Varro's influence with Pompey would protect him from Clodius and impending exile (*Ad Att.* 2.20.1; 2.21.6), and was angry at Varro's delay (*Ad Att.* 2.25.1). Once in exile, Cicero had hoped that Atticus would pressure Varro to intervene on his behalf with Pompey. Here too he was disappointed. Finally, Atticus engineered a rapprochement by suggesting that Cicero include Varro in one of his dialogues (*Ad Att.* 4.16.2). Thus, when in the fall of 47 Caesar had entrusted his libraries to Varro (Barwick notes [p. 301] Ritschl's suggestion in *Opusc.* III 451 f. that Varro then wrote *De bibliothecis* III), Cicero may have worried that he was losing Varro's attention, at the least. The two had visited in Tusculum in the happy days of their return to Italy, thanks to Caesar's *clementia* (*Ad fam.* 9.6.4). The *Academica posteriora*, a new four-book version with its dedicatory prompting to Varro and including Varro as a character, appeared sometime in June 45 (in between this and the return to Italy the *Brutus* had come out, with honorific mention of Varro at 205: "vir ingenio praestans omnique doctrina"). On the eleventh or twelfth of this month, Cicero wrote to Varro to remind him of his promise (*Ad fam.* 9.8.1). Barwick (p. 304) even suggests that Varro may have published the whole work after Cicero's death. The complex web of letters, dedications, alternate commissions, interventions of Atticus and no doubt Caesar, reveal just how prized an authority Varro was. (Caesar was an old hand at this sort of dedication: in 54 he had dedicated

his linguistic work, *De analogia*, to Cicero.) To have the old Pompeian within one's *amicitia* — and to make a public, literary display of that connection — was of great importance to Caesar and Cicero. No doubt Cicero hoped to be included in Varro's *Imagines* and would have worried about the epigram celebrating his exploits.

Elaine Fantham "Cicero, Varro, and M. Claudius Marcellus," *Phoenix* 31 (1977): 208–13, points out other sorts of influence and intervention between Cicero and Varro at this time. In the *Orator* (46 B.C.), for example, Cicero draws extensively from Varro. Fantham argues convincingly that Cicero knew Varro was dedicating his work *De sermone latino* (perhaps published in 46) to Marcellus, and so, for this reason, for political and personal reasons, and as a balance to Caesar, Cicero introduced him at *Brutus* 248–50. The interplay and rivalry between the works of these two continued even after Cicero's death. Lily Ross Taylor, "Varro's *De gente populi Romani*," *CP* 29 (1934): 221–29, following Hermann Peter's suggestion (*HRR* I xxiii ff.) that Caesar's comet and the prophecy of a new age occasioned the work, argued that Varro's work responded to Cicero, who at *Phil.* 1.13 had maintained that the deification of Julius Caesar was contrary to Roman precedent. The *De gente populi Romani* would thus be yet another installment in Varro's appropriation and support of the Caesars' account of Roman religion against the opposing opinions and publications of Cicero. Cicero's death may have made some writing easier, but Varro apparently did not hesitate to trespass upon Cicero's chosen subjects; in 45 he wrote a book, *De philosophia*, which enumerated 288 kinds of philosophy (Aug. *De civ. Dei* 19.1). Again the encyclopedist seems to have swallowed up Cicero's efforts: Varro's *libri disciplinarum* treated grammar, dialectic, and rhetoric.

15. Varro seems to have followed Cicero in naming his dialogues after Roman historical figures. Varro wrote a *Marius de fortuna* and a *Tubero de origine humana* and many others in the lost *Logisticorum libri LXXVI*, begun in 44 B.C.

16. See Frances V. Hickson, *Roman Prayer Language: Livy and the Aeneid* (Stuttgart: Teubner, 1993), 1–15.

17. See Glen Bowersock, *Augustus and the Greek World* (Westport, Conn.: Greenwood Press, 1981).

18. For an account of the rise of antiquarianism in the eighteenth century and its implications for historical method, see Arnaldo Momigliano, "Ancient History and the Antiquarian," *Journal of the Warburg and Courtauld Institutes* 19 (1950): 285–315.

19. The *liber annalis* appeared in 47 B.C. and immediately influenced Cicero's composition. Indeed, it made the *Brutus* possible (for Cicero's connection of Marcus with the republic's founder, Lucius Junius Brutus, see *Brutus* 53 and 331).

20. Nepos *Att.* 18.2. See Hans Josef Bäumerich, "Ueber die Bedeutungen der Genealogien in der römischen Literatur" (diss., Cologne, 1964), 63, citing F. Münzer, "Atticus als Geschichtsschreiber," *Hermes* 40 (1905): 50ff., who dated Atticus's genealogical monographs on the *gens Fabia* and the *gens Aemilia* to the latter half of 58 B.C. A useful survey, which demonstrates just how widespread the practice of mythic genealogies was, is T. P. Wiseman, "Legendary Genealogies in Late-Republican Rome," *G&R* 21 (1974): 153–64. Cicero could claim no connection of birth to the divine, but his writings, especially his poetry, advertised his ties to Marius and to Minerva (see *Ad Att.* 2.3.4 and the fragments of his poem *Marius*, fr. 8 and 18–22 in *FPL*, ed. Blänsdorf).

21. Messalla seems to have written of his outrage: "Exstat Messallae oratoris indignatio, quae prohibuit inseri genti suae Laevinorum alienam imaginem. Similis causa Messallae seni expressit volumina illa quae de familiis condidit, cum Scipionis Pomponiani transisset atrium vidissetque adoptione testamentaria Salvittonis — hoc enim fuerat cognomen — Africanorum dedecori inrepentes Scipionum nomini" (Pliny, *NH* 35.8).

On legendary genealogies, see Kaster, *Suetonius*, 305, and n. 20 above.

22. This Julia, Caesar's father's sister and the wife of Marius, died in 69, the year of Caesar's quaestorship. See Suet. *Caesar* 6.1; Plut. *Caesar* 5.1.

23. Servius, *Aen.* 5.389, refers to Hyginus's work. Bäumerich ("Genealogien," 34, n. 5) argues that Hyginus's book was probably written after Varro's *De familiis troianis* (and see p. 77 on Hyginus using material in Varro, citing [n. 2] Diehle *RE* 10, 629). Momigliano ("Ancient History and the Antiquarian," 289) points out one political aspect of Roman antiquarianism but treats it as unique: according to Aulus Gellius (13.12.2) the antiquarian Ateius Capito criticized the antiquarian Antistius Labeo for his *libertas* in requiring a republican precedent for Augustus's every action.

24. Quintilian 1.4 and 1.5 discusses pronunciation, but seems to assume that his students need no drills. No doubt students were corrected in the *progymnasmata*, the exercises of the grammar-school teacher that do not much concern the author of the *Institutio oratoria*. There are several indications of the variety of Latin pronunciation (aside from the variants of spelling on inscriptions), e.g., Cicero *Pro Archia* 10: "pingue quiddam sonantibus et peregrinum" and *Brutus* 171 (on different vocabulary found in Gallic Latin). Every reader of Catullus knows the mockery that can be produced by mispronunciation (poem 84, on the missing aspirate).

25. There was plenty of ancient writing on syntax, especially by Stoics. Varro himself devoted books 14 to 25 of the *De lingua latina* to this subject. These do not survive, but his tour de force was probably ety-

mology: early on he had raised etymology to a major historical method in the *Antiquities*, and in the present work provided a theoretical account of its method and ample demonstrations of its range.

26. *Cratylus* 397 D.

27. Remmius Palaemon referred to Varro as pig—*porcum*, no doubt because he wrote on everything, too unsystematically for the expert freedman (Suetonius, *De grammaticis* 23). See n. 58 below.

28. On Cicero's alleged antipathy to Caesar's exploitation, see Beard, "Cicero and Divination: The Formation of a Latin Discourse," 34.

29. It would take a long note to list the late republican and early imperial catalogues of Roman heroes. Cicero had changed the canon of historical exempla, and this would influence the heroes Virgil placed in the underworld. At the same time, Nepos wrote lives of eminent men and launched the tradition for Suetonius, among others. The sculptural program of the Augustan forum is the most famous gallery of *imperatores*. Perhaps as a rival project (see my Introduction, n. 4, on the location of the site and Suet., *Caes.* 44), Asinius Pollio set up a library at the Atrium Libertatis, which contained images of authors: "Primum autem Romae bibliothecas publicavit Pollio, Graecas simul atque Latinas, additis auctorum imaginibus in atrio quod de manubiis magnificentissimum instruxerat" (Isidore, *Orig.* 6.5.2, following Suetonius). Varro was the only author to have his bust put on display in his lifetime: "M. Varronis in bibliotheca, quae prima in orbe ab Asinio Pollione ex manubiis publicata Romae est, unius viventis posita imago est" (Pliny, *NH* 7.115). This may suggest that he was the curator of the library and that his *Imagines* was the textual analogue to the portrait busts of famous writers installed there. It may also suggest that Pollio was taking Pompey's, but especially Cicero's, Caesar's, and Octavian's, lead in appropriating the service of Varro. On this library, see F. Castagnoli, "Atrium Libertatis," *Rendiconti Lincei* 8.1 (1946): 276–91, and A. J. Marshall, "Library Resources and Creative Writing at Rome," *Phoenix* 30 (1976): 252–64.

30. Varro seems to have imitated Cicero's dialogic technique of representing an aporia of opposed Hellenistic schools solved by a Roman moderated synthesis. See below on the presentation of anomaly and analogy. An example of Cicero's technique is the *De finibus bonorum et malorum*, which presents the Old Academy on the greatest good after the foils of Epicureanism and Stoicism. Similarly, the *De natura deorum* devotes one book each to Epicureanism, Stoicism, and Academicism. Woldemar Görler, *Untersuchungen zu Ciceros Philosophie* (Heidelberg: C. Winter, 1974), 14, describes Cicero's technique of presenting contradictory viewpoints: "Bei Cicero dagegen [Carneades] ist die Tendenz positiv: Er will durch den Vergleich der Standpunkte zu einer mög-

lichst gesicherten Antwort vorstoßen." Sometimes the contrast is simply left without resolution; indeed, the opposing viewpoints are often incompatible. See especially Görler's discussion at pages 51–62, "Thematischer Ueberblick über die Anwendung des 'Stufenschemas.'"

31. Francesco Della Corte, *Varrone il terzo gran lume romano* (Florence: La Nuova Italia, 1970), traces the implications of all these passages, devoting his chapter 11 to the phase of their relations that resulted in mutual literary deference.

32. Della Corte, *Varrone*: rewriting of *Academica*, 155–58; presentation to Varro, 164–70; Varro's dedication of the *De lingua latina*, 174–75. In addition, one should note Caesar's (earlier) critical portrayal of Varro in book 2 of the *Bellum civile*; see Cynthia Damon, "Caesar's Practical Prose," *CJ* 89 (1994): 191–94.

33. Della Corte, *Varrone*, for instance, has written a model biography integrating the better-known political history and the slimly known and partially extant works of Varro. After stressing the importance of Varro's schooling under Accius, Della Corte presents chapters that consider Varro's relations to the leading autocrat of the day: for example, with the Sullan revolution Varro is back at Rome, and Della Corte concludes in the third chapter, though there is no evidence for Varro's relations to Sulla, that the anti-Gracchan, conservative Varro probably welcomed the reactionary movement (especially pp. 47–48). The subsequent chapters map literary composition against political events: chapter 4, titled "Al servizio di Pompeo," describes Varro as the happy collaborator, producing the *Ephemeris navalis ad Pompeium* and the Εἰσαγωγικός *ad Pompeium*, the manual of civil life and senatorial procedure. Chapter 5 treats the second installment of the *Ephemeris navalis*, produced on the occasion of Pompey's suppression of the pirates (in which campaign Varro served as a subordinate officer). Chapter 6 considers Varro's support of the triumvirate as manifested in his pamphlet Τρικάρανος. (This lost work has been interpreted as a spoof of the triumvirate, but Anderson sides with Della Corte; see William S. Anderson, *Pompey, His Friends, and Literature of the First Century B.C.*, University of California Publications in Classical Philology 19.1 [Berkeley and Los Angeles: University of California Press, 1963], 45.) His service on Caesar's commission of twenty to divide the *ager Campanus* led to the writing of the *De re rustica*. Five chapters treat the more Byzantine subjects of Varro's subsequent relations with Caesar and with Cicero, the last of which stresses the role of Atticus.

34. On the qualities of Roman personal abuse in public fora, see Catharine Edwards, *The Politics of Immorality in Ancient Rome* (Cambridge: Cambridge University Press, 1993).

35. The divisions of subject by book number included: 2, contra

etymology, 3, pro, 4, treating its nature; 5, place-names; 6, words pertaining to time; 7, abstruse words from the poets; 8, contra anomaly, 9, pro, 10, Varro's synthesis. Books 11–13 treated analogy, applied to the same categories as books 5–7. Syntax was discussed in 14–19 and perhaps in the remaining books. Cicero had an anti-analogistic section in the Brutus (258ff.) where Caelius and Pacuvius represent *mala consuetudo* but "Caesar autem rationem adhibens consuetudinem vitiosam et corruptam pura et incorrupta consuetudine emendat" (261). Cicero thus (re?)defines Caesar as a not so strict analogist.

36. Festus (p. 220) has much the same with slight variants and makes more of the sheep-grazing explanation (*pascens balare*) and sheep wandering (*palare*).

37. See C. O. Brink, *Horace on Poetry—Epistles Book II: Letters to Augustus and Florus* (Cambridge: Cambridge University Press, 1982), 85–86, on Varro's estimation of various poets. It is not my argument that he liked or disliked Ennius but that he disdains to value the poets and their teachers as culture authorities.

38. Joshua A. Fishman, *The Sociology of Language* (Rowley, Mass.: 1972), 20, notes that speech communities concerned with differentiating and authenticating their language become concerned with historicity, with creating an ancient ancestry and eliding recent influences.

39. Varro never uses the term *urbanitas*; indeed, he uses rustic Latin as the crucial link back to ancestral Latin; on this pointed contrast with Cicero, see Silvano Boscherini, "Città e campagna nella dottrina linguistica di Varrone," in *Atti del Congresso Internazionale di Studi Varroniani* (Rieti: Centro di studi varroniani, 1976), 319. The term remained in dispute: the Augustan poet Domitius Marsus wrote a book *De urbanitate* whose characterization of the *homo urbanus* Quintilian believed to be the elder Cato. See Quint. 6.3.102–12 and, for a collection of the relevant passages, Edwin Ramage, "The *De Urbanitate* of Domitius Marsus," *CP* 54 (1959): 250–55.

40. When Varro writes of his teacher Stilo, he makes use of established targets and polemics (including Naevius and his verbal attack upon the Metelli). Stilo was the client of the Metelli and counted the poet Naevius as one of his rivals. Varro employs known cultural antipathies to articulate his authority. One could invoke the connection of Lucilius and Scipio Aemilianus to bring in that circle, or the connection of Lucilius and Pompey to lead to Varro. At any rate, Varro's connections lead to Stilo and the Metelli against the poet Naevius and his interpreters, the grammarians.

41. 9.59: "Dei et servi nomina quod non item ut libera nostra transeunt, eadem est causa, quod ad usum attinet et institui opus fuit

de liberis, de reliquis nihil attinuit, quod in servis gentilicia natura non subest in usu, in nostris nominibus qui sumus in Latio et liberi, necessaria." The construction of such a hierarchy is not inevitable; it does not simply tumble down from the evidence—as is clear from the variety of things one could say about "Roman" nomenclature. Varro's focus is on Italy, perhaps even on constructing one Italy.

42. Actually, Varro, like Cicero in the *Brutus*, is in some difficulty on the topic of the people's judgment. They clearly have no authority: "homines imperiti et dispersi" (10.60) and "populo multiplici et imperito" (10.16), but, like Cicero, Varro is driven to acknowledge their importance. He cannot sever true Latin from the people without fragmenting Roman society, and he cannot emphasize *consuetudo* without acknowledging the people. Thus he displaces his target onto the nonnative experts.

43. Varro makes a second characterization of his technique in which he establishes a four-tiered system of etymology. Like Plato, the author stops short of claiming *noêsis* for his own work.

44. On their stigmatized social position and the desire of literary authors to distinguish themselves from these fee-taking professionals, see Robert Kaster, *Guardians of Language: The Grammarian and Society in Late Antiquity* (Berkeley and Los Angeles: University of California Press, 1988), 52–63.

45. Hellfried Dahlmann, *Varro und die Hellenistische Sprachtheorie* (1932; reprint, Berlin: Weidmann, 1964), 67. Eduard Norden, *Die Antike Kunstprosa*, vol. 1 (1898; reprint, Stuttgart: Teubner, 1958), 184–86, had suggested that teachers of analogy influenced the Scipionic circle in its development of pure Latin. This is no doubt true, as Hellenistic teachers all used analogy. See Albrecht Dihle, "Analogie und Attizismus," *Hermes* 85 (1957): 170–205.

46. Detlev Fehling, "Varro und die Grammatische Lehre von der Analogie und der Flexion," pt. 1, *Glotta* 35 (1956): 258–65, has demonstrated that Varro's assertion of the role of anomaly in etymology and the dependence of this thesis on preexisting linguistic theory are unsubstantiated. This demonstration has had a better reception from linguists than from classicists: Jan Pinborg, "Classical Antiquity: Greece," in *Current Trends in Linguistics*, ed. Thomas A. Sebeok, vol. 13, *Historiography of Linguistics* (The Hague and Paris: Mouton, 1975), 18: "It must not be forgotten that the discussion of linguistic topics did not take place between hermetically closed 'schools,' so that a Stoic answer and an opposing Alexandrian one exist for any grammatical question. I find, like Fehling, review of *Probleme der stoischen Sprachlehre und Rhetorik*, by Karl Barwick, *GGA* 212 (1958): 173, that it is more useful to look upon Hellenistic grammar as a unity, to the development of which each school contributed re-

search, but not totally different versions." Robert Henry Robins, "Varro and the Tactics of Analogist Grammarians," in *Studies in Greek, Italic, and Indo-European Linguistics*, ed. Anna Morpurgo Davies and Wolfgang Meid (Innsbruck: Innsbrucker Beiträge zur Sprachwissenschaft, 1976), 333–36, disputes Fehling's suggestion that Varro exaggerated the anomalist–analogist controversy on the flimsy ground of the number (but not the dates) of ancient sources on these topics. Detlev Fehling's work, cited above, supersedes much of the earlier bibliography, e.g.: Rudolph Dam, *De analogia: Observationes in Varronem grammaticamque Romanorum* (diss., Utrecht, 1930), chiefly useful as a description of Varro's linguistic vocabulary (Dam [p. 39] had already cast doubt on the assertions of the importance of anomalism for Stoic theories of language); especially valuable is Dihle, "Analogie und Attizismus," who appended an afterword (202–5) in response to Fehling, underscoring and agreeing that analogy and anomaly were not opposed in Hellenistic theory but that Roman Atticists used them as polar terms in their debate. Further, the Romans extended anomaly from flexion to word formation. For the Romans I would substitute Varro. Dihle (p. 200) makes clear that analogy provided the theoretical justification for the Atticists at Rome in the first century to separate themselves from a *consuetudo* that dictated *imitatio antiquitatis*.

47. The modern linguistic term is overgeneralization; see Jill G. de Villiers and Peter A. de Villiers, *Language Acquisition* (Cambridge, Mass.: Harvard University Press, 1978), 85.

48. Dahlmann, *Varro*, 54 and 69.

49. These contemporary influences are not given much weight in scholarship. Jean Collart, *Varron Grammairien Latin* (Paris: Les Belles Lettres 1954), 155, had recognized that Varro deformed the arguments of books 8 and 9 for the sake of the synthesis he presented in book 10. Collart stressed internal considerations to arrive at his conclusion: the absence of endorsed Roman sources; the aggressive stance attributed to the Stoics and the contempt they show for any compromise; the manifest respect for the masters of the two schools; the restriction of the polemic to the first half of the second century, when Crates and Aristarchus were in their prime. Collart follows Dahlmann in emphasizing the parallel procedure of argument of Sextus Empiricus.

50. In practice, Varro himself stays within the lines; he restricts the use of analogy so as to preserve traditional boundaries, e.g., at 9.100 the genera of the tenses are allowed their own authority: between verb forms of different tenses, irregularity such as *fui, sum, ero* need not be corrected (forced to conform to analogy).

51. Cicero, *De legibus* 2.59.

52. Suetonius, *De gramm.* 16. See Kaster, *Suetonius*, 188, who argues

well that Epirota's introduction of Virgil to the schools may not have been a sweeping change.

53. Suetonius relates in passing that Cornelius Nepos, Varro's contemporary and social peer, wrote a book distinguishing the erudite from the educated man (*De gramm.* 4: "Cornelius quoque Nepos libello quo distinguit litteratum ab erudito litteratos quidem vulgo appellari ait eos qui aliquid diligenter et acute scienterque possint aut dicere aut scribere, ceterum proprie sic appellandos poetarum interpretes, qui a graecis γραμματικοί nominentur"). The interesting inference for the present argument is that Nepos does not want the professional interpreters, the *grammatici*, to be called erudite. He is trying to restrict the appellation *litteratus* to the paid teacher. The sobriquet "erudite" he no doubt reserved for men like Varro—and himself. For a discussion of the various terms for teacher, see E. W. Bower, "Some Technical Terms in Roman Education," *Hermes* 89 (1961): 462–77.

54. See Kaster, *Guardians of Language*, 15–31, for the role of the grammarian in imperial times.

55. Pliny, *Ep.* 4.13. Suetonius's own career is that of a *scholasticus*, a habitué of the schools: see Kaster, *Suetonius*, xxi.

56. Kaster, *Suetonius*, xxvi–xxvii, demonstrates the lack of precedent for the *De grammaticis*. On the original form of the work and the historian's methods, see Andrew Wallace-Hadrill, *Suetonius: The Scholar and His Caesars* (London: Duckworth, 1983), 50–59.

57. This is also a topos for Greek philosophers.

Suetonius put, as the second element of his biographies, following the grammarian's name, an indication of his status (i.e., *libertus* or alleged *ingenuus* or *expositus*) and of his allegiances (place of birth, names of patrons and students often follow). The instances of doubtful birth are: Gnipho, exposed (7); L. Orbilius Pupillus, an orphan (9); P. Valerius Cato, called by some a freedman, who asserted in his own book that he was a freeborn orphan (11); Lenaeus (diligent defender of his patron, Pompey), kidnapped from Athens, who eventually tried to buy his freedom but was given it "ob genium atque doctrinam" (15); C. Julius Hyginus, Spaniard or Alexandrian? (20); C. Melissus, exposed by his parents, who remained in servitude to Maecenas rather than reclaiming his freedom through his mother, "quare cito manumissus, Augusto etiam insinuatus est" (21).

The double naming of the freedmen likewise draws attention to their artificial and ambitious status. Saevius Nicanor, the first grammarian of Suetonius's series, made a riddling poem of his two names (5); Suetonius reports two spellings of Aurelius Opilius's name (6); "Ateius Praetextatus . . . ad summam Philologus ab semet nominatus," Pollio wrote with disdain (10); Cornelius Epicadus claimed to be the freedman of both Sulla and one of Sulla's son (12); Lucius Crassicius changed his cognomen from Pasicles to Pansa (18). Their names are as shifty as their birth, such notices imply. The charges of plagiarism emphasize the dangerous, extremely fluid movement of names. Servius stole some of his father-in-law's books; Suetonius tells of his consequent suicide (3). Orbilius republished Gnipho's works under the rightful author's name (7). On the Roman practice of double (or more) *cognomina*, see Kaster, *Suetonius*, 109–11.

58. For a precis of the distinguished classicists who have written on this question, see Daniel J. Taylor, "Palaemon's Pig," *Historiographica Linguistica* 8 (1981): 191–93. Kaster, *Suetonius*, 237, finds none of the suggested explanations convincing.

59. Compare the elite aristocratic circle of critics and their withering one-liners that Seneca includes in his account of the declaimers (see Chapter 4).

60. Suetonius reports the following instances of poverty-stricken teachers: M. Pompilius Andronicus (8); Lucius Orbilius Pupillus wrote of his extreme poverty and achieved at Rome greater fame than profit ("maiore fama quam emolumento," 9); P. Valerius Cato died in poverty (11); Hyginus died poor, according to his friend Clodius Licinus, the historian and consular (20).

Notes to Chapter 3

1. J. P. Postgate, "Phaedrus and Seneca," *CR* 33 (1919): 23, n. 2, found very little to fault: "There is little in the idioms or diction of Phaedrus to suggest the foreigner. His use of abstract nouns is certainly pushed beyond the Latin norm." But the norm of the contemporary schools and declamatory halls was rich in such abstract nouns, as Seneca the Elder and Valerius Maximus attest.

The monographs on Phaedrus's style attest to his "correct" Latinity, that is to say, they find parallels in the poets for unprosaic diction or syntax. See, for example, A. von Sassen, "De Phaedri Sermone" (diss., Marburg, 1911), and C. Causeret, "De Phaedri sermone grammaticales observationes" (diss., Paris, 1886). Likewise, the efforts to find vulgarity or popularity have had limited results; J. Bertschinger, "Volkstümliche Elemente in der Sprache des Phädrus" (diss., Bern, 1921), and Mariarosaria Pugliarello, "Appunti di sintassi fedriana," *SRIL* 4 (1981): 109–121, assert the artistic intent (variety, dignity for the new genre) of the features of colloquial or archaic Latin found in Phaedrus. H. MacL. Currie, "Phaedrus the Fabulist," *ANRW* II, 32.1 (1978): 504, found the fables "the last survival of the *sermo urbanus* in Latin poetry."

For full accounts of Phaedrus's careful and archaizing meter, see A. Guaglianone, "Fedro e il suo senario," *RSC* 16.1 (1968): 91–104, and D. Korzeniewski, "Zur Verstechnik des Phaedrus," *Hermes* 98 (1970): 430–58. The fundamental work on Phaedrus's meter remains the appendix in the edition of Louis Havet, *Phaedri Augusti Liberti Fabulae Aesopiae* (Paris: Hachette, 1895), 147–224. Havet's observations swept away many readings.

2. Morten Nøjgaard, *La Fable Antique 2: Les Grands Fabulistes* (Copenhagen: Nordisk, 1967), repeatedly remarks on this feature (e.g., 79: "La société des animaux figure les relations sociales," and 110–11, 172–73).

3. At the cost of her downfall the cicada overvalues her voice (3.16.16: "simul gaudebat vocem laudari suam"), as does the ass his braying, in 1.11. Two poems after the cicada, the peacock is in peril, in a fable entitled *Pavo ad Iunonem de voce sua*. Phaedrus locates two such fables at Roman games. A mimer named Princeps mistakes the crowd's hurrah for the Princeps as a bravo for him (5.7). The crowd itself is no judge of proper voice: when a *scurra* proposes a new type of entertainment, pig calling, the audience gives first prize to a human imitator and not to the farmer who snuck a pig under his cloak. Phaedrus points out that the *vocem naturae* (5.5.33) was not as well received by the partisan crowd.

4. These statements about his new genre consistently present Phaedrus as the Roman not the Greek, although envious critics (*Livor*) try to deny his claim. The very language of the claim comes from Catullus and Horace: e.g., "hanc [the material of Aesop] ego polivi versibus senariis" (1 Prologue 2); the epilogue to book 2 mentions Aesop and the Athenians' reception of the ex-slave and then contrasts "quodsi labori faverit Latium meo, / plures habebit quos opponat Graeciae" (8). The exhortation of the third prologue to have Eutychus read his work (which opposes the busy, serious reader and the *otium* of the poet and his work, and which Martial in 5.80 follows) again presents an accuser, this time the evil Sejanus, then notes the poet's own Thracian beginnings, and concludes by banishing *Livor*. The epilogue to book 4 echoes the prologue's boast that Phaedrus's poems are being copied into the addressee's notebooks: "quare, vir sanctissime, / Particulo, chartis nomen victurum meis, / Latinis dum manebit pretium litteris, si non ingenium, certe brevitatem adproba" (4 Epilogue 4–6). The consistent rhetoric of the prologues and epilogues asserts that, against the critics who would return him to his Greek origins, in birth or genre, the poet's brief speech enrolls him in Latin literature.

5. With this story Phaedrus seeks to redirect the doxographical tradition about the poet Simonides. The biographers of the poets repre-

sented Simonides as one who would sell his praise to the highest bidder. Phaedrus is interested only in emphasizing the return for poetic merit, which he so characteristically couches as the merit due voice, the true and abiding personal characteristic that can survive catastrophe.

6. So the editors write from the readings of PR' and D: FEDRI AUGUSTI LIBERTI LIBER FABULARUM and PHEDI AUG LIBER I AESO-PIARU.

7. P. R. C. Weaver, *Familia Caesaris: A Social Study of the Emperor's Freedmen and Slaves* (Cambridge: Cambridge University Press, 1972), 2–3, citing L. R. Taylor, "Freedmen and Freeborn in the Epitaphs of Imperial Rome," *AJP* 82 (1961): 113, notes that the abbreviations *Aug lib* or *Aug l* constituted a status symbol even in "the first c. A.D. when the freedmen of private citizens were ceasing to use any form of freedman indication at all" and concludes: "The fact is that the Familia Caesaris, consisting especially of the private staff of the emperor who came to perform public or semipublic functions, broke through all the traditional categories belonging to the *familia* of a *privatus* and came to form what was virtually an *ordo libertorum et servorum principis*, a new 'estate' or status-group in the hierarchy of Roman Imperial society" (115).

8. Taylor, "Freedmen," 29–130, argued that freedmen's motivation in leaving stone records was to display their Roman status. Elizabeth A. Meyer, "Explaining the Epigraphic Habit in the Roman Empire: The Evidence of Epitaphs," *JRS* 80 (1990): 74–96, has demonstrated that provincials (North Africans) were animated by the same motivation.

9. See above, n. 5. Susan Treggiari, *Roman Freedmen during the Late Republic* (Oxford: Oxford University Press, 1969), 11, stresses the importance slaves born in the master's house accorded this circumstance of birth. This and not race or national origin was their prime means of self-identification and of status.

10. Observing the great discrepancy between the intellectual and the social rank of the literate Roman freedman, Johannes Christes, "Reflexe erlebter Unfreiheit in den Sentenzen des Publilius Syrus und den Fabeln des Phaedrus," *Hermes* 107 (1979): 200, posed the fundamental question of their cultural allegiances.

11. Seneca, hoping to win his recall to Rome through flattery of the influential imperial freedman Polybius, urged Claudius's minister to try putting fables to verse, an "intemptatum Romanis ingeniis opus" (*Ad Polyb.* 8.3). This statement reflects either ignorance or abuse of our author (and possibly of others too—the elder Seneca at *Suas.* 7.12 commemorates a fabulist: "Surdinus, ingeniosus adulescens, a quo Graecae fabulae eleganter in sermonem Latinum conversae sunt"). Slander of Phaedrus, whose phrasing Seneca borrowed in his dramas, as Postgate, "Phaedrus

and Seneca," has shown, is part of the flattery of Claudius's freedman—only the worthy Polybius can be a Roman *littérateur*. In addition, Seneca would not have been sympathetic to Phaedrus's manner or style, as the dramatist's own *senarii* indicate. His resentment of the educational influence of freedmen is clear from *Epist.* 127.7.

12. I am not arguing that Phaedrus's target here was a freedman, only that oathbreaking is a recurrent concern, one which the poet presents as moving him to speech: Phaedrus sets himself in contrast to the garrulous characters of 3.13, "Hanc praeterissem fabulam silentio, / si pactam fuci non recusassent fidem."

13. See Alan Watson, *The State, Law, and Religion: Pagan Rome* (Athens, Ga., and London: University of Georgia Press, 1992), 45–46. For a direct connection with the poems, see Keith Bradley, *Slaves and Masters in the Roman Empire* (New York: Oxford University Press, 1984), 152, who suggests that Phaedrus 1.8 is reminiscent of the contract for manumission.

14. Drawing the attention of a listener to the correctness of speech of the speaker or another speaker is peculiar, the action perhaps of the boor, the social snob, or the pedagogue. Phaedrus's self-advertisement will not fit these categories. Freedmen in Petronius's pages take a different tack by pointing out the impropriety of their own speech and trying to "correct" their speech—a well-documented phenomenon.

15. On Phaedrus's innovative use of epimythia, see B. E. Perry, "The Origin of the Epimythium," *TAPA* 71 (1940): 408–12 and idem, trans., *Babrius and Phaedrus* (Cambridge, Mass.: Harvard University Press, 1984), xv–xvi.

16. In writing this way, Phaedrus refers back to the situation of Aesop telling his fables (in the *Life of Aesop*, for example, the threatened slave tells them to hostile listeners as his defense) more than he does to the actual fables as collected by Demetrius of Phalerum and preserved by the *Augustana*.

17. See notes 19 and 22 below.

18. N. Festa, "Su la favola di Fedro," *Rendiconti dell R. Accademia Nazionale dei Lincei* 33 (1924): 40, had observed the frequency of *calumnia* and the *calumniator* in Phaedrus.

19. The hyperbolically abused target of iambs is, of course, generic, as Archilochus and Callimachus had ensured. This generic connection of *vituperatio* and iambic verse has not impeded the reconstruction of Phaedrus's life, enemies, and addressees. Attilio de Lorenzi's biography of the poet, *Fedro* (Florence: La Nuova Italia Editrice, 1955), is more imaginative but of the same technique as the ancients' lives that have been attached to so many manuscripts.

Pierre Grimal, "Du nouveau sur les *Fables* de Phèdre?" in *Mélanges de littérature et d'épigraphie latines d'histoire ancienne et d'archéologie. Hommage à la memoire de Pierre Wuilleumier* (Paris: Les Belles Lettres, 1980), 143–49, illustrates well the methodology of identifying the poems' contexts and personae. Abandoning an earlier identification—F. Buechler, "Coniectanea," *RhM* 38 (1883): 333ff., citing Josephus *Ant. Jud.* 19.256ff., had identified Eutychus as the cook of Caligula, a conclusion refuted by Louis Havet in his edition and by Hausrath, *RE* 19 (1938): 1476, as Grimal notes, 143 n. 4—which Grimal considered indefensible because Phaedrus's Eutychus, unlike Caligula's, is a man of importance, the scholar advances the case of a different Eutychus (*CIL* 6. 9105, a freedman of Claudius). This inscription names the freedman's wife (Claudia Peloris). Grimal proceeds by assuming that Claudia Peloris became Eutychus's wife in 54, i.e., was freed after Claudius's death. But we do not know this. The inscription identifies her as "Octaviae divi Claudi f lib," which means only that the inscription was erected after 54. Grimal then asserts that Phaedrus's prologue (which refers to Eutychus's wife) was therefore written after the fall of 54 and finally searches for allusions to post-54 political events in book 3. For example, he claims that (pp. 145–46) the fable of the drunken old women pertains to the spirit of increased liberty of the debut of the *quinquennium* and (p. 146) Agrippina exiled under Gaius is the panther stuck in a ditch who returns under Nero to gobble up her victims.

Rival identifications have not led to scholarly consensus and are easy to mock: Festa, "Su la favola di Fedro," 46, n. 2, wrote of Havet's reconstructions of the poet's targets and juggling of Phaedrus's lines, "Non è possibile seguire l'acrobatismo critico del filologo francese."

20. *Contumelia* represents the active harm inflicted on another that manifests the disdain of the agent: "contumelia a contemptu dicta est, quia nemo nisi quem contempsit, tali iniuria notat" (Sen. *Dial.* 2.11.2). Contumely is not the same as injury; for, in treating the victim as beneath oneself, it involves a social sneer, as Pacuvius makes clear: "patior facile iniuriam, si est vacua a contumelia" (preserved in Nonius, p. 430). The idiom *contumeliam dicere* or *iacere* demonstrates that contumely is often verbal and so overlaps with calumny, which can mean trickery, malicious prosecution (see Kaster, *Suetonius*, 303), or insult; like contumely, it swings between words and action. Cicero sees *contumelia* as the foundation of verbal insult: "maledictio autem nihil habet propositi praeter contumeliam" (*Pro Caelio* 6). *Malum* is the passive harm suffered by the practitioners of insult and derisive injury if Jupiter or some other just patriarch is listening, or by their victims if the accuser's false testimony is believed by a credulous or unjust superior.

21. This is, of course, the Augustan imperial position on the Roman republic; cf. Maternus in Tacitus's *Dialogus*. For violence attendant upon social confusion in the plots of Phaedrus, see, for example, what happens to the lowly ass when he treats the boar as an equal (1.29); once the eagle and the lowly sow come to fear the status and the position of the other, the social interloper can destroy their families; they fear that their tree home will be leveled and act as if they were on the same level; thus violence, not the deference of status and relative role, guides their action (2.4); the lofty goat comes to destruction when he is talked down a well by a fox stuck at the bottom (4.9). Verticality (especially the use of *celsus* and *humilis*) is essential to Phaedrus's brief presentation of his plots, and to their interpretation. *Celsus* signals the favored, socially superior position from which the fable, and harm, will devolve.

22. The log-king and his serpent successor have been interpreted as representing Augustus and Tiberius. Certainly, the fable's characterization of republicanism as social disorder is Augustan. A political, metaphorical reading of fable may well have been inevitable in a literary culture characterized by the mime and by partisan historiography (contrast Velleius Paterculus and Cremutius Cordus). Indeed, wherever animal hierarchy is depicted, political or social interpretations are natural—this is an essential characteristic of fable. But the crucial question is whether a particular fable is simply an analogy or is a parable, whether it stands as a mask for particular social or political dissent and lampoon or whether its target and moral are different. I should like to avoid the two extremes of denying that a fable can be read as a sort of equation (snake $= x$, frog $= y$) and also of adopting the reductive position that the ambiguity and mask of fable (of any text?) allow both or all readings at the same time. Phaedrus is here orthodoxly Augustan in his political views, while throughout the poems he maintains both this socially conservative stance and, in 2.5, it should be noted, tells a tale to the credit of Tiberius. Finally, whether or not the emperors lurk behind these fabulous monarchs (and a Greek slave from Thrace or from the East generally would have known of many dynasts and tyrants), this poem's concerns with social order, insult, and ambition mark the rest of Phaedrus's books.

23. Common syntax and narrative structure, as well as common diction, connect these two poems. For instance, both rely on simple epithet, predominantly the participle, economically to signal transition in interpretive viewpoint and in plot: e.g., *procax* and *petulans* in the first poem, echoed and expanded in the second poem: *tumens, contemnens, impudenti, mulcatus, maerens, repulsus*. Phaedrus's self-vaunted brevity owes much to this narrative technique.

24. Pierre Hamblenne, "Le Choucas chez les Paons (Phaedr., 1, 3): Phèdre, Séjan ou Pallas?" *LEC* 49 (1981): 128, nn. 13 and 14, cites Valerius Maximus (*De repulsis*, 7.5.1) for "notatus . . . repulsa," the sad comment on Quintus Aelius Tubero's disappointment in the praetorian election. Compare also Valerius Maximus on Marius, at 6.9.14. *Calamitas*, in the final line of this poem, also connects the world of the fable with the sphere of Roman politics, for *calamitas* can mean a defeat at court.

25. Cicero observes, in self-serving fashion in the *Philippics*: "nulla contumelia est, quam fecit dignus" (3.22).

26. Seneca gives the prevailing ancient etymology: "contumelia a contemptu dicta est, quia nemo nisi quem contempsit, tali iniuria notat" (*Dial.* 2.11.2). Note that Trimalchio's bad joke and bad scholarship (*Satyricon* 56, *contumelia* as from *contus cum malo*) is so bad and funny because the two possible etymologies are so obvious.

27. Gabriella Moretti, "Lessico giuridico e modello giudiziario nella favola fedriana," *Maia* 34 (1982): 227–46, has investigated Phaedrus's legal language and remarked on the peculiar preoccupation of the poet: "i processi, in Fedro, trattano sempre, infatti, di furto, frode, e in ogni caso di contenziosi riguardo alla proprietà di una *res*" (228). The wolf had just appeared as the sheep's *fraudator*, falsely promising surety, in 1.16.

28. Perry, *Babrius and Phaedrus*, xcii–xciii, noted that, alone of the ancient fabulists, Phaedrus represents the occasion of a particular fable of Aesop. John Winkler, *Auctor et Actor: A Narratological Reading of Apuleius's* The Golden Ass (Berkeley and Los Angeles: University of California Press, 1985), 282, has emphasized the contrast in the ancient life of Aesop of the fable teller's ugliness as symbol of his slavery to his handsomely named but by comparison insubstantial master, the philosopher Xanthos.

29. See above, nn. 20 and 26.

30. Phaedrus's popular wisdom is often paralleled in the early dramatists. Compare the lion's sentiment to Caecilius *com.* 4: "facile aerumnam ferre possum, si inde abest iniuria: etiam iniuriam, nisi contra constat contumelia . . ."; and Pacuvius *trag.* 279: "patior facile iniuriam, si est vacua a contumelia."

31. Phaedrus uses the words *calumnia, calumniari,* and *calumniator* only in his narratorial voice: 1 prol. 5 imagines a critic involved in calumny; 1.17.2 describes in an epimythium the dog of the fable as a *calumniator*; Aesop is said at 3. prol. 37 to have evaded others' calumny through fable; Augustus dispels the murk of calumny at 3.10.42. Likewise, Phaedrus uses the root *fraud-* in his narratorial comments (initially at 1.10.1, 1.16.1, and 2.4.5; a *sententia* at 3.10.53; to summarize the fox's motives at

4.9.7; cf. 4.26.17). In three places, however, the animals recognize what is happening to them and use the word themselves (1.17.9, 3.15.8, 4.21.19).

32. In addition, in the second fable, two passersby speak with the lion: a *praedator* (2) and a *viator/innoxius* (4/5). Only the humble traveler, who in a double contrast to the robber does not try to take what is not his and does not even presume to speak to his superior, receives a share of the spoils. Phaedrus has taken his diction from Virgil's first book of the *Georgics*, where *improbus* is a most important word, most famously characterizing labor (145–46) but also the goose (1.119) and the importunate crow: "Tum cornix plena pluviam vocat improba voce" (*Georgics* 1.388).

33. Of course, credulous characters must make these mistakes to make a fable possible, just as the plots, deceptions, and misidentifications of New Comedy all depend on easy credit (the game-giver's money, the character's belief, the audience's belief, the old man's or miser's money, the tokens of identity finally produced to restore true credit). Phaedrus is doing more than playing with the folkloric extremes of credulity and cleverness, with Simple Simon and the fox. Like New Comedy's negotiation between the miserly and the overgenerous, Phaedrus associates the credulous and the deceiver with the fictions that bind society.

34. Part of this unnatural calamity and part of the humor of the poem is the (unstated) consequence of the tortoise's fall—the literary precedent. Aeschylus, the doxographic tradition maintained, was struck and killed by a falling tortoise. The literary precedent of Pindar as eagle and his critics as carping crows helps to locate the crow as the not-so-high flier.

35. Treggiari, *Roman Freedmen*, gives the comprehensive account of the legal and social position of freedmen in the early empire. As she stresses, only in the major cities did freedmen constitute a large, even dominating, portion of the population (p. 36), and it was in the city of Rome under Augustus that freedmen, especially those with literary training, found their position and opportunities the best they had ever been (p. 123).

36. See Weaver, *Familia Caesaris*, and Treggiari, *Roman Freedmen*.

37. See Weaver, *Familia Caesaris*, 2, on imperial freedmen's hold on the imperial civil service.

38. For an account of the official honors granted freedmen and the limits to their social promotion, see Gérard Boulvert, *Domestique et fonctionnaire sous le Haut-Empire romain: La condition de L'affranchi et de l'esclave du prince* (Paris: Les Belles Lettres, 1974), 208–14. Treggiari, *Roman Freedmen*, 37–86, discusses the issues of freedmen's legal status.

39. Boulvert, *Esclaves et affranchis imperiaux sous le Haut-Empire ro-*

main (Naples: Jovene, 1970), 343 and 353, has collected the testimonia of this resentment.

40. References are to B. E. Perry, *Aesopica* (Urbana: University of Illinois Press, 1952), and C. Halm, *Fabulae Aesopicae collectae* (Leipzig: Teubner, 1852).

41. Phaedrus makes a similar change at 4.9 (*Vulpis et caper*). The first two sentences of Aesop 9 present the characters paratactically. The lines and independent sentences begin with the agents: fox . . . goat. . . . Phaedrus subordinates the fox, as his grammar mirrors the characters' initial positions. Phaedrus is consistent in this revision of Aesop. At 1.5 he has not followed the Greek (Aesop 339; Halm 258; see also Babrius 67), whose parataxis and alternate, abstract abilities he eschews; instead of θῆρας ἐθήρευον λέων καὶ ὄναγρος, ὁ μὲν λέων διὰ τῆς δυνάμεως ὁ δὲ ὄναγρος διὰ τῆς ἐν ποσὶ ταχύτητος, Phaedrus has "Vacca et capella et patiens ovis iniuriae / socii fuerunt cum leone in saltibus."

42. Compare that other literary outsider and threat to society, the miserly Knemon of Menander's *Dyskolos*, who falls down a well (line 627).

43. As Giordana Pisi, *Fedro traduttore di Esopo*, Università degli Studi di Parma, Pubblicazioni della Facoltà di Magistero 4 (Florence: La Nuova Italia Editrice, 1977), 56, observed.

44. On freedmen's letters of appointment and recommendation, see now J. E. Lendon, "Perceptions of the Prestige and the Working of Roman Imperial Government" (Ph.D. diss., Yale University, 1991), 21ff. and 321.

45. Pisi, *Fedro traduttore di Esopo*, 27, noted that this phrase is Phaedrus's addition. The well-deserving client might receive a *praemium* but ought not to put a dollar value (*pretium*, which, as Pisi, 31, n. 22, writes, is "ricompensa commerciale") on his service. This section of Pisi brings out well Phaedrus's innovative style. Consider especially the contrast of the Greek, which is at times proverbial (see 27, n. 2, which compares Greg. Cypr. 2.8: ἐκ λύκου στόματος and Zen. 3.48, ἐκ λύκου στόματος) and the legal and mercantile Latin (p. 32, for instance, notes that *flagitare* is often used of debtors).

46. Remember the stag's similar confusion about an abstract noun (1.12.6: "crurumque nimiam *tenuitatem* vituperat").

47. Compare Seneca, *De beneficiis* 2.11.2.

48. S. F. Bonner, *Roman Declamation in the Late Republic and Early Empire* (Liverpool: Liverpool University Press, 1949), 84–132.

49. The Roman who was legally liable for ingratitude was the freedman who failed to discharge the services owed his former master. The master's exact power over his former slave (legal and otherwise) has been

disputed; see W. W. Buckland, *The Roman Law of Slavery: The Position of the Slave in Private Law from Augustus to Justinian* (1908; reprint, New York: AMS Press, 1970), 71; Arnold Duff, *Freedmen in the Early Roman Empire* (Cambridge: Cambridge University Press, 1958), 37, 40ff.; Treggiari, *Roman Freedmen*, 68–80. The ungrateful, like the misanthropes of New Comedy, are outside of society, hoarders of capital—status and real, respectively.

50. Antonio La Penna, "Introduction," in *Fedro: Favole*, ed. Agostino Richelmy (Turin: Giulio Einaudi, 1978), xliii, observes that fables with more than three characters are an innovation, though he credits this departure from the Greek to a "Western" tradition. Phaedrus, as his moral shows, is figuring a society (and not simply an agreement of two) where there can be none.

51. For the Stoic Seneca, men did not have to be of the same station to confer and receive *beneficia*—the slave's service to the master can be a *beneficium* (*De beneficiis* 3.18). For Phaedrus, both parties of the social contract must recognize their relation, their like status. Compare 1.22 and 1.31. In the former, a weasel caught by a man tries to avoid his fate by contracting out his mice-eating services. The man denies that these constitute *gratum* or even *beneficium*: "noli imputare vanum beneficium mihi." The weasel, whom the poet labels *improbam*, is then killed. Not everybody recognizes that such offers are empty. A kite unable to catch some doves turns to false contract: "consilium raptor vertit ad fallaciam / et genus inerme tali decepit dolo." The kite asks the doves to make him king by compact, *icto foedere* (though perhaps we should read *ficto foedere*). Once they have entrusted themselves (*credentes*) to the deceiver, they are eaten.

52. Paul, *Digest* 17.1.1.4: "contrarium ergo est officio merces," cited by Boulvert, *Domestique et fonctionnaire*, 187, in his discussion of the language of the freedman's obligations and relations.

53. The praise of body parts involves a social reckoning, as when Menenius Agrippa told the plebeians, who out of disgust with the senate had seceded to the Aventine Hill, the parable of the all-important stomach. Such "folklore" presents a social hierarchy as natural. Cf. the blazon of feminine parts in Elizabethan poetry; Patricia Parker, "Rhetorics of Property: Exploration, Inventory, Blazon," in *Literary Fat Ladies: Rhetoric, Gender, Property* (London and New York: Methuen and Co., 1987), 126–54.

54. Compare the boar's response to the ass who called him brother: "ille indignans repudiat / officium" (1.29.5–6). For the boar the salutation was *contumelia*, which will only arouse *periculum* for the abuser (2) and not *officium*.

55. *Anus ad amphoram*, 3.1.2: "adhuc Falerna faece e testa nobili" (an old woman can tell from the dregs what a noble wine this jug contained).

56. Phaedrus uses the word *nobilis* in two other passages, in its technical civic meaning. In both cases he simply refers to a *quidam nobilis* who was the giver of games (5.5.4 and 5.7.16).

57. The context of such identification and misidentification is not always literary. Indeed, it is ubiquitous, from the ass who misappraises his voice to the brave soldier who says he would have been misled by his cowardly compatriot's words had he not seen his fellow turn his back and run (5.2). Phaedrus points interpretation toward his own condition and draws together the themes of self and poetic misappraisal in the prologues (discussed below).

58. As La Penna, "Introduction," xxx–xxxi notes, the Cynics had made not only Socrates but Simonides into an exemplar of *autarkeia*.

59. Phaedrus has declared his moral from the start: "Homo doctus in se semper divitias habet" and has also signaled the poet's worth, his *genus*: Simonides is here introduced as the one "qui scripsit *egregium* melos." One other fable (5.1) enacts the proper treatment due a poet. Demetrius of Phalerum (as Perry, trans., *Babrius and Phaedrus*, 351, says, "in all probability, confused and conflated with his successor in the regency of Athens, the Macedonian Demetrius Poliorcetes") is flattered by the leading Athenians; then the artists and men of leisure come to pay court to their new tyrant. From afar Demetrius sees the effeminate and luxuriant Menander and demands: "'Quisnam cinaedus ille in conspectu meo audet cevere?' responderunt proximi 'Hic est Menander scriptor.' mutatus statim 'Homo' inquit 'fieri non potest formosior.'" The poet turns the tyrant into a flatterer. This tyrant's good judgment is clear: Phaedrus is following his prose collection of Aesop's fables.

60. This was Attilio de Lorenzi's suggestion; *Fedro* (Florence: La Nuova Italia Editrice, 1955), 145, approved by Perry, lxxvi. I too find it plausible, but it is important to state the exact, circumstantial evidence: Eutychus is a slave name (as Taylor, "Freedmen and Freeborn," 125, states, the second most common slave name); he is described as preoccupied with business, which the poet contrasts to his addressee's domestic affairs (3. prol.); Phaedrus is identified in the manuscript title as an imperial freedman; another poem (2.5) is set at Tiberius's estate and has to do with an ambitious member of the imperial household.

61. Phaedrus would then have been the first to do so. Boulvert, *Domestique et fonctionnaire*, 208, lists, in addition to Martial and Statius, the following literary dedications to imperial freedmen: Scribonius Largus's *Compositiones* to Calliste and Josephus's *Contra Apionem* to Epaphroditus.

62. Of course, the joke is not to be taken literally, as imperial freed-men could not expect to be named in the emperor's will. Perhaps in addition to reminding his addressee of their status, Phaedrus's *Particulo* is meant to echo the names of the parasites of New Comedy (Peniculus, Parmeno, Curculio). In both cases Phaedrus and his addressee are sharers in another's birthright. Michael Kaplan, *Greeks and the Imperial Court, from Tiberius to Nero* (New York: Garland, 1990), 141–45, concluded that Eutychus, Particulo, and Philetus were fictitious addressees.

63. Compare Horace's boast: "Parios ego primus iambos / ostendi Latio" (*Epist.* 1.19.23–24).

64. This is the barb of the jibe of *Patavinitas*, which the Roman noble Asinius Pollio threw at the northern Italian Livy, who from an aris-tocratic point of view remained a provincial in speech or outlook and had not been born to Roman history.

65. *Livor* does unite two groups: poets and those who wrote or bought epitaphs. Both strive to avoid the abuse of their readers and to assert their own legitimacy.

66. Such "autobiographical criticism" can be found in de Lorenzi, *Fedro*.

67. Standard practice has been to list Phaedrus as yet another victim of Sejanus; see, for instance, La Penna, "Introduction," xii. But Phaedrus does not say as much. Grimal, "Du nouveau sur les *Fables* de Phèdre?" 148, observed (following F. Vollmer, "Beiträge zur Chronologie und Deu-tung der Fabeln des Phaedrus," *SBAW* [1919]: 9–24) that in the pur-portedly autobiographical "Quodsi accusator alius Seiano foret" the poet has written *foret*, not *fuisset*, and suggests this could be an image we are to interpret: "si l'accusateur était différent d'un Séjan. . . ." Indeed, the future tenses of this entire section, like those of the end of the epilogue to book 2 (where the *exilium* is prospective), place the unjust judge and the dire consequences in the realm of the poet's imagination.

68. *Ars poetica* 333–34: "Aut prodesse volunt, aut delectare poetae, / aut simul et iucunda et idonea dicere vitae."

Notes to Chapter 4

1. See now Mary Beard, "Looking (Harder) for Roman Myth: Dumézil, Declamation and the Problem of Definition," in *Mythos in mythenloser Gesellschaft: Das Paradigma Roms*, ed. Fritz Graf (Stuttgart and Leipzig: Teubner, 1993), 44–64, on declamation as a cultural negotiation of social and familial conflict.

2. The exact title is not sure; I have given what Janet Fairweather, *Seneca the Elder* (Cambridge: Cambridge University Press, 1981), 4, n. 3, calls "the least garbled version of the title." The ten books of *controversiae* were probably not followed by two of *suasoriae*, of which only one is extant. Michael Winterbottom, trans., *The Elder Seneca*, 2 vols. (Cambridge, Mass., and London: Harvard University Press, 1974), xxi, n. 1, argued, from a reference in *Suas.* 6.27 to the coming end of the book, that "there were never more than seven declamations." William A. Edward, *The Suasoriae of Seneca the Elder* (Cambridge: Cambridge University Press, 1928), xxx, n. 1, had maintained that originally there were more than one book of *suasoriae* because "MSS. B, V, D end the book of *Suasoriae* thus: 'liber primus explicit, incipit liber secundus.'" The colophon is an unsteady guide to the contents of manuscripts. One especially suspects that school works could be tacked on to a canonical author.

3. Seneca has been fortunate in his most recent editors and translators: Michael Winterbottom's Loeb volume (n. 2 above) ensured that this author was read in decades not sympathetic to Silver Latin. L. Håkanson's edition (*L. Annaeus Seneca Maior, oratorum et rhetorum sententiae divisiones colores* [Leipzig: Teubner, 1989]) is a model for the presentation of a text that survives in full and in excerpted versions.

4. Janet Fairweather, *Seneca the Elder*, 54–55 and 69.

5. Charles W. Lockyer, "The Fiction of Memory and the Use of Written Sources: Convention and Practice in Seneca the Elder and Other Authors" (Ph.D. diss., Princeton University, 1970), pushed to the extreme the doubts many had held of Seneca's protestations of memory. Since the work of Frances Yates (*The Art of Memory* [Chicago: University of Chicago Press, 1966]), ancient memory techniques have been better understood, and Seneca's claims for the power of his memory are credible, which does not mean that his account of the composition of the work is credible. As Lockyer and others have pointed out, it was an ancient topos to maintain the fiction of a dialogue, to write as if one were speaking— i.e., without reference to prior written works. Seneca's use of written sources is discussed by Lockyer, 158–90 and by Fairweather, *Seneca the Elder*, 39–42 and 47–49. Fairweather doubts Seneca would go through the "cumbrous process of looking up references" in papyrus rolls, but see my suggestions on the use of slave or freedman labor in the composition of ancient books, in *Valerius Maximus and the Rhetoric of the New Nobility* (Chapel Hill and London: University of North Carolina Press, 1992), 59–61.

6. Collections of exempla date from Nepos and Varro. For exegesis of a speech, compare what Fronto preserves of Tiro on Cato, which may be from the preface to Tiro's publication of Cicero's speeches.

7. Seneca, *Contr.* 2 pr. 3: "facilis ab hac [eloquentia] in omnes artes discursus est."

8. On Seneca and Agrippina, and more generally on Seneca's attachment to the circle of Sejanus, see Zeph Stewart, "Sejanus, Gaetulicus, and Seneca," *AJP* 74 (1953): 70–85.

9. Tacitus, *Annales*, 16.17: "petitione honorum abstinuerat per ambitionem praeposteram ut eques Romanus consularibus potentia aequaretur; simul adquirendae pecuniae brevius iter credebat per procurationes administrandis principis negotiis." Tacitus resents Mela's means of acquiring wealth and fame: he did not undertake the traditional *cursus honorum*, and so the historian has in all probability misrepresented Mela's motives in not seeking the consulship; two brothers had reached the consulship, a third honor might make the family too conspicuous, perhaps even dynastic, in its ambitions. If Mela was the emperor's procurator, he may have been following his father's lead: H. de la Ville de Mirmont, "Les Déclamateurs espagnols au temps d'Auguste et de Tibère," *Bulletin Hispanique* 14 (1912): 13, suggested that Seneca returned to Spain to discharge an imperial procuratorship and that Tacitus "forgets" that his father-in-law's grandfathers were of this station, imperial procurators in Cisalpine Gaul.

10. Seneca, fragment 98: "si quaecumque composuit pater meus et edi voluit, iam in manus populi emisissem, ad claritatem nominis sui satis sibi ipse prospexerat: nam nisi me decepit pietas, cuius honestus etiam error est, inter eos haberetur, qui ingenio meruerunt ut puris titulis nobiles essent."

11. Helvia's aunt married C. Galerius, prefect of Egypt from A.D. 16 to 31. Perhaps Seneca the philosopher aimed above this equestrian pinnacle.

12. Horace refers to Accius's trimeters as noble (*Ars poetica* 259), but this word is infrequently applied to artistic works. Propertius, punning on the meanings of the word, ironically warns Cynthia not to become a *nobilis historia* (1.15.24). Elsewhere, Propertius stretches the usage of the word by applying it to places (like the forum, 4.9.20, which would have been filled with *nobiles*, living and statuary). He refers to a ivory decoration of the Temple of Apollo as *Libyci nobile dentis opus* (2.31.12), a phrase followed by Ovid.

13. *Ann.* 13.42: "simul studiis inertibus et iuvenum imperitiae suetum livere iis qui vividam et incorruptam eloquentiam tuendis civibus exercerent. . . . veterem ac domi partam dignationem subitae felicitati sumbitteret." Compare the abuse of Seneca by Dio 61.10.

14. Ronald Syme, "The Senator as Historian," in *Ten Studies in Tacitus* (Oxford: Oxford University Press, 1970), 8.

15. Having mentioned the ever-senatorial Tacitus's condescension

toward Seneca, I should point out the similarity of their stations. If, as Syme suggested, Tacitus was of provincial background, we may well imagine his grandfather to have been very like the elder Seneca—a Western provincial and wealthy landowner, interested in education and in sending Tacitus or his father to Rome to complete his education. The rise of the sons through marriage and public speaking would be a common route to distinction. Syme, *Ten Studies in Tacitus*, 10, suggested that Tacitus's assumption of *nobilitas* has fooled posterity and that Asinius Pollio is a good parallel. If the elder Seneca was Pollio's client (dependent friend), Tacitus might have judged him and his family unequals, despite their similarities to modern eyes. Aulus Gellius alludes to an ancient resentment: "some characterized Seneca's learning and style as *vulgaria* and *vernacula et plebeia*" (*Noct. Att.* 12.2.1). On Suillius' status, see Syme, "Personal Names in *Annals* 1–6," *JRS* 39 (1949): 16–17; and idem, *Tacitus* 373 n.5 and 581.

16. Syme, *Ten Studies in Tacitus*, 8, points out that Tacitus uses *felicitas* only twice, at 13.42 and 14.53—the two passages (discussed above) that employ criticism of the younger Seneca (and his philosophical "felicity").

17. Lockyer, "The Fiction of Memory," 195–99, catalogs the instances of Roman literary works in which the author addresses his son. For such dedications in late antiquity (and the literary convention dating from the elder Cato) see Kaster, *Guardians of Language*, 67–68, who notes that no professional grammarian dedicated a work to his son.

18. Seneca shares the disdain of this circle for the professional teacher. Suetonius (*De gramm.* 4) records the attitude of Messala: "Eosdem litteratores vocitatos Messala Corvinus in quadam epistula ostendit, non esse sibi dicens rem cum Furio Bibaculo, ne cum Ticida quidem aut litteratore Catone; significat enim haud dubie Valerium Catonem, poetam simul grammaticumque notissimum."

19. He refers once to a tutor of Nero, a Lepidus, whose name indicates attachment to the house of Nero's aunt Lepida, where the future emperor lived until his adoption by Claudius (February 25, 50). This notice, like those of Pollio educating his grandson or Messala conducting declamation at home, may suggest the connection of the elder Seneca with Lepida's household. The dating and type of Nero's adoption are discussed by K. R. Bradley, *Suetonius' Life of Nero: An Historical Commentary*, Collection Latomus, vol. 157 (Brussels, 1978), 53.

20. Suetonius, writing of late republican times, indicates the variety of primary education available: "temporibus quibusdam super viginti celebres scholae fuisse in urbe tradantur" (*De grammaticis* 3)

21. Cestius is my suggestion. See Lockyer, "The Fiction of Memory," for written sources.

22. See Stanley F. Bonner, *Roman Declamation in the Late Republic*

and Early Empire (Liverpool: Liverpool University Press, 1949), 51–70. This overview, however, shares the method, found in so much Roman institutional history, of combining chronologically distinct and, at times, polemical sources to produce a synthesis.

23. Describing an exceptional teacher who instructed both grammar and rhetoric, Suetonius writes that this teacher removed his pulpit in the afternoon so as to declaim (*De grammaticis* 4).

24. E.g., Cassius Severus at Cestius's school; he was asked to leave (*C.* 3 pr. 16).

25. Seneca describes Albucius's sketchy private declamations, his form of instruction, in the preface to book 7. He writes that when Albucius declaimed in public *ter bucinavit* (*C.* 7 pr. 1), which seems to imply that he spoke at night, when the night watch sounded a trumpet every three hours. On Albucius, see Kaster, *Suetonius*, 313–16.

26. As does Petronius (*Sat.* 6), who has Encolpius harangue Agamemnon who has just finished performing inside and has been succeeded by another declaimer.

27. Seneca has drawn most of Pollio's speech from occasions that are clearly *recitationes*. Indeed, we see Pollio leaving the recitation of a Spanish poet. Seneca manages to weave in such different forms of discourse as forensic speech, recitation, and historiography in his digressions, those notices of criticism that serve to delineate proper declamation.

28. At *S.* 4.5., Seneca says that Fuscus declaimed more often in Greek than in Latin, yet Seneca's text has no Greek *sententiae* from Fuscus (once, at *C.* 1.7.14, the scribes have omitted Fuscus's quotation of *Iliad* 24.478–79, but this is the only Greek he speaks). The *suasoriae* do have Greek *sententiae*, but Seneca seems unwilling to have Fuscus, the model of the *suasoriae*, speak Greek.

29. Fairweather, *Seneca the Elder*, 106–31, describes in detail that, contrary to Seneca's account, ample evidence attests to a Hellenistic practice of declamatory training, i.e., declamation was not born with Seneca, and the *controversia* is not a novel form; in particular (117–19), Cicero declaimed theses, abstract philosophical questions. Seneca has been misled by Cicero's terminology (he refers to declamations as *causae*) and has ignored Cicero's references to his own declaiming.

30. Their importance has been recognized by A. D. Leeman, *Orationis ratio* (Amsterdam: A. M. Hakkert, 1963), 224: "Of these prologues it can be said without exaggeration that they are indispensable for a right understanding of the whole literary production of Imperial Rome."

31. Miriam Griffin, "The Elder Seneca and Spain," *JRS* 62 (1972): 16, adds epigraphical support to Syme's notice of the "Spanish look" of Fabianus's name (*HSCP* 73 [1968]: 222, quoted by Griffin). Griffin finds

Fabianus's style fluent, but "by comparing what the two Senecas say, we can see that Fabianus' oral and written style was cold, flat, and lacking in point, brilliance and precision." See the younger Seneca's *Epist.* 100 for Fabianus's writings.

32. Tacitus makes an unreliable guide: he is highly prejudiced against such equestrians as Haterius, Seneca, and Cassius Severus.

33. Compare the similar treatment and position of the Greek exempla in Valerius Maximus's chapters in Bloomer, *Valerius Maximus and the Rhetoric of the New Nobility*, 17 and 28.

34. For the possibility that Fuscus was the main figure of the preface to the *Suasoriae*, see Lewis A. Sussman, "Arellius Fuscus and the Unity of the Elder Seneca's *Suasoriae*," *RhM* 129 (1977): 310–13. For the disparities of judgment, see G. Hoffa, "De Seneca patre selectae quaestiones" (diss., Göttingen, 1909), 23, for Gallio, and 12, for Latro. Fairweather pointed out that Seneca praised Gallio's *idiotismos* (*C.* 7 pr. 6), his use of colloquial but not vulgar style.

35. In fact, Tacitus has Vipstanus Messala describe Gallio in these terms (*Dial.* 26.1).

36. Henri Bornecque, *Les Déclamations et les déclamateurs d'après Sénèque le Père* (1902; reprint, Hildesheim, 1967).

37. He is admired by that difficult critic Cassius Severus (*S.* 6.11). Jerome called him sublime (*Epist. Ad Jovin.* 1.28).

38. Seneca writes, somewhat misleadingly, of this practice: "[Pollio] primus omnium Romanorum advocatis hominibus scripta sua recitavit" (*C.* 4 pr. 2). Alexander Dalzell, "C. Asinius Pollio and the Early History of Public Recitation at Rome," *Hermathena* 85 (1955): 26, concludes: "Pollio's innovation was the establishment of public recitations on a more formal basis." See now Florence Dupont, "Recitatio," *Roman Cultural Revolution* (Cambridge: Cambridge University Press, in press).

39. Compare the literary social gesture of Cicero saying he met Cato in the library of the young Lucullus's house (*De Fin.* 3.7), a dialogic fiction not to be believed but a social fiction uniting the uppercrust, the *boni omnes*.

40. Even if the line "Defendus Cicero est Latiaeque silentia linguae" drove Pollio out, Seneca takes pride in this Spanish poet Sextilius Ena. Seneca identifies him as his *municeps*, the same distinction he granted the playwright Statorius Victor (*S.* 2.18).

41. Syme, *Ten Studies in Tacitus*, 136, pointed out that Pollio's grandfather, leader of the Marrucini, fought against Rome (Livy, *Per.* 73) and see Syme, *Tacitus*, 569, on Pollio's independence: "The Italian *novus homo* had no cause for indulgence towards the Roman aristocracy."

42. Votienus seems to have broken ties with his hometown: he was

accused before Augustus by Vinicius on behalf of the citizens of Narbonne (7.5.11). He also advertised his status as a Roman *patronus*: he published his defense of Galla Numisia before the centumviral court (*C.* 9.5.15).

43. One thinks of the "thick sounding" poets of Spain alluded to by Cicero at *Pro Archia* 26.

44. My general conclusions disagree with Griffin, "The Elder Seneca and Spain," who argues from Seneca's disapproval of some Spaniards that "Seneca does not allow his keen interest in the speakers of his province to cloud his judgment" (12). In addition, the wrong question lies behind the conclusion that no sense of Spanish nationalism ("national consciousness," 15) animated Seneca. As Griffin noted, the Senecas returned to Spain, married Spanish ladies, and, I would argue, advanced their Spanish friends. All of which is consistently the action of a Roman *patronus*, if we understand the Senecas' attitudes and behavior from the perspective of Roman provincialism rather than provincial nationalism. To be nationalist, besides the anachronism, would require a stance as an outsider, recognizable in Tacitus's Arminius but not in a provincial landowner.

45. Murredius was possibly Cestius's student, according to Bornecque, *Les Déclamations et les déclamateurs d'après Sénèque le Père*, 181.

46. Norden, *Die Antike Kunstprosa* (1898; reprint, Stuttgart: Teubner, 1958), 292.

47. Fabianus is praised by the consulars Messala and L. Vinicius (*C.* 2.4.10 and 2.5.19, respectively). His teacher, the philosopher Sextius, according to the younger Seneca (*Brev. vit.* 10.1), called Fabianus "non ex his cathedraris philosophis, sed ex veris et antiquis." This praise smacks of the elder Seneca's language that distinguished the Greek from the Roman.

48. If, at 10 pr. 12, one adopts <*magistro*> *Latroni* for *misero Latroni*, as Hoffa, "De Seneca patre selectae quaestiones," 21, emends following *nescioquis*, as Håkanson writes in his apparatus.

49. See Nietzsche's essay "The History of Greek Eloquence," in *Friedrich Nietzsche on Rhetoric and Language*, ed. and trans. Sander L. Gilman, Carole Blair, and David J. Parent (Oxford and New York, 1989), 213: "To no task did the Greeks devote such incessant labor as to eloquence. . . . Devotion to oratory is the most tenacious element of Greek culture and survives through all the curtailments of their condition. . . . Hellenic culture and power gradually concentrate on oratorical skill [Reden-können]." Nietzsche knew the contradictions inherent in this teleology: the loss of Hellenic power accompanies the rise of words. In writing this claim Nietzsche ignores the Romans.

50. Bonner, *Declamation*, 5–6.

51. Compare the plot of Plautus's *Rudens* with the example of an old-fashioned *controversia* in Suet., *De rhetoribus* 1.

52. "Facile est accusare luxuriem" (Cicero, *Pro Caelio* 29).

53. The severe speakers calculate the public *aestimatio* of the woman in a way reminiscent of Caesar's pretext for dismissing his wife.

54. The *divisio* of 2.5 ("Torta a tyranno uxor. . . . Ingrati actio est") also calculates *beneficia*, which in this case are so strong that Gallio can ask whether husbands and wives can give *beneficia* or are these considered *officia* (2.5.13). Seneca's compressed allusion to Latro's treatment of another case (7.4.3, where mother and father have rival claims to their son's behavior: "Latro hanc controversiam quasi tota offici esset declamavit") suggests just how commonplace such an understanding of a *controversia* was. Similarly, 4.8 analyzes what social name—*officium*, *opera*, or something worse—to give to behavior of double obligation: a patron asks his freedman for services from which the patron had earlier exempted him (*Patronus operas remissas repetens*). Significantly, the freedman is the target of universal abuse (*Extra*: "Omnes invecti sunt in libertum"), for he tries to hold his former master to contractual terms rather than honoring social obligation. Such is the point of the concluding *sententia* in the case against the freedman: "Nihil est venali misericordia turpius," to which Winterbottom (1974) compares the younger Seneca, *De beneficiis* 4.25.3: "pudeat ullum venale esse beneficium."

55. The cases of insanity should also be understood in their social terms, for the accusers allege dementia on the grounds that father-defendant has acted other than his social-familial role, e.g., 2.6: "Quidam luxuriante filio luxuriari coepit. Filius accusat patrem dementiae" and 7.6, "Demens qui servo filiam iunxit."

56. George Kennedy, *The Art of Rhetoric in the Roman World* (Princeton, N.J.: Princeton University Press, 1972), 334, has pointed out "the recurring question of the relationship of children to adults" within declamation.

57. E.g., at 2.2.6 Latro criticizes an additional oath, for it ignores the *invidia* attendant of the declaimer's fiction. At 2.4.8 the severe Messala disapproves, but most everyone else was misled by the sympathetic declaimer: "Albucius ethicos, ut multi putant, dixit—certe laudatum est cum diceret." The *prudentes*, who calculated the effect upon a real jury, were displeased with the harsh color of Hispanus (7.1.24), who had proposed, instead of the usual sewing up of the bad brother in a sack, to expose him to the sea so that "ipse poenam suam spectet."

58. Poetic rhythms were to be avoided. On the faults of Fuscine style, see Fairweather, *Seneca the Elder*, 200–2 and 214, and Norden, *Die Antike Kunstprosa*, 292–93.

59. At 9.2.24 Seneca attributes a *sententia* thought to be Latro's to his student Florus because of the facile verbal play and the effeminate *compositio*.

60. See Arno Reiff, *Interpretatio, imitatio, aemulatio: Begriff und Vorstellung literarischer Abhängigkeit bei den Römern* (Würzburg: Triltsch, 1959). Håkanson reads *surripere* for *corrumpere* here.

61. On Roman resentment toward the *grammatici* who taught Latin literacy and preliminary rhetoric, see my Chapter 2 above.

62. Q. Caecilius Epirota, the freedman of Atticus, is said to have introduced contemporary poets into the schools' curriculum (Suet., *De grammaticis* 16).

63. See note 57 above.

64. Seneca's distinction of vulgarity from low style, *verba sordida* from *verba cottidiana*, follows a familiar pattern. Vibius Rufus (9.2.25) is cleared of the charge of vulgarity when Seneca relates that Asinius Pollio did not "rule out" his *sententia*. Seneca then makes a transition to those who are faulted for vulgarity by invoking Livy's quotation of the rhetorician Miltiades' *sententia* on orators who ferret out old vulgar words. Murredius, Licinius Nepos, and Saenianus are quoted as examples of bad taste. At 1.2.22 a praetorian is detected in his plagiarism and silenced by Scaurus's interruption, an allusion to Ovid, *Priap.* 3.8. Scaurus attributed this fault (vulgarity) to the Greek declaimers. He cites Greek plagiarists; Murredius is again censured, and again Vibius Rufus is delivered from the charge: he used everyday but not sordid language. At 7 pr. 3, Seneca attributes Albucius's vulgarity to his abundance and adds the explanation that Albucius used *verba sordida* because "timebat ne scholasticus videretur." Seneca's circle thus escapes the charges of vulgarity and is excluded from the ranks of the scholastic Greeks. The Roman praetorian who plagiarized remains anonymous.

65. Porcellus *grammaticus* criticized a line of Cornelius Severus for an alleged solecism, but Seneca disagrees (*S.* 2.13).

66. Nicetes pointed out Cestius's anachronism in using Demosthenes' words for Thermopylae (*S.* 2.14). Seneca faults Tuscus (the foolish historian who had accused Scaurus Mamercus of treason in A.D. 34 (see Tac. *Ann.* 6.29) for using Caesar's *veni vidi vici* in this *suasoria* (2.22).

67. Other faults reveal Seneca's concern with restraint: faults that seem technical collapse genre distictions: (1) punning *sententiae* are taken over from the mime, that emblem of low life (e.g., Murredius is again the villain, using a stupid *color* and a Publilian *sententia* at 7.3.8—the unsympathetic Cassius Severus is made to defend both the use of puns and Publilian *sententiae*); (2) rhythm and repetition are faults that seem to confuse poetic with prose practice (Latro is invoked at 7.4.10 to correct the *scholastici*'s fondness for well-sounding epigram and "maxime quia Triarius compositione verborum belle cadentium multos scholasticos delectabat"); (3) overuse of *exempla*, in addition to trespassing into history,

may have been a kind of anachronism or simply automatic (not specific, germane) composition (7.5.12–13 may be censure of Valerius Maximus: Seneca says a sickness for learning exempla and fitting them in a *controversia* has seized the schoolmen. He lists as an example Musa, who in this *controversia* mentioned Croesus's son [cf. Valerius Maximus 5.4. ext. 3]. Musa is roundly pilloried by Haterius, Maecenas, and Cassius Severus).

Finally, Seneca mollifies the censure of Votienus Montanus's repetition by the wit Scaurus by citing repetition in Ovid (*C.* 9.5.15–17).

68. So once Seneca reattributes to Florus a *sententia* alleged to be Latro's because of its "mollem compositionem" (9.2.24).

69. Indeed, he even engages in a sort of *aemulatio* with past censors. In *S.* 1.12, a certain Dorion spoke the "most corrupt thing." Maecenas censured Dorion by comparison with Virgil. Seneca trumps this: "Multo corruptiorem sententiam Menestrati cuiusdam, declamatoris non abiecti suis temporibus, nactus sum in hac ipsa suasoria" (*S.* 1.13). Seneca's *nactus sum* contrasts strongly with the usual *memini* with which he vouches for the authenticity of his material. The episode also contrasts with the consensus opinion that Dorion's was the most corrupt *sententia*. Seneca's research has found one worse.

70. The philosopher learned from his father: Stewart, "Sejanus, Gaetulicus, and Seneca," 81–83, described the politically animated choice of subject of the *Consolatio ad Marciam*, wherein the author seeks to distance himself from any connection with the fallen *Sejaniani* (newly oppressed by Caligula after the conspiracy of Lepidus and Gaetulicus) by addressing Cremutius Cordus's daughter. In playing father to the bereaved Marcia, the philosopher assumes a noble status.

Notes to Chapter 5

1. Sen., *Epist.* 114.1: "talis hominibus fuit oratio qualis vita." Of course, armed with this interpretive legacy and shaped by his experience of Domitian, Tacitus does not express any sympathy for court speech. We can imagine from comparison with other cultures some of the social context of the "highly rhetorical" qualities of literature, and no doubt speech, among the elite of Julio-Claudian Rome. Frank Whigham, *Ambition and Social Privilege: The Social Tropes of Elizabethan Courtesy Theory* (Berkeley and Los Angeles: University of California Press, 1984), 36–38, traces the essentials: the court produced the need for continual performance and self-presentation, especially in conversation and judgment of other's conversation. At the same time, style becomes more opaque, more in need of

an interpreter. In short, the self resists being read in any straightforward, literal fashion.

2. Cicero, *De orat.* 3.19: "ea [res et verba] divisit quae seiuncta esse non possunt." Of course, the orator is trained to adapt his gestures to his words; indeed, he watches his audience to see the effect of his speech upon their faces, as Quintilian reports that Cicero had directed (12.10.56: "Nam id quoque plurimum refert, quomodo audire iudex velit, atque eius vultus saepe ipse rector est dicentis, ut Cicero praecipit").

3. On the interactions of the emperor and his audience in Tacitus, see Shadi Bartsch, *Actors in the Audience* (Cambridge, Mass.: Harvard University Press, 1994), esp. 10–11.

4. For example, F. R. D. Goodyear, "Tiberius and Gaius: Their Influence and View of Literature," *ANRW* II 32.1 (1984): 603–4, follows an established if polemical line in decrying Tiberius's influence on Roman literature.

5. Scholarly lament, following Tacitean lines, seems especially to distort the early imperial writing of history. See Bloomer, *Valerius Maximus and the Rhetoric of the New Nobility*, 147–50.

6. Tiberius was of course a trained and experienced speaker. He began early, speaking his father's *laudatio* at the age of nine in 33 B.C. (Suet., *Tib.* 6.4).

7. N. P. Miller, "Tiberius Speaks: An Examination of the Utterances Ascribed to Him in the Annals of Tacitus," *AJP* 89 (1968): 1–19. For Tacitus's attribution of archaic language to Tiberius, see Ronald Syme, "The Political Opinions of Tacitus," in *Ten Studies in Tacitus* (Oxford: Clarendon Press, 1970), 130, n. 3.

8. Ammianus Marcellinus, 16.10.10.

9. Tacitus gives the epithet *minitabundus* (2.10) to Arminius, the traitor and enemy of Rome, in that confrontation with his brother, the loyal Flavus, which recalls the duel of Quadrigarius's Gaul and Torquatus (Quadrigarius, fr. 10B, preserved by Aulus Gellius 9.13.6). The future participle is archaic or colloquial: Quintilian writes (1.6.42) apropos of those using obsolete words on the basis of their author's *auctoritas*: "Neque enim tuburchinabundum et lurchinabundum iam nobis quisquam ferat, licet Cato sit auctor." Perhaps even for Naevius the form of the word could add to a joke: "Risi egomet mecum *cassabundum* ire ebrium" (fr. 21 Ribbeck, preserved by Varro, *De lingua latina* 7.53).

10. Tiberius always spoke openly with Sejanus (4.1); this intimate speech has, of course, nothing to recommend it.

11. Suetonius puts the quotation more intelligibly: "Agrippinam . . . manu apprehendit Graecoque versu, 'Si non dominaris,' inquit, 'filiola, iniuriam te accipere existimas?' " (*Vita Tiberii* 53).

12. Tacitus points the contrast: Tiberius did not attend Germanicus's and Drusus's games, unlike his father's practice (1.76: "Augustus comiter interfuisset"). Also cf. 1.54, where Augustus is said to have tolerated the theater "et civile rebatur misceri voluptatibus vulgi." *Comitas*, of course, is an essential attribute of Germanicus (e.g., 1.33, 2.72). So the people understand Tiberius's *animus* upon Germanicus's death: "displicere regnantibus civilia filiorum ingenia" (2.82).

One consequence of this new hermeneutics of suspicion is that the speaker increasingly emphasizes his own claims to verity; see Bartsch, *Actors in the Audience*, 148–49, on the attempts of Pliny's *Panegyricus* to prove its own sincerity.

13. "Hidden" or "concealed" is the recurrent and essential metaphor for Tacitus's appraisal of Tiberius's style. Cf. 4.19: "proprium id Tiberio fuit scelera nuper reperta priscis verbis obtegere." The charge here is also typical: Tiberius confuses the new and the old and consequently destroys the bond between words and things. While he subverts the law, Tiberius keeps a rigorous hold on appearances, especially his own; Tacitus describes him thus: to the conspiring Libo, Tiberius "non vultu alienatus, non verbis commotior" (2.28), and at the accusation Tiberius is unmoved (2.29: "immoto eius vultu"). Viewing the face of empire becomes the people's concern: before Cn. Piso's trial, the people wonder "satin cohiberet ac premeret sensus suos Tiberius haud alias intentior populus plus sibi in principem occultae vocis aut suspicacis silentii permisit" (3.11). Tacitus's preoccupation with the emperor's expression leads him to include as a reason for Tiberius's withdrawal to Capri embarrassment for his looks (4.57).

14. This is a recurrent reaction to Tiberius's words, whose dissimulation effects a corresponding dissimulation of applause and credit. At 1.52, Tacitus characterizes Tiberius's speech to the senate for the dead Germanicus: "magis in speciem verbis adornata quam ut penitus sentire crederetur. Paucioribus Drusum et finem Illyrici motus laudavit, sed intentior et fida oratione." Tiberius receives a sort of inverse reading: the more rhetorical and enthusiastic he is, the less he is believed. Cf. 4.8, where Tiberius's words on Drusus's death would have been credited had he not continued to speak of the restoration of the republic.

15. Of course, flattery can follow Tiberius's speech, but this he resists so that his audience is reduced to nonverbal expression. Often silence, but at 2.38 (Tiberius's rejection of that scion of republican oratory M. Hortalus, grandson of Hortensius) this is mixed with murmur: "plures per silentium aut occultum murmur excepere." Silence does not please the emperor; indeed, it poses a great threat. When Lucius Piso declares his *secessio* (2.34), the emperor is upset, as Nero will be with Thrasea

Paetus's withdrawal. Total silence gives the lie to the fiction of a working senate; the *vultus*, charade of speech, must go on. Silence does not simply exclude the senator from the community or intimate that community's falsity but also suggests a different allegiance, to Stoicism perhaps, but at any rate total independence from the patron emperor.

16. For the increasing number of trials through the course of the *Annals*, see Ronald Martin, *Tacitus* (Berkeley and Los Angeles: University of California Press, 1981), 134–38.

17. However, in the crossed rhetoric that Tiberius speaks and presents, error is easy and dangerous. Domitius Celer counsels Piso to return to Syria, identifying Agrippina with rumor and the *vulgus*, Piso with Tiberius's hidden desires (2.77). This reading of the emperor will not be borne out.

18. Above all Tiberius seeks to maintain his composure, which only literalism (see 4.42), death, and criticism can shake. Tacitus attributes the absence of Livia and Tiberius at the funeral of Germanicus to their fear of showing their *vultus*; Germanicus's funeral has no *imagines*—masks are banned, and so the duplicitous duo cannot appear. On Tiberius's control of women as signifiers (Antonia mysteriously is absent), see below, p. 170. The moments of the rupture of Tiberius's control correspond to those natural intrusions that disrupt Germanicus's planning (mutiny, tempest, death). At the funeral of Germanicus, men's partisan attachment penetrates the shell of Tiberius (3.4). Tacitus also has the people sense Tiberius's difficulty at the trial of Cnaeus Piso.

19. Hispo follows the first case of *maiestas* (1.73), but he and Caepio Crispinus truly anticipate the coming trials in their attack upon a senator (the first trial had involved two equestrians), and one who was the accuser's patron or superior, Granius Marcellus, the governor of Bithynia, whom Caepio served as quaestor.

20. Tiberius wants above all to keep his rhetoric, his premeditated composition of all things, intact: "Nihil aeque Tiberium anxium habebat quam ne composita turbarentur" (2.65).

21. Tiberius's vulnerability to unmasked, direct criticism recurs at 4.42: with difficulty Tiberius *componeret animum* on the report of Votienus's slanders.

22. Tacitus confronts Tiberius with the scion of eloquence itself. The contrast of that descendant of republican oratory and the imperial interloper into rhetoric may have been more strongly felt by the senators because Tiberius inhabited Hortensius's ancestral place, literally: Augustus lived in the house of Hortensius (Suet., *Aug.* 72).

23. I should note that, as 2.35 overtly declares, Asinius Gallus and

Gnaeus Piso engage in the display (*species*), not the old republican reality of free speech.

24. Tacitus associates failed attempts to direct water, especially, with the Julio-Claudians. The Tiber, the German tempest among others, Nero's artificial lake and his contrived, unsuccessful matricidal shipwreck all show the Julio-Claudian failure to control the medium.

25. Tacitus's Tiberius seems to worry that he has a new Fulvia, a gender-confused and -confusing woman revolutionary on his hands. Velleius Paterculus had written of Fulvia: "Ex altera parte uxor Antonii Fulvia, nihil muliebre praeter corpus gerens, omnia armis tumultuque miscebat" (74).

26. Tacitus imagines Tiberius's invidious thoughts toward Agrippina: "conpressam a muliere seditionem, cui nomen principis obsistere non quiverit" (1.69). Again, the emperor worries about his name coming second to that of a woman.

27. Joel Fineman, "The History of the Anecdote: Fiction and Fiction," in *The New Historicism*, ed. H. Aram Veeser (New York and London: Routledge, 1989), 49–76, has pointed out the significance of Thucydides' phrase.

28. A new census ends this mutiny when the soldiers hand over these same agents: "Tum ut quisque praecipuus turbator conquisiti . . ." (1.30). The narrative of the German mutiny contains the same sort of final census taking—e.g., "seditiosissimum quemque vinctos" (1.44), and at 1.48, Caecina and his inner circle set a time to kill "foedissimum quemque et seditioni promptum. . . . nullo nisi consciis noscente quod caedis initium, quis finis."

29. The mutinous soldiers recognize the nominaliam of imperial language; to Drusus the troops complain, "Tiberium olim nomine Augusti desideria legionum frustrari solitum" (1.26).

30. Noise but not words characterizes mob signification in Tacitus (e.g., of the mutinous crowd here *Adstrepebat*, at 1.25 "murmur incertum, atrox clamor et repente quies," and, at 1.28, upon the eclipse the soldiers *strepere*).

31. The German rebellion starts from the *vernacula multitudo* with their "multa seditionis ora vocesque" (1.31), which as Mommsen showed means a legion raised from the noncitizens of the city mob. In addition to any technical meaning, this "vernacular mob" speaks a vulgar Latin as if the theater crowd and its license had been transferred to the field. As a Latin-speaking audience, it can hear the nominalism of imperial speech and appreciate, or perhaps even make possible, Germanicus's *Quod nomen* speech (on which see below). Tacitus's diction again underscores the con-

cern with language as an index to action and behavior. The leader of a
theater faction is replaced by the theatrical audience he had tried to sway.

32. Noise, direct and comprehensible, characterizes this soldiery
too: at 1.35, on Germanicus's first, unsuccessful speech, "atrocissimus
veteranorum clamor oriebatur." By 1.41, Germanicus's miserable column
of female relatives elicits sympathetic emotion and expression from the
soldiers: "Non florentis Caesaris neque suis in castris, sed velut in urbe
victa facies, gemitusque ac planctus. . . ." This also achieves what his words
could not, for the troops divide: "pars Agrippinae occursantes, plurimi
ad Germanicum regressi."

33. In addition, he acts like Drusus, the emperor's blood son, in
composing a letter *nomine principis*. In forging the emperor's name, he
follows the practice of Tiberius himself; his reliance on the shield of a
name follows Tiberius and Augustus. Forgery is a broader symptom and
consequence of the emperor's nominalism: accusations falsely signed, and
even unsigned, come to be believed; names are added to wills as outright fakes or, in the case of the Caesars, as unwanted interlopers. Julia's
letters to Augustus criticizing Tiberius were believed to have been written by Gracchus (1.53). Tacitus himself engages in unmasking forgeries:
Drusus's answer to Piso was crafted by Tiberius—so Tacitus concludes, as
the naive young Drusus now employs an old man's craft (3.8). The rhetoric of Tiberius is perfectly inverted; it makes the young old.

34. Indeed, they are so literal that in their desire to control signification they wish to possess the signs; so they will wake the sleeping
Germanicus and demand the *vexillum* (1.39).

35. For a similar return of rhetorical control, compare Tacitus's account of the dissolution of the soldiers' panic at the eclipse of the moon.
Quintilian saw the precedent for this action in just such terms: "cum Sul-
picius ille Gallus in exercitu L. Paulli de lunae defectione disseruit, ne
velut prodigio divinitus facto militum animi terrerentur, non videtur usus
esse oratoris officio?" (1.10.47).

36. At 2.12 Tacitus presents Germanicus as interpreter, first of the
report that the Germans were planning a night raid, second of his own
troops' feelings. At 2.20 the reader is advised that Caesar knew all—i.e.,
this penetrating reader knows the hidden stratagems of the Germans as,
in his nocturnal escapade, he knows the words and feelings of his men.

37. Tacitus here echoes Sallust, who has desire lay hold of Marius
(*cupido*, at *Jugurtha* 89.6). The author of the Ps.-Sallustian letters *De re-
publica* imitated the typically Sallustian use of *invadere*, but with *torpedo*
at 2.8.7, which Tacitus then reused at *Histories* 3.63.2. See also *Cat.* 31.1
of *tristitia*; *Jug.* 35.9, of *metus*; Livy 2.9.5, of *terror*; and Caesar, *Bellum*

Civile 1.14. In the present passage from the *Annals*, Tacitus's echo ushers in the moral monograph on Germanicus.

38. Of course, Caecina's troops replay the earlier mutiny. Like Germanicus, he is forced to melodramatic action after speech fails: at 1.66 he throws himself before the camp's gate to prevent its abandonment. Then comes a successful speech, heard in silence (1.67), and a new constitution of society: "equos dehinc, orsus a suis, legatorum tribunorumque nulla ambitione fortissimo cuique bellatori tradit, ut hi, mox pedes in hostem invaderent." In the ensuing battle, the Germans prove poor interpreters: they are overawed by the sound and *fulgor*, which they had not expected.

39. Tacitus makes calculations of order very difficult, in his tempest in particular. Not only is social hierarchy impossible (for the good cannot be discerned from the bad, and like the good man's effort in Thucydides' plague, his effort is unavailing), but the storm, whose dimensions a classical treatment indicates by a number of technical means (figures of speech; narrator's intervention, e.g., *mirabile visu*), can only be appreciated by a sort of multiplication of the known, a proportional extension of the reported geographical extreme; i.e., 2.24 states not only that this is not simply the worst storm ever, it is worse proportionally as Ocean is worse than all other seas and as Germany is ill-climed.

40. This mob scene shares the unknowable, indistinguishable quality of other mob scenes. At Brindisi, for example, upon Agrippina's arrival, the wailing of men cannot be told from that of women. This gender confusion is one variation of the difficult-to-read mixture of such scenes. Mutinous speech arises in the murkiness of twilight "flexo in vesperam die" (1.16). In their concerted action, the soldiers reverse the confusion: they treat the half-awake enemy with no quarter, no distinction: "Non sexus, non aetas miserationem attulit; profana simul et sacra et celeberrimum illis gentibus templum quod Tamfanae vocabant solo aequantur. Sine vulnere milites, qui semisomnos, inermos, aut palantis ceciderant" (1.51.2–3). Just earlier their violence toward themselves was a melee the like of which has never been known: "Diversa omnium, quae umquam accidere, civilium armorum facies" (1.49).

41. Livy presents how Romans are supposed to grieve. In the good old days of the republic a woman's face mirrored the prospects of the republic; see 22.7.12–14 for the visibility of emotion, especially women's, in a dire period of the Punic wars: "inde varios vultus digredientium ab nuntiis cerneres, ut cuique laeta aut tristia nuntiabantur. . . ."

42. Indeed, the destructive tempest comes at the equinox, where a classical reading would expect equal, balanced nature.

Notes to Chapter 6

1. "Pilgrimage" is an appropriate term for Petronius's text whether or not one accepts the interpretation of the novel as a mock Odyssey driven by the *ira Priapi* (first proposed by Eilimar Klebs, "Zur Komposition von Petronius' Satirae," *Philologus* 47 [1889]: 623–35; for bibliography, see Slater, *Reading Petronius* [Princeton, N.J.: Princeton University Press, 1990], 40). The freedmen in their commonplaces treat the present as an unholy age alienated from the divine and wish for a return to the old relations with the gods. Ganymedes complains that prayer is no longer efficacious; once upon a time the women prayed for rain and returned from the altar wet as rats, as he puts it (44). Even if the three heroes are not fleeing Priapus, they are figures of bad fortune (on Encolpius as a satiric hero, see Amy Richlin, *The Garden of Priapus*, rev. ed. [Oxford and New York, 1983]: 191–92). As Fortune's victims, they make a claim to their hosts' generosity and long for a return to the high style. At the least, they treat grand living as their due from which they have been parted. So, as shipwrecked travelers they appeal to the charity of the pious—if the text would only provide some pious characters. They will be rescued and victimized time and again by characters playing the role of august host, saving patron, dutiful priestess.

2. See my discussion above, Chapter 1.

3. Peter George, "Style and Character in the *Satyricon*," *Arion* 5 (1966): 336, attributed the critical fascination with, indeed overemphasis on, the *Cena* to the pedantic interest in linguistic deviance from classical Latin.

4. The legal prescriptions about freedmen's dress only prevented confusion with (ex)magistrates and equestrians. The freedman was barred from offices and statuses that had distinctly high-status marking, the magistracies with the purple-fringed toga, fasces, axes, and for the most part the rank of equestrian, which was signaled by the wearing of a gold ring and by serving on juries.

5. The critical faculties of the freeborn trio seem impaired before the *Cena*: when Quartilla says *embasicoetas*, Encolpius thinks she means "cup"; she meant and delivers a *cinaedus* (24.2). For all his guest's disdain, Trimalchio's visual and verbal puns fool Encolpius again and again. Slater, *Reading Petronius*, 46, discerned the connected errancy of language and plot: "Loss of control of the meaning of words and loss of freedom of action go hand in hand."

6. Most famously, Bakhtin has emphasized the generic embrace of the novel, and especially its relations to epic (*The Dialogic Imagina-*

tion [Austin: University of Texas Press, 1981], 6–7). The "novelization of genres" does not emphasize the use to which Petronius puts the generic voices: he is engaged in a technique of literary indirection and dilation.

7. It was once maintained that Petronius employed two levels of style; see, for bibliography and a corrective to the editors' standardization of the narrator's style, Hubert Petersmann, *Die Römische Satire* (Darmstadt: Wissenschaftliche Buchgesellschaft, 1986), 401–10. J. P. Sullivan, *The* Satyricon *of Petronius: A Literary Study* (Bloomington: Indiana University Press, 1968), 164, distinguished the *sermo urbanus* of the narrative from the *sermo plebeius* of the *Cena* and added a third, the elaborate style of literary and rhetorical passages. To this degree, the old reading was true, the narratorial voice stands in contrast to the narrated voices, but the characters' condescension and ambition in speech draw attention to the high style as a stance. Stylistic crossing tends to undermine the alleged distance and conflate viewpoint. Contamination with freedmen culture undermines the high and stilted language and objectivity of the character narrator Encolpius and his fellow freemen. Beck, in "Encolpius at the *Cena*," *Phoenix* 29 (1975): 272–76, explained the contrast in styles by arguing for a young Encolpius of the narrative and an older Encolpius the narrator, a thesis which responds to the shifting style of the narratorial voice but does not account for the contexts of those changes and indeed the naiveté of the (older) narrator. P. Veyne, "Le 'Je' dans le *Satiricon*," *REL* 42 (1964): 301–6, saw Encolpius's expressions of wonder in the *Cena* as feigned naiveté. Like much of the scholarship, these approaches seek a consistency of character and narrator. However, Slater (*Reading Petronius*, 53) has noted that the many shifts in the *Satyricon* frustrate the reader's efforts at consistency-building (the term from Iser).

For a precis of the freedmen's linguistic peculiarities, see Martin S. Smith, ed., *Petronii Arbitri Cena Trimalchionis* (Oxford: Oxford University Press, 1975), xxix–xxx and 220–24. See also Donald C. Swanson, *A Formal Analysis of Petronius' Vocabulary* (Minneapolis: The Perine Book Co., 1963). On distinct styles as dissonant voices, see Froma Zeitlin, "Petronius as Paradox: Anarchy and Artistic Integrity," *TAPA* 102 (1971): 645. Both Slater and Zeitlin rightly stress the importance and thoroughgoing quality of disruption in the *Satyricon* and thus do not attempt to plot variety of style exclusively in terms of characterization.

8. See Brent Vine's review article of Bret Boyce's *The Language of the Freedmen in Petronius'* Cena Trimalchionis, *Gnomon* 67 (1995): 112–17.

9. Hugh Kenner, *Joyce's Voices* (Berkeley and Los Angeles: University of California Press, 1978), 15–16, and for the Eumaeus episode, 35–38.

10. George ("Style and Character," 350) had observed that Encolpius suits his style to his addressee. This shows the rhetorician in action

and also the fluidity and interdependence of styles in this text. The narrator and his brothers can change sexual orientation as well as social status. Amy Richlin (*The Garden of Priapus*, 191) points out that the trio's sex-role switching reflects "an attitude that is usually a mark of low income."

11. Richlin (*The Garden of Priapus*, 190) has described the *Satyricon*'s relationship to the Greek novel as "a sort of literary *contaminatio*" and suggests that the reader's identification with the disreputable narrator "is a staining joke on the reader," and that Petronius is staining a genre (191–92).

12. The narrator is taken in: Encolpius mistakes the procuress for a goddess (at 7.2, as Slater, *Reading Petronius*, 33, points out, anticipated by Richlin in her first edition in 1983, 194). Along with Trimalchio, who passes off mime players as *Homeristae*, Encolpius misreads the vulgar as the epic. For a precis of the Homeric allusions, see Richlin, *The Garden of Priapus*, 192. Slater, *Reading Petronius*, 82, has stressed the significance of the narrator's loss of position for the interpretation of the work: "In tandem with the destabilization of the privileged positions of narrator and reader runs the destabilization of sign systems in the *Cena*."

13. Patricia A. Parker, *Inescapable Romance: Studies in the Poetics of a Mode* (Princeton, N.J.: Princeton University Press, 1979), 7, describes error as one of the metaphors that romantic texts from the *Aeneid* to *Paradise Lost* provide for their own description: "The fertile multiplicity of the meanings of 'error'—mental, geographical, and narrative—with varieties of 'de-viation,' inform not only the wandering structure of the poems of Ariosto and Spenser but also the devious romance of figure and trope which Mallarmé identifies with the 'erreur' of poetry itself." Petronius's text, however, makes much of the sterility of infinite repetition.

14. Compare Encolpius's characterization of Ascyltos as "stupro liber, stupro ingenuus" (81). On the incongruity between speakers and their fine moral or literary sentiments, see Sullivan, *The* Satyricon *of Petronius*, 215–16. For prostitution as a character trait linking the freedmen and the freeborn trio, see Thomas K. Hubbard, "The Narrative Architecture of Petronius' *Satyricon*," *AC* 55 (1986): 207.

15. On the connection of romance and the dilation of closure, see Parker, *Inescapable Romance*, 9–10 and 31–39.

16. One expression travels from narrator to freedman: the steward picks up Encolpius's *sine dubio* (30), an expression he could not have heard, of course, but his repetition complicates our reading of the narratorial voice. Encolpius had delivered one of his typical, introductory statements of wonder, "sine dubio paulisper trepidavimus." The steward echoes this with "Tyria sine dubio." The freedman is trying to impress his

guests and is no doubt inflating the value of his lost clothes. Part of the travel of the expression derives from the reader's perspective, for both the narrator and the steward are here playing the scene straight, assuring the listener of the genuineness of their emotion, or their cloth. Neither the narrator's nor the steward's audience believes the assurance of verity. We are forced to doubt, as each pronouncement of truth-telling and of wonder occasions skepticism in the reader. For other borrowings of the freedmen's style in this early and orienting scene in Trimalchio's house, cf. narrative *quisquis* (31.7), an echo of syntax of 28.7 (Trimalchio's sign: *quisquis servus*) and the narrator's *valde lauta* (31.8, *valde* frequently appears on the freedman's lips). See note 22 below for additional examples of *contaminatio*. At times, perhaps, we cannot judge whether a low form in the narrational voice constitutes seepage from the surrounding stories or scribal error; e.g., at 26, "Gitona libentissime servile officium tuentem usque hoc iubemus in balneo sequi," I would suggest the use of *hoc* for the literary *huc* (see Friedlaender, *Petronii Cena Trimalchionis* [Leipzig: S. Hirzel, 1906], 27), and *in balneo* for *in balneum* reflects the servile drag put on by the *ingenuus* Giton. The editors disagree: Müller excises *usque hoc* and adopts Heraeus's *balneum*. I do not have the temerity to defend the Trau manuscript's accuracy, but scholars have used as a principle of editing "restoration," which applies well if the narrating voice is to be granted authority and distance. Another example may help. In the narrator's Latin the Trau manuscript three times refers to trumpet players: at 53.12 they are the vulgar *cornices*, so too at 78.6; but H reads *cornicipes* at 78.5, an obvious scribal slip for *cornicines*, the literary Latin plural. Müller has simply printed *cornicines* in all three places. Petersmann, *Die Römische Satire*, 403, argued that the first and last instance should be the vulgar form, suited to Trimalchio: *cornices* in fact occurs in the host's reported speech; only 78.5 is actually from Encolpius's mouth. Thus viewpoint and not the absolute distinction of direct speech and narratorive frame determined morphology. The report of overheard vulgarisms may be the first inroad into the narratorial voice. Petronius seems careful in his morphological/phonological contrasts: Encolpius has *caupones* and *plaudebat* against the freedmen's *coda* and *plodo* (98.1 and 70.10 versus 44.12 and 45.13).

Along with a sense of restoring linguistic propriety to the narrator, Müller's recognition of the excerptor's interpolation, detected by Fraenkel especially, has led scholars to accept strong revision of the manuscripts generally. These are of course separate issues. On interpolation, see Müller, xxxix–xlvii. On the Trau ms. (H), see idem, xxviii–xxxiii (in Latin), a full account of the manuscript tradition in Müller and Wilhelm Ehlers, eds. and trans., *Petronius Arbiter Satyrica* (Munich: E. Heimeran,

1965), 381–430 (in German); for a photographic image of this MS with diplomatic copy, see S. Gaselee, *A Collotype Reproduction of the Trau Manuscript* (Cambridge: Cambridge University Press, 1915).

17. This had long been a trite expression: Plautus puts Orcus in the mouth of Ergasilus in the *Captivi* (283), in a speech of banal philosophizing.

18. On *novi generis labyrinthi* at 73.1, see Slater, *Reading Petronius*, 78, n. 67, and 87; Rick M. Newton, "Trimalchio's Hellish Bath," *CJ* 77 (1982): 315–16; and P. Fedeli, "Petronio: Il viaggio, il labirinto," *MD* 6 (1981): 91–117.

19. For result clauses that usher in death, cf. "potantibus ergo et accuratissime nobis lautitias mirantibus larvam argenteam attulit servus sic aptatam, ut articuli eius vertebraeque laxatae in omnem partem flecterentur" (34.8); "sic orbis vertitur tamquam mola, et semper aliquid mali facit, ut homines aut nascantur aut pereant" (39.13); "et haec ideo omnia publico, ut familia mea iam nunc sic me amet tamquam mortuum" (71.3); finally, [Eumolpus] "ego sic semper et ubique vixi, ut ultimam quamque lucem tamquam non redituram consumerem" (99.1). Related are the class of asseverations that also use *sic* or *ita* and *ut* but where the dependent clause seeks to reify and verify the wish of the main clause (see below, note 22).

20. Trimalchio's reuse and exaggeration of this sentence type is part of his general odyssey in search of credibility. He reassures excessively that his stories are worthy of *fides*. On the errancy of *fides*, see below, note 38.

21. Much of the humor depends on the substitution, in the first clause, of "profit" or "sexual exploitation" in place of "gods" or "life." In the present example, *bene moriar* makes two substitutions, inverting "as surely as I wish to live or prosper" and contaminating this with *bene* from the freedmen's phrase *bene esse* or *bene habere*, to be well, to be living well.

22. For examples of the syntax of this sentence type (*sic* or *ita* with the subjunctive . . . *ut* with the indicative) see Hofmann-Szantyr, no. 341e, p. 634, and Kuhner-Stegmann, no. 47.11, I pp. 190–91, *TLL* 7.2.526.23 and 60–61 (the last analyses Petr. 58.12 as a contamination of *ita lucrum faciam, ut te persequar*, and *ita me lucrum transeat, nisi* . . .). This sentence type is often found in Plautus, in wishes invoking the gods, e.g., *Captivi* 622–24: "at ita me rex deorum atque hominum faxit patriae compotem, ut istic Philocrates non magis est quam aut ego aut tu." This example itself varies the typical (clearly colloquial) "ita me di ament / amabunt, ut . . ." "so help me god the following is true. . . ." Petronius's freedmen substitute money making for god's help: "so may I grow fat, as the following is true. . . ." Translate "Damn, I'll get you." "For damn sure, that guy isn't Philocrates." A parallel for these expressions of violent threat

is found in Roman curse tablets; the *defixiones* record wishes for physical harm to come to others (often the destruction or withering of the body parts of a rival in love). The sympathetic magic of the formulas is straightforward: the word *defigo* applies to the inscribed lead foil buried in the ground and the enumerated body parts of the intended victim, or the formula "as surely as such and such is true, so may my victim be harmed" links the action with desired result. In fact, the *defixiones* offer a close syntactic parallel to the freedmen's abusive threats: "Ita uti mortuos nec ad deos nec ad homines acceptus est, seic Rhodine aput M. Licinium accepta sit et tantum valeat quantum ille mortuos quei istic sepultus est" (a republican or Augustan example found just outside Rome, off the Via Latina, *CIL* 6:140); Audollent, *Defixionum Tabellae* (1904; reprint, Frankfurt: Minerva, 1967), 139; Degrassi, *Inscriptiones Latinae Liberae Rei Publicae* (Florence: La Nuova Italia, 1963), 1144.

23. Bernstein, *Bitter Carnival,* 88, notes that in literature the abject figures "regularly turn to insult as a means of breaking out of their entrapment in buffoon's motley." Hermeros tries to break out through homophobic language: calling Ascyltos a fruit, a *nocturnus*, someone not worth his own piss, and one who cannot escape Hermeros's pisser (57: "Ad summam, si circumminxero illum, nesciet qua fugiat"). *Toga perversa*, the commentators all point out, refers to the magistrate's reversal of dress before doing violence, passing the sentence of capital punishment. The sexual connotations of dress reversal should be clear. This is yet another instance of the freedmen's appropriation of dress and roles above their station, and perhaps too of an idiom above their station, which they misuse and misunderstand.

24. Ganymedes' complaint, just above, of the present ball-less state of affairs, anticipates the sexual connotation of *fruniscar*: "Sed si nos coleos haberemus, non tantum sibi placeret" (and perhaps, too, by "haec colonia retroversus crescit tamquam coda vituli"). The evil times are thus ascribed to lack of virility or backward virility, and then to the gods, on the assurance of what the problematical *vir* Ganymedes will do to Encolpius.

25. Hermagoras makes another such sexual threat at 58.6: "recte, venies sub dentem: aut ego non me novi, aut non deridebis, licet barbam auream habeas. Athana tibi irata sit curabo, et <ei> qui te primus 'deuro de' fecit."

26. Cf. his misunderstanding of *salvo*, which also redounds to his discredit: "Attonitis admiratione universis 'Salvo' inquit 'tuo sermone' Trimalchio 'si qua fides est, ut mihi pili inhorruerunt, quia scio Niceronem nihil nugarum narrare'" (63).

27. An apparently nonthreatening instance of this sentence type

comes at 61: "'omne me' inquit 'lucrum transeat, nisi iam dudum gaudi-monio dissilio, quod te talem video.'" Niceros is delighted by Trimal-chio's notice and invitation to speak. This strained politeness, which seeks to assure the auditor of the genuineness of the speaker's emotion, ex-presses that assurance in terms of self-explosion. While this sentence does not threaten the auditor, Niceros does threaten himself with rupture—in turn a threat if the host will not believe his guest. Generally, this sen-tence type abounds in sexual threat; cf. "Sic me salvum habeatis, ut ego sic solebam ipsumam meam debattuere, ut etiam dominus suspicaretur" (Trimalchio at 69).

28. The freedmen offend linguistically in proxemic terms as well (proxemics is that branch of sociolinguistics which studies the distance between speakers). They speak too close—Fortunata and Habinnas's wife are far too close, as are Trimalchio and at least one of his interlocutors, the boy who rides on his back while asking him the questions of the *bucca* game. Encolpius and his neighbor are perhaps too close, but this enables their intimate exchange: the indiscreet, frank information about Fortunata, for example. Such knowledge should be shared *only* when speakers are close, but exactly this sort of information, the account of rags-to-riches rise, the mercantile lowdown on Trimalchio, insinuation about his sexual career, is told out loud and from a respectable distance by the *host*.

29. On this term, see R. A. Hudson, *Sociolinguistics* (Cambridge: Cambridge University Press, 1980), 43: social dialects or sociolects "refer to non-regional differences."

30. Hermagoras, thinking Giton is a slave, calls him this at 58.3. The name comes from an imperative and from the function of the slave, just like the name of Trimalchio's carver (the dumb pun of whose name En-colpius doesn't get). Both names blur the call to heed the master's words and to serve his body.

31. Ogling may well have begun other scenes, such as the meeting of Agamemnon and Encolpius. The narrative does seem to link physical, sexual, and visual wandering—and not just in the scene of the ooh's and aah's of those gaping at the narrator's prick. When Encolpius wanders about town, lost or in pursuit of Giton, he says of his wandering: "Post-quam lustravi oculis totam urbem" (11). His *lustratio* is no procession of purification (as the Roman farmer was supposed to walk around his field in the old rite) but a reconnoitering that lands him in a brothel (Horace tries to defend himself from his slave's accusations of sexual perversity: he has engaged in *otium*, not *mala lustra* [*Sat.* 1.6.68]). Trimalchio de-fends his own infatuation with an idiom similar to Encolpius's: "Non est dignus quem in oculis feram?" (75). For additional examples of the word

"eye" used with a sexual meaning, cf. Habinnas of his *puer* Alexandrinus, who is cross-eyed: "sicut Venus spectat. Ideo nihil tacet, vix oculo mortuo umquam" (68), and the expression *ego me apoculo* (67; and cf. 62, the pun or alternate etymology of *culus* reinforces the vulgar connotations). Later in their night wanderings, Encolpius as Theseus needs Giton-Ariadne's chalk marks to recover his way. The text in these episodes of lost and recovered homosexual love presents its movement as passing from ogling to action; the fulfillment and frustration of desire progresses as character moves from spectator to participant, or even *spectandus*. This narrative patterning applies to all the spectacles of this text, even the verbal performances of the *Cena*, where speaking itself is an attempt to escape being laughed at. Of course, the attempts to speak simply turn into more spectacle—derisible matter for the next speaker. Thus episodes in the *Cena* replay not just the same themes but the same need to speak.

32. Agamemnon and Encolpius have a mutual infatuation; see George Kennedy, "Encolpius and Agamemnon in Petronius," *AJP* 99 (1978): 173.

33. The town is thoroughly commercial: "In hac enim urbe non litterarum studia celebrantur, non eloquentia locum habet, non frugalitas sanctique mores laudibus ad fructum perveniunt, sed quoscumque homines in hac urbe videritis, scitote in duas partes esse divisos. Nam aut captantur aut captant" (116). This town of crows and corpses, the topography and figures of freedmen, recalls Phaedrus's fabulous anti-landscape, the place Latium would be if it did not recognize the poet. Phaedrus's text, of course, gives the poet his due: see Simonides' and Menander's receptions (4.23 and 5.1).

34. He also anticipates Trimalchio as a naive rhetor or reader, as he describes rhetoricians as comic parasites and then literalizes this sententia by running along to dinner and bringing uninvited his would-be critics and rivals in speech.

35. Kennedy, "Encolpius and Agamemnon in Petronius," 173, argued that Agamemnon also was a visitor to the school.

36. Here, too, Petronius allies his characters by their economic attitude: the gossip rates Glyco dumb because he plans to execute his own freedman; this is *se traducere*. Echion is smart to have his boy/son/slave educated; this is, one infers, *se augere*. In the freedman economy of value, sexual conduct and sociofamilial relations have everything to do with self-inflation.

37. The freedmen fail precisely in switching codes: they do not have the language to speak of education; but the language they do have usurps and destabilizes the proper code. Scholars have moved away from reading the *Satyricon* as a binary code switching from narrator to narrated, but

the movement cannot be to a unitary language. (Trimalchio tries hardest at code switching: he changes his voice, tries to speak a literary Greek, but it all comes out as the [eunuch's] singsong.)

38. Petronius's indications of the reception of Niceros's story are nicely ironic: "Attonitis admiratione universis 'salvo' inquit 'tuo sermone' Trimalchio 'si qua fides est, ut mihi pili inhorruerunt.'" Petronius often begins an episode with a notation of the confused or ludicrous universal reaction of the characters, e.g., *Consternati nos* . . . or *Saturi*. In addition, Trimalchio here indulges in one of these overemphatic wishes: "may your story be sound, if there is any credibility, as surely as my hair stood on end." The humor, then, lies in Trimalchio's confusion over the meaning of *salvo sermone*, in his use of this freedman's overly emphatic form of speech, and in the simple fact that the corroborating clause of his wish, his hair standing on end, has not occurred. The course of Trimalchio's diction in this section again illustrates *contaminatio*. After Trimalchio's story of witches, the audience acts like him: they maintain that they believe the preceding story. The narrator Encolpius picks up both Trimalchio's initial statement, "si qua fides est," and his final exhortation, "Rogo vos, oportet credatis." At the beginning of 64 he reports (ironically?) "Miramur nos et pariter credimus," and at the beginning of 65, "Hanc humanitatem insecutae sunt matteae, quarum etiam recordatio me, si qua est dicenti fides, offendit." Further, the narrator reports he has been restored by the speech ("Recreatus hoc sermone"—Trimalchio in turn will, at 68, wish himself safe and sound, *salvum*). The narrator picks up the diction of believability and the confession of belief from the most unbelievable character.

39. Laughter irrepressible gives away the free men as it would return its target to servile status: Echion reacts by impugning Ascyltos's free birth (57: "quid habet quod rideat? numquid pater fetum emit lamna? eques Romanus es; et ego regis filius. 'quare ergo servivisti? . . .'"). After Echion parades his biography, Giton, laughing but in slave dress, becomes the target: "'tu autem' inquit 'etiam tu rides cepa cirrata? io Saturnalia, rogo, mensis december est?'" (58). Laughter from a slave is unimaginable outside the Saturnalia or the comic stage, and so Echion's language attempts to fix Giton in the status advertised by his clothes.

40. Encolpius addresses Agamemnon at 49, but Trimalchio leaps in to forestall the rhetorician's reply. "At non Trimalchio . . ." follows Encolpius's direct speech; the narrator has turned away from Agamemnon, not allowing him to respond to Encolpius's private remarks ("inclinatus ad aurem Agamemnonis") and instead bringing on Trimalchio berating the cook.

41. Elsewhere the narrator's notices of speech type may communicate outright disdain, e.g., 47: "Eiusmodi fabulae vibrabant," where stories and not Virgilian weapons fly through the air. Mock epicism in-

volves the narrator in the mockery as surely as such first-person notices as *garrimus*.

42. One thinks of Servius in Macrobius's *Saturnalia* as almost done out of a role when the noble guests decide what aspect of Virgil they will expound; see Kaster, *Guardians of Language*, 62. It is not simply that the pedant makes bad company: his speech precludes that of others.

43. Whether Petronius narrated Agamemnon's declamation is far from clear. The first fragment begins with Encolpius outside the school, declaiming against declamation. Agamemnon refers to his own earlier performance: "Non est passus Agamemnon me diutius declamare in porticu, quam ipse in schola sudaverat" (3). Sweating, the verb *sudare*, occurs in sexual encounters in Petronius's text. Agamemnon's inviting of the three heroes to Trimalchio's dinner may, like his praise of Encolpius's speech, be the recompense for sexual favors. He would thus anticipate that other lettered teacher Eumolpus in his attitude toward students, and perhaps too in his exclusion from his audience: perhaps he has been driven from the hall as Eumolpus is stoned in the art gallery. Otherwise, one expects the declaimer to remain to hear his rivals and learn who wins the contest or what the critics thought. In Seneca the Elder's collection, declaimers comment upon each other's performance; presumably there was discussion after the performances.

44. He is a mouthpiece for Cicero at 3.2: Agamemnon quotes *Pro Caelio* 41.

45. For the extreme, comic statement of this Athenian social protocol, see Bella Zweig, "The Mute Nude Female Characters in Aristophanes' Plays," in *Pornography and Representation in Greece and Rome*, ed. Amy Richlin (Oxford and New York: Oxford University Press, 1992), 73–89.

46. See Chapter 1 for a discussion of ideal speech roles for the freedman at Rome.

47. Quintilian (1.12.17) belittles the monetary calculation of the benefits of education—although he knows parents think this way. In the praise of his boy's education, Habinnas shows similar pride, and ignorance that he has been in the wrong circles: "Habinnas et numquam, inquit, didicit, sed ego ad circulatores eum mittendo erudibam" (68). The result of such an education is aping; the boy imitates (mule drivers and street vendors) beautifully.

48. Characteristically, Trimalchio envies the transparent reading of these experts. They can see beyond the surface. A soothsayer impresses Trimalchio for the same reason: the Greekling *mathematicus* "intestinas meas noverat" (76). Slater, *Reading Petronius*, 70, has pointed out the thematic connections of doctors and money changers in this passage with semiology.

49. Part of the appeal of this speech stems from its frankness. Bern-

stein, *Bitter Carnival*, 16, writing of what he terms the Saturnalian dialogue, describes a moment that is exactly unconventional, disconcerting,
and sympathetic: "At the center of the *agon* there is always a moment of
absolute reversal when it is the slave, like Horace's Davus, who calls his
master 'O totiens servus.'" The master, in Horace's or Petronius's satire
and beyond, is always something of a straight man for this melodramatic
criticism.

50. Trimalchio prices himself with an expression that he has not
quite understood: after praising his silver cups, he delivers this *aestimatio*:
"Meum enim intellegere nulla pecunia vendo" (52.3). Note that the freedmen's pricing also involves the language of fables: Trimalchio describes
his metamorphosis as that of frog to king (77); Fortunata, on the other
hand, has more threatening forms: "inflat se tamquam rana" (74), she is a
kite (75) and a viper (77). Trimalchio, we are to understand, is the busy bee
whose wealth grew "tamquam favus" (76). Hermeros praises the under-
taker similarly (38: he dined like a king and was "fantasia, non homo").

51. One should neither assume that *aestimatio* was a set process nor
read the Roman statements of *aestimatio* as objective reports. The stern
old Cato, according to Polybius (31.25), complained that in the present,
corrupt age a pretty boy cost more than a plot of land and that a jar of
pickled fish was held more dear than a plowman. Such a report of topsy-
turvy *aestimatio* is itself complicated by narrative context. Polybius has
just reported L. Aemilius Paullus's laudable poverty. This praise of the
old-fashioned mores and judgment of his patron's father anticipates Polybius's first-person account of Scipio Aemilianus's *aestimatio* of Polybius
and their friendship.

52. See Israel Shatzman, *Senatorial Wealth and Roman Politics*, Collection Latomus 142 (Brussels, 1975), 47–74.

53. Trimalchio tries to defend his kissing of a slave by praising the
boy's learning (75: "decem partes dicit, librum ab oculo legit") and virtue,
but his high-sounding *aestimatio* soon sounds even more ridiculous and
does not conceal his lust. Talk of education does not fool the wives Fortunata and Scintilla. In the freedmen's stories, female calculation is canny
and threatening: the widow of Ephesus fools all and comes up with the
final trick (swap of dead for living); the witches are not harmed by the
large-limbed, sword-wielding *baro* and swap mannequin for child.

54. Ascyltos's proposal may partake of folklore (cf. Solomon's solution to double claims on a child) but certainly has the ring of the rhetorical schools' exercise, the *divisio*: "Age nunc et puerum dividamus" (79).

55. For similarly abusive characterizations, see Quint. 8.6.53, and
Seneca, *Contr.* 7.4.8.

56. In addition, the economic utopia the freedmen long for differs

strikingly from the aristocratic ideal. On a number of occasions, the freed-men speak nostalgically of the old days, not when virtue had its reward or status could be clearly seen, but when credit was easy and goods were cheap. Ganymedes contrasts the expensive price of grain today with the old days: "interim nemo curat, quid annona mordet. . . . Itaque illo tem-pore annona pro luto erat" (44). In the story of the unbreakable glass, the emperor has the inventor killed from fear of the disastrous effect on the economy: "si scitum esset, aurum pro luto haberemus" (51). In this series of economic ruminations, Habinnas concludes: "Mulieres si non essent, omnia pro luto haberemus; nunc hoc est caldum meiere et frigidum po-tare" (67). The dirt-cheap economy is prevented by corrupt magistrates, the emperor, and women—each target is named by the speaker.

57. On the "abject" as a critical term, see Bernstein, *Bitter Carnival*, 18 and 28–29.

58. Generosity is a patron's virtue, but the freedmen reveal a par-ticular viewpoint: the magistrate Norbanus is censured for his parsimo-nious games and so will get no return on his expenditure. Trimalchio praises Fortunata for selling all her jewelry on the shipwreck of Trimal-chio's cargo—she has realized a multiple return. Chrysanthus has spoilt his capital by bequeathing it outside his family, whence it will not return. Norbanus and Chrysanthus, unlike Fortunata, failed to recognize who was their own (*suus*). Such an attitude distorts the high Roman ideal, and practice. The patron left his property to many; he recognized his clients and friends, even his equals or betters, by naming them in his will. Real and status capital were thus traded within a finite circle. The freedmen as imagined by Petronius have no such broad conception; they have only their own family—wife and children, not the extended aristocratic *fa-milia*—as the devoted domestic scenes and sentiments of freedmen's and freedwomen's inscriptions reveal.

59. Compare the hotheaded irruptions of the diners. The freedmen, as always, cannot contain themselves. It is not clear that Phileros disap-proves of Chrysanthus's excesses: his report includes what an upper-class Roman would never have admitted as praiseworthy.

60. Note also that Hermeros makes his critic's paternity an issue elsewhere: "Iam scies patrem tuum mercedes perdidisse, quamvis et rhe-toricam scis" (58.8). Hermeros has neither father nor rhetoric and tries to set at naught the freeborn's possession of these. Likewise he denies Ascyltos the schoolmaster's authority by calling him "mufrius non magis-ter" (58).

61. The names Phileros/Hermeros/Ganymedes are interchangeable; there is nothing significant in the name change—the names imply con-fused, multiple attachments. Love is father, and the sons take as close to

a patronymic as they can. But they are also brother to the master, Ganymedes to Zeus, and, as in the narrated autobiography, adulterous lover of the mistress. Thus they name with approval other freedmen as jacks-of-all-trades, bastard bisexuals: Habinnas describes his favorite as an educated man with an expression that also means a bisexual, "omnis musae mancipium" (68); Phileros praises the dead Chrysanthus "Immo etiam pullarius [or, as H reads, puellarius] erat, omnis Minervae homo" (43). Both riddles recommend that the reader, the riddle solver, know himself or his own place. The first is clear: he who flees his own (family, station) flees far. The second is not. Hermeros seems to echo the earlier truism, replacing fleeing with approaching. If both riddles have sexual meanings, the first would mean "he who flees unions with his own kind errs greatly." The second puts the same thought in harder terms: "I who come afar, come swellingly/ambitiously"—Hermeros has relied on puns to riddle the first truism. Hermeros's further explanation of the riddle seems to apply as well to penis as to the usual solutions of foot, eye, and hair: "dicam tibi, qui de nobis currit et de loco non movetur; qui de nobis crescit et minor fit."

62. F. Zeitlin, "Petronius as Paradox," 665, has argued that the inadequacy of the standards of literary culture, its failure to regulate the chaos of the world, mocks the aristocracy that gives rise to this culture and the freedmen who get it so wrong.

63. Equally, the reader comes to distrust the freeborn's moralizing about money. Trimalchio may seem ridiculous "Credite mihi: assem habeas, assem valeas; habes, habeberis" (77.6), but only because he voices the sentiment that motivates all (the sentiment is vulgar and proverbial; Horace voices it in the Satires: " 'Nil satis est' inquit 'quia tanti quantum habeas sis' " (Sat. 1.62), and see A. Otto, Die Sprichwörter und sprichwörtlichen Redensarten der Römer (1890; reprint, Hildesheim, 1965), 157. Ascyltos maintains the free and noble sentiment that money corrupts, so he justifies in verse his fear of taking his suit to court: "Quid faciunt leges ubi sola pecunia regnat / . . . Nonnumquam nummis vendere verba solent" (14.2). But the trio are really worried about being discovered. It is they who are in search of lost treasure (did they steal this?) and who sell their words, profiting from their standing as educated men. Only Trimalchio is naive enough to name his gods Profit (60.8: Cerdo, Felicio, Lucrio). The free and savvy Encolpius simply buys off the priestess after his sacrilege (again after delivering verse). The first scene with Eumolpus (88) shows the poet taking up this tired locus: money has ruined art.

64. Literary expertise distinguishes the travelers, both at the dinner party and, for example, at the unliterary town of Croton; indeed, Petronius may have wanted his reader to recognize the pretensions of the traveling scholar in his protagonists. Pace Slater, Reading Petronius, 31, n. 12: "The pose of critic is just another of Encolpius's roles."

65. The soiling of literature with hard cash characterizes the free as well: apprehended in sacrilege, the goose-slaying Encolpius turns to his wallet, an offer that moves the priestess to verse: "Quisquis habet nummos, secura navigat aura . . ." (137). The poem continues with mythological and historical examples so as to prove that the moneyed man may be anything, specifically a lettered professional (poet, declaimer, or lawyer: "Carmina componat, declamet, concrepet omnes / et peragat causas sitque Catone prior. / Iurisconsultus . . .").

66. On the ironic connections of the poem and the narrative setting, see Roger Beck, "Eumolpus *Poeta*, Eumolpus *Fabulator*: A Study of Characterization in the *Satyricon*," *Phoenix* 33 (1979): 248. More generally on these poems, see F. Zeitlin, "Petronius Romanus: A Study of the *Troiae Halosis* and *Bellum Civile*," *Latomus* 30 (1971): 56–82 who argues for the *Bellum Civile* as a subversion of Virgil and the *Troiae Halosis* as a particular response to *Aeneid*, books 1 and 2. Earlier, debate focused on the relation of the *Bellum Civile* to Lucan's work (see Beck, "Eumolpus *Poeta*," 239–53 and the bibliography cited at 239, n. 1) and that of the *Troiae Halosis* to Seneca and Virgil (Sullivan, *The* Satyricon *of Petronius*, 186–89).

67. Trimalchio maintains he has gone to school (48: "solebam ego haec puer apud Homerum legere"), but like the rest of the freedmen clearly he has not; when he says, at 63, "vitam Chiam gessi," we know he has led the life of the dissolute not the poet.

68. Acts of reading abound within the text in, for instance, the ubiquitous *tituli* and *signa*, but Trimalchio shows particular, naive faith in the written word. He cannot resist producing an *inscriptio* for an occasion. His calendar is written out for all to see, as are warnings to slave, labels to pictures, forged labels to wine, punning labels on after-dinner gifts. In the end the guests are force-fed his texts: an *actuarius* reads out the daily register, and finally all are treated to a reading of the host's will. While other freedmen quote *tituli* (advertisements) and Petronius is here exploiting freedmen's attachment to them and the obvious pride that freedmen and -women felt in inscribing their tombstones with a record of their lives proclaiming their and their descendants' free status, and considering that part of the humor derives from the pride and faith of those who are the first members of their class or family to become literate, Trimalchio takes all of this to an extreme. Petronius presents him as a naive reader and composer, delighted in fooling his guests with gastronomic, visual, and verbal puns but at the same time overly credulous of the very written word he insistently explains or cooks up. Perhaps the man who literalizes Plato by making ecphrasis edible actually believes the awful poem he delivers was really Lucilius's, in which case he has been misled by a label, the wrong name affixed to a work. Significantly, the only real offense and punishment (and one remembers that there are no or very few real punishments

of slaves on the comic stage, although see P. G. Walsh, *The Roman Novel* [Cambridge: Cambridge University Press, 1970], 26, for real slave punishment as Roman entertainment) is a verbal one: the *actuarius* reads out that a slave has been crucified "quia Gai nostri genio male dixerat" (53).

69. See note 40, above.

70. 63: "Attonitis admiratione universis 'Salvo' inquit 'tuo sermone' Trimalchio 'si qua fides est, ut mihi pili inhorruerunt, quia scio Niceronem nihil nugarum narrare.'"

71. Trimalchio speaks a most scholastic, almost puerile rhetoric. His figures include ecphrasis (e.g., his account inspired by the skeleton), the priamel of the wretched poem *rictu marcent* ("priamel," although not an ancient term, was a highly recognizable, perhaps even trite poetic form—this would have been assured by Horace *Carmen* 1.1—everybody who had gone to school would know this beginning, as surely as the scribblers of graffiti at Pompeii knew the opening lines of Virgil's first and second books of the *Aeneid*). Like his little comedies involving double names of his slaves, his exegesis of the astrological menu displays his fondness for puns and *figurae etymologicae*. Trimalchio's analysis of Agamemnon's *controversia* is a rhetorical *divisio*. Throughout, the role of namer is the master's role: a naive belief in the power of words animates Trimalchio's rhetoric. He is fascinated with words that mean two things yet everywhere tries to inscribe himself unambiguously. Pots, pictures, and freedmen bear his name. He is stuck on names like that of Carver, which he repeats to himself again and again. Most of all he loves to hear and see his own name: on his dishes, on his slave's lips, on his epitaph, in his freedmen's names.

72. Trimalchio must be absent for speech to be pleasant. Once he has gone, "Nos libertatem sine turanno nacti coepimus invitare convivarum sermones" (41). The narrator strongly marks these divisions of pleasurable and Trimalchionian speech, for he signals the end of the pleasant speech with "Eiusmodi fabulae vibrabant, cum Trimalchio intravit" (47). Trimalchio, a constipated figure, is almost synonymous with interruption. (On the connection of self-containment and the abject, see Bernstein, *Bitter Carnival*, 29, who cites Julia Kristeva, *Power of Horror: An Essay on Abjection*: "Linked primordially to the body's excretions, the abject 'is something rejected from which one does not part,' a horror that violates 'identity, system, order.'") Encolpius asks his neighbor for an account of his host and hostess, which he finds enjoyable until the host interrupts: "Interpellavit tam dulces fabulas Trimalchio" (39). The narrator uses *excepit* (42) to introduce one freedman's tale but otherwise lets the freedmen speak for themselves, i.e., this portion of the narrative the narrator makes dramatic and almost seamless. The narrator thus seems to

return with Trimalchio. The Virgilian heft of *vibrabant* and the hyperbole of *tam dulces* contribute some irony to these narratorial comments; nonetheless, they signal the descent to bathos, the ensuing subordination to Trimalchio as master of speech.

73. On the mixture of genres in the *Satyricon* as a duplication of the banquet of Trimalchio (with confrontation and mixture of Eastern and Western forms), see Daniel L. Selden, "Genre of Genre," in *The Search for the Ancient Novel*, ed. J. Tatum (Baltimore: Johns Hopkins University Press, 1994), 42.

74. The free speakers do not fare much better: Petronius repeatedly mocks their efforts at speech. For example, the introductory sentence at 115, "Audimus murmur insolitum," leads to discovery of Eumolpus writing deathbed verse. The imminent shipwreck and the melodramatic parting speech of the lovers had prepared the reader for the groans of the ship striking aground with timbers snapping. As so often, the first-person sensory report was misleading, and the narrative also refuses to let the free speak too long or to have their speech or verse credited as anything but noise.

75. Note, too, that as characters they are allied to Trimalchio in our voyeuristic reading. Just as they never meet Trimalchio (instead they oversee him playing games in the bath), so the reader never meets the free characters, a feature that cannot be laid to the fragmentary nature of the text but instead arises from its episodic declarations. New characters enter as surprises or chance discoveries. We overhear the meeting with Agamemnon (while these characters are outside the declamatory hall, overhearing the speeches inside), as we do Encolpius's meeting with Eumolpus (itself a scene of interrupted overlooking: Eumolpus is gazing at the pictures). See Christopher Gill, "The Sexual Episodes in the 'Satyricon,'" *CP* 68 (1973): 172–85, on literary voyeurism in the *Satyricon*, and Walsh, *The Roman Novel*, 93–94, on the effect upon Encolpius of the paintings with subjects of mythological homosexual love.

76. He is not alone, but he is the most credulous. On Encolpius as an unreliable narrator, see Beck, "The *Satyricon*: Satire, Narrator, and Antecedents," *MH* 39 (1982): 206. The reactions to Trimalchio's speech are (pseudo-)literary: "sophos universi clamamus" (40); a different production had staged another genre from the flatterers: the guests were prompted to a *laudatio* (35 and 47). Petronius presents the response to the signs and texts of Trimalchio in first-person narratorial comments. The guests almost always display a unanimous reaction to Trimalchio's signification, although on occasion Encolpius is the only guest misled (cf. 30: "quod praecipue miratus sum"; 47: "ego putabam . . . sed Trimalchio expectatione discussa"; and compare 65: "Ego maiestate conterritus"). The

first-person plural pronouncements nonetheless have a full share of irony (e.g., 31: "Obligati tam grandi beneficio"), especially as they are repeated. The beginning of the dinner orients us to this disingenuous naiveté: following the *symphoniacus* playing in Trimalchio's ear, Encolpius makes this self-characterization: "admiratione iam saturi" (28). The course of signs and interpretation continues with the *libellus* on the door post, then the talking magpie with the first-person singular interjection *omnia stupeo*, the *canis . . . pictus* and Encolpius's literal reading of *Cave canem*. Here occurs one of those occasions that isolates Encolpius as the naive reader: his *collegae* laugh at him. After the "venalicium cum titulis pictum," the exegesis of the *atriensis* and the procurator's accounts, "in postibus triclinii fasces," on the other post the inscription *C Pompeio Trimalchioni*, one calendar on either doorpost, the trio tries to enter the dining room "His repleti voluptatibus . . ." (30). For first-person notices as responses to reading, compare "Dum titulos [of the wine] perlegimus, complosit Trimalchio manus"; these signs and the host's truisms produce the usual effect: "nobis . . . mirantibus" (34). At times the trio may be caught up in wonder (40: "Necdum sciebamus <quo> mitteremus suspiciones nostras, cum extra triclinium clamor sublatus est ingens"), but it is Encolpius who stands in need of an interpreter (41: "duravi interrogare illum interpretem meum," and for the general contrast of guests and Encolpius, see 60: "Consternatus ego . . . convivae mirantes"). Encolpius comes off as badly as Trimalchio, the only other character so misled by signs: "Mirabatur haec [the acrobats] solus Trimalchio" (53). Encolpius also, like Trimalchio, earns the freeborn's laughter: he thinks the drunken Habinnas is the praetor; "Risit hanc trepidationem Agamemnon . . ." (65).

77. Steve Johnstone, "On the Uses of Arson in Classical Rome," in *Studies in Latin Literature and Roman History VI*, Collection Latomus 217 (Brussels, 1992), 41–69.

78. Kenneth Rose, "Time and Place in the *Satyricon*," *TAPA* 93 (1962): 402–9.

79. Kenner, *Joyce's Voices*, 59, notes that the title "Ulysses" is "the sole *remark* the author . . . permits himself"; Joyce removed the chapter headings before publication, but the reader supplies them. In Petronius, characters' names are the sole remarks the narrator provides, although we recognize Homeric situation and allusion as surely and curiously as in *Ulysses*. Michael André Bernstein, *The Tale of the Tribe: Ezra Pound and the Modern Verse Epic* (Princeton, N.J.: Princeton University Press, 1980), 21, writes of Pound's reaction to these effaced subtitles: "in the Paris Letter of June 1922 (*The Dial*), Pound wrote: 'The correspondences with Homer are part of Joyce's medievalism and are chiefly his own affair, a scaffold, a means of construction, justified by the result and justifiable by

it only.'" Pound's attitude seems to stem from his understanding of that novel as satire, not epic, and surely denies the incompleteness, the failure of correspondence that the satiric epics so trumpet.

80. For Horace's association of the indecorous and the feminine, see Ellen Oliensis, "Canidia, Canicula, and the Decorum of Horace's *Epodes*," *Arethusa* 24 (1991): 107–38.

81. Displacement, where the author gets his characters lost, is one aspect of literary disconnection. On the repetition of displacement, see especially Susan Stewart, *Nonsense: Aspects of Intertextuality in Folklore and Literature* (Baltimore: Johns Hopkins University Press, 1979), 131. See Richlin, *The Garden of Priapus*, 255, for bibliography.

82. Of course, Rome had literatures of vulgarity. The Priapean poem of plain Latin could, however, be relegated to a minor, though not a despised, genre (unlike the mime, which was recognized as vulgar but without pretensions). On the mime, see Elaine Fantham, "Mime: The Missing Link in Roman Literary History," *CW* 82 (1989): 153–63, and Gerald N. Sandy, "Scaenica Petroniana," *TAPA* 104 (1974): 329–46, with the bibliography cited at 329, n. 1. For the Priapea, see E. M. Connor, *Symbolum Salacitatis: A Study of the God Priapus as a Literary Character*, Studien zur klassischen Philologie 40 (Frankfurt, 1989); G. Luck, *The Latin Love Elegy* (London: Methuen, 1959), 92–93, on the *novi poetae* and Priapus; and Richlin, *The Garden of Priapus*, 116–27. Priapeia were assigned in antiquity to Virgil: 86 poems were appended to his MSS. Even here the Latin is not so plain: poeticized vulgarity lies distinctly in the realm of sophisticated, literary play. The prose of Petronius, despite the most assiduous searches of the source critics, had no such established pedigree. I will not rehearse the bibliography on the "sources" of Petronius, an issue wherein scholars have located and contested the origin of the novel. Bakhtin has shifted the perspective of this issue by arguing that the novel distinctively has all origins; it subjects canonical genres and styles to parodying stylization (Bakhtin, *The Dialogic Imagination*, 6). Thus any *Quellenforschung* for motif, character, theme, and diction will be overabundantly fulfilled, and miss the point. As a literary genealogist, Petronius is not to be trusted, especially when he has a character quote the authority for the "literature" recited. The scazons and hexameters of 5 are not those of Lucilius; the *senarii* of 55 are not from Publilius's hand. When Trimalchio sings a song from the mime *The Silphium Gatherers*, the joke is in the title, for Silphium is an abortifacient. Trimalchio can produce nothing genuine or fertile.

83. Pliny, *Epist.* 5.3.6, wrote for public consumption a defense of his own early writing of scandalous verse. Cicero had similarly defended the riotous life of Caelius as customary adolescent high living. No doubt,

Caelius pushed such a defense to the limits, but it is important that Cicero assumed the jurors would allow youth a period of indulgence (*Pro Caelio* 11). Similarly, Valerius Maximus depicts the life of Sulla as juvenile debauchery immediately giving way to military genius and industry when the young man goes as praetor to Marius in Africa (6.9.6). On *apologiae* for the writing of obscene verse, see Richlin, *The Garden of Priapus*, 2–13.

84. Not unlike Aper in Tacitus's *Dialogus*. The mouthing of classical esthetics should not be confused with the author's position. See Froma I. Zeitlin, "Petronius as Paradox," 639, who points out that Agamemnon and Eumolpus do not follow their own literary strictures.

85. For a reading of Petronius's text as parody of Seneca, see Sullivan, *The Satyricon of Petronius*, 172–79.

86. A. S. Gratwick, ed., *Menaechmi* (Cambridge: Cambridge University Press, 1993), 41, recognizes the posturing of Horace's iambs in the *Epodes*: he calls them a writing of Greek, not Latin, and compares Horace's complaints in the *Ars poetica* about the old Greek dramatists' style of invective. Certainly, Horace draws attention to the non-Romanness of his composition, in an almost self-conscious fashioning of an opening for literature, one he disapproves of, both in the final judgment of the *Ars poetica* and in the self-mockery and Greekness of the *Epodes*. Whether or not Phaedrus knew the *Epodes* were Horace's first work, he tries to inaugurate his own literary career with iambs made safe by other gestures and apologetics.

87. See Kenneth Burke's discussion of literary politenesses and "the mimetics of social inferiority" in *A Rhetoric of Motives* (New York: Prentice-Hall, 1950), 123–24. Burke's analysis arises from William Empson's *English Pastoral Poetry*: "Empson is concerned with a kind of expression which . . . aims rather at a stylistic transcending of conflict. . . . He examines typical social-stylistic devices whereby spokesmen for different classes aim at an over-all dialectic designed to see beyond the limitations of status." Frank Whigham offers a detailed, social study of the Renaissance literatures of politeness in *Ambition and Social Privilege: The Social Tropes of Elizabethan Courtesy Theory*.

Bibliography

Aarlseff, Hans. *The Study of Language in England, 1780-1860.* Princeton, N.J.: Princeton University Press, 1967.

Anderson, William S. *Pompey, His Friends, and Literature of the First Century B.C.* University of California Publications in Classical Philology 19.1. Berkeley and Los Angeles: University of California Press, 1963.

Asmis, Elizabeth. "Crates on Poetic Criticism." *Phoenix* 46 (1992): 138-69.

Audollent, Augustus. *Defixionum tabellae.* 1904. Reprint, Frankfurt: Minerva, 1967.

Axelson, Bertil. *Unpoëtische Worter.* Lund: H. Ohlssons, 1945.

Badian, Ernst. "Ennius and His Friends." *Ennius. Entretiens sur l'antiquité classique* 17 (1972): 151-208.

Bakhtin, M. M. *The Dialogic Imagination.* Austin: University of Texas Press, 1981.

Bardon, Henri. *Le Vocabulaire de la critique littéraire chez Sénèque le Rhéteur.* Paris: Les Belles Lettres, 1940.

————. *La Littérature latine inconnue.* Paris: Klincksieck, 1956.

Bartsch, Shadi. *Actors in the Audience.* Cambridge, Mass.: Harvard University Press, 1994.

Barwick, Karl. "Die sogennante Appendix Probi." *Hermes* 54 (1919): 409-22.

————. "Widmung und Enstehungsgeschichte von Varros *De lingua latina.*" *Philologus* 101 (1957): 298-304.

Bäumerich, Hans Josef. "Ueber die Bedeutungen der Genealogien in der römischen Literatur." Diss., Cologne, 1964.

Beacham, Richard C. *The Roman Theater and Its Audience.* London: Routledge, 1990.

Beard, Mary. "Cicero and Divination: The Formation of a Latin Discourse." *JRS* 76 (1986): 33-46.

————. "Looking (Harder) for Roman Myth: Dumézil Declamation and the Problem of Definition." In *Mythos in mythenloser Gesellschaft. Das Paradigma Roms,* ed. Fritz Graf, 44-64. Stuttgart and Leipzig: Teubner, 1993.

Beck, Roger. "Encolpius at the *Cena.*" *Phoenix* 29 (1975): 270-83.

————. "Eumolpus *Poeta,* Eumolpus *Fabulator*: A Study of Characterization in the *Satyricon.*" *Phoenix* 33 (1979): 239-53.

———. "The *Satyricon*: Satire, Narrator, and Antecedents." *MH* 39 (1982): 206–14.

Bernstein, Michael André. *The Tale of the Tribe: Ezra Pound and the Modern Verse Epic*. Princeton, N.J.: Princeton University Press, 1980.

———. *Bitter Carnival: Ressentiment and the Abject Hero*. Princeton, N.J.: Princeton University Press, 1992.

Bertschinger, J. "Volkstümliche Elemente in der Sprache des Phädrus." Diss., Bern, 1921.

Bing, Peter. *The Well-Read Muse: Present and Past in Callimachus and the Hellenistic Poets*. Hypomnemeta: Untersuchungen zur Antike und zu ihrem Nachleben 90. Göttingen: Vandenhoeck and Ruprecht, 1988.

Blank, David L. *Ancient Philosophy and Grammar*. Chico, Calif.: Scholars Press, 1982.

Bloch, R. Howard. *Etymologies and Genealogies: A Literary Anthropology of the French Middle Ages*. Chicago: University of Chicago Press, 1983.

Bloomer, W. Martin. *Valerius Maximus and the Rhetoric of the New Nobility*. Chapel Hill and London: University of North Carolina Press, 1992.

Bömer, F. "Thematik und Krise der römischen Geschichtsschreibung im 2. Jahrhundert v. Chr." *Historia* 2 (1953): 189–208.

Bonner, Stanley F. *Roman Declamation in the Late Republic and Early Empire*. Liverpool: Liverpool University Press, 1949.

Bornecque, Henri. *Les Déclamations et les déclamateurs d'après Sénèque le Père*. 1902. Reprint, Hildesheim, 1967.

Boscherini, Silvano. "Città e campagna nella dottrina linguistica di Varrone." In *Atti del Congresso Internazionale di Studi Varroniani*, 317–20. Rieti: Centro di studi varroniani, 1976.

Boulvert, Gérard. *Esclaves et affranchis imperiaux sous le Haut-Empire romain*. Naples: Jovene, 1970.

———. *Domestique et fonctionnaire sous le Haut-Empire romain: La condition de l'affranchi et de l'esclave du prince*. Paris: Les Belles Lettres, 1974.

Bourdieu, Pierre. *Distinction*. Trans. Richard Nice. Cambridge, Mass.: Harvard University Press, 1984.

Bower, E. W. "Some Technical Terms in Roman Education." *Hermes* 89 (1961): 462–77.

Bowersock, Glen. *Augustus and the Greek World*. Westport, Conn.: Greenwood Press, 1981.

Boyce, Bret. *The Language of the Freedmen in Petronius' Cena Trimalchionis*. Leiden and New York: E. J. Brill, 1991.

Bradley, K. R. *Suetonius' Life of Nero: An Historical Commentary*. Collection Latomus 157. Brussels, 1978.

————. *Slaves and Masters in the Roman Empire.* New York: Oxford University Press, 1987.

Brunt, P. A. "'Amicitia' in the Late Roman Republic." In *The Crisis of the Roman Republic*, ed. R. Seager, 199–218. Cambridge: Cambridge University Press, 1969. Originally published in *PCPhS* 11 (1965): 1–20.

Buckland, W. W. *The Roman Law of Slavery: The Position of the Slave in Private Law from Augustus to Justinian.* 1908. Reprint, New York: AMS Press, 1970.

Buecheler, F. "Coniectanea." *RhM* 38 (1883): 132–33.

Burke, Kenneth. *A Rhetoric of Motives.* New York: Prentice-Hall, 1950.

Carter, John. "Civic and Other Buildings." In *Roman Public Buildings*, ed. I. M. Barton, 31–97. Exeter: University of Exeter, 1989.

Castagnoli, F. "Atrium Libertatis." *RAL* 8.1 (1946): 276–91.

Causeret, C. "De Phaedri sermone grammaticales observationes." Diss., Paris, 1886.

Christes, Johannes. "Reflexe erlebter Unfreiheit in den Sentenzen des Publilius Syrus und den Fabeln des Phaedrus." *Hermes* 107 (1979): 199–220.

Ciaffi, V. "Intermezzo nella 'Cena' Petroniana." *RFIC* 33 (1955): 113–45.

Collart, Jean. *Varron Grammairien Latin.* Paris: Les Belles Lettres, 1954.

C[orpus] I[nscriptionum] L[atinarum]. 16 vols. Berlin, 1863–.

Courtney, Edward. *The Fragmentary Latin Poets.* Oxford: Oxford University Press, 1993.

Currie, H. MacL. "Phaedrus the Fabulist." *ANRW* II, 32.1 (1984): 497–513.

Dahlmann, Hellfried. *Varro und die Hellenistische Sprachtheorie.* 1932. Reprint, Berlin: Weidmann, 1964.

Dalzell, Alexander. "C. Asinius Pollio and the Early History of Public Recitation at Rome." *Hermathena* 86 (1955): 20–28.

Dam, Rudolph. *De analogia: Observationes in Varronem grammaticamque Romanorum.* Diss., Utrecht, 1930.

Damon, Cynthia. "Caesar's Practical Prose." *CJ* 89 (1994): 191–94.

Davies, A. Morpurgo. "Language Classification in the Nineteenth Century." In *Current Trends in Linguistics*, ed. Thomas A. Sebeok, 618–22. Vol. 13, *Historiography of Linguistics*. The Hague and Paris: Mouton, 1975.

Degrassi, Atilius. *Inscriptiones Latinae liberae rei publicae.* Florence: La Nuova Italia, 1963.

Della Corte, Francesco. *Varrone il terzo gran lume romano.* Florence: La Nuova Italia, 1970.

————. 1981. *La filologia latina dalle origini a Varrone.* Florence. Reprint of the original text of Turin, 1937, updated with minor subtractions and additions.

Dihle, Albrecht. "Analogie und Attizismus." *Hermes* 85 (1957): 170–205.

Douglas, A. E. *Cicero*. Greece and Rome New Surveys in the Classics, no. 2. Cambridge: Cambridge University Press, 1968.

Duff, Arnold. *Freedmen in the Early Roman Empire*. Cambridge: Cambridge University Press, 1958.

Dupont, Florence. "Recitatio." In *The Roman Cultural Revolution*, eds. Thomas Habinek and Alessandro Schiesaro. Cambridge: Cambridge University Press, forthcoming.

Edward, William A. *The Suasoriae of Seneca the Elder*. Cambridge: Cambridge: Cambridge University Press, 1928.

Edwards, Catharine. *The Politics of Immorality in Ancient Rome*. Cambridge: Cambridge University Press, 1993.

Empson, William. *Some Versions of Pastoral*. 1935. Reprint, New York: New Directions, 1974.

Fabre, G. *Libertus. Recherches sur les rapports patron-affranchi à la fin de la république romaine*. Rome: Coll. Ecole Française à Rome, 1981.

Fairweather, Janet. *Seneca the Elder*. Cambridge: Cambridge University Press, 1981.

Fantham, Elaine. "Cicero, Varro, and M. Claudius Marcellus." *Phoenix* 31 (1977): 208–13.

——. "Mime: The Missing Link in Roman Literary History." *CW* 82 (1989): 153–63.

Fedeli, P. "Petronio: Il viaggio, il labirinto." *MD* 6 (1981): 91–117.

Fehling, Detlev. "Varro und die Grammatische Lehre von der Analogie und der Flexion." Parts 1 and 2. *Glotta* 35 (1956): 214–70; 36 (1957): 48–100.

——. Review of *Probleme der stoischen Sprachlehre und Rhetorik* by Karl Barwick. *GGA* 212 (1958): 161–73.

Ferrero, Leonardo. "La voce pubblica nel proemio degli Ann. di Tacitus." *RFIC*, n.s. 24 (1946): 50–86.

Festa, N. "Su la Favola di Fedro." *Rendiconti dell R. Accademia Nazionale dei Lincei*, vol. 33, 1924.

Fineman, Joel. "The History of the Anecdote: Fiction and Fiction." In *The New Historicism*, ed. H. Aram Veeser, 49–76. New York and London: Routledge, 1989.

Fraenkel, Eduard. *Elementi Plautini in Plauto*. Florence: La Nuova Italia, 1960. Originally published as *Plautinisches im Plautus*. Berlin: Weidmann, 1922.

F[ragmenta] P[oetarum] L[atinorum]. Ed. Jürgen Blänsdorf. Stuttgart and Leipzig: Teubner, 1995.

Friedlaender, Ludwig. *Petronii Cena Trimalchionis*. Leipzig: S. Hirzel, 1906.

Gaselee, S. *A Collotype Reproduction of the Trau Manuscript*. Cambridge: Cambridge University Press, 1915.

George, Peter. "Style and Character in the *Satyricon*." *Arion* 5 (1966): 336–58.

Giamatti, A. Bartlett. *Exile and Change in Renaissance Literature*. New Haven and London: Yale University Press, 1984.

Gill, Christopher. "The Sexual Episodes in the *Satyricon*." *CP* 68 (1973): 172–85.

Gilman, Sander L., Carole Blair, and David J. Parent, eds. and trans. *Friedrich Nietzsche on Rhetoric and Language*. Oxford and New York: Oxford University Press, 1989.

Goodyear, F. R. D. "Tiberius and Gaius: Their Influence and View of Literature." *ANRW* II, 32.1 (1984): 603–10.

Goold, George P. "A Greek Professorial Circle at Rome." *TAPA* 91 (1961): 168–92.

Görler, Woldemar. *Untersuchungen zu Ciceros Philosophie*. Heidelberg: C. Winter, 1974.

Greenberg, R. A. "Ruskin, Pugin, and the Contemporary Context of *The Bishop Orders His Tomb*." *PMLA* 84 (1960): 1588–94.

Griffin, Miriam T. "The Elder Seneca and Spain." *JRS* 62 (1972): 1–19.

———. *Seneca*. Oxford: Oxford University Press, 1975.

Grimal, Pierre. "Du nouveau sur les *Fables* de Phèdre?" In *Mélanges de litterature et d'epigraphie latines d'histoire ancienne et d'archeologie: Hommage à la memoire de Pierre Wuilleumier*, 143–49. Paris: Les Belles Lettres, 1980.

Gruen, Erich. *Culture and National Identity in Republican Rome*. Ithaca, N.Y.: Cornell University Press, 1992.

Guaglianone, A. "Fedro e il suo senario." *RSC* 16 (1968): 91–104.

Håkanson, Lenart. *L. Annaeus Seneca Maior, Oratorum et rhetorum sententiae divisiones colores*. Leipzig: Teubner, 1989.

Halm, C. *Fabulae Aesopicae collectae*. Leipzig: Teubner, 1852.

Hamblenne, Pierre. "Le Choucas chez les Paons (Phaedr., 1,3): Phèdre, Séjan ou Pallas?" *LEC* 49 (1981): 125–33.

Hausrath, August. "Phaedrus." *RE* 19.2 (1938): 1475–1505.

Häussler, R. *Nachträge zu A. Otto: Die Sprichwörter und sprichwörtlichen Redensarten der Römer*. Hildesheim: Georg Olms, 1968.

Havet, Louis. *Phaedri Augusti Liberti Fabulae Aesopiae*. Paris: Hachette, 1895.

Hervieux, Léopold. *Les Fabulistes latins depuis le siècle d'Auguste jusqu'à la fin du moyen âge*. Paris: Firmin-Didot, 1883–99.

Hexter, Ralph, and Daniel Selden, eds. *Innovations of Antiquity.* New York: Routledge, 1992.

Hickson, Frances V. *Roman Prayer Language: Livy and the Aeneid.* Stuttgart: Teubner, 1993.

Hoffa, G. "De Seneca patre selectae quaestiones." Diss., Göttingen, 1909.

Hubbard, Thomas K. "The Narrative Architecture of Petronius' *Satyricon.*" *AC* 55 (1986): 190–212.

Hudson, R. A. *Sociolinguistics.* Cambridge: Cambridge University Press, 1980.

Jocelyn, H. D. "The Poet Cn. Naevius, P. Cornelius Scipio and Q. Caecilius Metellus." *Antichthon* 3 (1969): 32–47.

Johnson, R. R. "Ancient and Medieval Accounts of the 'Invention' of Parchment." *CSCA* 3 (1970): 115–22.

Johnstone, Steve. 1992. "On the Uses of Arson in Classical Rome." *Studies in Latin Literature and Roman History VI*, 41–69. Collection Latomus 217. Brussels, 1992.

Kaplan, Michael. *Greeks and the Imperial Court from Tiberius to Nero.* New York and London: Garland, 1990.

Kaster, Robert A. *Guardians of Language: The Grammarian and Society in Late Antiquity.* Berkeley and Los Angeles: University of California Press, 1988.

———. ed. and trans. *Suetonius,* De grammaticis et rhetoribus. Oxford: Oxford University Press, 1995.

Kennedy, George. *The Art of Rhetoric in the Roman World.* Princeton, N.J.: Princeton University Press, 1972.

———. "Encolpius and Agamemnon in Petronius." *AJP* 99 (1978): 171–78.

Kenner, Hugh. *Joyce's Voices.* Berkeley and Los Angeles: University of California Press, 1978.

Klebs, Eilimar. "Zur Komposition von Petronius' Satirae." *Philologus* 47 (1889): 623–35.

Kleijwegt, Marc. 1991. *Ancient Youth: The Ambiguity of Youth and the Absence of Adolescence in Greco-Roman Society.* Amsterdam: Gieben, 1991.

Konstan, David. *Roman Comedy.* Ithaca, N.Y.: Cornell University Press, 1983.

Korzeniewski, D. "Zur Verstechnik des Phaedrus." *Hermes* 98 (1970): 430–58.

Kroll, Wilhelm. *Studien zum Verständnis der römischen Literatur.* Stuttgart: Metzler, 1924.

Kuhner, R. and Carl Stegmann. *Ausfuhrliche Grammatik der lateinischen Sprache.* Revised by Andreas Thierfelder. Hannover: Hahn, 1955.

Langbaum, Robert. *The Poetry of Experience: The Dramatic Monologue in Modern Literary Experience.* London: Chatto and Windus, 1957.

La Penna, Antonio. Introduction to *Fedro: Favole*, ed. Agostino Richelmy. Turin: Giulio Einaudi, 1978.

Laurand, L. *Etudes sur le style des discours de Cicéron.* 4th ed. Amsterdam: A. M. Hakkert, 1965.

Leeman, A. D. *Orationis ratio.* Amsterdam: A. M. Hakkert, 1963.

Lendon, J. E. "Perceptions of the Prestige and the Working of Roman Imperial Government." Ph.D. diss., Yale University, 1991.

Leumann, Manu, Johann Hoffmann, and Anton Szantyr. *Lateinische Grammatik.* Munich: C. H. Beck, 1977–79.

Lockyer, Charles W. "The Fiction of Memory and the Use of Written Sources: Convention and Practice in Seneca the Elder and Other Authors." Ph.D. diss., Princeton University, 1970.

Lorenzi, Attilio de. *Fedro.* Florence: La Nuova Italia Editrice, 1955.

Luck, Georg. *The Latin Love Elegy.* London: Methuen, 1959.

Marshall, A. J. "Library Resources and Creative Writing at Rome." *Phoenix* 30 (1976): 252–64.

Martin, Ronald. *Tacitus.* Berkeley and Los Angeles: University of California Press, 1981.

Meyer, Elizabeth A. "Explaining the Epigraphic Habit in the Roman Empire: The Evidence of Epitaphs." *JRS* 80 (1990): 74–96.

Miller, N. P. "Tiberius Speaks: An Examination of the Utterances Ascribed to Him in the *Annals* of Tacitus." *AJP* 89 (1968): 1–19.

Mirmont, H. de la Ville de. "Les Déclamateurs espagnols au temps d'Auguste et de Tibère." *Bulletin Hispanique* 14 (1912): 11–29.

Momigliano, Arnaldo. "Ancient History and the Antiquarian." *Contributo alla Storia degli Studi Classici* 67 (1955): 67–106. Originally published in *Journal of the Warburg and Courtauld Institutes* 13 (1950): 285–315.

Mommsen, Theodor. *The History of Rome.* Translated by William Dickson. New York: Scribners, 1895.

Moretti, Gabriella. "Lessico giuridico e modello giudiziario nella favola fedriana." *Maia* 34 (1982): 227–46.

Mounin, Georges. *Histoire de la linguistique des origines au XXe siècle.* Paris: Presses universitaires de France, 1967.

———. "Bréal vs. Schleicher: Linguistics and Philology during the Latter Half of the Nineteenth Century." In *The European Background of American Linguistics*, ed. H. M. Hoenigswald, 63–106. Dordrecht: Foris Publications, 1979.

Müller, Konrad. *Petronii Arbitri Satyricon.* Munich: Ernst Heimeran, 1961.

Müller, Konrad, and Wilhelm Ehlers, eds. and trans. *Petronius Arbiter Satyrica*. Munich: E. Heimeran, 1965.

Münzer, Friedrich. "Atticus als Geschichtsschreiber." *Hermes* 40 (1905): 50–100.

Newton, Rick M. "Trimalchio's Hellish Bath." *CJ* 77 (1982): 315–16.

Nøjgaard, Morten. *La Fable Antique 2: Les Grands Fabulistes*. Copenhagen: Nordisk, 1967.

Norden, Eduard. *Die Antike Kunstprosa*. 1898. Reprint, Stuttgart: Teubner, 1958.

O'Connor, E. M. *Symbolum Salacitatis: A Study of the God Priapus as a Literary Character*. Studien zur klassischen Philologie 40. Frankfurt: Lang, 1989.

Oliensis, Ellen. "Canidia, Canicula, and the Decorum of Horace's *Epodes*." *Arethusa* 24 (1991): 107–38.

Otto, A. *Die Sprichwörter und sprichwörtlichen Redensarten der Römer*. 1892. Reprint, Hildesheim, 1965.

Pagnini, Rossana Valenti. *Il potere e la sua imagine: Semantica di species in Tacito*. Studi e testi dell'antichità 19. Naples: Soc. Ed. Napoletana, 1987.

Parker, Patricia A. *Inescapable Romance: Studies in the Poetics of a Mode*. Princeton, N.J.: Princeton University Press, 1979.

———. *Literary Fat Ladies: Rhetoric, Gender, Property*. London and New York: Methuen, 1987.

Perry, B. E. "The Origin of the Epimythium." *TAPA* 71 (1940): 408–12.

———. *Aesopica*. Urbana: University of Illinois Press, 1952.

———., trans. *Babrius and Phaedrus*. Cambridge, Mass.: Harvard University Press, 1984.

Peter, Hermann, ed. *Historicorum Romanorum reliquiae*. 2 vols. Leipzig: Teubner, 1906–14.

Petersmann, Hubert. *Die Römische Satire*. Darmstadt: Wissenschaftliche Buchgesellschaft, 1986.

Pinborg, Jan. "Classical Antiquity: Greece." In *Current Trends in Linguistics*, ed. Thomas A. Sebeok, 69–126. Vol. 13, *Historiography of Linguistics*. The Hague and Paris: Mouton, 1975.

Pisi, Giordana. *Fedro traduttore di Esopo*. Università degli Studi di Parma, Pubblicazioni della Facoltà di Magistero 4. Florence: La Nuova Italia Editrice, 1977.

Postgate, J. P. "Phaedrus and Seneca." *CR* 33 (1919): 19–24.

Pugliarello, Mariarosaria. "Appunti di sintassi fedriana." *SRIL* 4 (1981): 109–21.

Ramage, Edwin. "The *De urbanitate* of Domitius Marsus." *CP* 54 (1959): 250–55.

Rawson, Elizabeth. *Intellectual Life in the Late Roman Republic*. London: Duckworth, 1985.

———. *Roman Culture and Society*. Oxford: Oxford University Press, 1991.

Reekmans, T. "Vultus, vox en silentium in Tacitus' historische Werke." *Kleio* 14 (1984): 161–69.

Reiff, Arno. *Interpretatio, imitatio, aemulatio: Begriff und Vorstellung literarischer Abhängigkeit bei den Römern*. Würzburg: Konrad Triltsch, 1959.

Reynolds, L. D., ed. *Texts and Transmission*. Oxford: Oxford University Press, 1983.

Reynolds, L. D., and N. G. Wilson. *Scribes and Scholars: A Guide to the Transmission of Greek and Latin Literature*. 2d ed. Oxford: Oxford University Press, 1974.

Richlin, Amy. *The Garden of Priapus*. Rev. ed. Oxford and New York: Oxford University Press, 1992.

Richmond, H. M. "Personal Identity and Literary Persona: A Study in Historical Psychology." *PMLA* 90 (1975): 209–19.

Robins, Robert Henry. "Varro and the Tactics of Analogist Grammarians." In *Studies in Greek, Italic, and Indo-European Linguistics*, ed. Anna Morpurgo Davies and Wolfgang Meid, 333–36. Innsbruck: Innsbrucker Beiträge zur Sprachwissenschaft, 1976.

———. *A Short History of Linguistics*. 3d ed. London: Longman, 1990.

Rocher, Ludo. "Les Philologues classiques et les debuts de la grammaire comparée." *RUB* 10 (1957–58): 251–86.

Romeo, Luigi, and Gaio E. Tiberio. "Historiography of Linguistics and Rome's Scholarship." *Language Sciences* 17 (1971): 23–44.

Rose, Kenneth. "Time and Place in the *Satyricon*." *TAPA* 93 (1962): 402–9.

Ross, David O. *Style and Tradition in Catullus*. Cambridge, Mass.: Harvard University Press, 1969.

Ruskin, John. *Modern Painters*. Vol. 4. 1856. In *The Works of John Ruskin*, vol. 6, ed. E. T. Cook and Alexander Wedderburn. New York: Longmans, 1913.

Ryberg, I. S. "Tacitus' Art of Innuendo." *TAPA* 73 (1942): 383–404.

Saller, Richard. *Personal Patronage under the Early Empire*. Cambridge: Cambridge University Press, 1982.

Sandy, Gerald N. "Scaenica Petroniana." *TAPA* 104 (1974): 329–46.

Sassen, A. von. "De Phaedri sermone." Diss., Marburg, 1911.

Scullard, H. H. *Roman Politics 220–150 B.C.* Oxford: Oxford University Press, 1973.

Selden, Daniel L. 1994. "Genre of Genre." In *The Search for the Ancient*

Novel, ed. J. Tatum, 39–64. Baltimore: Johns Hopkins University Press, 1994.

Shatzman, Israel. *Senatorial Wealth and Roman Politics*. Collection Latomus 142. Brussels, 1975.

Shaw, W. David. *The Dialectical Temper: The Rhetorical Art of Robert Browning*. Ithaca, N.Y.: Cornell University Press, 1968.

Skutsch, Otto, ed. *The Annals of Quintus Ennius*. Oxford: Oxford University Press, 1985.

Slater, Niall W. *Plautus in Performance*. Princeton, N.J.: Princeton University Press, 1985.

Smith, Martin S., ed. *Petronii Arbitri Cena Trimalchionis*. Oxford: Oxford University Press, 1975.

Sochatoff, A. F. "The Basic Rhetorical Theories of the Elder Seneca." *CJ* 34 (1938–39): 345–54.

Stewart, Susan. *Nonsense: Aspects of Intertextuality in Folklore and Literature*. Baltimore: Johns Hopkins University Press, 1979.

Stewart, Zeph. "Sejanus, Gaetulicus, and Seneca." *AJP* 74 (1953): 70–86.

Sullivan, J. P. *The Satyricon of Petronius: A Literary Study*. Bloomington: Indiana University Press, 1968.

Sumner, G. V. "The Family Connections of L. Aelius Sejanus." *Phoenix* 19 (1965): 134–46.

Sussman, Lewis A. "The Elder Seneca as a Critic of Rhetoric." Ph.D. diss., University of North Carolina, 1969.

———. "The Elder Seneca's Discussion of the Decline of Roman Eloquence." *CSCA* 5 (1972): 195–210.

———. "Arellius Fuscus and the Unity of the Elder Seneca's *Suasoriae*." *RhM* 120 (1977): 303–23.

———. *The Elder Seneca*. Mnemosyne Suppl. 51. Leiden: E. J. Brill, 1978.

Swanson, Donald C. *A Formal Analysis of Petronius' Vocabulary*. Minneapolis: The Perine Book Co., 1963.

Syme, Ronald. "Personal Names in *Annals* 1–6." *JRS* 39 (1949): 6–18.

———. *Tacitus*. Oxford: Oxford University Press, 1958.

———. *Ten Studies in Tacitus*. Oxford: Oxford University Press, 1970.

Taylor, Daniel J. "Palaemon's Pig." *Historiographia linguistica*. 8 (1981): 191–93.

Taylor, Lily Ross. "Varro's *De gente populi Romani*." *CP* 29 (1934): 221–29.

———. "Freedmen and Freeborn in the Epitaphs of Imperial Rome." *AJP* 82 (1961): 113–32.

Treggiari, Susan. *Roman Freedmen during the Late Republic*. Oxford: Oxford: Oxford University Press, 1969.

Veyne, P. "Le 'Je' dans le *Satiricon*." *REL* 42 (1964): 301–24.

Vine, Brent. Review of Bret Boyce, *The Language of the Freedmen in Petro-nius*' Cena Trimalchionis [Leiden and New York: E. J. Brill, 1991], in *Gnomon* 67 (1995): 112–17.

Vollmer, F. "Beiträge zur Chronologie und Deutung der Fabeln des Phae-drus." *SBAW* (1919): 9–24.

Wallace-Hadrill, Andrew. *Suetonius*. London: Duckworth, 1983.

Walsh, P. G. *The Roman Novel*. Cambridge: Cambridge University Press, 1970.

Watson, Alan. *The State, Law and Religion: Pagan Rome*. Athens and Lon-don: University of Georgia Press, 1992.

Weaver, P. R. C. *Familia Caesaris. A Social Study of the Emperor's Freedmen and Slaves*. Cambridge: Cambridge University Press, 1972.

Wellesley, K. "*Suggestio falsi* in Tacitus." *RhM* 103 (1960): 272–88.

Whigham, Frank. *Ambition and Social Privilege: The Social Tropes of Eliza-bethan Courtesy Theory*. Berkeley and Los Angeles: University of California Press, 1984.

White, Peter. *Promised Verse: Poets in the Society of Augustan Rome*. Cam-bridge, Mass., and London: Harvard University Press, 1993.

Williams, Gordon W. *Tradition and Originality in Roman Poetry*. Oxford: Oxford University Press, 1968.

Winkler, John. *Auctor et Actor: A Narratological Reading of Apuleius's* The Golden Ass. Berkeley and Los Angeles: University of California Press, 1985.

Winterbottom, Michael, trans. *The Elder Seneca: Declamations*. 2 vols. Cambridge, Mass., and London: Harvard University Press, 1974. (Loeb Classical Library.)

Wiseman, T. P. *New Men in the Roman Senate, 139 B.C.–A.D. 14*. Oxford: Oxford University Press, 1971.

———. "Legendary Genealogies in Late-Republican Rome." *G&R* 21 (1974): 153–64.

Woodman, Tony, and David West, eds. *Quality and Pleasure in Latin Poetry*. Cambridge and New York: Cambridge University Press, 1974.

Woolford, John, and Daniel Karlin, eds. *The Poems of Browning*. Vol. 2. Harlow, Essex, England, and New York: Longman, 1991.

Yates, Frances A. *The Art of Memory*. Chicago: University of Chicago Press, 1966.

Zeitlin, Froma I. "Petronius as Paradox: Anarchy and Artistic Integrity." *TAPA* 102 (1971): 631–82.

———. "Petronius Romanus: A Study of the *Troiae Halosis* and *Bellum Civile*." *Latomus* 30 (1971): 56–82.

Zetzel, James E. G. *Latin Textual Criticism in Antiquity*. New York: Arno Press, 1981.

Ziolkowski, Jan, ed. *On Philology*. University Park and London: Pennsylvania State University Press, 1990.

Zweig, Bella. "The Mute Nude Female Characters in Aristophanes' Plays." In *Pornography and Representation in Greece and Rome*, ed. Amy Richlin, 73–89. Oxford and New York: Oxford University Press, 1992.

Index of Passages

General Index

Cimon, 141
Cinna, 70
Claudius, 70, 92
clientela, 12, 239
Clodius, 53, 154
Constantius II, 159
contaminatio, 201, 203–5, 224
copia: goal of classical orator, 156; of
  Tiberius, 159; in declamation, 113,
  137, 138, 151
Cordus, Cremutius, 175
correctio: in the elder Seneca, 154; in
  Cicero's *Pro Caelio*, 154; in Tacitus's
  Annales, 155, 157
Corvinus, Messala, 70, 72
Crates of Mallos, 38–40, 41, 42, 43, 69,
  250 n.1
Craton, 148
curse tablets. See *Defixiones*

Dante, 43; *On Vulgar Eloquence*, 43
declamation: as Roman cultural and
  linguistic prescription, 110–53;
  as role-playing, 138–39; and Roman comedy, 138–39; mistakes
  in, as social failing, 142–53; in the
  schools, 110–11, 118–19, 136; the
  elder Seneca's history of, 110–14;
  ambitions of the prefaces to Seneca's
  history, 120–28; lost prefaces of
  Seneca's history, 125–28; social
  function of, 135–42
declinatio, 64
defixiones, 292 n.22
Demetrius, tyrant of Athens, 74
Demosthenes, 135
pseudo-Demosthenes, 146
Dionysius of Halicarnassus, 47
Domitian, 156, 194
Drusus, 178
dubitatio, 165–67, 180, 190, 191

Ennius, 13, 18, 21, 29, 30, 37, 41, 61, 64,
  69, 71; authorial persona of, 24–28;
  compared to Naevius, 27; epitaph
  of, 26, Roman citizenship of, 246
  n.8
ephebeia, 3
Epirota, Q. Caecilius, 67, 70
Erasmus, 43; *De duplici copia verborum
  ac rerum*, 6

etymology, 49–50; as arbiter of Roman identity in *De lingua latina*,
  41–42, 55–62; Caesar's use of, in
  construction of genealogy, 49;
  etymology as history in Varro's
  Antiquities, 49
Eutychus, 102, 105
Evander, 58

Fabianus, 122–23, 125–27, 130–32, 139
Fabius Pictor, 18, 245 n.2
Fenestella, 111
Figulus, Nigidius, 45, 48
figura etymologica, 56, 82
Flavius, Alfius, 131, 144
Florus, 132, 147
freedman/men, 10, 24, 27, 29, 35, 36,
  92–93, 135, 138, 143, 148; as poet
  (Phaedrus), 75–76; as experts, 8,
  198; as embodiment of emancipa-
  tory potential of literature, 27–28;
  Bathyllus, freedman of Maecenas,
  133; epitaphs as markers of their
  status, 6, 75–76, 197; scapegoats in
  Roman culture, 198; vs. freeborn,
  in the *Satyricon*, 196–97, 200; and
  the traffic of their speech in the
  Satyricon, 203–12
Fronto, 139
Fuscus, 124, 126, 131, 132, 145–47

Gallio, Junius, 115–17, 124, 126, 127,
  129, 130, 132, 133, 145
Gallus, Asinius, 70, 134, 165–68, 170
Gallus, Vibius, 130, 131, 141
Geminus, Varius, 127, 128, 131, 132
Glycon, 148
grammar, comparative, 15–16, 244 n.9
grammaticus/i, 16, 40, 59–60, 63,
  67–72, 197
Grimm, Jacob, 15, 244 n.9
gymnasium, 3

Hannibal, 22
Haterius, Quintus, 123, 125, 145
Hellenismos, 1, 243 n.1; and *latinitas*,
  1–3
Herodotus, 58; *Histories*, 56–57; and
  Tacitus, 162, 164
Hesiod, 82
Hispanus, Cornelius, 127

DATE DUE

GAYLORD

PRINTED IN U.S.A.